Potential of AI to Replace Teachers' Expertise:

Ethics and Challenges

Shahnawaz Khan
https://orcid.org/0000-0002-3675-4467
Bahrain Polytechnic, Bahrain

Philippe Pringuet
https://orcid.org/0009-0009-0925-0309
Bahrain Polytechnic, Bahrain

IGI Global
Scientific Publishing
Publishing Tomorrow's Research Today

Vice President of Editorial Melissa Wagner
Director of Acquisitions Mikaela Felty
Director of Book Development Jocelynn Hessler
Production Manager Mike Brehm
Cover Design Jose Rosado

Published in the United States of America by
IGI Global Scientific Publishing
701 East Chocolate Avenue
Hershey, PA, 17033, USA
Tel: 717-533-8845 | Fax: 717-533-7115
Website: https://www.igi-global.com E-mail: cust@igi-global.com

Library of Congress Cataloging-in-Publication Data

Names: Khan, Shahnawaz, editor. | Pringuet, Philippe, 1982- editor.
Title: Potential of AI to replace teachers' expertise : ethics and challenges / [edited by] Shahnawaz Khan, Philippe Pringuet.
Description: Hershey, PA : IGI Global Scientific Publishing, 2026. | Includes bibliographical references and index. | Summary: "This book aims to serve as a comprehensive resource for applying artificial intelligence (AI) in education"-- Provided by publisher.
Identifiers: LCCN 2025012919 (print) | LCCN 2025012920 (ebook) | ISBN 9798337303963 (hardcover) | ISBN 9798337303970 (paperback) | ISBN 9798337303987 (ebook)
Subjects: LCSH: ChatGPT. | Artificial intelligence--Educational applications--Bahrain. | Education--Effect of technological innovations on--Bahrain. | Teacher effectiveness--Bahrain.
Classification: LCC LB1028.43 .P68 2026 (print) | LCC LB1028.43 (ebook) | DDC 379.285/63095365--dc23/eng/20250418
LC record available at https://lccn.loc.gov/2025012919
LC ebook record available at https://lccn.loc.gov/2025012920

British Cataloguing in Publication Data
A Cataloguing in Publication record for this book is available from the British Library.

Table of Contents

Detailed Table of Contents

autonomy, guarantees equity, and fosters inclusivity. The book advocates for a collaborative future where instructors and AI synergistically enhance assessment processes and student results.

This work demonstrates that AI offers significant potential for personalizing learning pathways, providing immediate feedback, and increasing educational access. Its effective implementation requires maintaining the irreplaceable human elements of teaching, establishing robust ethical frameworks Integrating Kolb's experiential learning theory with AI and human teachers creates a dynamic educational environment where students engage in hands-on activities, reflect on their experiences, form abstract concepts, and test these concepts in new situations. AI enhances the process by providing personalized learning experiences and immediate feedback, supporting reflective observation with active experimentation. Human teachers complement AI by offering emotional support, mentorship, and imbibing critical thinking, guiding students through reflective observation and encouraging deeper insights. However, ethical considerations are crucial in this integration, ensuring AI systems are fair, protecting privacy, maintaining accountability, prioritizing transparency, and well-being of learners.

Application of AI in the teaching learning process has raised questions on how it can supplement or supplant part or the entire function of a tutor.. However, the main disadvantage of implementing AI to replace the human-based and context-sensitive sensible judgement of a teacher is a number of ethical and practical consequences. It is evident that AI cannot emulate human emotions, therefore, there remains no empathy and touch, there exists a potential transmission of undesirable algorithmic bias, and, finally, the absence of human touch devaluates the possibilities of creating thinking, imagination, and ethical personality. Moreover, there are questions concerning data privacy. This study has highlighted that AI should support the activities teachers perform; when appropriate, integrated should be ethical and offer the same advantages learners. These are the challenges that future research has to solve to gain the best opportunity for uniting the AI and human values for education. This chapter purpose is to determine if and how AI can replicate and enhance educational processes.

This chapter examines the increasing role of Artificial Intelligence (AI) in higher education, focusing on its integration, implementation strategies, and the ethical challenges that arise. It provides insights into how generative AI (GenAI) tools and large language models (LLMs) can be used effectively in classrooms, offering educators and administrators practical guidance for navigating this evolving landscape. The chapter also highlights potential future developments of AI in higher education and explores professional development opportunities to help institutions adapt. By addressing both the benefits and challenges of AI, the chapter aims to empower higher education professionals with the knowledge and tools needed to use AI to enhance teaching, learning, and overall educational experiences. Ultimately, it provides a guide for effectively incorporating AI to support and transform educational practices.

The learning process, a fundamental component of educational achievement, has been significantly enhanced by the rapid advancement and proliferation of Artificial Intelligence (AI) technologies. These developments play a crucial role in addressing complex challenges in the educational system. Educators, as the cornerstone of this system, possess extensive expertise cultivated through years of dedicated practice, continuous professional development, and commitment to their profession. This chapter provides a comprehensive examination of AI's role in education, illustrating how it can complement and enhance the instructional functions performed by teachers. The discussion critically evaluates the advantages AI brings to diverse educational settings while also acknowledging its limitations in fully replicating human instruction. By highlighting the unique and irreplaceable aspects of human

Subsequent sections will explore AI as a supplementary tool within traditional educational frameworks.

Preface

The evolution of Artificial Intelligence (AI) has ushered in a transformative era. AI has rapidly become an inseparable part of almost every aspect of our lives. AI has been reshaping economies, industries, and societies worldwide. The field of education is no exception. Education stands at a pivotal juncture, confronting the immense potential and complex challenges presented by AI. This book explores the evolving dynamic landscape of AI by bring together the diverse perspectives and cutting-edge research from the researchers around the world. It also highlights the influence of AI on teaching, learning, and the very essence of education. This book is not just a collection of academic exercises, it brings the vast experience and critical exploration of how the educators from around the world can harness AI to build an innovative, creative, and enabling teaching and learning environment for our learners.

In this rapidly evolving and advancing technological world, traditional learning and teaching methods sometimes may struggle to equip our learners with the dynamic skill set required for the future and the technological demands of today and the next generation's industry. Employers of today need problem-solvers, critical thinkers and innovators. This book explores the areas how the gaps of the traditional educational system can be bridged to enable the learners being ready for the industry 4.0. AI can enrich and enable the learning and teaching environment for the learners of the next generation. AI can aid in developing tailored learning pathways for each learner and finding engaging ways to impart the knowledge of the complex concepts, etc. AI can aid the educators and educational administrations to managing administrative load, and other matters so that they can focus on what truly matters: our learners.

This book is structured to guide you through the exciting and sometimes challenging landscape of AI in education. It commences by looking at AI's direct influence on learning and pedagogy. You'll find fascinating discussions on how AI tools, like ChatGPT, are being used to develop practical work skills, especially within our hospitality and vocational programs. Then, it explores how innovative concepts like an "AI Helmet" can be utilized to track learner performance in workshops. Furthermore, it also explores how AI can enhance Problem-Based Learning (PBL), and how aligning with Bloom's Digital Taxonomy can foster deeper understanding and boost employability. Additionally, it also considers how complex disciplines, such as forensic accounting, are adapting their pedagogical approaches in this AI-driven era.

CHAPTER OVERVIEW

The opening chapter, *The AI Classroom Genie Effect: Empowering Educators for Smarter Teaching and Personalized Engagement*, sets the stage by examining how artificial intelligence is reshaping higher education. Through lived experiences of educators across diverse contexts, the chapter introduces the AI-LPE (Learning, Pedagogy, Ethics) framework, which highlights AI's dual role as a transformative teaching partner and an institutional challenge. By foregrounding the themes of enhanced learning tools, pedagogical evolution, and ethical governance, the chapter emphasizes the importance of human-centered AI integration that prioritizes both innovation and responsibility.

Chapter 2, *AI as an Educational Partner: Potential, Ethical Dilemmas, and the Future of Teaching*, continues this exploration by framing AI not as a substitute but as a collaborator in the teaching process. Intelligent tutoring systems, automated grading tools, and personalized learning platforms are presented as ways to enhance rather than replace the human educator's role. The chapter highlights the ethical dilemmas inherent in this transformation and argues for a balanced approach that harnesses technological potential while safeguarding the human values that define education.

Shifting focus to the domain of student services, Chapter 3, *AI Enhanced School Guidance Interventions: Promises, Threats, and Future Directions*, explores how guidance offices have adapted in the wake of the pandemic and how AI tools such as chatbots and digital platforms are beginning to reshape counseling and career guidance. While AI can extend accessibility and anonymity in student support, the chapter raises important concerns about its implications for the human element of guidance, reminding us that technology must augment, not diminish, the counselor–student relationship.

Chapter 4, *Enhancing Assessment with AI: Strategies for Complementing Teacher Expertise*, examines the transformative role of AI in educational evaluation. Moving beyond efficiency, the chapter situates AI-driven assessments within cognitive and constructivist learning theories and demonstrates how adaptive analytics and feedback systems can enhance learning. Yet the argument remains clear: effective assessment must preserve teacher autonomy, equity, and inclusivity. This chapter presents a vision of collaborative assessment where educators and AI systems work together to support student success.

In Chapter 5, *The Role of AI in Experiential Learning: Balancing Ethics and Expertise*, the discussion turns to Kolb's experiential learning cycle as a lens for exploring AI's role in shaping hands-on, reflective, and iterative learning. AI is shown to offer personalized pathways and immediate feedback, while educators provide the critical human touch such as mentorship, emotional support, and ethical guidance. Importantly, this chapter underscores the ethical imperatives that must frame AI's use, ensuring fairness, privacy, accountability, and learner well-being.

Chapter 6, *The Role of AI in Education: Challenges and Ethical Implications to Enhance Teachers' Expertise*, offers a critical examination of the risks and limitations of AI in teaching. While AI can replicate certain instructional processes, it cannot emulate empathy, creativity, or ethical discernment. The chapter highlights dangers such as algorithmic bias and loss of human connection, calling for future research that focuses on integration strategies where AI supports rather than supplants teachers. This chapter reinforces the centrality of human judgment in meaningful education.

Focusing on higher education, Chapter 7, *Artificial Intelligence Integration and Higher Education Faculty: Tools, Ethics, Challenges, and Pedagogical Insights*, provides practical strategies for navigating the rise of generative AI and large language models in classrooms. It highlights the professional development needs of faculty, ethical considerations of adoption, and the pedagogical opportunities these technologies bring. By bridging present challenges with future possibilities, the chapter equips higher education leaders with a roadmap for thoughtful and effective AI integration.

Chapter 8, *The Role of AI in Education, Complementing or Competing with Teachers?*, revisits the central question of whether AI serves as a collaborator or a competitor in the learning process. The chapter affirms the irreplaceable value of educators, whose expertise, mentorship, and professional commitment cannot be duplicated by machines. While acknowledging AI's ability to address systemic challenges and provide instructional support, the chapter underscores that education thrives most when AI is positioned as a complement to, rather than a substitute for, human teaching.

Chapter 9, *Redefining the Role of Educators, Not Replacing Them: Strategies for Creating Content with AI*, provides a forward-looking model for how educators can embrace AI without losing pedagogical control. Building on the TPACK framework, the chapter introduces five educator roles in an AI-enhanced environment: Innovators, Instructional Designers, Facilitators of Critical Thinking, Ethical and Moral Guides, and Social-Emotional Mentors. Practical applications in lesson planning, curriculum development, and assessment demonstrate how educators can leverage

AI tools to expand possibilities while ensuring the centrality of human connection and ethical oversight.

Finally, Chapter 10, *Artificial Intelligence in Education: Partner or Replacement for Teachers?*, offers a comprehensive synthesis of the recurring theme across this volume, the indispensability of human educators. While recognizing the ways AI can enhance teaching and streamline instructional processes, the chapter emphasizes the limitations of technology in replicating empathy, adaptability, and authentic human interaction. In doing so, it reinforces a central message of this collection: AI is best positioned not as a replacement but as a partner in advancing the goals of education.

The application of AI is not limited to classroom strategies only, this book also examines the role of AI in educational enhancement and assessment. You'll find fascinating insights into AI models for evaluating learner engagement in online classes. Moreover, it explores specialized scales for measuring educational quality, a topic of great importance in Saudi Arabia. The captivating discussion on the transformative "AI Classroom Genie Effect" highlights how AI empowers educators to teach smarter and engage learners more personally. Furthermore, this book delves into utilizing AI as a true educational partner, acknowledging its immense potential to enrich learning. At the same time, it also takes into account the ethical considerations and the critical role of the human element in teaching.

Additionally, this book addresses the growing need for AI literacy and research in education. It presents comprehensive reviews on AI literacy in higher education. The review emphasizes the need for interdisciplinary approaches and robust policy development. It also explores the integration of Large Language Models (LLMs) in academic writing and practical frameworks like RAISE to promote AI literacy, to safeguard academic integrity, and to inspire innovative assessment methods. It also provides insight upon the broader digital transformation in education, with a specific focus on the impactful changes taking place in India.

The role of AI in enhancing educational practices and learner skills cannot be overlooked. This book explores a wide range of topics, from AI-enhanced school guidance interventions to smart strategies for supporting teachers with assessment. A captivating discussion on pedagogical approaches, that strengthen the reasoning and analytical skills of the learners and encourage them to think "Beyond AI Dependence", cultivates genuine critical engagement and intellectual courage.

While we discuss the applications and utilizations of AI, we must confront the ethical considerations of AI in education. This book meticulously explores the ethical implications of data collection and usage, emphasizing privacy, consent, transparency, and the crucial issue of bias. This book also delves into the ethical and practical applications of AI in experiential learning, examining the challenges and implications of using it to enhance teacher expertise. The ongoing debate about whether AI serves as a partner or a replacement for teachers has also been thoroughly analyzed. It also introduces a framework for ethical, interpretable AI language, underscoring the importance of preserving meaningful, human-centered dialogue in an age of autonomous systems.

In conclusion, this book is not just a collection of research on AI in teaching and learning, it is a testament to the collaborative spirit of academicians striving to navigate this new frontier of artificial intelligence. It is also an invitation for educators, policymakers, researchers, and students across the Middle East and globally to engage in thoughtful dialogue, critically assess our current practices, and collectively shape a future where AI genuinely elevates the learning experience for all.

Chapter 1

The AI Classroom Genie Effect:

Empowering Educators for Smarter Teaching and Personalized Engagement

Harris Saseendran
https://orcid.org/0000-0001-7386-8001
Bahrain Polytechnic, Bahrain

Sonia Selwin
https://orcid.org/0000-0001-9606-3839
Andrews University, USA

Koteswara Rao Vemavarapu
https://orcid.org/0009-0009-8325-0171
Bahrain Polytechnic, Bahrain

Devi Manikeswari
https://orcid.org/0000-0002-5014-9423
Bahrain Polytechnic, Bahrain

Anand Soni
https://orcid.org/0009-0001-4896-0639
Bahrain Polytechnic, Bahrain

ABSTRACT

The rapid integration of Artificial Intelligence (AI) in higher education is redefining the role of educators and institutional functions. Using hermeneutic phenomenology

DOI: 10.4018/979-8-3373-0396-3.ch001

and Interpretative Phenomenological Analysis (IPA), this study explores how AI technologies influence learning, through the lived experiences of educators from various countries. The findings showcase the AI-LPE (Learning, Pedagogy, Ethics) framework to critically examine AI's dual potential, as a powerful teaching assistant and a source of institutional challenge. Findings highlight three thematic areas including AI-Driven Learning Tools, enhancing student engagement, creativity and personalization; Pedagogical Integration, where faculty evolve toward mentorship and adaptive instruction; and Ethical Governance, addressing concerns over data privacy, algorithmic bias, and academic integrity. This chapter offers practical, research-informed strategic solutions for academic leaders, educators and policymakers, underscoring the importance of human-centered AI implementation for institutional effectiveness.

1. BACKGROUND OF THE STUDY: AI IN EDUCATION

What does the future look like? This question has intrigued thinkers, philosophers, and scientists throughout the ages. Today, we live in a time marked by extraordinary progress. Technologies that were once considered pure science fiction just a few decades ago have now become part of our everyday life. Slowly but surely, the way we learn and educate also has kept pace with these breakthroughs. With recent breakthroughs in generative AI and large language models, artificial intelligence (AI) has evolved into a powerful tool across various fields including human resources, banking, learning and education (Selwin et. al., 2024; Hwang et al., 2020; Li & Gu, 2023). Today we have futuristic AI tools including chatbots and virtual assistants that can generate learning materials, address student queries for 24/7 support, provide targeted feedback as well as streamline administrative work (Holmes et al., 2019; Winkler et al., 2023a). As AI brings us new and improved applications in education, the shift towards a student-centred learning environment is accelerating (Aad & Hardey, 2025; Winkler et al., 2023b). While some may imagine a future where AI takes a central role in education, many researchers emphasize that AI's purpose cannot be to replace human teaching, but rather to enhance and support their efforts. While algorithms can effectively handle tasks like grading or resource curation, the empathic, creative, and critical-thinking dimensions of teaching remain uniquely human. Human-centred AI (HCAI) frameworks reinforce the importance of accountability, equity, and transparency in technology integration (Shneiderman, 2020a; Shneiderman, 2020b; Li & Gu, 2023; Chedrawi et al., 2024).

This paper contends that AI via smart prompts, personalized activities, and interactive engagement can function as an "ultimate teaching assistant" when applied along with sound pedagogical design (Abdelwahab et al., 2023). Drawing on existing literature and fresh insights from qualitative interviews with academicians, we outline how educators can merge AI tools with established learning theories while safeguarding ethical standards. AI in classrooms can reduce the manual labour of grading and curating resources, freeing teachers for one-on-one mentoring (Aad & Hardey, 2025; Adelaide Now (2025)). Pedagogical value in using GENAI tools and Scaffolding techniques and improving students comprehension of Visual Learning analytics (VLA) is highlighted by Yan et al. (2024a). Their findings show that AI agents improve learning by providing structured support instead of replacing traditional instructions.

One academician we interviewed highlighted AI's amazing capability to "deliver immediate and personalized feedback to every single one of his students at once" reducing long turnaround times. Another interviewee noted, "My 120 students get instant clarifications even at 2 AM," highlighting AI's round-the-clock availability. Traditional teaching emphasizes nuanced human interaction, empathy, and cultural context. These are dimensions an AI may overlook if not carefully trained or validated (Floridi et al., 2018; Esplugas, 2023; Li & Gu, 2023). Many faculty we interviewed felt that "personal bonding and emotional cues can never be fully automated." Therefore, a hybrid model where AI handles repetitive tasks while educators ensure holistic support emerges as best practice (Shneiderman, 2020b).

Table 1. Synthesizing Literature on AI Integration in Education

Author	Focus Area	Methodology	Key Findings	Challenges Identified	Recommendations	Implications
Ghimire & Edwards (2024)	Policy Frameworks	Policy analysis	Formal AI policies are not found in many institutions. schools are less proactive than higher education	Lack of proactive planning; absence of formal frameworks	All levels require detailed AI policies	Points out that AI governance is required in schools
McDonald et al. (2024)	Policy Frameworks	Policy content analysis	Institutions promote AI use but not enough instructions	Ambiguity in implementation practices	Develop clear, actionable guidelines	Require detailed policy development
Jin et al. (2025)	Institutional Readiness	Survey & document analysis	Universities hesitantly integrating AI technologies in the absence of structured frameworks	No proper guidelines and no proper implementation	Support structured AI integration strategies globally	Focus on readiness assessment before full-scale implementation

continued on following page

Table 1. Continued

Author	Focus Area	Methodology	Key Findings	Challenges Identified	Recommendations	Implications
Yan et al. (2024a)	Ethical Challenges for Large Language Models in Education (LLM)	Scoping review	Ethical issues in using AI in classrooms	Low technological readiness, lack of replicability and transparency, Data privacy	Innovations with state of the art models, open-sourcing models/ systems, human centred approach	Improve reporting standards to develop educational technologies using LLM.
Yan et al. (2024b)	Educational Tools	Experimental study	AI agents improved students' comprehension of visual data	Need for effective scaffolding	Use AI as supplement, not substitute for instruction	Highlights pedagogical value of GenAI tools
Labadze et al (2023)	AI Chatbots in Education	Systematic Literature Review	AI chatbots are used for student engagement, administrative tasks and tutoring.	Ethical concerns, privacy issues, lack of standardization, and limited pedagogical integration.	Develop regulatory guidelines, integrate pedagogy, ensure transparency and ethics	Educational institutions need to adapt to policies and practices to support students using educational chatbots.
Adelaide (2025)	Infrastructure/EdTech Use	Journalistic reporting	AI reduces admin workload, boosts efficiency	Teacher overload, unclear path to integrate AI	Use AI to relieve teacher burnout & optimize workflow	Administrative benefits of AI
Gichuki (2025)	Global AI Education Initiatives	Comparative Review	Overview of AI integration efforts in countries like China, South Korea, and UAE	Entrenched inequalities and regulatory gaps.	Implement inclusive policies and invest in teacher training	Displays a global perspective on AI adoption in education
Nyaaba (2025)	Educational Tools	Design Case Study	Developed a localized AI tool supporting pre-service teachers with curriculum-aligned content	Limited corpora in indigenous languages and access barriers due to premium subscriptions	Collaborate with AI developers to expand access and assess usage across diverse contexts	Demonstrates the importance of culturally responsive AI tools in teacher education.
Vesna et al. (2025)	Digital Divide	Literature Review	AI integration has transformed education but exacerbated the digital divide	Technological infrastructure gaps, socio-economic barriers, and policy constraints	Increase investment in digital infrastructure and develop inclusive policies	Emphasizes the need for equitable access to AI-powered educational tools

While there is increased enthusiasm among national policy-makers, students, parents, teachers and educational institutions to integrate artificial intelligence (AI) into educational settings, there are many challenges that institutions face related to infrastructure, policy, and faculty preparedness. UNESCO (2021a) highlights that one of the key issues that hinder AI adoption among low and middle-income countries are unequal access to digital tools and underinvestment in educational technology infrastructure. As this technology is new and changing at a drastic pace, another issue is that teachers often lack the knowledge and skills needed to adopt AI, and also fail to understand the its need thus leading to challenges find it challenging to find structured professional development opportunities to build AI-related pedagogical and ethical competencies (Winkler, Koehler, & Theodore, 2023a; Celik, 2023; Algerafi et. al., 2023; Bhimwala et. al.; Alwaqdani, 2025) and technological infrastructure gaps and lack of resources and investment (Nyaaba, 2025; Vesna et al. (2025). Another concern is the fact that institutional policies relating to AI usage, standardisation, transparency, ethics, data privacy, and academic integrity are usually namesake, inconsistent or absent in many higher education settings (Chedrawi, Kazoun, & Kokkinaki, 2024; Ghimire & Edwards, 2024; McDonald et al., 2024; Labadze et al, 2023). These systemic issues raise critical questions about institutional readiness (Jin et al., 2025) and policy alignment that needs to be addressed to ensure ethical and sustainable integration of AI in education and to develop localised AI tools through collaboration with AI to expand access to usage across diverse settings including people with disabilities. (Gichuki, 2025; Labadze et al, 2023).

2. OBJECTIVES OF THE STUDY

Despite the presence of studies addressing AI in educational institutions, there remains a distinct lack of qualitative research using hermeneutic phenomenology (for data collection) and interpretative phenomenological analysis to explore the challenges and the use of AI in Business Management Education. Most of the existing research used quantitative analysis, while we advocate constructivist ontology and interpretivist epistemology to better understand the lived experiences of teachers using AI.

This study tries to address this gap by examining the rapidly evolving role of artificial intelligence in business education to propose a conceptual framework that can support enhanced student engagement and learning outcomes. While the original aim of this study was to explore educators' lived experiences with AI in business education, key themes such as institutional readiness, ethical governance, and faculty capacity-building emerged inductively during the interpretative process. Consistent with hermeneutic phenomenology and IPA methodology, these areas were not pre-defined but were recognized through deep engagement with participant narratives. Drawing on interpretative phenomenological analysis and triangulated with international trends, the objectives of this research are to:

1. To explore the lived experiences of business educators as they engage with AI tools in their teaching practices.

2. To understand how educators perceive the influence of AI-enabled learning tools on student engagement, creativity, feedback, and skill development.
3. To investigate the ethical concerns and academic integrity issues raised by educators in the context of AI integration in higher education.
4. To examine educators' views on institutional preparedness, infrastructure, and professional development support for AI adoption in business education.
5. To situate educators' narratives within broader trends in AI policy, market developments, and global best practices, and use these insights to inform the development of an integrative conceptual framework for ethical and effective AI use in education.

3. RESEARCH METHODOLOGY AND DATA ANALYSIS

This research adopts a constructivist ontology and interpretivist epistemology to gain deeper insights into the role of AI as a teaching assistant, The research design adopted was qualitative study and stratified random sampling was used. Hermeneutic phenomenology was selected as it allows a deeper engagement with the subjective experiences of educators, when collecting information within their institutional and sociocultural contexts (Creswell, 2013). Interpretative Phenomenological Analysis (IPA) was used to analyze how educators make sense of AI integration, while attention was also given for both personal reflection and environmental factors (Smith, Flowers, & Larkin, 2022). This approach allowed for taking care of ethical concerns, perceptions of faculty roles and understanding institutional readiness for AI integration in higher education. Through in depth interviews the lived experiences of nine business studies educators across various areas of expertise from universities in Bahrain, the United States, and India (Tamil Nadu) were studied (Table 2). Semi-structured interview protocols were used to explore their experiences, challenges, and expectations regarding AI integration in business education. The interviews followed constructs from the TPACK, UTAUT and Adaptive Learning frameworks to align questions with educators' lived experiences. Key focus areas included AI adoption in lesson delivery, research, student engagement, ethical considerations, and institutional infrastructure. Open-ended questions were used so that participants could elaborate on unanticipated issues, such as data privacy concerns or changing faculty roles. The IPA approach allowed our research team to accommodate these emerging concerns, due to its inductive nature of phenomenological inquiry (Smith & Osborn, 2008). Interviews lasted 30–45 minutes and were mostly conducted virtually due to geographical differences.

Table 2. Respondent Demographic Profile

Sl. No	Pseudo Names	Area of Expertise of Tutors	Age Group	Teaching Experience	Location	Highest Education
1	Nagaraj	Strategic Management	41-50	25	Bangalore, India	Doctorate
2	Aqeela	Marketing	31-40	11	Bahrain	Masters
3	Adam	Finance	31-40	7	Maryland, USA	Doctorate
4	Sarah	Entrepreneurship	41-50	17	Michigan, USA	Doctorate
5	Mohammed	Finance	51-60	23	Bahrain	Masters
6	Megha	Human Resource Management	31-40	8	Chennai, India	Doctorate
7	Thomas	Business Analytics	41-50	22	Maryland, USA	Masters
8	Khadija	Marketing	31-40	8	Bahrain	Doctorate
9	Sheela	Finance	41-50	13	India	Doctorate

Market Studies as Supplementary Insight: To strengthen the analytical depth and contextual relevance of this study, recent global market studies were reviewed alongside the primary qualitative data. These supplementary sources helped position the lived experiences of educators within broader international trends in AI integration across higher education. Key reports consulted included publications from EDUCAUSE (2025b), Jisc (2023), UNESCO (2021a), and national education councils from the United States, United Kingdom, Australia, and Finland. Insights from these reports were inductively synthesized to inform the development of the AI-LPE conceptual model, with further focus on the "Impact & Solutions" quadrant revealing strategic domains to guide the mapping of practical interventions presented in Section 6. This triangulated approach enabled a more comprehensive interpretation of institutional readiness, policy evolution, and pedagogical transformations.

Data Analysis: Interpretative Phenomenological Analysis (IPA) is a qualitative research method to study meaning of lived experiences. It emphasizes the double hermeneutic process, where participants interpret their experiences and the researchers interpret those interpretations (Smith et al., 2022). Using IPA, we are able to form themes and patterns, enriching our understanding of the tools and impact of AI on educators and students. Respondent feedback was recorded, and the transcripts were used for analysis of the data (Smith et al., 2022; Smith & Osborn, 2008). The first step of the analysis began with reading and re-reading the transcripts, followed by developing Exploratory Notes. We then constructed Experiential Statements from these notes, which was followed by clustering Experiential Statements and searching for connections from them. Based on these connections, Personal Experiential

Themes (PETs) were developed. Finally, a Cross Case Analysis was conducted to group together matching PETs under Group Experiential Themes (GET) across cases. The flexibility of the IPA method allowed the researchers to remain open to unexpected findings. For example, while our initial coding focused on pedagogical utility, emergent themes such as institutional unpreparedness, lack of AI governance policies, and long-term academic integrity concerns were included in the GETs "Angels and Demons" and "Super Guru." Thus, IPA supported in capturing complex institutional, infrastructural and ethical dynamics that go beyond issues related to classroom practices (Smith & Osborn, 2008).

Constructing Experiential Statements: The experiential statements are the condensed summary or points extracted from the transcript that directly reflect the experiences of the participants. Apart from the participants' original words, our interpretations are also included in these experiential statements and hence consists of both description as well as interpretation. The statements were refined to analyse and reflect a deeper understanding of the available data (Smith et al., 2022). This approach ensured that not only the functional benefits of AI such as lesson design and grading support were captured, but also the more nuanced concerns highlighted by educators about surveillance, plagiarism, students' over-dependence on AI tools, and the absence of clear institutional AI use guidelines and policies. A sample of Experiential Notes and Statements is shown in Table 3.

Table 3. Exploratory Notes and Experiential Statements (Sample Excerpts)

Pseudo Name	Transcript Excerpt	Exploratory Notes	Experiential Statement
Aqeela	"I find it easier to **prepare** my **lessons** now. I can just ask the AI to **summarize** a chapter, and it gives me points I might've **missed**."	Depends on AI for lesson preparation; finds it efficient; discovers new angles	Easy to prepare lessons Ask AI to Summarise chapters
Sarah	"We had a university event last month, and my students used AI to **design** the **entire program**, from concept to roles. I was impressed!"	AI supports student engagement and creativity; encourages autonomy	Design entire program
Thomas	"I'm concerned about plagiarism. Some students are clearly using AI to prepare their assignments, and it's getting **harder** to **detect**. I came to know that there are tools to mask AI detection as well…"	Concerned about academic integrity; existing tools may be insufficient	Hard to detect (Plagiarism) Tools to mask AI detection
Megha	"I **don't think AI** and new tech can ever **replace the role of a real teacher.** AI can certainly support us to perform our job, but in the end, **students need a human for support and guidance**, as we can understand their emotional and academic needs. The human touch is important."	She feels that AI lacks emotional and intuitive depth; limits of automation in student mentoring. AI cannot replicate human empathy and individualized mentorship in student development	Can't replace teachers Need human for support and guidance

Based on the Table 3 findings of the above notes and statements from respondents, similar themed statements were clubbed together after various rounds of reviews to form Personal Experiential Theme (PET) and Group Experiential Theme (GET). The below Table 4 shows a sample of how these themes were formed.

Table 4. Formation of Personal and Group Experiential Themes from Sample Experiential Statements

Experiential Statement/Emergent Themes	Personal Experiential Theme (PET)	Group Experiential Theme (GET)
Easy to prepare lessons Ask AI to Summarise chapters	PET 2.1: *Future-proof Training*	GET 2: *Super Guru*
Design entire program	PET 1.3: *Creative Soup*	GET 1: *AI Gives You Wings*
Hard to detect (Plagiarism) Tools to mask AI detection	PET 2.4: *Guarding the Grade*	GET 2: *Super Guru*
Can't replace teachers Need human for support and guidance	PET 2.5: *Enhanced Avatar*	GET 2: *Super Guru*

Below table 5 shows the complete list of all Personal Experiential Themes (PET) and Group Experiential Themes (GET) that are derived in this study.

Table 5. Clustering PETs and GETs - Theme-wise Summary of Responses

Group Experiential Themes (GET)	Personal Experiential Theme (PET)	Key Respondents	Indicative Response Summary
GET 1: AI Gives You Wings	PET 1.1: Supportive Secretary	Khadija, Sheela, Adam	Students use AI for simplifying concepts, summarizing study material, and keeping up with market trends.
	PET 1.2: Smart Feedback	Aqeela, Sarah	Students get quick feedback, structure assignments, and refine their submissions using AI tools.
	PET 1.3: Creative Soup	Sarah, Mohammed, Aqeela, Sheela	AI supports students in planning events, dividing tasks, and generating creative ideas for university activities.
GET 2: Super Guru	PET 2.1: Future-proof Training	Aqeela, Megha, Adam	AI enables educators to prepare teaching materials, slides, and case studies quickly and in a customized manner.
	PET 2.2: Engaging Gen Z	Khadija, Aqeela	AI helps make classes more engaging through creative activities, simulations, and gamified learning.
	PET 2.3: Research Unlimited	Nagaraj, Sheela	Educators use AI to support literature reviews, referencing, and generating summaries, though manual fact-checking is still required.
	PET 2.4: Guarding the Grade	Thomas, Sarah, Megha, Khadija	Concerns raised over student misuse of AI, challenges in detecting AI-written content, and the need to rethink assessment formats.
	PET 2.5: Enhanced Avatar	Nagaraj, Mohammed, Megha	AI reduces routine tasks, allowing faculty to focus more on mentoring and personalized student support.
GET 3: Angels and Demons	PET 3.1: One-Eyed Robot	Megha, Adam	AI may reproduce bias due to flawed data. Business ethics education should address AI bias awareness.
	PET 3.2: Data Robber	Mohammed	Fear over misuse of user data by AI companies; need for better data protection measures.
	PET 3.3: Mirage in the Desert	Sarah, Sheela, Khadija	Difficulty in verifying AI-generated information; institutions must establish clear policies on AI-generated academic content.
	PET 3.4: Walking the Tight Rope	Aqeela, Nagaraj, Khadija	Educators stress the need for human involvement in grading and mentoring, as AI lacks emotional intelligence and contextual understanding.

4. FINDINGS AND INTERPRETATION

Based on the responses given by the respondents, as shown in Table 5, the below Group Experiential Themes (GET) and Personal Experiential Theme (PET) themes were designed. All inter-related similar points were clubbed together as PET that were then classified under a common GET. Below descriptions provide an overview of the various themes to showcase the impact and support that AI provides educators in educational institutions:

Group Experiential Theme 1: AI Gives You Wings - This theme explores how AI is transforming the way students learn their courses, making education more accessible, efficient, and personalized to provide instant feedback and tailor learning experiences. Students develop real-world business skills through AI-powered activities that mimic professional work environments.

a) **PET 1.1: Supportive Secretary** – This theme reveals that many students in business courses use generative AI tools like ChatGPT and Gemini to understand difficult concepts, summarize reports and learning materials, as well as prepare for exams. AI's ability to simplify complex concepts into easy-to-understand bite-sized explanations makes it a preferred learning aid, sometimes even over textbooks and lecture notes. It also supports students to be aware of market trends, so that they can move ahead in life to be better prepared for their chosen career roles.
b) **PET 1.2: Smart Feedback–** The theme highlights how AI is used by students to proofread their reports, structure their assignments, and generate personalized feedback. Instead of waiting for instructor feedback, students use AI- tools to receive feedback and improve the quality of their papers and reports before submission. The downside here is that if the student is not careful, the work submitted might not fulfil the course and assessment requirements.
c) **PET 1.3: Creative Soup-** The theme shows how students use AI-powered ideas and recommendations to engage in decision-making when preparing for activities and university events. It supports them to organize their plans, divide roles between team members, design programs based on specific requirements and engage in creative ideas, thereby enhancing the overall quality of their activities.

Existing research has uncovered similar findings, for example, recent studies highlight that most students are already using AI tools like ChatGPT and other machine learning technologies (Vorobyeva et. al., 2025) primarily due to its ability to give tailored feedback (Merino-Campos (2025a). This shift from traditional standardised teaching to individualised learning points to the start of a new era of educational practices. (Aristanto et al., 2023)

Group Experiential Theme 2: Super Guru - AI is revolutionizing how instructors design lesson plans, learning material, and student engagement activities as well as developing assessments, doing research and playing a more enhanced role for students. This theme focuses on educators' ability to use AI to reshape the way they teach and assess students, while also developing themselves. Numerous studies have highlighted AI's ability to tailor content and feedback to individual learners' needs (Merino-Campos, 2025b).

a) **PET 2.1: Future-proof Training –** AI tools help instructors prepare study material quicker and more effectively for engaging PowerPoint slides, handouts and other support material. This theme reveals how professors also use AI to summarize textbook chapters and generate customized teaching notes and slides. AI-generated case studies integrate the latest industry data, company insights, and news articles, to help students learn by analysing real-world business challenges and issues. Some instructors highlighted how they use AI to generate case studies specific to multinational corporations and industry trends in HR, marketing or business management. While curriculum integration and teacher preparation remain significant concerns, many educators believe that pedagogical challenges should be prioritized over technology implementation (Vorobyeva et al., 2025).
b) **PET 2.2: Engaging Gen Z–** Teachers today are able to turn their classes into appealing sessions, that achieve course learning outcomes while delivering a fun experience. AI is able to use its vast resources of best practices to recommend a more impactful way of ensuring that the lesson has been delivered. Teachers informed how they found that using AI they are able to make unique connections to reveal how a particular topic in the course can be best delivered through innovative pedagogical approaches that the tutors may not otherwise try. Class activities and games, interactive role-plays, simulations, and real-world problem-solving scenarios are therefore becoming much more common, thanks to creative AI suggestions and results that provide clear instructions and steps on how to proceed for a selected topic of study.
c) **PET 2.3: Research Unlimited –** The theme reveals that educators can do a lot more effective and efficient research using AI to support their continuous professional development (CPD). AI tools are used to summarize and list the important points of relevant journal articles while also supporting in preparing referencing and citations. These tools help them in preparing literature reviews, summarizing papers articles and even online videos, as well as generating drafts of business reports. However, educators also stressed the need to manually fact-

check and avoid AI-generated misinformation as some of the respondents had found various errors in AI generated results which rendered them unusable.

d) **PET 2.4: Guarding the Grade–** The theme highlights respondent concerns for universities and educational institutions to apply relevant AI detection tools to monitor plagiarism in student work. With the ease of using AI tools, teachers informed that they are facing a new challenge of grading reports that had a lot of AI content. Students were finding new ways to mask their AI usage through various online applications. Also, another concern was that with increased usage of AI, teachers worried that real learning might be impacted as students would do less research for preparing their assignments and reports. Teachers discussed that such a change might lead to more and more students graduating without actually achieving course intended learning outcomes, as they take a "short-cut" towards easy grades. Some teachers also suggested that it might be time for educational institutions to look at assessments in a completely new light to do away with traditional assignments and report-writing and focus on more practical presentations and viva-voce type assessments, so as to minimize the impact of AI tools.

e) **PET 2.5: Enhanced Avatar–** With AI being able to handle many of the routine roles that occupied a lot of the time educator used to spend in their professions, it opens up the ability of the teachers to focus more on mentorship, critical analysis and support of their students' work. The theme shows that today's teachers can focus more on individual one-on-one support and guidance roles for their students, to ensure their development by focusing on their specific learning styles and learning tools.

Group Experiential Theme 3: Angels and Demons - This theme highlights the moral and ethical implications of AI adoption in education. As AI becomes a standard tool for usage across the board, students and educators must be aware of its bias, privacy concerns, and ethical limitations in decision-making.

a) **PET 3.1: One-Eyed Robot –** As students and tutors directly use a lot of information taken from AI-generated content, the theme highlights the importance of reflecting on the historical biases that exist in information available based on business decisions that have been made in the past. For example, if data is entered for a HR talent acquisition application to choose the best candidate for a technical position, the AI may favour male candidates for the role due to biased or skewed training data. It's necessary to ensure that Business ethics courses now include AI bias detection and mitigation strategies as core learning objectives to ensure that students learn to comprehend what the results might mean.

b) **PET 3.2: Data Robber –** As tutors and students become more dependent on AI generated analysis, care needs to be taken to ensure confidential organizational and personal data is handled appropriately. Just as social media companies sell and profit from user-data, the theme reveals the respondents' fears of how their data is used by AI-based companies for making a profit.

c) **PET 3.3: Mirage in the Desert:** The theme highlights concern about how realistic today's data and research are. With AI tools being able to mimic realistic information and provide summaries on reports and quote studies, the question is how to judge the veracity of the information being generated. Educational institutions must establish policies on what AI-generated content can be shared, stored, or cited in academic research.

d) **PET 3.4: Walking the Tight Rope –** While AI can perform a lot of academic processes, institutions must be careful when automating grading of assessments, and planning for AI based tutoring or chatbots for student support as it cannot replace human intuition and insight in critical decision-making. Educators emphasize the importance of their roles in learning as being essential to ensure overall learner development.

Collectively these experiential themes reveal how educators are navigating the possibilities and pitfalls of AI in higher education. They need to succeed in everything from enhancing instructional design and student engagement to handling institutional readiness, reduced critical thinking, ethical dilemmas, data privacy risks as well as algorithmic bias. They highlight the urgency of developing responsive, ethical, and context-sensitive strategies that match pedagogical values and institutional priorities (Merino-Campos, 2025a; Vorobyeva et al., 2025; Alwaqdani, 2025; Walter, 2024).

5. CONCEPTUAL MODEL: OVERVIEW OF THE AI-LPE FRAMEWORK

The AI-Enhanced Learning Pedagogy and Ethics (AI-LPE) framework in Figure 1 synthesizes three core theoretical lenses: TPACK (Technological, Pedagogical, and Content Knowledge), Adaptive Learning Theory, and the UTAUT model (Unified Theory of Acceptance and Use of Technology) with the empirical themes that emerged from this study. The framework illustrates how AI-Driven Learning Tools (ADLT), Pedagogical Integration & Adaptation (AIPS), and Ethical Concerns in AI Education (EC-AI) collectively shape teaching and learning outcomes. Finally, it proposes impact areas and solutions for the effective integration of AI in higher education settings.

Figure 1. AI-Enhanced Pedagogy and Ethics (AI-LPE) Framework

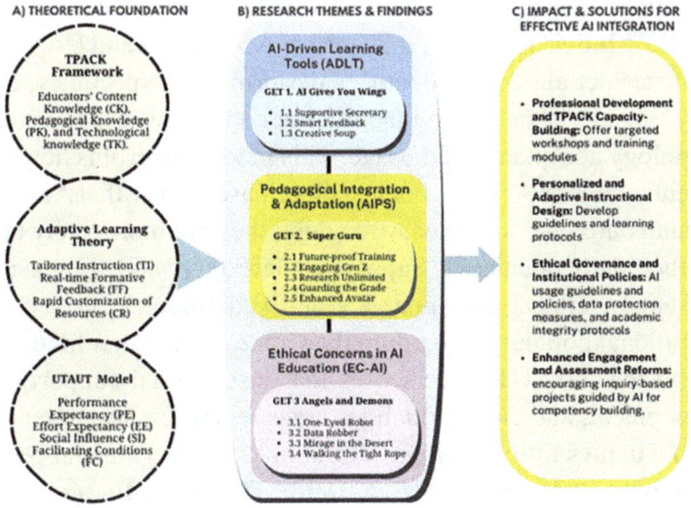

A) **Theoretical Foundation -** Three learning theories were identified and applied in this study as follows:

  i. **TPACK Framework**: TPACK (Mishra & Koehler, 2006) underscores that meaningful technology integration occurs at the intersection of educators' content knowledge (CK), pedagogical knowledge (PK), and technological knowledge (TK). This theory is applicable to our study as it highlights how teachers must align AI functionalities (e.g., automated feedback, rapid content generation) with sound pedagogical strategies and mastery of subject-specific content. As educators move toward "Super Guru" roles (see AIPS theme), their TPACK competence enables them to design authentic learning experiences that leverage AI without losing human empathy or oversight. Vorobyeva et. al. (2025) highlights that there is a need for thorough professional development activities for teachers and AI tools for especially targeted instruction.

  ii. **Adaptive Learning Theory**: Adaptive Learning Theory (Chen, 2014) posits that instructional methods should dynamically adjust to each learner's progress, often facilitated by data-driven platforms. The theory naturally supports tailored instruction, real-time formative feedback, and rapid customization of resources, evident in themes such as "AI Gives You Wings" (enabling student autonomy and creativity) and "Smart Feedback." However, Sheela also emphasizes the educator's responsibility to maintain equitable standards, ensuring that all learners benefit from adaptive features while mitigating algorithmic biases (linked to the Ethical Concerns theme).

iii. **UTAUT Model**: The Unified Theory of Acceptance and Use of Technology (Venkatesh et al., 2003) identifies performance expectancy, effort expectancy, social influence, and facilitating conditions as key determinants of technology acceptance and usage. This model underpins how teachers and students embrace AI tools. For instance, if users sense that AI supports better learning outcomes and is easy to adopt, they are more likely to integrate it into their daily practices ("Supportive Secretary" and "Enhanced Avatar"). Conversely, ethical dilemmas ("One-Eyed Robot," "Data Robber") and institutional policies ("Guarding the Grade") can either hinder or facilitate acceptance. UTAUT underscores that institutional support, professional development, and clear guidelines are essential for sustained AI adoption.

B) **Research Themes and Findings-** The study's themes are clubbed as follows:

i. **AI-Driven Learning Tools (ADLT): The main-theme AI Gives You Wings,** shows that students leverage AI to access on-demand clarifications and streamlined content summaries. By asking targeted questions or requesting concise explanations, learners receive immediate feedback to increase efficiency of the learning process while enabling students to explore topics more deeply, giving a sense of autonomy and confidence. The sub-themes, **Supportive Secretary & Smart Feedback** shows that AI serves as a "support system" for both educators and learners by automating repetitive tasks, such as organizing reading materials, suggesting assignment structures, or proofreading papers. The ability of AI technology to spot errors or offer real-time critique saves time on both sides. As a result, educators can concentrate on higher-order teaching and mentoring, while learners can refine their drafts before submission, ultimately raising the quality of academic work. The other sub-theme, **Creative Soup** reveals that AI goes beyond routine tasks, AI stimulates creativity by offering fresh ideas and novel solutions for student-led projects, university events, or collaborative endeavors. Here we see that AI acts as a catalyst for exploration, where students can brainstorm event concepts, design promotional materials, and prototype project outcomes with AI-driven suggestions, sharpening their creative thinking.

ii. **Pedagogical Integration & Adaptation (AIPS):** The main-theme **Super Guru** reveals that when educators delegate time-consuming tasks like administrative duties or preliminary content reviews to AI tools, they free themselves to assume a more hands-on, mentorship-oriented role. Thus, teachers can focus on guiding critical thinking and facilitating meaningful discussions to enhance the classroom experience beyond rote instruction. The sub-themes **Future-proof Training** and **Engaging Gen Z** support this by revealing that AI-driven resources help instructors design curricula, lesson plans and real-time case studies or interactive simulations, to ensure that the course content stays relevant to evolving industry trends. By aligning their class pedagogy to match and support Gen Z's digital fluency, learners remain motivated and are better prepared for the workplace. The sub-themes **Research Unlimited** and **Guarding the Grade** reveal the use of AI in enabling both teachers and students to conduct research and literature reviews with more efficiency. For example, AI is able to quickly review a complete paper to check that all in-text citations are accurately referenced. Such tasks which usually take a long time are now stream-lined, allowing the educators and students to focus more time on enhancing their overall knowledge of their subject and work domain. However, key challenges revolve around plagiarism issues and academic integrity. As AI writing keeps improving, educators and institutions must implement improved strategies, tools and policy reforms to ensure authenticity and overall skill development. The sub-theme **Enhanced Avatar** reveals that while AI can replicate a lot of the roles performed by educators, it cannot imitate the emotional intelligence and moral judgement that humans apply in teaching and student support and guidance. The human factor ensures empathy for students to motivate them to continue their learning journey. Therefore, AI is a useful tool for education and not a replacement.

iii. **Ethical Concerns in AI Education (EC-AI):** The main-theme is titled **Angels and Demons** to highlight the dual nature of AI's application. On one hand, AI tools are powerful and time-saving solutions that improve productivity among both teachers and students. However, on the other hand, it provides powerful, time-saving solutions that enhance productivity and engagement. On the other, there are data privacy concerns on how user-data is being used while also negatively impacting academic integrity. The sub-themes, **One-Eyed Robot** and **Data Robber** reveal that as AI tools depend on access to vast amounts of data sets, there is an increased likelihood of their results amplifying existing biases and discriminatory ideas in society, while also leaking sensitive and personal information. Therefore, strong data governance policies are important to ensure ethical standards are being maintained. Finally, the sub-themes, **Mirage in the Desert** and **Walking the Tight Rope** reveal AI's capability to generate realistic content that might be false, incomplete or inaccurate, taking information out of context. Some teachers informed about AI generating completely fabricated citations during research, raising concerns about misinformation and academic dishonesty. Without clear institutional guidelines and mechanisms being followed for verification of data being used, students may rely on inaccurate information. Academicians are faced with having to find ways to balance AI's efficiency with the need for ethical oversight, critical thinking, and an appropriate pedagogy to achieve their learning outcomes. Our findings are supported by Alwaqdani (2025), whose research in Saudi Arabia confirmed the dual nature of AI in education, where it can save time and personalize learning, while also warning of risks such as reduced creativity and compromised critical thinking, while also leading to job displacements. Merino-Campos (2025a) also emphasizes the growing ethical and data privacy concerns associated with widespread AI adoption in educational contexts. Similarly, Walter (2024) stresses that AI systems are statistical machines and therefore not 'truth-generators', a fact we must remind ourselves to be aware of their limitations.

6. DISCUSSION AND IMPLICATIONS: SOLUTIONS FOR EFFECTIVE AI INTEGRATION

While the previous sections revealed the conceptual model and thematic findings, this section moves the focus from theoretical exploration to applied implications. Given the challenges and insights shared by educators, there is a critical need to convert these findings into actionable strategies. The strategic interventions designed here are based on the Impact & Solutions quadrant within the AI-LPE conceptual framework (from Figure 1). While reflecting on these solutions, this section also looks at current industry trends and international best practices to successfully integrate AI into higher educational institutions. Figure 2 illustrates the four strategic domains derived from the lived realities of educators in this study, representing the core pathways to achieving ethical, effective, and inclusive AI integration: (i) Professional Development and TPACK Capacity-Building, (ii) Adaptive Instruction and Student Engagement, (iii) Ethical Governance and Institutional Policies, and (iv) Assessment Innovations and Academic Integrity.

Figure 2. AI-LPE in Action: Strategic Domains for Ethical AI Integration in Higher Education

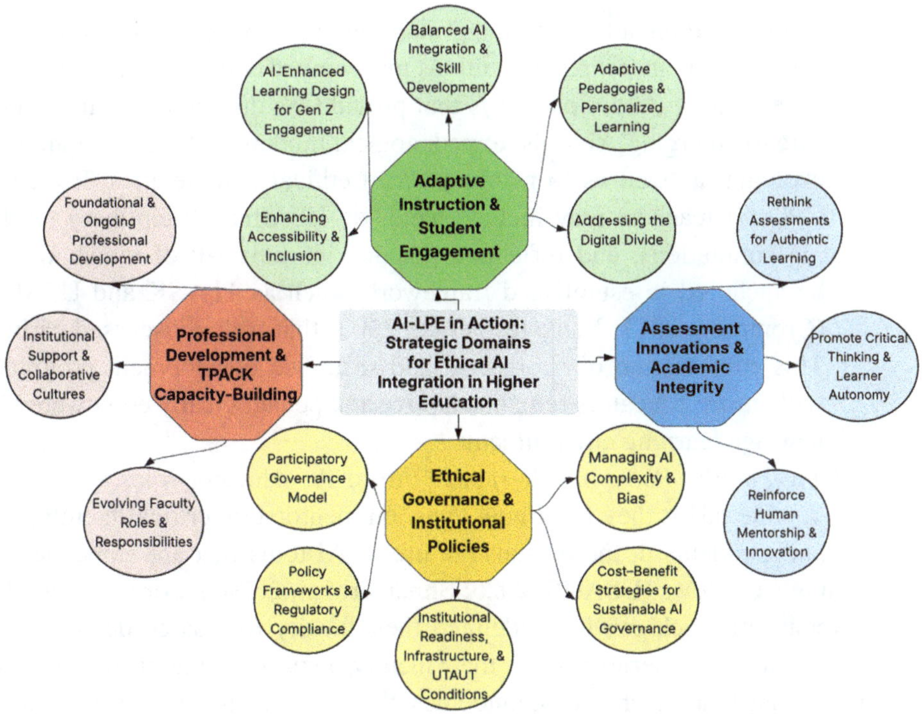

6.1 Professional Development and TPACK Capacity-Building

Within a short period, AI has been moving from being a supplementary tool to becoming a pedagogical partner. For this change to be successful, we require an appropriate shift in faculty expertise and institutional ecosystems as well. In our study, educators highlighted the value of collaborative learning in building digital confidence.

- *Foundational and Ongoing Professional Development:* To effectively integrate AI into higher education, faculty must develop a foundational literacy that extends beyond basic tool usage to include pedagogical, ethical, and cognitive competencies. This foundational training should be supported through structured programs such as case-based workshops, prompt engineering techniques, instructional design strategies and ethical decision-making frameworks (Digital Education Council, 2025a; Alwaqdani, 2025). For example,

Jisc, a UK-based tertiary education institute provides micro-credentials and toolkits that help educators apply AI tools responsibly within their disciplines (Jisc, 2023).

However, foundational training alone may not be enough in a rapidly evolving AI landscape. Institutions must embed continuous professional development (CPD) pathways that provide faculty with ongoing exposure to emerging AI tools, to pedagogical models that are continuously evolving, as well as to resolve related ethical complexities. Effective CPD for teachers may include hands-on labs, interdisciplinary teaching simulations, and reflective practice journals, all of which would be anchored in established frameworks such as TPACK and UTAUT (Crompton, 2017; Venkatesh et al., 2003) that we've discussed earlier. This combination of short-term and sustained development programs will ensure educators remain adaptive and pedagogically empowered in new-age learning environments.

- *Evolving Faculty Roles and Responsibilities:* As educator roles evolve beyond routine tasks, they must now focus on mentorship, critical facilitation, and guide students in the responsible use of AI tools that are embedded in learning workflows (USAHS, 2025; Shneiderman, 2020a). For example, the University of Michigan has redefined their faculty role as co-designers of digital learning experiences. As their faculty begin building customized AI applications that match course outcomes, they use the university's generative AI suite, including 'U-M GPT' and 'Maizey' for content creation, personalized instruction and student engagement (Maher, 2024). Also, the University of Florida is another institution that expects their faculty to embed AI tools across course curricula and focus on continuous professional development to keep themselves updated with evolving technologies (University of Florida, 2023).
- *Institutional Support and Collaborative Cultures:* While one can understand the importance for faculty members to be 'AI-ready', the fact is that they thrive in institutions that foster collaborative learning cultures and provide technological infrastructure. Institutions should offer AI-dedicated support hubs and interdisciplinary think-tanks to promote shared learning and innovation (Digital Education Council, 2025b). This aligns with TPACK principles, which emphasize the integration of technological, pedagogical, and content knowledge (Mishra & Koehler, 2006). For example, the California State University (CSU) partnered with OpenAI to roll out 'ChatGPT Edu' to cater to the needs of more than 460,000 students and 63,000 faculty across their 23 campuses. This collaborative culture has supported faculty in the

CSU system to use this tool to create tailored teaching aids, interactive simulations and formative feedback systems (Alba, 2024).

6.2 Adaptive Instruction and Student Engagement

This section is aligned with the second pillar of the AI-LPE framework. It focuses on how educators can redesign learning experiences using AI to be adaptive to the needs of students for better engagement, addressing inclusivity, motivation, and their needs for differentiated instruction. Although AI can enhance personalization, it needs to be framed within adaptive pedagogical strategies that reinforce human values.

- *Adaptive Pedagogies and Personalized Learning*: AI can support personalization by tailoring content and feedback based on learner profiles, using adaptive learning theory to guide instruction. Interviews revealed that educators are using AI to tailor instructional content, generate dynamic feedback, and co-design flexible learning paths. Adaptive Learning Theory supports these strategies by enabling real-time customization based on learner profiles (Chen, 2014). An American entrepreneurship professor in our study used AI tools to allow students to choose weekly readings based on their area of business interests, increasing autonomy and engagement. This approach matches with the point highlighted by Merino-Campos (2025b), that emphasizes the importance of tailoring content and feedback to the individual needs of each learner.
- *Enhancing Accessibility and Inclusion*: AI tools aligned with Universal Design for Learning (UDL) have expanded accessibility for students with disabilities and for neurodiverse learners. Tools like real-time captioning, speech-to-text, language translation and screen-reading applications support visual, auditory, and cognitive challenges (OECD, 2024; Garg & Sharma, 2020; U.S. Department of Education, 2023). There was a time when learners with disabilities had to rely on specialized assistive technologies. Today, modern AI solutions have democratized access to education by embedding inclusive features directly into mainstream platforms. Institutions such as the University of Michigan are integrating neurodiverse-focused adaptive platforms, while Australia's education standards promote inclusive AI design (Commonwealth of Australia, 2022).
- *AI-Enhanced Learning Design for Gen Z Engagement*: With technology progressing at a fast pace, the gaps between generations have become more pronounced than ever. As 'Generation Z', the people born between 1997 and 2012 pursue higher education, there is a need to align the use of AI and pedagogy with this generation's preferences and interactive design elements.

AI-infused pedagogy can student engagement through simulations, gamified exercises, and scenario-based learning. Participants in this study highlighted increased interest from Gen Z students when AI was used to generate fun class-activities, real-world problem scenarios or gamify revision modules. Applying AI provides educators with a host of world-class tools that not only boost student interest but also deepens their engagement with learning outcomes (Digital Education Council, 2025b). At the University of Applied Sciences Burgenland in Austria, role-playing game mechanics was integrated into the curriculum for Master's in Cloud Computing Engineering. Students engaged in simulated business scenarios to enhance decision-making and deepen theoretical understanding and critical thinking (Stampfl, Geyer, Deissl-O'Meara, & Ivkić, 2024). Similarly, the University of the Philippines Open University (UPOU) enhanced its MOOCs by incorporating AI gamification elements like progress bars, badges, and leaderboards, leading to a notable 28.86% course completion rate and improved learner satisfaction among Gen Z learners, as they were more familiar with digital game-based environments (Moldez, Crisanto, Cerdeña, Maranan, & Figueroa, 2024).

- *Addressing the Digital Divide*: Despite its benefits, AI can worsen educational inequities. Students from under-resourced communities may lack reliable internet or computing device access, furthering the digital divide between the 'haves' and the 'have-nots'. Institutions must consider investing in equitable infrastructure which may include device-lending programs and low-bandwidth solutions (University of Maryland College of Education, 2024). Universities may also consider tying up with charitable organizations to support engagement. 'Solve Education!', a global education technology NGO, launched "Dawn of Civilization," a city-building mobile game powered by AI to create immersive, motivating, and inclusive learning pathways that improves literacy and numeracy among out-of-school youth (Solve Education!, 2025).
- *Balanced AI Integration and Skill Development*: While applying the latest AI tools has many benefits, a key challenge is ensuring the transfer of required knowledge, skills and abilities to the learner. Thus, there is a pedagogical need to strike a balance between leveraging AI tools and developing core academic skills. There is a risk of educators focusing too much on AI tools that might undermine students' analytical capacities and creativity. When using AI-generated content, educators must design classroom pedagogies that encourage critique, comparison, and reflective engagement (Hennekeuser et al., 2024). Faculty in our study mostly reflected that their use of AI was appropriate and does not over-emphasize its use.

6.3 Ethical Governance and Institutional Policies

Aligned with the third solution proposed in the AI-LPE model (Figure 1), this section addresses the institutional, ethical, and policy frameworks essential for effective AI governance in higher education.

- *Institutional Readiness, Infrastructure, and UTAUT Conditions*: Several educators in our study noted absent or incomplete formal AI governance structures in their institutes. This aligns with EDUCAUSE (2025a), which found fewer than 50% of institutions have formal AI strategies in place. Therefore, the need of the hour is Infrastructure investment, faculty training, and cost-modelling as essential components of institutional readiness (Winkler, Koehler, & Theodore, 2023c). Higher education institutions must meet the facilitating conditions (FC) of the UTAUT model by ensuring that technology such as strong Wi-Fi, dedicated AI platforms, and cross-disciplinary AI support teams are accessible and integrated within faculty workflows (Venkatesh et al., 2003).
- *Policy Frameworks and Regulatory Compliance*: Clear institutional AI policies are essential to reduce misuse and ensure accountability, so as to address transparency, fairness, and bias issues (World Bank, 2024). With AI having access to sensitive, personal student and faculty data, it is critical to ensure compliance with global standards like the General Data Protection Regulation (GDPR). Institutions could adopt Data Protection Impact Assessments (DPIAs) and integrate 'privacy-by-design' protocols to ensure regulatory compliance (European Parliament, 2020; Merino-Campos, 2025b). For example, the University of Texas at Austin has introduced detailed institutional guidance on AI usage, outlining acceptable use standards for generative AI tools and prohibits the processing of sensitive or confidential data on non-institutionally vetted platforms (University of Texas at Austin, n.d.). Across the European Union, the Artificial Intelligence Act (AI Act), which entered into force in August 2024, complements the GDPR by establishing risk-based governance for AI applications. Educational institutions operating within EU jurisdictions must now prepare for compliance obligations, with key requirements for high-risk AI systems coming into effect between 2025 and 2027 (European Commission, 2024). Institutions operating in other parts of the world could voluntarily choose to comply with such international standards, to ensure effectiveness and fairness in all their systems.
- *Participatory Governance Model*: Unless educational institutions involve diverse stakeholders in policy development including faculty, IT staff, student representatives, top management, public-sector officials and legal experts,

their strategic plans for AI implementation might be unsustainable and irrelevant (OECD, 2024). In Finland, initiatives like the *Elements of AI* course, developed by the University of Helsinki and MinnaLearn, aim to educate at least 1% of EU citizens on the basics of AI, promoting widespread AI literacy and engagement (University of Helsinki & MinnaLearn, n.d.). Additionally, participatory research projects improve AI-based public sector services, emphasizing the importance of involving citizens in AI development processes (Aalto University, 2021). Singapore's approach to AI governance, outlined in its *Model AI Governance Framework*, emphasizes transparency, fairness, and human-centric values (Personal Data Protection Commission, 2020).

- *Managing AI Complexity and Bias:* The increasing complexity of AI poses risks related to misinformation, data hallucination, and algorithmic bias. A notable case of AI-induced bias occurred in the United Kingdom in 2020, when an algorithm used to grade A-level exams disproportionately downgraded students from disadvantaged backgrounds. This led to widespread protests and the eventual abandonment of the algorithmic grading system. The case highlights the potential for AI to worsen existing inequalities if not carefully managed (Wakefield, 2020). A study by the University of Texas revealed that predictive algorithms used to assess student success rates were less accurate for Black and Hispanic students compared to their white counterparts. These inaccuracies could lead to misinformed decisions regarding grades, student support and resource allocation (Gándara et al., 2023). Stanford University's Human-Centered Artificial Intelligence (HAI) initiative found that AI detectors designed to identify AI-generated text were more likely to flag essays written by non-native English speakers as AI-generated, raising concerns about fairness and the potential for unjust academic penalties (Liang et al., 2023). To address these challenges, institutions need to implement safeguards such as real-time content verification and bias detection protocols. Accrediting bodies may consider policy audits on AI integration practices (Floridi et al., 2018).
- *Cost–Benefit Strategies for Sustainable AI Governance:* Although the upfront costs of AI adoption such as licensing, infrastructure, and faculty training can be significant, they need to be viewed as strategic investments that will improve profitability and success in the long run rather than as wasted expenses. Global organizations report that over time, AI integration can lead to enhanced student engagement, streamlined administrative tasks, and improved instructional efficiency (OECD, 2024; UNESCO, 2021b). Institutions must adopt a dual-pronged approach that upholds ethical AI use while ensuring long-term financial sustainability. This includes establishing clear usage protocols, academic integrity policies, and deploying AI detection tools to safe-

guard educational standards (U.S. Department of Education, 2023). Some of our participants highlighted the challenge with grading student work, as their institutions did not provide access to AI-detection software applications. By aligning ethical policy design with return-on-investment evaluations, institutions can create governance models that are both responsible and financially sustainable.

6.4 Assessment Innovations and Academic Integrity

Aligned with the last pillar of the AI-LPE model, this section focuses on reforming assessment practices to align with evolving academic integrity standards and student-centered evaluation.

- *Promote Critical Thinking and Learner Autonomy:* The widespread use of generative AI tools in higher education raises concerns about declining student autonomy and the erosion of critical engagement. With instant access to AI-generated information at their fingertips, students may be tempted to accept surface-level outputs instead of developing their own in-depth reasoning and applying their problem-solving skills when preparing their assignments. This shift not only threatens academic integrity but also challenges the broader mission of higher education to cultivate independent thought, employability skills, and civic responsibility among the future workforce.

One solution is to design structured tasks that require students to analyse, evaluate, and make ethical decisions about AI-generated content, essential for restoring learner agency (Hennekeuser et al., 2024). The risk is that students may outsource even higher-order academic tasks to AI, thereby bypassing the intellectual rigor traditionally expected in university education. Reflective assessment models, such as those at Bournemouth University, help counter this trend by training students to critique and contextualize AI outputs, reinforcing analytical and self-regulatory competencies (Bournemouth University, 2023). Some educators are now incorporating AI into the early stages of assignments while requiring students to revise and refine their work through human-led critique and reflection. This two-phase approach encourages responsible AI use while preserving originality and deeper thinking (Digital Education Council, 2025a).

- *Rethink Assessments for Authentic Learning:* A recent Bloomberg article (2025) cautions that "assignments that once demanded days of diligent research can be accomplished in minutes," making it increasingly difficult for educators to distinguish between original student work and AI-generated content. This growing concern has prompted many faculty members to redesign assessments in ways that better reflect authentic learning and achievement of course outcomes.

Our interviews revealed that educators are moving away from traditional essays and standard reports, opting instead for oral presentations, viva-voce and Q&As, inquiry-based projects, hand-written exams, and other formats that limit opportunities for AI misuse. At the University of Warwick, students are permitted to use AI tools during submission of their essays but must submit the prompts they used and explain how they built upon the AI-generated content to demonstrate learning (University of Warwick, 2025). These strategies encourage critical engagement and transparency. This shift is also evident in the growing adoption of performance-based formats such as role-plays, debates, case simulations, and presentations. These methods align more closely with higher-order learning objectives and demand that students actively construct and demonstrate knowledge (Esplugas, 2023; University of Warwick, 2025). The emphasis on deeper engagement echoes reflective practices discussed earlier, underscoring the need for assessment tasks that support both ethical AI use and authentic learner development.

- *Reinforce Human Mentorship and Innovation*: While AI can assist with administrative and low-level cognitive tasks, educators in our study emphasized that the human dimensions of teaching remain irreplaceable as qualities such as empathy, ethical judgment, and contextual understanding are essential to the learning process. Faculty can continue to play a critical role in mentoring students, offering personalised feedback, and guiding learners through complex academic, professional, and ethical challenges (Shneiderman, 2020b). In response to these demands, some institutions are embedding AI literacy within the curriculum in ways that promote innovation while maintaining academic rigour. At University College London (UCL), for example, students explore how AI is transforming real-world professional practices within their field. This type of engagement supports deeper learning by fostering ethical reflection and critical application of AI tools in authentic contexts (University College London, 2023).

As mentors, faculty can redesign curricula that supports their evolving roles. Curricula that are designed to include structured stages such as AI-assisted ideation followed by human critique and refinement can help students understand how to use AI responsibly without compromising originality. These practices, supported by guidelines from the Digital Education Council (2025b), encourage students to think critically about the role of AI in their learning and professional development.

Educators also pointed to the need for higher education to equip students with future-facing skills that remain valuable in an increasingly automated workforce. The example of IBM, which recently reduced thousands of jobs in its human resources division due to AI integration, highlights the growing impact of automation even in traditionally people-centered domains (Yadav, 2025). This trend underscores the importance of developing distinctly human capacities such as creativity, ethical reasoning, communication, and collaboration. By nurturing these innovative abilities, educators can prepare students to work effectively alongside AI systems, rather than be displaced by them.

7. CONCLUSION

As artificial intelligence becomes an embedded force in higher education, this study illustrates how its integration is redefining the landscape of business education from routine automation to pedagogical transformation. Drawing from the lived experiences of educators across diverse national contexts, this research uncovered how AI supports learning personalization, rapid content generation, and creative engagement, while also raising significant concerns around academic integrity, data ethics, and institutional preparedness.

Based on the findings of this study, the AI-LPE (AI-Enhanced Learning, Pedagogy, and Ethics) framework was developed which reveals the experiential themes, *AI Gives You Wings*, *Super Guru*, and *Angels and Demons*, showing how AI acts both as an enabler and a disruptor. Students benefit from on-demand feedback and creativity-enhancing tools, while educators leverage AI for curriculum design, student engagement, and professional growth. Yet, risks such as data misuse, bias, and over-reliance on generative content demand critical scrutiny and policy responses. The conceptual integration of TPACK, Adaptive Learning Theory, and the UTAUT model highlights that sustainable AI adoption must go beyond technology to include pedagogical purpose, ethical frameworks, and supportive institutional conditions. The four strategic domains derived from this research, Professional Development and TPACK Capacity-Building; Adaptive Instruction and Student Engagement; Ethical Governance and Institutional Policies; and Assessment Innovations and Academic Integrity, offer a roadmap for institutions to move from AI awareness to AI maturity.

Ultimately, the findings underscore that while AI can enhance educational efficiency and innovation, it cannot replace the human elements of mentorship, critical reflection, and ethical judgment. The future of AI in higher education will depend not on how smart the systems become, but on how wisely institutions and educators choose to use them to co-create meaningful, innovative and ethical learning journeys.

REFERENCES

Aad, S., & Hardey, M. (2025). Generative AI: Hopes, controversies and the future of faculty roles in education. *Quality Assurance in Education*, *33*(2), 267–282. DOI: 10.1108/QAE-02-2024-0043

Aalto University. (2021, March 29). Participatory research to improve artificial intelligence-based public sector services and empower citizens. https://shorturl.at/LO2zm

Abdelwahab, H. R., Rauf, A., & Chen, D. (2023). Business students' perceptions of Dutch higher educational institutions in preparing them for artificial intelligence work environments. *Industry and Higher Education*, *37*(1), 22–34. DOI: 10.1177/09504222221087614

Adelaide Now. (2025, May 26). More efficient and easier: How AI can help teachers spend less time on things other than teaching. *Adelaide Now*. https://shorturl.at/DUSBv

Alba, D. (2024, February 4). Cal State is bringing ChatGPT to all of its campuses. *Axios*. https://www.axios.com/2025/02/04/california-state-university-chatgpt-openai

Alwaqdani, M. (2025). Investigating teachers' perceptions of artificial intelligence tools in education: Potential and difficulties. *Education and Information Technologies*, *30*(3), 2737–2755. DOI: 10.1007/s10639-024-12903-9

Aristanto, A., Supriatna, E., Panggabean, H. M., Apriyanti, E., Hartini, H., Sari, N. I., & Kurniawati, W. (2023). The role of Artificial Intelligence (AI) at school learning. *Consilium: Education and Counseling Journal*, *3*(2), 2. Advance online publication. DOI: 10.36841/consilium.v3i2.3437

Bloomberg Editorial Board. (2025, May 27). *Does college still have a purpose in the age of ChatGPT?* Bloomberg. https://www.bloomberg.com/opinion/articles/2025-05-27/does-college-still-have-a-purpose-in-the-age-of-chatgpt

Bournemouth University. (2023, August 2). Using artificial intelligence to support assignments or assessments. https://www.bournemouth.ac.uk/news/2023-08-02/using-artificial-intelligence-support-assignments-or-assessments

Celik, I. (2023). Towards intelligent-TPACK: An empirical study on teachers' professional knowledge to ethically integrate artificial intelligence (AI)-based tools into education. *Computers in Human Behavior*, *138*, 107468. Advance online publication. DOI: 10.1016/j.chb.2022.107468

Chedrawi, C., Kazoun, N., & Kokkinaki, A. (2024). The role of AI agents in fostering inclusivity for HEIs' students with special needs against backdrops of the accreditation trend. *Quality Assurance in Education, 32*(4), 582–596. Advance online publication. DOI: 10.1108/QAE-01-2024-0010

Chen, C. M. (2014). Intelligent web-based learning system with personalized learning path guidance. *Computers & Education, 56*(1), 209–222. DOI: 10.1016/j.compedu.2010.08.001

Commonwealth of Australia. (2022). *Disability standards for education review: Final report.* https://www.education.gov.au/disability-standards-education-2005/resources

Creswell, J. W. (2013). *Qualitative inquiry and research design: Choosing among five approaches* (3rd ed.). SAGE.

Crompton, H. (2017). *Mobile learning and educational theory: Integrating pedagogical strategies with learning technologies.* Routledge.

Digital Education Council. (2025a). *Annual report on digital learning innovations.* Digital Education Council Publications.

Digital Education Council. (2025b). Empowering faculty to experiment, share and learn: Advancing AI literacy in higher education. https://www.digitaleducationcouncil.com/post/empowering-faculty-to-experiment-share-and-learn-advancing-ai-literacy-in-higher-education

EDUCAUSE. (2025a). *2025 EDUCAUSE AI landscape study.* https://library.educause.edu/resources/2025/2/2025-educause-ai-landscape-study

EDUCAUSE. (2025b). *Teaching and learning workforce in higher education.* https://www.educause.edu/content/2025/teaching-and-learning-workforce-in-higher-education

Esplugas, M. (2023). The use of artificial intelligence (AI) to enhance academic communication, education and research: A balanced approach. *The Journal of Hand Surgery, European Volume, 48*(8), 819–822. DOI: 10.1177/17531934231185746 PMID: 37417005

European Commission. (2024). *Artificial Intelligence Act: A European approach to excellence and trust.* https://digital-strategy.ec.europa.eu/en/policies/regulatory-framework-ai

European Parliament. (2020). *The impact of the General Data Protection Regulation (GDPR) on artificial intelligence.* https://www.europarl.europa.eu/RegData/etudes/STUD/2020/641530/EPRS_STU(2020)641530_EN.pdf

Floridi, L., Cowls, J., Beltrametti, M., Chatila, R., Chazerand, P., Dignum, V., Luetge, C., Madelin, R., Pagallo, U., Rossi, F., Schafer, B., Valcke, P., & Vayena, E. (2018). AI4People—An ethical framework for a good AI society: Opportunities, risks, principles, and recommendations. *Minds and Machines*, *28*(4), 689–707. DOI: 10.1007/s11023-018-9482-5 PMID: 30930541

Gándara, D., Anahideh, H., Ison, M. P., & Picchiarini, L. (2023). Inside the black box: Detecting and mitigating algorithmic bias across racialized groups in college student-success prediction. *arXiv preprint* arXiv:2301.03784. https://arxiv.org/abs/2301.03784

Ghimire, P., Kim, K., & Acharya, M. (2024). Opportunities and challenges of generative AI in the construction industry: Focusing on adoption of text-based models. *Buildings (Basel, Switzerland)*, *14*(1), 220. DOI: 10.3390/buildings14010220

Gichuki, L. (2025). AI goes to school: The global AI education race, opportunities and perils. *DevelopmentAid*. https://www.developmentaid.org/news-stream/post/194647/ai-transforming-education

Hennekeuser, D., Vaziri, D. D., Golchinfar, D., Schreiber, D., & Stevens, G. (2024). Enlarged education – Exploring the use of generative AI to support lecturing in higher education. *International Journal of Artificial Intelligence in Education*. Advance online publication. DOI: 10.1007/s40593-024-00424-y

Holmes, W., Bialik, M., & Fadel, C. (2019). *Artificial intelligence in education: Promises and implications for teaching and learning*. The Center for Curriculum Redesign.

Hwang, G. J., Xie, H., Wah, B. W., & Gašević, D. (2020). Vision, challenges, roles and research issues of artificial intelligence in education. *Computers & Education: Artificial Intelligence*, *1*, 100001. DOI: 10.1016/j.caeai.2020.100001

Jin, Y., Yan, L., Echeverria, V., Gašević, D., & Martinez-Maldonado, R. (2025). Generative AI in higher education: A global perspective of institutional adoption policies and guidelines. *Computers and Education: Artificial Intelligence*, *8*, 100348. DOI: 10.1016/j.caeai.2024.100348

Jisc. (2023). *AI in tertiary education: Challenges and opportunities*. https://www.jisc.ac.uk/reports/artificial-intelligence-in-tertiary-education

Labadze, L., Grigolia, M., & Machaidze, L. (2023). Role of AI chatbots in education: A systematic literature review. *International Journal of Educational Technology in Higher Education*, *20*(1), 56. Advance online publication. DOI: 10.1186/s41239-023-00426-1

Li, S., & Gu, X. (2023). A risk framework for human-centered artificial intelligence in education: Based on literature review and Delphi–AHP method. *Journal of Educational Technology & Society*, *26*(1), 187–202.

Liang, P., Bommasani, R., & Zelikman, E. (2023). AI-detectors biased against non-native English writers. *Stanford HAI*. https://hai.stanford.edu/news/ai-detectors-biased-against-non-native-english-writers

Maher, M. (2024, May 8). U-M launches first university-built generative AI tools. *The Michigan Daily*. https://www.michigandaily.com/news/administration/umich-becomes-first-major-university-to-develop-its-own-generative-ai/

McDonald, N., Johri, A., Ali, A., & Hingle, A. (2024). Generative artificial intelligence in higher education: Evidence from an analysis of institutional policies and guidelines. *arXiv preprint arXiv:2402.01659*. https://arxiv.org/abs/2402.01659

Merino-Campos, C. (2025a). Privacy by design: Building a data protection culture in higher education institutions. *EDUData Journal*, *11*(1), 45–60.

Merino-Campos, C. (2025b). The impact of artificial intelligence on personalized learning in higher education: A systematic review. *Trends in Higher Education*, *4*(2), 17. DOI: 10.3390/higheredu4020017

Mishra, P., & Koehler, M. J. (2006). Technological pedagogical content knowledge: A framework for teacher knowledge. *Teachers College Record*, *108*(6), 1017–1054. DOI: 10.1111/j.1467-9620.2006.00684.x

Moldez, C., Crisanto, M. A., Cerdeña, M. G. R., Maranan, D. S., & Figueroa, R. (2024). Innovation in education: Developing and assessing gamification in the University of the Philippines Open University Massive Open Online Courses. *arXiv preprint* arXiv:2409.03309. https://arxiv.org/abs/2409.03309

Nyaaba, M. (2025). *Glocalizing Generative AI in Education for the Global South: The Design Case of 21st Century Teacher Educator AI for Ghana*. arXiv preprint arXiv:2504.07149. https://arxiv.org/abs/2504.07149 DOI: 10.2139/ssrn.5212321

OECD. (2024). The future of education and skills: AI in learning. https://www.oecd.org/education/ai-in-education.pdf

Personal Data Protection Commission. (2020). *Singapore's approach to AI governance: Model AI governance framework* (2nd ed.). https://www.pdpc.gov.sg/help-and-resources/2020/01/model-ai-governance-framework

Selwin, S., Saseendran, H., Vemavarapu, K. R., Shaikh, I., Shaikh, Z. H., & Harris, S. B. (2024). AI-Driven Employee Engagement: Transforming Banking Workforce Dynamics Using the BEULA Model. In Awwad, B. (Ed.), *The AI Revolution: Driving Business Innovation and Research. Studies in Systems, Decision and Control* (Vol. 525). Springer., DOI: 10.1007/978-3-031-54383-8_32

Shneiderman, B. (2020a). Bridging the gap between ethics and practice: Guidelines for reliable, safe, and trustworthy human-centered AI systems. *ACM Transactions on Interactive Intelligent Systems*, *10*(4), 1–31. DOI: 10.1145/3419764

Shneiderman, B. (2020b). Human-centered AI. *Interactions (New York, N.Y.)*, *27*(4), 76–81. DOI: 10.1145/3388440

Smith, J. A., Flowers, P., & Larkin, M. (2022). *Interpretative phenomenological analysis: Theory, method and research* (2nd ed.). SAGE. DOI: 10.1037/0000259-000

Smith, J. A., & Osborn, M. (2008). Interpretative phenomenological analysis. In Smith, J. A. (Ed.), *Qualitative psychology: A practical guide to research methods* (2nd ed., pp. 53–80). SAGE.

Solve Education! (2025). *Dawn of civilization: Bridging educational gaps through gamification*. Solve Education! Publications.

Stampfl, R., Geyer, B., Deissl-O'Meara, M., & Ivkić, I. (2024). Revolutionising role-playing games with ChatGPT. *arXiv preprint* arXiv:2407.02048. https://arxiv.org/abs/2407.02048

UNESCO. (2021a). *AI literacy and the new digital divide: A global call for action*. https://www.unesco.org/en/articles/ai-literacy-and-new-digital-divide-global-call-action

UNESCO. (2021b). *Guidance for AI and education: Recommendations for governments*. https://unesdoc.unesco.org/ark:/48223/pf0000376709

University College London. (2023). *Assessment ideas for an AI enabled world*. https://www.ucl.ac.uk/teaching-learning/sites/teaching_learning/files/assessment_menu_040723.pdf

University of Florida. (2023). *AI Across the Curriculum – AI2 Center*. https://ai.ufl.edu

University of Helsinki & MinnaLearn. (n.d.). *Elements of AI*. https://www.elementsofai.com/

University of Maryland College of Education. (2024). *Bridging digital divides in AI-enabled classrooms*.

University of Texas at Austin. (n.d.). *Guidance for using artificial intelligence.* https://tech.utexas.edu/governance/guidance-for-ai

University of Warwick. (2025). *AI and assessment.* https://warwick.ac.uk/fac/cross_fac/academic-development/ai/assessment/

U.S. Department of Education. (2023). *Artificial intelligence and the future of teaching and learning.* https://www.ed.gov/sites/ed/files/documents/ai-report/ai-report.pdf

USAHS. (2025). *AI in higher education: How AI is reshaping higher education.* https://www.usa.edu/blog/ai-in-higher-education-how-ai-is-reshaping-higher-education/

Venkatesh, V., Morris, M. G., Davis, G. B., & Davis, F. D. (2003). User acceptance of information technology: Toward a unified view. *Management Information Systems Quarterly, 27*(3), 425–478. DOI: 10.2307/30036540

Vesna, L., Sawale, P. S., Kaul, P., Pal, S., & Murthy, B. S. N. V. R. (2025). Digital divide in AI-powered education: Challenges and solutions for equitable learning. *Journal of Information Systems Engineering & Management, 10*(21s). https://www.jisem-journal.com/index.php/journal/article/view/3327

Vorobyeva, K. I., Belous, S., Savchenko, N. V., Smirnova, L. M., Nikitina, S. A., & Zhdanov, S. P. (2025). Personalized learning through AI: Pedagogical approaches and critical insights. *Contemporary Educational Technology, 17*(2), ep574. DOI: 10.30935/cedtech/16108

Wakefield, J. (2020, August 17). A-levels and GCSEs: How did the exam algorithm work? *BBC News.* https://www.bbc.com/news/technology-53810658

Walter, Y. (2024). Embracing the future of artificial intelligence in the classroom: The relevance of AI literacy, prompt engineering, and critical thinking in modern education. *International Journal of Educational Technology in Higher Education, 21*(1), 15. Advance online publication. DOI: 10.1186/s41239-024-00448-3

Winkler, C., Hammoda, B., Noyes, E., & Van Gelderen, M. (2023a). Entrepreneurship education at the dawn of generative artificial intelligence. *Entrepreneurship Education and Pedagogy, 6*(4), 579–589. DOI: 10.1177/25151274231198799

Winkler, J., Koehler, M. J., & Theodore, R. (2023b). Reimagining professional development for AI-driven classrooms. *Educational Technology Research and Development, 71*(2), 355–373. DOI: 10.1007/s11423-023-10102-9

Winkler, R., Koehler, M. J., & Theodore, R. M. (2023c). Empowering educators to be AI-ready: Opportunities and cost considerations. *Journal of Educational Technology Policy and Practice, 21*(2), 115–134. DOI: 10.1007/s12345-023-00678-x

World Bank. (2024). *Artificial intelligence in education: Challenges and opportunities*. https://documents1.worldbank.org/curated/en/099734306182493324/pdf/IDU152823b13109c514ebd19c241a289470b6902.pdf

Yadav, N. (2025, May 27). *IBM is cutting around 8000 jobs likely because of AI, major losses in HR department*. India Today. https://www.indiatoday.in/technology/news/story/ibm-is-cutting-around-8000-jobs-likely-because-of-ai-major-losses-in-hr-department-2544873-2025-05-27

Yan, L., Martinez-Maldonado, R., Jin, Y., Echeverria, V., Milesi, M., Fan, J., Zhao, L., Alfredo, R., Li, X., & Gašević, D. (2024b). *The effects of generative AI agents and scaffolding on enhancing students' comprehension of visual learning analytics*. arXiv preprint arXiv:2409.11645. https://arxiv.org/abs/2409.11645

Yan, L., Sha, L., Zhao, L., Li, Y., Martinez-Maldonado, R., Chen, G., Li, X., Jin, Y., & Gašević, D. (2024a). Practical and ethical challenges of large language models in education: A systematic scoping review. *British Journal of Educational Technology*, *55*(1), 90–112. DOI: 10.1111/bjet.13370

Chapter 2
AI as an Educational Partner:
Potential, Ethical Dilemmas, and the Future of Teaching

Anand Soni
https://orcid.org/0009-0001-4896-0639
Bahrain Polytechnic, Bahrain

Satya Ratnakaram
https://orcid.org/0000-0002-8908-302X
Bahrain Polytechnic, Bahrain

Om Prakash Yadav
https://orcid.org/0000-0003-0802-8684
Lovely Professional University, India

Harris Saseendran
https://orcid.org/0000-0001-7386-8001
Bahrain Polytechnic, Bahrain

Zakir Hossen Shaikh
https://orcid.org/0000-0003-4733-4166
College of Business Administration, Bahrain

ABSTRACT

Rapid advancements in Artificial Intelligence (AI) are dramatically reshaping various sectors, with education at the forefront of this transformation. AI-driven technologies, including intelligent tutoring systems, automated grading tools, and personalized learning platforms—are revolutionizing traditional teaching methodologies by

DOI: 10.4018/979-8-3373-0396-3.ch002

delivering tailored educational experiences and streamlining administrative tasks (Francesc et al., 2019). This paper investigates AI's potential as an essential educational partner rather than a substitute for human teachers, highlighting its role in enhancing personalized learning and freeing educators to focus on mentorship and critical thinking. This study discusses the ethical concerns, issues/ impact and future of teaching in an AI-assisted environment, advocating for a balanced approach that leverages technological advancements while preserving the indispensable human element in education. The paper calls for responsible AI deployment to support and enhance the core values of teaching and learning.

1. INTRODUCTION

In 1959, Arthur Samuel coined machine learning as "the ability to learn without being explicitly programmed," marking an early milestone in AI. While AI can exist without machine learning, doing so demands extensive manual coding. Deep Learning, a subfield of machine learning, uses layered neural networks to extract meaningful patterns from data. AI heavily relies on big data, defined as datasets too large for conventional tools, characterized by Volume, Variety, and Velocity (Manyika et al., 2011). In education, Educational Data Mining and Learning Analytics use data to improve teaching, predict learner behaviors, and provide real-time feedback for enhanced learning outcomes *(Francesc et al., 2019).*

1.1 Background and Context

Artificial Intelligence (AI) is reshaping education by transforming traditional teaching models into dynamic, personalized systems. From intelligent tutors to adaptive learning platforms, AI addresses demand for individualized instruction and administrative efficiency (Sierra, 2024). Tools like ChatGPT, virtual assistants, and learning analytics provide real-time feedback and help identify learning gaps, especially in technical fields like medicine and engineering (Mirza et al., 2025; Varghese et al., 2025).

However, this progress brings ethical concerns, including data privacy, bias, and reduced teacher autonomy (Jafari, 2024).

AI in education has changed from rule-based systems to psychologically intelligent tools that actively adopt learning (Lucietto & Peters, 2024). However, limited access in less focused areas highlights ongoing equity challenges (Sapohov, 2024). As AI becomes a collaborative classroom partner, it restyles traditional teaching roles and responsibilities (Ka & Colloton, 2024). Ethical venture of AI in education demands clear and strong digital literacy between the educators and learners (Eshaghi, 2024).

In response to the growing demand for unbiased, reachable, and tailored learning experiences in the global education sector, this study explores the use of AI's transformative potential while emphasizing the need of ethical, inclusive, and responsible implementation to ensure technological innovations benefit all stakeholders of an educational systems (UNESCO, 2023).

1.2 Rationale for the Study

Artificial Intelligence (AI) is redesigning education by developing individualized learning and advancing instructional proficiency (Sierra, 2024). However, its rapid incorporation raises important concerns about algorithmic bias, surveillance, and unequal access (Jafari, 2024). As AI evolves from a helpful tool to a joint classroom partner, it challenges traditional teaching roles and *demands* adaptive and rational strategies from both educators and learners (Ka & Colloton, 2024). This study responds to these challenges by examining AI's transformative probable in education while highlighting the need for ethical, wide-ranging, and responsible implementation to ensure that innovation benefits all stakeholders in the educational system.

1.3 Objectives of the Chapter

1. **To examine the pedagogical potential of Artificial Intelligence (AI)** AI is becoming a genuine partner in the classroom, helping individualize learning, catalyst engagement, and supporting teachers in meeting diverse student needs.
2. **To critically analyze the ethical dilemmas** associated with AI addition in education, including concerns of data privacy, algorithmic bias, academic integrity, teacher autonomy, and unequal access to technological resources.
3. **To explore future trajectories for AI in education**, offering evidence-based recommendations for educators, policymakers, and technologists on the responsible, equitable, and pedagogically sound deployment of AI systems in classrooms.

1.4 Scope and Limitations

Scope of the Study

This chapter explores the integration of Artificial Intelligence (AI) as a partner in modern education, emphasizing its pedagogical potential, ethical implications, and future impact on teaching and learning practices. The focus is both theoretical and practical, examining AI tools such as intelligent tutoring systems, generative AI (e.g., ChatGPT), learning analytics, and adaptive learning platforms. The study encompasses K–12 and higher education settings, drawing on global examples to provide a comprehensive overview ((Akgun & Greenhow, 2021). It engages with literature from 2020 to 2025, emphasizing emerging technologies, teacher-student dynamics, and institutional adoption models.

Limitations of the Study

While the chapter aims for broad relevance, several limitations are acknowledged:

- Geographical scope is general rather than region-specific, which may overlook local cultural, infrastructural, and policy differences affecting AI deployment.
- The study is qualitative and conceptual, relying on secondary data and literature review rather than empirical fieldwork or experimental validation.
- Rapid advancements in AI may outpace current literature, potentially making some conclusions subject to change.
- Focus is primarily on educational settings, corporate training or informal

2. LITERATURE REVIEW

2.1 Evolution of AI in Educational Contexts

Artificial Intelligence in education has evolved from early rule-based systems in the 1980s to modern deep learning models capable of natural language understanding and real-time student interaction. Early intelligent tutoring systems like PLATO laid the groundwork for AI-enabled personalized learning (f et al., 2016). The evolution was catalyzed by advancements in machine learning, NLP, and cloud computing, enabling AI to scale within digital learning platforms (Holmes et al., 2019). Today, AI contributes to pedagogical shifts, supporting adaptive learning and data-driven instruction (Chen et al., 2020). Also In smart education, wearable devices may involve the integration of AI to deliver personalized feedback that encourages students to critically analyze and deepen their understanding (Pavan et al., 2024). The historical trend suggests AI has transitioned from a passive tool to an active learning agent (Baker et al., 2019; Ka & Colloton, 2024).

2.2 AI-Powered Tools and Platforms in Use Today

Current AI tools include virtual assistants, learning analytics dashboards, automated essay scoring systems, and generative tools like ChatGPT. Platforms such as Carnegie Learning and Century Tech (CLCT) retain rational algorithms to individualize content delivery (Zawacki-Richter et al., 2019). AI is also used for automated marking/grading and in day-to-day administrative work (Luckin et al., 2016). Generative models like GPT-4 are being explored for individualize student feedback and creative writing support (Holmes et al., 2022). AI tools are increasingly integrated into Learning Management System (LMS) in the educational environments and enhancing student and educator engagement (Sierra, 2024).

2.3 Impact of AI on Teaching and Learning

AI changes learning by improving access, enabling individualized monitoring, and identifying knowledge gaps. Research shows that students using AI-assisted platforms exhibit improved performance and retention (Chen et al., 2020). Teachers at different levels benefit from AI-generated insights into student learning behaviors (Xia et al., 2022). However, concerns remain about trusting too heavily on automation, reducing significant human interaction in the classroom (Luckin et al., 2016). While AI can boost engagement and support formative assessment, it could be used to enhance the teaching aids do not replace the natural human touch that is focal point to effective teaching and learning (Mirza et al., 2025).

2.4 The Role of Teachers in AI-Integrated Classrooms

In these days we can witness that classroom at any educational organization supported by AI, teachers are evolving from traditional content deliverers roles to facilitators and learning designers (Holmes et al., 2022). As AI reshapes directions/ instruction, teacher training in AI literacy becomes essential (Zawacki-Richter et al., 2019). Yet, concerns about losing autonomy persist (Jafari, 2024), highlighting the need to involve educators in AI design to preserve pedagogical integrity (Ka & Colloton, 2024; Lucietto & Peters, 2024).

2.5 Ethical Considerations in AI for Education

AI in education introduces ethical dilemmas/ a confusion around student and educator's privacy, surveillance system, bias, and transparency. Predictive analytics, while useful, may inadvertently reinforce stereotypes or socio-economic disparities (Baker & Smith, 2019). Data governance frameworks are often lacking, leading to ethical vulnerabilities (Holmes et al., 2019). Teachers and students express discomfort with opaque AI decisions and lack of control over data (Eshaghi, 2024; Jafari, 2024). Equity concerns are especially pressing in low-resource settings with limited AI access (Sapohov, 2024).

2.6 Gaps in Existing Research

Despite increasing AI adoption, gaps remain in longitudinal studies on learning outcomes, the psychological impact of AI use, and policy frameworks guiding AI ethics. Few studies explore how AI affects student agency and teacher identity (Zhao et al., 2024). Most research is also concentrated in high-income countries, leaving out diverse contexts (Ka & Colloton, 2024; Sapohov, 2024). Furthermore, there's limited interdisciplinary work that bridges educational theory with AI technical development (Holmes et al., 2022).

This chapter explores how the relationship between AI technology and education can be transformed by addressing ethical boundaries and integrating evolutionary updates into the governing rules of the digital landscape, particularly within the education sector.

3. RESEARCH QUESTIONS

3.1 Primary Research Question

- **RQ1:** What is the potential of Artificial Intelligence (AI) to function as a collaborative partner in modern teaching and learning environments?
- **RQ2**: What are the key ethical challenges associated with the integration of AI in educational contexts, particularly concerning equity, privacy, and teacher autonomy?
- **RQ3**: How might the evolving relationship between AI and educators reshape the future of teaching roles, curriculum design, and classroom practices?

3.2 Sub-Questions

- How do current AI-powered tools (e.g., ChatGPT, adaptive platforms) influence students' learning outcomes across different educational levels?
- What are educators' perceptions of AI's role in enhancing or limiting pedagogical effectiveness?
- How do data privacy regulations and algorithmic transparency affect the trustworthiness of AI systems in educational use?
- In what ways do AI tools contribute to or mitigate educational inequalities in under-resourced institutions?
- What competencies do teachers need to effectively integrate AI tools while maintaining ethical and instructional standards?

4. RESEARCH METHODOLOGY

4.1 Research Design

This study adopts a qualitative, exploratory research design utilizing secondary data analysis. The research aims to critically examine existing academic literature, policy documents, technical reports, and institutional case studies that discuss the integration of Artificial Intelligence (AI) in educational contexts. This design is suitable for synthesizing diverse sources to identify thematic patterns, ethical issues, and pedagogical implications without direct interaction with human participants (Johnston, 2014).

By analyzing previously published peer-reviewed literature and institutional publications from 2020–2025, the study explores how AI has influenced teaching and learning practices, teacher roles, and educational equity. A narrative synthesis approach is employed to interpret trends, contradictions, and gaps within the selected studies (Pope & Mays, 2006). The design allows for a broad yet critical overview of AI's evolution in education, emphasizing cross-disciplinary insights.

Table 1. Research Design Linkage

Research Question	Linked Objective	Research Design Link
RQ1: What is the potential of AI as a collaborative partner?	Objective 1 & 3	Secondary data analysis of case studies and literature on AI-based tools and personalization
RQ2: What are the key ethical challenges of AI in education?	Objective 2	Review of policies, ethics literature, and reports on AI bias and privacy
RQ3: How might AI reshape teaching roles and curriculum?	Objective 1 & 3	Synthesis of studies on teacher roles, AI-driven pedagogy, and curriculum models

Source: Created by author from the above details given in sections 2 and 3.

Figure 1. Visual linkage- Research questions objectives and design

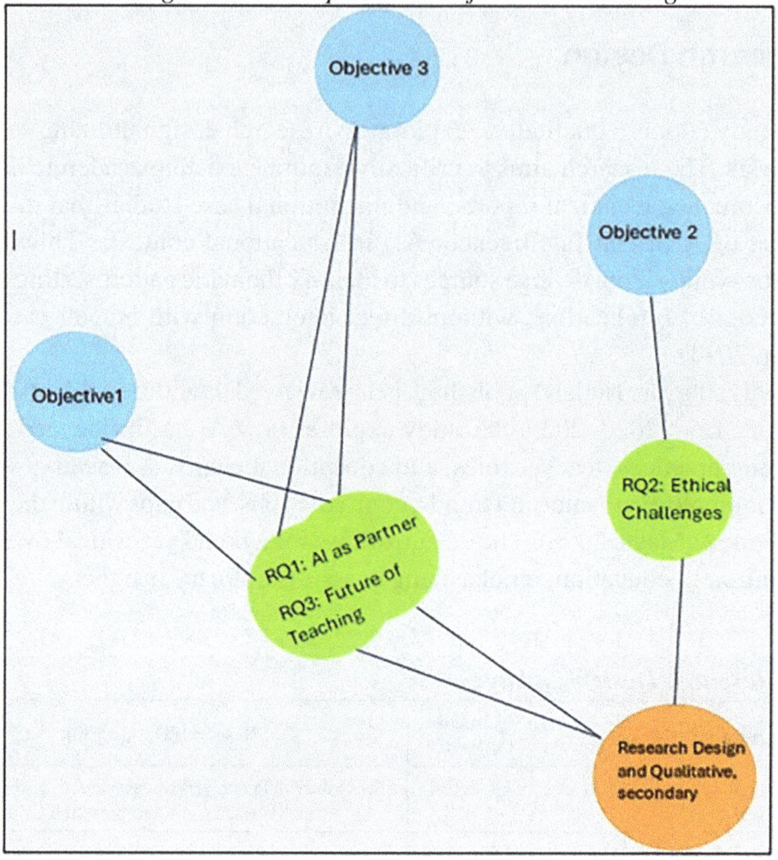

(source: created by author)

Table 1 and Figure 1 illustrate the alignment between the research questions (both primary and sub-questions) and the chapter objectives, offering a structured overview of how the study is conceptually and methodologically grounded. The purpose of developing these visual and tabular representations is to clarify the logical connections between the study's inquiries and its intended contributions.

By mapping these relationships, the table and diagram support the study's qualitative, secondary-data-based research design.

4.2 Ethical Considerations

Although the study is based on secondary data, ethical research principles still apply. All data sources are obtained from publicly available academic journals, conference proceedings, open-access policy papers, and credible online databases.

There is no involvement of human subjects, thereby eliminating the need for institutional review board (IRB) approval (Bishop, 2007).

To maintain academic integrity, proper citation practices are rigorously followed, and intellectual contributions are acknowledged in accordance with APA 7 referencing standards. Additionally, care is taken to critically evaluate the credibility, relevance, and bias of each source to ensure accurate representation of original findings (Eynden, et al., 2011). Where sensitive topics (e.g., algorithmic bias or equity) are discussed, the study emphasizes balanced interpretations based on evidence rather than speculative claims.

5. DISCUSSION AND FINDINGS

5.1 Role of AI as a Learning Facilitator in Education.

AI is increasingly identified in the education sector not just as a tool, but as an active learning facilitator in modern classrooms. Adaptive systems like Carnegie Learning and AI tutors such as ChatGPT personalize instruction, adjust pacing, and offer real-time support to students based on their individual progress (Chen et al., 2020). AI also helps streamline access to educational resources, reducing cognitive overload and allowing students to focus on higher-order thinking (Zawacki-Richter et al., 2019). AI's rational and supportive role is especially helpful in large, diverse classrooms, where modifying lessons to individualistic needs is often challenging for teachers to do alone (Luckin et al., 2016). It is important to note that the value of artificial intelligence in the education market is estimated at US$10.25 billion in 2024, with projections indicating a significant compound annual growth rate (CAGR) of 33.51%, reaching approximately US$43.47 billion by 2029 (Research and Markets, 2024).

5.2 Teacher Perspectives on AI Integration

Teachers hold mixed views on AI integration. While many appreciate the administrative support and diagnostic feedback AI offers, concerns remain about the erosion of pedagogical autonomy and the impersonal nature of AI interactions (Holmes et al., 2022). Some educators fear that over-reliance on AI may be deskill teachers or marginalize their professional expertise (Jafari, 2024). On the other hand, when appropriately trained, teachers often report enhanced instructional creativity and better student engagement due to AI-enabled insights (Ka & Colloton, 2024). The UK has set an ambitious goal to support over 1,000 government-funded PhD researchers in AI by 2025, alongside the launch of Turing Fellowships aimed at nurturing early-career AI researchers. In contrast, China initiated a five-year university project in April 2018, which successfully trained at least 500 teachers and 5,000 students in AI technologies (Research and Markets, 2024).

5.3 Student Experiences with AI Tools

Students generally report positive experiences with AI tools, especially those that offer personalized learning paths and instant feedback (Varghese et al., 2025). AI has been shown to reduce academic stress by providing self-paced learning environments and enhancing student motivation through gamified systems (Xia et al., 2022). However, some students express skepticism, particularly around the accuracy of AI assessments and the lack of human emotional intelligence (Mirza et al., 2025). Artificial Intelligence enhances education by automating grading, offering personalized tutoring, and providing constructive feedback. It reshapes the teacher's role from instructor to facilitator and supports trial-and-error learning by creating adaptive, low-risk environments, ultimately improving both instructional efficiency and student engagement in the learning process (Fahimirad & Kotamjani, 2018).

Table 2. Use of Gen AI tools to enhance educational experiences.

Country	Use of AI in Education
Singapore	68%
India	68%
UAE / KSA	50%
Canada	48%
Australia / New Zealand	44%
United States (US)	44%
United Kingdom / Ireland	36%
Japan	22%

Source: EY 2023 International Survey on Digital Transformation in Higher Education

The table 3: shows the adoption of AI in education across eight countries or regions. Singapore and India lead the way with a high adoption rate of 68%, indicating strong national strategies or institutional readiness for AI-enhanced learning. UAE/KSA (50%) and Canada (48%) follow closely, reflecting significant regional efforts in modernizing education. Countries like Australia/New Zealand and the US show moderate levels at 44%, suggesting ongoing integration. Meanwhile, UK/Ireland (36%) and Japan (22%) exhibit relatively lower usage, possibly due to regulatory, infrastructural, or cultural factors. Overall, AI usage in education shows a positive trend globally, with notable leadership in Asia and the Middle East.

5.4 Benefits Observed in AI-Assisted Learning

AI-supported classrooms have demonstrated notable gains in academic performance, knowledge retention, and skill acquisition. In STEM and medical fields, simulations powered by AI offer realistic practice environments that improve technical competencies (Pohn et al., 2025). Additionally, AI can assist students with disabilities by providing customized interfaces and content, making education more inclusive (Sierra, 2024). Its real-time feedback system/ loops along with analytics tools facilitate optimization learning which is supporting the needs of all types of learners. These days AI in education transforms the knowledge transfer style, instruction mechanism and research by enabling modern technologies like as neural networks, machine learning, and CALL etc., mentioned were not feasible in traditional classrooms, across diverse learning contexts (Holmes et al., 2019; Hwang et al., 2020).

Table 3. Case studies reflecting the use of AI in Education

#	Title	Discussion
1	Explainable AI in Intelligent Tutoring Systems	AI in intelligent tutoring systems across multiple institutions (Khosravi et al. (2022). The AI has not only assessed student performance but also offered a customized explanation for its feedback, by enhancing transparency. In the study it mentioned that students who are using a math ITS received traceable reasoning behind the AI's problem-solving steps. Teachers has applied this as an insight to adjust individualize instruction in real-time. Students reported have increased trust and motivation when AI recommendations were made explainable.it had resulted into learning more collaborative and enhanced the clarity in algorithmic assessments.
2	AI-Enhanced Inclusive Reading in Japan	In Japanese inclusive classrooms using an AI-powered reading system called Reading Skill Builder (Toyokawa et al. (2023). The system used natural language processing (NLP) to trace a student's reading level, then adapted content and provided rational questions aligned to their skills and capabilities. Visual learners received texts was image-supported, while slower readers were offered audio versions. The AI also alerted teachers to students who required additional support. The intervention proved especially effective for students with dyslexia and attention problems, enabling individualized reading strategies in mainstream education.
3	AI Ecosystem for Engineering Students in Lithuania	This study focused on engineering programs at Lithuanian universities integrating an AI-driven platform for sustainable design projects. Students used the system to simulate smart city layouts, test renewable energy scenarios, and evaluate their environmental impact using AI-driven optimization. The ecosystem included dashboards that tracked teamwork, progress, and environmental efficiency scores. Professors used predictive analytics to forecast student success and provide early interventions. The case highlighted how AI can bridge sustainability education with technical skill-building in engineering domains. Paulauskaite-Taraseviciene, A., et al. (2022).

Source: Created by author.

5.5 Investment on use of AI in the Education sector and future trends.

As per the report of (Research and Markets, 2024) Artificial intelligence in the education market is worth US$10.248 billion in 2024. It is projected to exhibit a remarkable CAGR of 33.51%, reaching a market value of US$43.467 billion by

2029. Also, studies reveal that over the past five years, AI investment in education has increased exponentially, with both governments and private sectors contributing to infrastructure, digital tools, and talent development.

5.6 Ethical Dilemmas Identified

Despite its advantages, AI in education raises complex ethical concerns. Privacy violations, algorithmic bias, and data commodification are prominent issues (Jafari, 2024). There is also a risk of deepening digital divides, as schools in under-resourced areas may lack the infrastructure needed to adopt AI equitably (Sapohov, 2024). Moreover, AI systems often function as "black boxes," making it difficult for educators to understand or challenge the rationale behind automated decisions (Holmes et al., 2022).

Member States of UNESCO are encouraged to foster the development of foundational or "prerequisite skills" essential for AI education. These include basic literacy, numeracy, coding, digital competencies, and media and information literacy, alongside critical and creative thinking, collaboration, communication, socio-emotional intelligence, and AI ethics awareness. Particular emphasis should be placed on regions or countries where significant gaps in these skill areas persist within the education system (UNSCO, 2021).

5.7 Conceptual Model for AI Integration in Education

The conceptual framework guiding this study (see Figure 2) maps the interrelationship between AI tools, teacher roles, student agency, and ethical governance. It reflects how AI serves as a mediating agent between learners and content, while simultaneously interacting with teacher strategies and ethical oversight.

Figure 2. Conceptual model for AI integration in Education

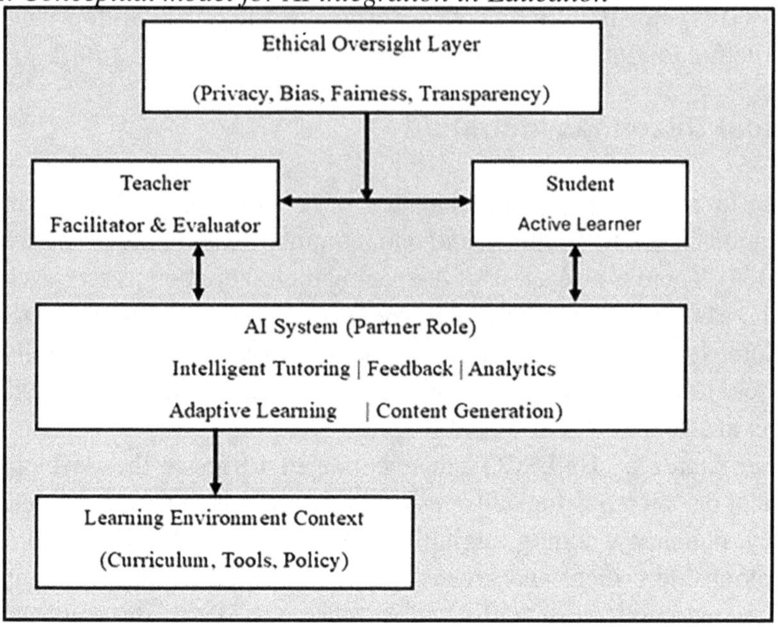

Source: created by author.

This model positions AI as a strategic partner that operates within human-guided and ethically monitored environments. The teacher remains an instructional leader, the student becomes an empowered learner, and the AI system bridges both—provided it functions within clear ethical and contextual boundaries.

Core Elements of Model

Figure 3. Core Elements of conceptual model

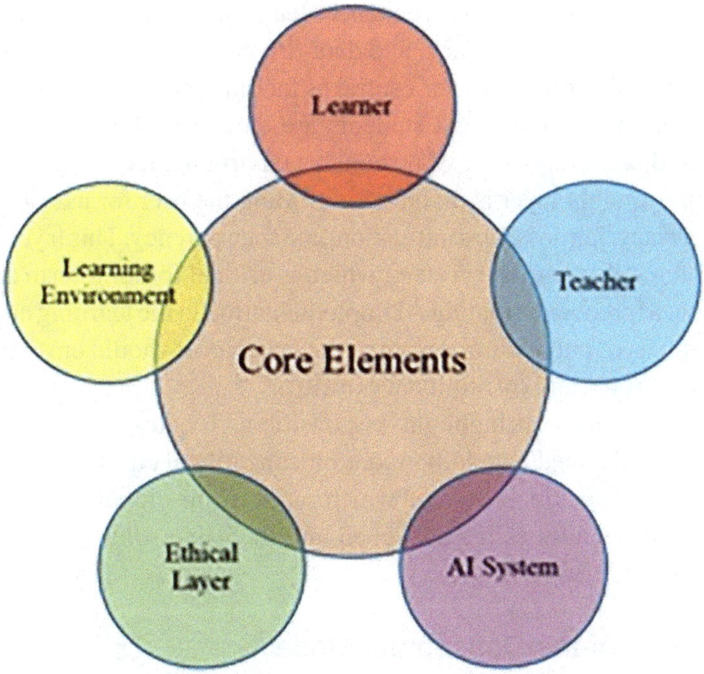

(source: created by author)

Explanation of model's core elements shown in picture 2.

- Student: Receives personalized learning support, feedback, and pacing via AI systems. Gains agency in learning processes.
- Teacher: Acts as a guide, curriculum designer, and ethical supervisor of AI interventions. Maintains pedagogical and emotional intelligence.
- AI System: Delivers adaptive content, assesses performance, suggests pathways, and supports diagnostics through tools like ChatGPT, LMS bots, etc.
- Ethical Oversight Layer: Enforces responsible AI usage, data protection, transparency, and equitable access.
- Learning Environment Context: Institutional policies, classroom setup, infrastructure, and socio-cultural dynamics enabling or restricting AI use.

The effective coloration of AI in the education sector, as illustrated in the framework, depends on a synergistic interaction and coordination among students, teachers, and in the different units of AI systems, all should be within a well-defined ethical and contextual infrastructure facilities. By positioning/inducing AI as a partner rather than a replacement, the system enhances learning through intelligent tutoring, adaptive content, real-time feedback, and data-driven individualize analytics. Educators/ teacher remain core factors or central as facilitators and evaluators, ensuring pedagogical alignment, other hand students are empowered as active learners in personalized and highly dynamic & responsive environments.

The ethical oversight layer is pivotal, it's guiding the user for use of AI through principles of privacy, fairness, bias mitigation, and transparency. This layer introduces trust and accountability into the system, which is critical for long-term adoption of AI in education. Moreover, initiating AI implementation in the learning environment context in the areas of curriculum design, policy, and tools should ensure alignment with educational goals and institutional priorities.

Altogether, this framework highlights responsible and context-aware AI integration but still it can be enhanced by adding more on educational equity, personalization, and efficiency. It's a sustainable model which supports the global education sector's evolving needs, especially as it seeks open and inclusive solutions in the face of widening access and quality gaps.

Critical Analysis of the Conceptual Model: AI as an Educational Partner

The conceptual model visually represents the interconnected dynamics among the different units of AI systems. It incorporates educators, learners, ethical governance, and institutional frameworks in the context of modern education. This model emphasizes a collaborative and ethically conscious educational ecosystem, where AI acts as a facilitative agent rather than a replacement for human actors.

1. AI as a Mediator: Not a Substitute

At the core of the model is the AI System in a "Partner Role", presenting intelligent tutoring, adaptive learning, analytics, and content generation areas/functions of teaching and learning mechanism. These functions are necessary for:

- Personalizing instruction for students, enabling self-paced learning.
- Supporting teachers through real-time feedback and performance tracking.

However, the model avoids techno-determinism by rejecting the idea of AI replacing educators. As an alternative, teachers remain facilitators and evaluators, ensuring that instructional collaboration AI and human judgment are preserved especially in human areas requiring empathy, critical discussion, and ethical reasoning (Holmes et al., 2022).

2. **The Learner's Agency and Equity Implications**

The learner is positioned as an active participant, benefiting from AI's responsiveness and adaptability. While this increases learner autonomy and engagement, it also raises concerns about equity:

- Students from under-resourced settings may lack access to high-quality AI tools (Zou et al., 2023).
- Over-reliance on algorithmic paths could reduce exposure to diverse learning methods or limit critical thinking.

Thus, teacher mediation and ethical oversight are crucial to ensuring AI does not inadvertently reinforce educational inequalities.

3. **Ethical Oversight as a Non-Negotiable Layer**

The Ethical Oversight Layer—encompassing privacy, fairness, transparency, and bias mitigation—sits above all human-AI interactions. It ensures:

- Teachers and students interact with AI in a safe, accountable, and transparent manner.
- AI decisions, especially in grading or content filtering, are explainable and contestable.

Without this layer, the risk of algorithmic harm, surveillance, and erosion of agency would significantly increase (Jafari, 2024).

4. **Contextual Embeddedness: Policy, Curriculum, and Tools**

Learning Environment Context layer of the model recognizes that AI does not function in isolation. As it needs to be aligned with curriculum standards, institutional policies, and technological infrastructure shape:

- What can AI do?

- How it is used,
- And by whom.

This contextual grounding ensures the model reflects real-world applicability, reinforcing that any AI integration strategy must be tailored to institutional, cultural, and curricular realities (Zawacki-Richter et al., 2019).

5. Implications for Practice and Research

The model is not just descriptive but prescriptive. It supports for:

- Teacher training in AI literacy.
- Policy development that includes ethical AI governance.
- Inclusive access strategies to ensure all learners benefit equitably.

For researchers, this model offers a valuable starting point to explore how AI is shaping education. It assists through studies that examine not just effectiveness, but also whether these innovations promote equality, access, and ethical responsibility in teaching and learning environments.

5.7 Limitations of AI in Current Educational Settings

These days, AI continues to spark excitement in education, its widespread adoption faces real-world challenges in the different areas of education including both inside and beyond classroom activities. Major limitation lies in AI's inability to grasp context the way human teachers do. Unlike educators, AI lacks emotional awareness, cultural awareness and sensitivity, and the capacity to read non-verbal indicators/ cues elements that are highly important for classroom environment connection and responsive teaching (Roll & Wylie, 2016). Another hurdle is the preparedness of teachers. Many educators are still in the navigating mode from digital shift and often lack the training needed to fully integrate AI into their teaching understandings (Hwang et al., 2020). In the absence of knowledge to use relevant and rational tools effectively, AI risks being underutilized or mismanaged. Undoubtably AI-generated feedback is fast and data-rich but still requires human interpretation especially in nuanced areas like individual creativity, ethics, or situation based critical thinking. There's also the issue of unequal access. Educational organizations in the underdeveloped areas often do not have the required infrastructure as compared to developed or urban areas. Generally, education organizations in underdeveloped areas suffer with the lack of required equipment, IT support and internet facilities to apply most of AI technology (Zou et al., 2023). It results in the development of a new gap which reflects that some students highly benefited from cutting-edge learning environments, while others fall further much behind. Overall, these challenges show that how AI's role in education must be carefully and thoughtfully implemented to truly enhance learning, AI needs to be supported by inclusive policies, ongoing teacher development, and a firm commitment to maintaining the human element that defines great teaching.

6. CONCLUSION

This chapter highlights how AI is becoming a true partner in education and enhances personalized learning, supporting teachers, and offering data-driven insights to improve instruction. There are tools like intelligent tutors and learning analytics that are already helping boost student engagement and assessment (Chen et al., 2020; Xia et al., 2022). But still there are many challenges remaining around ethics, teacher autonomy, and unequal technical and other infrastructural access (Holmes et al., 2022; Jafari, 2024). These insights highlight the vital blending of AI innovation with human-centered teaching and strong educational institution support for responsible implementation.

6.1 Contributions to Educational Research and Practice

This study contributes value by introducing a conceptual framework that brings together the teaching, tech, and ethical aspects of AI in education. It goes beyond AI's practical use, exploring how it affects both teacher identity and student empowerment (Ka & Colloton, 2024; Lucietto & Peters, 2024). At its core, it emphasizes that AI should support—not replace—educators, helping them thrive as facilitators enriched by thoughtful use of technology (Zawacki-Richter et al., 2019; Varghese et al., 2025).

6.2 Recommendations for Policy Makers and Educators

1. Support ethical and equitable AI integration, it is recommended that:
2. Institutions develop transparent AI policies with clear accountability mechanisms (Holmes et al., 2019; Roberts et al., 2021).
3. Educators engage in continuous professional development focused on responsible AI use and critical data literacy (Luckin et al., 2016; Yin & Jones, 2021).
4. Students and teachers be included in AI co-design processes to ensure the technology aligns with educational values (Baker & Smith, 2019; Eshaghi, 2024).

6.3 Directions for Future Research

The long-term effects of AI on learning and cognition, especially across different disciplines and age groups (Roll & Wylie, 2016; Chen et al., 2020). Cross-national comparisons on AI implementation and its impact on educational equity (Zawacki-Richter et al., 2019; Sapohov, 2024).

REFERENCES

Akgun, S., & Greenhow, C. (2021). Artificial intelligence in education: Addressing ethical challenges in K-12 settings. *AI and Ethics*, *2*(3), 431–440. DOI: 10.1007/s43681-021-00096-7 PMID: 34790956

Baker, T., Smith, L., & Anissa, N. (2019, February 20). *Educ-AI-tion rebooted? Exploring the future of artificial intelligence in schools and colleges*. Nesta. https://www.nesta.org.uk/report/education-rebooted/

Bishop, L. (2007). A Reflexive Account of Reusing Qualitative Data: Beyond Primary/Secondary Dualism. *Sociological Research Online*, *12*(3), 43–56. DOI: 10.5153/sro.1553

Chen, L., Chen, P., & Lin, Z. (2020). Artificial Intelligence in Education: A Review. *IEEE Access : Practical Innovations, Open Solutions*, *8*, 75264–75278. DOI: 10.1109/ACCESS.2020.2988510

Eshaghi, S. (2024, August). *Cooperative Play in Historic Preservation Education: A Theoretical Framework and Game Implementation at the Silk Roads Using Unreal Engine*. Tdl.org. https://ttu-ir.tdl.org/items/a7f435f5-e8f8-4a7b-8bab-4b10912370c8

Eynden, V. V. den, Corti, L., Woollard, M., Bishop, L., & Horton., L. (2011). *MANAGING AND SHARING DATA BEST PRACTICE FOR RESEARCHERS*. UK Data Archive.

Fahimirad, M., & Kotamjani, S. S. (2018). A Review of the Application of Artificial Intelligence in Teaching and Learning in Educational Contexts. *International Journal of Learning and Development*, *8*(4), 106. DOI: 10.5296/ijld.v8i4.14057

Francesc, P., Migue, F., & Paula, V. (2019). *Artificial intelligence in education: challenges and opportunities for sustainable development*. Unesco.org. https://unesdoc.unesco.org/ark:/48223/pf0000366994

Holmes, W., Bialik, M., & Fadel, C. (2019). Artificial Intelligence. In *Education Promises and Implications for Teaching and Learning*. The Center for Curriculum Redesign.

Hwang, G.-J., Xie, H., Wah, B. W., & Gašević, D. (2020). Vision, challenges, roles and research issues of Artificial Intelligence in Education. *Computers and Education: Artificial Intelligence*, *1*, 100001. DOI: 10.1016/j.caeai.2020.100001

Jafari, E. (2024). Artificial intelligence and learning environment: Human considerations. *Journal of Computer Assisted Learning*, *40*(5), 2135–2149. Advance online publication. DOI: 10.1111/jcal.13011

Johnston, M. (2014). *Secondary Data Analysis: A Method of which the Time Has Come. Qualitative and Quantitative Methods in Libraries*. QQML.

Ka, C., & Colloton, T. (2024). *Generative AI in Higher Education*. Routledge., DOI: 10.4324/9781003459026

Khosravi, H., Shum, S. B., Chen, G., Conati, C., Tsai, Y.-S., Kay, J., Knight, S., Martinez-Maldonado, R., Sadiq, S., & Gašević, D. (2022). Explainable Artificial Intelligence in education. *Computers and Education: Artificial Intelligence*, *3*(3), 100074. DOI: 10.1016/j.caeai.2022.100074

Lucietto, A. M., & Peters, D. (2024). Engineering technology and engineering: Incorporating the humanities into the classroom. *Frontiers in Education*, *9*, 1534407. Advance online publication. DOI: 10.3389/feduc.2024.1534407

Luckin, R., Holmes, W., Griffiths, M., & Forcier, L. B. (2016). *Intelligence Unleashed: An argument for AI in Education*. Pearson Education.

Manyika, J., Chui, M., Brown, B., Bughin, J., Dobbs, R., Roxburgh, C., & Hung Byers, A. (2011). *Big Data: The Next Frontier for Innovation, Competition, and Productivity*. McKinsey Global Institute. https://www.mckinsey.com/~/media/McKinsey/Business%20Functions/McKinsey%20Digital/Our%20Insights/Big%20data%20The%20next%20frontier%20for%20innovation/MGI_big_data_exec_summary.pdf

Mirza, A., & Syed, N. Fatmi, & Pohn, B. (2025). *Integrating artificial intelligence into pre-clinical medical education*. Frontiers in Education. https://www.frontiersin.org/journals/education/articles/10.3389/feduc.2025.1570389/full

Paulauskaite-Taraseviciene, A., Lagzdinyte-Budnike, I., Gaiziuniene, L., Sukacke, V., & Daniuseviciute-Brazaite, L. (2022). Assessing Education for Sustainable Development in Engineering Study Programs: A Case of AI Ecosystem Creation. *Sustainability (Basel)*, *14*(3), 1702. DOI: 10.3390/su14031702

Pavan, S. (2024). *Devi Manikeswari, Shaikh, Z. H., Mahapatra, D. M., Mohanty, B. S., & Soni, A*. Advances in Educational Technologies and Instructional Design Book Series. Wearables and AI-Smart Technologies., DOI: 10.4018/979-8-3693-7817-5.ch002

Pohn, B., Mehnen, L., Fitzek, S., & Choi, K. (2025). Integrating AI into medical education: Opportunities and challenges. *Frontiers in Education, 10*, •••. https://www.frontiersin.org/articles/10.3389/feduc.2025.1570389/full. DOI: 10.3389/feduc.2025.1570389

Research and Markets. (2024, November 18). *Artificial Intelligence in Education Market Report 2024-2029: Investments in AI-Driven Learning Platforms Fuel Growth with North America Leading*. GlobeNewswire News Room; Research and Markets. https://www.globenewswire.com/news-release/2024/11/18/2982495/28124/en/Artificial-Intelligence-in-Education-Market-Report-2024-2029-Investments-in-AI-Driven-Learning-Platforms-Fuel-Growth-with-North-America-Leading.html

Research and Markets. (2024, November 18). Artificial Intelligence in Education Market Report 2024-2029: Investments in AI-Driven Learning Platforms Fuel Growth with North America Leading. GlobeNewswire News Room; Research and Markets. https://www.globenewswire.com/news-release/2024/11/18/2982495/28124/en/Artificial-Intelligence-in-Education-Market-Report-2024-2029-Investments-in-AI-Driven-Learning-Platforms-Fuel-Growth-with-North-America-Leading.html

Roll, I., & Wylie, R. (2016). Evolution and Revolution in Artificial Intelligence in Education. *International Journal of Artificial Intelligence in Education, 26*(2), 582–599. DOI: 10.1007/s40593-016-0110-3

Sapohov, M. (2024). The characteristics of the educational and digital environment of US universities. *Педевтологія, 2*(1), 51–58. DOI: 10.31652/3041-1203-2024(1)-51-58

Sierra, C. (2024). A Historical Perspective on Artificial Intelligence in Higher Education. https://doi.org/DOI: 10.13140/RG.2.2.34113.26727

Toyokawa, Y., Horikoshi, I., Majumdar, R., & Ogata, H. (2023). *Challenges and opportunities of AI in inclusive education: a case study of data-enhanced active reading in Japan*. Smart Learning Environments., DOI: 10.1186/s40561-023-00286-2

Varghese, N. N., Jose, B., Bindhumol, T., Cleetus, A., & Nair, S. B. (2025). The power duo: Unleashing cognitive potential through human-AI synergy in STEM and non-STEM education. *Frontiers in Education, 10*, 1534582. Advance online publication. DOI: 10.3389/feduc.2025.1534582

Zawacki-Richter, O., Marín, V. I., Bond, M., & Gouverneur, F. (2019). Systematic review of research on artificial intelligence applications in higher education – where are the educators? *International Journal of Educational Technology in Higher Education, 16*(1), 39. Advance online publication. DOI: 10.1186/s41239-019-0171-0

Chapter 3
AI Enhanced School Guidance Interventions:
Promises, Threats, and Future Directions

Marie Grace Avelino Gomez
https://orcid.org/0000-0003-0180-9875
University of the Philippines, Philippines

ABSTRACT

School guidance offices traditionally offer face-to-face support for students' academic, personal, social, and career development. The COVID-19 pandemic disrupted these services, necessitating a shift to remote modalities like video counseling and digital apps. The emergence of artificial intelligence (AI) presents both opportunities and challenges for guidance services. AI-powered chatbots can offer conversational support, mental wellness activities, career guidance, and even preliminary mental health screenings. While AI provides anonymity and accessibility, its increasing sophistication raises questions about its role alongside traditional human counselors and the potential impact on the human element of guidance.

INTRODUCTION

The school's guidance office provides vital support services to the student body. These services help students cope with their issues and concerns, get to know themselves better, access information on wellness and mental health, and plan for future career endeavors (Octaviani et al., 2021).

Traditionally, these services are provided face-to-face. Guidance offices always accept clients who need help. Students or clients visit the guidance office for

DOI: 10.4018/979-8-3373-0396-3.ch003

wellness activities, counseling, psychological assessment, career education, and various information that can help them with their academics (Dianovi et al., 2022). The counselors build a therapeutic alliance with their clients to help address their needs (Zeren et al., 2022).

The COVD-19 pandemic restricted accessibility to guidance offices because of school closures imposed by the government to suppress contagion (Astuti, 2021). However, these lockdowns made it challenging to access services. The inability to get immediate help, having loved ones die due to the virus, loss of jobs, and isolation resulted in mental health issues (Savitz-Romer et al., 2021).

Many guidance offices shifted to video counseling through various video conferencing platforms to address some issues (Karaman, 2021). Those with connectivity issues had to use messenger chat or cellphone calls. Digital apps that address wellness and mental health issues were also available on the Google Play or Apple Market.

Technological advances have led to the emergence of artificial intelligence (AI). This technology has made significant contributions in the field of guidance by providing tools that support mental health practitioners and their clients. AI-powered chatbots utilize natural language processing (NLP) mechanisms to offer conversational support and practical counseling (Tewari et al., 2021). These chatbots provide mindfulness activities, self-reflection, mood tracking, psychoeducation, and referral support. Some clients resort to seeking intervention from chatbots for anonymity.

AI platforms such as ChatGPT and Google Gemini can provide support by giving numbers of nearby mental health facilities (Ajlouni et al., 2023). Cognitive behavior therapy(CBT)-based interventions are also discussed. These can even show empathy to the client by showing statements such " I am sorry to hear that.", "I hope you will be ok soon." "Get well." and "Get some help." Voice features can also be activated the client can engage in a dialogue. There are times when worksheets can be given to the client needing counseling.

AI platforms can also provide career education. They can identify career trends and prospective salaries, suggest colleges, and provide the academic track record of various institutions. They can identify companies or the best places where work can be found. They can give tips for job interviews and help prepare for board examinations.

Assessment tools that serve as AI platforms give screeners for various mental health conditions. The screening tools can be used to identify symptoms of depression, anxiety, learning disabilities or a developmental delay.

AI poses both a threat and a support mechanism for counselors. As AI becomes more sophisticated, more and more people are getting intervention from them. Some would rather trust the AI service than go to the guidance office and wait for their turn. For those who want the human touch, they will still resort to traditional guidance services.

PURPOSE/OBJECTIVES OF THE BOOK CHAPTER

First, the chapter examines school guidance services across three periods: pre-pandemic, during the pandemic, and post-pandemic. Before COVID-19, guidance programs relied on in-person interactions for personal counseling, career guidance, and mental health support (Leatherman, 2024). The pandemic disrupted these traditional methods, prompting a rapid shift to remote counseling and digital solutions (Pedroso et al., 2022). Online counseling, teletherapy, and digital mental health resources became essential for service continuity during lockdowns (Garza Schuster, 2022). Post-pandemic, hybrid models combining in-person and digital tools have enhanced accessibility and efficiency (Stato et al., 2022). This shift highlights the increasing reliance on technology and paves the way for AI's potential role in school guidance (Grassini, 2023).

Secondly, it explains how the increase in technology usage for delivering guidance services acted as a precursor to the acceptance of AI applications in this field. The pandemic-driven shift to digital platforms normalized virtual counseling, chat-based interventions, and self-help apps, leading to a reduction in skepticism about technology in guidance services (Su et al., 2024). Standard tools such as online appointment systems and virtual counseling rooms laid the groundwork for AI-powered solutions (Thurupathi, 2025). Rising demands for efficiency, personalization, and 24/7 access have propelled the adoption of AI applications, including automated assessments, chatbot consultations, and predictive analytics for identifying at-risk students (Ping, 2024).

Third, it discusses various apps and AI applications used in guidance services. AI-powered chatbots like Woebot and Wysa provide immediate emotional support, addressing mental health concerns at scale (Lee, 2025). CiCi, a personalized AI, offers nonjudgmental interactions based on knowledge from Cognitive Behavior Therapy (Li et al.,, 2025). Predictive analytics tools assess academic performance and emotional well-being, enabling early interventions (Xuam Lam et al., 2024). AI-driven platforms like Replika and Ellie engage students in reflective conversations to help manage stress and anxiety (Romael Haque & Rubya, 2023). These tools enhance accessibility and efficiency, complementing human counselors rather than replacing them.

Fourth, it describes the potential threat of AI to guidance counselors. While AI expands access to counseling, over-reliance on it may dehumanize guidance services, as AI lacks genuine empathy, cultural sensitivity, and nuanced understanding (Rubin et al., 2024). There is also a risk of job displacement if institutions prioritize cost-effective AI over human professionals (Ofem et al., 2025; Wong, 2024). Ethical concerns, including data privacy, algorithmic bias, and misinformation, raise doubts about the reliability of AI-driven counseling (Farhud & Zukaei, 2021). Without proper regulation, AI could undermine the human-centered nature of school guidance, making clear ethical and professional boundaries essential (Adams, 2024).

Fifth, it illustrates how AI can be utilized for future guidance services within the context of the VUCAD (volatile, uncertain, complex, ambiguous, and diverse) world. AI offers benefits but also presents risks, including over-reliance on automated counseling and diminished human involvement (Karan & Angadi, 2023; Akingbola et al., 2024). Concerns about AI's empathy deficit, cultural sensitivity, and ethical risks, such as data privacy and misinformation, remain pressing (Tilala et al., 2024). Without proper safeguards, AI could erode the human-centric foundation of school guidance, emphasizing the need for responsible integration (Adams et al., 2022).

The Pre-COVID 19 Pandemic Setting: Traditional Face-to-Face Services of the Guidance Office

Traditional school guidance services are vital in supporting students' academic, personal, and career development giving direct, face-to-face interactions (Alfaris et al., 2021). School counselors offer personalized support, assisting students in navigating challenges, making informed decisions, and accessing necessary resources, thus are uniquely positioned to meet the students' needs (Farrell, 2022). The in-person nature of these services builds trust, enables immediate feedback, and strengthens the counselor-student relationship, making guidance programs an essential component of student success both in the academic and personal domains (Ngeno, 2022).

School Counseling. Traditional school counseling involves direct, personal interactions between students and guidance counselors to address a variety of concerns related to academics, finances, and daily living issues (Peterson, 2019). These intervention sessions cover a wide range of personal, social, and academic challenges. Counselors create a safe and confidential environment, encouraging students to express their difficulties, develop coping strategies, and improve their self-awareness (Bulmer et al., 2022). This in-person setting provides immediate feedback, customized support, and helps build strong relationships, which are crucial for effective intervention. Additionally, licensed counselors and mental health professionals have honed their skills over many years and have met stringent state or national requirements.

Psychological Assessment. Psychological assessment in traditional counseling often involves administering standardized tests in person. Counselors and other mental health professionals have invested countless hours studying assessment procedures and various standardized test protocols. An in-person approach to assessment allows counselors to observe students' behavior, ensure proper test administration, and provide immediate feedback (Himelfarb, 2019). Such assessments yield significant insights into a student's cognitive abilities, personality traits, and emotional well-being, which aid in developing tailored interventions and support strategies (Fadli, et al., 2022) In-person interaction is crucial for accurately interpreting the results to the clients.

Career Education. Traditional career education in a guidance office involves direct interactions through workshops, individual counseling sessions, and career fairs. Counselors assist students in exploring career options, assessing their interests and skills, and developing career plans (Rezaiee & Kareshki, 2024). Students receive personalized counseling on career pathways and lattices, job market trends, resume building, and informed career decision-making about their future.

Information Services. Traditionally, guidance offices have served as essential resources for sharing important information with students and parents. They provide details on academic requirements, college applications, scholarship opportunities, and community services (Habsy, 2024). Information is typically communicated through printed materials, bulletin boards, and personal consultations, ensuring accessibility and clarity. This in-person approach enables guidance counselors to confirm that students understand the information provided.

Referral. In a conventional guidance office, the referral process connects students and their families with appropriate external resources such as therapists, medical professionals, or social service agencies (Jannah et al.,2023). In-person meetings allow counselors to thoroughly assess students' needs, clarify the referral process, and ensure a smooth transition to outside support systems. This personal interaction fosters a sense of support and ongoing care.

Research. Conventional research in guidance offices focuses on assessing program effectiveness, understanding student needs, and guiding decision-making (Gardner et al., 2023). This approach typically consists of administering surveys, conducting interviews, and analyzing data gathered from both students and staff. Engaging in face-to-face interactions while collecting data provides deeper, more detailed insights, which bolster evidence-based practices and enhance the ongoing development of guidance services. Face-to-face interactions can also better show the authenticity of some qualitative research procedures (Pagliarin et al., 2023).

Traditional school guidance services have historically relied on personal interactions, which provide students with customized support and significant relationships. Although advancing technology introduces novel methods to improve counseling services, the human aspect is essential for building trust, empathy, and profound understanding. As schools consider new approaches in guidance, maintaining a balance between technological progress and the foundational principles of tailored and student-focused support is crucial.

Effects of the COVID-19 Pandemic on School Guidance Services

The COVID-19 pandemic forced a rapid shift in school guidance services, increasing reliance on cellphone-based and online counseling. With school closures and social distancing, traditional face-to-face counseling was no longer feasible, prompting guidance counselors to adopt phone calls, text messaging, video conferencing, and email to support students remotely (Pedroso, 2022; Campo et al., 2022). This transition ensured service continuity and expanded access for students hesitant about in-person counseling.

The pandemic also accelerated the development and use of cellphone and web-based applications for wellness, counseling, and assessment (Campo et al., 2022). As demand for remote support grew, mental health professionals and developers enhanced digital tools offering self-help resources, mood tracking, mindfulness exercises, virtual counseling, and online mental health assessments (Mielgo-Conde et al, 2021). These apps provided immediate, convenient support, complementing school guidance services.

Additionally, the crisis spurred the widespread creation and dissemination of IEC materials on student well-being (Sanni, 2024). Schools and guidance departments responded to rising stress and anxiety by sharing resources on coping strategies, mental health maintenance, and support services through digital platforms (Ye, 2021). These materials aimed to raise awareness, empower students and families, and proactively address pandemic-related challenges.

AI and the Delivery of Various School Guidance Services

AI can enhance school counseling by equipping counselors with valuable tools and insights. AI-powered chatbots and virtual assistants can provide initial support, answer common questions, and offer psychoeducational resources, enabling counselors to focus on more complex cases. Natural Language Processing (NLP) allows AI to analyze student communications (with ethical and privacy safeguards) to detect emotional distress, notifying counselors about those who need intervention (Wong et al., 2023). Additionally, AI can personalize support by suggesting coping strategies tailored to student needs.

AI is increasingly integrated into educational settings to support the psychosocial well-being of students, particularly those with emotional and behavioral concerns, ADHD, and autism. In Su et al.'s (2024) study, AI-driven tools can provide personalized interventions tailored to individual student needs, enhancing engagement and learning outcomes. For students with ADHD, AI applications can assist in maintaining focus and organization through customized reminders and task management strategies. In the case of autism, AI technologies can facilitate social skills development by simulating social interactions and providing immediate feedback. Additionally, AI-powered systems can monitor behavioral patterns, enabling early detection of issues and timely intervention by educators and mental health professionals. By offering consistent and non-judgmental support, AI tools can help reduce anxiety and build confidence among students facing psychosocial challenges. Overall, the integration of AI in educational environments holds promise for creating more inclusive and supportive learning experiences for students with diverse needs (Su et al., 2024).

The use of NLP can predict client satisfaction. In Hornstein et al. (2025) study in a 24/7 youth chat counseling service, their team analyzed 2,609 anonymized chat transcripts from a German counseling platform, focusing on messages exchanged within 72 hours before clients completed feedback questionnaires. They employed machine learning models to assess linguistic features, such as sentiment and complexity, to determine their correlation with client satisfaction ratings. The study found that certain linguistic patterns, including positive sentiment and empathetic language, were strong predictors of higher satisfaction scores. These findings suggest that NLP techniques can effectively evaluate counseling interactions and potentially guide counselors toward more effective communication strategies. However, the study acknowledged limitations, including the inability to share data due to privacy concerns and the need for further research to generalize findings across different counseling contexts. Overall, the research highlights the potential of AI in enhancing the quality and effectiveness of digital mental health services (Hornstein et al., 2025).

In psychological assessment, AI improves efficiency and provides deeper insights. AI can quickly score standardized assessments and identify patterns signaling concerns (Tutun et al., 2023). While not replacing professionals, AI streamlines initial evaluations and flags risks for further assessment (Meier, 2025). AI chatbots can even offer preliminary diagnoses for underlying mental health conditions (Jayabhaduri et al., 2024).

AI is increasingly integrated into school counseling assessments, providing tools that enhance the efficiency and objectivity of evaluating student performance. In Krach & Corcoran's (2024) research, AI-powered systems, such as automated essay scoring, deliver consistent and unbiased grading, reducing potential human error and bias. These technologies also enable real-time feedback, allowing school counselors and educators to identify and address students' learning needs promptly. Furthermore, AI facilitates the analysis of large datasets to monitor academic progress and predict outcomes, aiding in the early identification of students at risk of underperforming. However, implementing AI in assessment raises ethical concerns, including issues of transparency, fairness, and data privacy, necessitating the development of guidelines to ensure responsible usage. Overall, while AI presents significant opportunities to transform educational assessment, careful consideration is required to balance technological benefits with ethical responsibilities (Krach & Corcoran, 2024).

For career education, AI offers personalized pathways. It analyzes students' interests, skills, and academic performance to suggest career options, educational opportunities, and skill requirements (Sun & Pratt, 2024). AI also connects students with mentorships, internships, and labor market insights (Westman et al., 2021), helping them make informed decisions.

AI is increasingly utilized in academic counseling to assist high school seniors in selecting suitable tertiary education paths. Majjate et al. (2023) analyzed students' academic histories and preferences using AI systems that can predict the likelihood of admission to chosen universities and recommend alternative institutions that align with their profiles. For instance, a counseling system developed in Morocco employed the Huber Regressor model, achieving a high R-squared value of 0.9306, to provide accurate admission predictions. This system includes two main modules: a recommendation module using popularity-based and content-based approaches, and a prediction module for admission likelihood. The integration of AI in this context enables personalized guidance, helping students make informed decisions about their academic futures. However, challenges such as data privacy, the need for comprehensive training, and the risk of over-reliance on technology must be addressed to ensure ethical and effective implementation. Overall, AI has the potential to significantly enhance the efficiency and personalization of academic counseling services (Majjate, 2023).

AI enhances information services in school guidance by providing instant access to policies, academic resources, mental health support, and scholarship details through chatbots and intelligent search engines (Chiu, 2021). Available 24/7, these tools reduce administrative burdens and personalize information delivery based on individual student needs (Maghsudi et al., 2021).

In referrals, AI streamlines access to external resources. It maintains updated databases of community organizations and mental health professionals, matching students with appropriate support based on their needs (Ouédraogo, 2024). This ensures timely and effective assistance (Anuyah et al., 2023).

Habichit et al. (2023) developed an AI-enabled self-referral chatbot to enhance accessibility to mental health services, particularly for minority groups facing additional barriers. In a study involving 129,400 patients across 28 NHS Talking Therapies services in England, the chatbot led to a 15% increase in total referrals, surpassing the 6% increase observed with traditional methods. Notably, referrals from non-binary individuals rose by 235%, bisexual individuals by 30%, and ethnic minority individuals by 31%. The tool's human-free nature and its ability to improve the perceived need for treatment were identified as key factors in reducing barriers for these groups. These findings suggest that AI chatbots can significantly improve access to mental health services, especially for disadvantaged populations.

Finally, AI strengthens research in school guidance. By analyzing student data while adhering to privacy regulations, AI identifies trends, evaluates interventions, and informs program development (Bagunaid et al., 2022). This data-driven approach improves guidance services and student outcomes.

AI is increasingly being used in school counseling research to enhance the effectiveness and accessibility of mental health support for students. The study by Jaiswal et al. (2025) demonstrates that AI technologies, such as chatbots and virtual assistants, provide personalized and immediate assistance, enabling students to access support at any time. These tools can analyze large volumes of data to identify patterns indicative of emotional distress, facilitating early intervention strategies. For instance, AI-driven systems have been developed to assist high school seniors in selecting suitable academic paths by analyzing their profiles and preferences. Additionally, AI-based platforms have been implemented to support elementary students with emotional disorders, significantly improving social-emotional competencies. However, ethical considerations, privacy concerns, and adequate training must be addressed to ensure responsible AI integration. Overall, AI holds substantial potential to transform school counseling by providing efficient, personalized, and accessible mental health support (Jaiswal et al., 2025).

The Impact of AI on Industry 4.0 and School Guidance

Rapid technological advancements have interconnected various fields, leading to unprecedented industrial changes known as Industry 4.0 (Yola et al., 2024). As the successor to previous industrial revolutions, Industry 4.0 is driven by cyber-physical systems and intelligent computing (Chaka, 2020). A key component of this transformation is AI, which has sparked both optimism and concern regarding its societal impact (Nkedishu et al., 2024). While AI enhances efficiency and convenience, some fear it may pose a threat to jobs by outperforming human labor (Roubini, 2023).

AI's influence extends to education and guidance, where it is reshaping learning and student support systems (Putri et al., 2024). AI-powered tools offer personalized learning, intelligent feedback, career guidance, and mental health assistance (Guerra, 2023). In school guidance, AI improves accessibility, responsiveness, and overall effectiveness, providing valuable support for students and counselors alike (Yola et al., 2024).

AI is increasingly integrated into academic settings to support students' decision-making processes. Al Maqbali and Tahir's (2024) study states that offers tools that assist in various academic and administrative tasks. However, this reliance on AI presents several risks, including diminished human decision-making capabilities, increased laziness among users, and heightened security and privacy concerns. Studies indicate that AI's role in automating tasks can lead to a significant reduction in students' ability to make independent decisions. Furthermore, the convenience provided by AI may contribute to decreased motivation and effort among students, potentially impacting their learning outcomes. Security and privacy issues are also prominent, as the use of AI involves the collection and analysis of sensitive personal data, raising concerns about data protection and potential breaches. To mitigate these risks, it is recommended that AI technologies in education be designed with strong ethical considerations, incorporating secure algorithms to protect user data. Additionally, reducing dependency on AI for decision-making and providing comprehensive training for both teachers and students can help preserve human cognitive abilities and ensure responsible use of AI in academic environments (Al Maqbali & Tahir, 2024).

In career guidance, AI streamlines decision-making, helping students navigate their educational and professional paths more efficiently (Monreal & Palaoag, 2023). Additionally, AI has proven beneficial in mental health support, with AI-driven apps like Wysa significantly reducing anxiety and depression symptoms, especially during the pandemic (Sinha et al., 2023).

AI's rapid evolution marks a significant technological milestone, making advanced tools easily accessible online. Its capabilities—such as problem-solving, personalized support, and automation—extend across multiple sectors, including school guidance. By offering tailored solutions to student concerns and easing counselors' workloads, AI holds immense potential to enhance student well-being and academic success.

AI-Powered Chatbots and Technologies in School Guidance

Discussing mental health remains taboo due to stigma, prejudice, and discrimination (Thomicroft et al., 2022). AI chatbots provide anonymous interactions, allowing users to seek support without fear or anxiety. Their ability to simulate natural conversation makes them a valuable tool for students and professionals, offering immediate, non-judgmental guidance in a way that feels personal rather than robotic.

AI is widely recognized for its chatbots and computer programs designed for automated, interactive conversations with humans (Gisonna, 2025). Various AI chatbots exist, including Google's Gemini Advanced, Jo Aggarwal's mental health app Wysa, Woebot, and the widely used ChatGPT by OpenAI. These AI-driven tools are increasingly relevant in school counseling, assisting practitioners with workloads and providing a safe space for students who may be uncomfortable with face-to-face consultations (Crandall, 2024).

ChatGPT, the most popular chatbot, records approximately 2.3 billion visits per month as of March 2024 (Liu et al., 2024). It operates as a large language model trained on vast datasets to generate accurate, human-like responses (Isakova et al., 2023). With its NLP capabilities, ChatGPT enables fluid, text-based conversations, making it a valuable tool for both education and counseling by fostering an engaging and supportive interaction for users.

Another popular chatbot is Gemini. Developed by Google, Gemini is a multimodal AI trained on images, video, and audio, rather than just text, setting it apart from other chatbots (Carlà et al., 2024). This allows it to generate context-aware responses and process various forms of information, enhancing its potential in school guidance and counseling (Imran & Amulsharraf, 2024).

Wysa and Woebot are AI-powered chatbots that specialize in mental health support. According to Wysa's official website, it provides personalized, immediate care for individuals, organizations, and healthcare providers using AI-driven CBT techniques (Malik, 2022). Wysa combines AI responses with human support, where its AI coach learns from user interactions, while emotional health professionals offer additional guidance.

Sinha et al. (2023) present a study on how Wysa functions. Wysa is an AI-enabled, chat-based mental health app designed to build resilience by promoting a positive self-view and self-reflection. It offers a conversational agent and various intervention tools based on evidence-based practices, such as CBT, mindfulness, and guided behavioral reinforcement. These features aim to assist users in managing issues like stress, anxiety, and depression. However, Wysa has limitations, including the lack of human therapists, which may impact the depth of therapeutic engagement. Additionally, while it provides immediate support, it may not be suitable for individuals with severe mental health conditions who need personalized care (Sinha et al., 2023).

Yeh et al. (2025) study shows that Woebot is an AI-driven chatbot designed to provide mental health support by automating CBT techniques . Accessible through platforms like Facebook Messenger and mobile apps, it helps users monitor symptoms and manage episodes of anxiety and depression. Woebot engages users through structured conversations, primarily using predetermined response buttons, while its natural language processing capabilities allow for some open-ended inputs . While studies have shown that interactions with Woebot can lead to reductions in depression scores among university students, similar decreases in anxiety scores were observed in both Woebot and control groups . However, limitations include technical glitches, user experience issues, and language barriers, which can affect user acceptance and engagement (Yeh et al., 2025). This technology provides judgment-free support, making mental health assistance more accessible. Similarly, Woebot functions as an automated therapist, utilizing AI to deliver CBT-based interventions (Brown, 2021).

Abby. Abby is a free, AI-powered therapy assistant offering 24/7 mental health support through personalized, non-judgmental conversations. Utilizing advanced natural language processing, Abby engages users to understand and respond to their emotions, providing tailored insights and guidance. While it serves as an accessible supplement to traditional therapy, Abby does not replace professional mental health services and cannot diagnose conditions. The platform prioritizes user privacy with encrypted and anonymized interactions, ensuring confidentiality (Abby.gg, 2025).

CiCi Bot. Muthmainna's (2024) study on CiciBot, an AI-powered conversational tool, enabled Indonesian English as a Foreign Language (EFL) students with a supportive, low-pressure environment to practice speaking English, aiming to alleviate speaking anxiety. By offering personalized feedback and simulating interactions akin to those with native speakers, AI-CiciBot serves as a therapeutic aid to build students' confidence and oral proficiency. The study observed a significant improvement in students' speaking skills, with mean scores rising from 49.17 in pre-tests to 90.47 in post-tests, and noted increased student engagement and willingness to participate in speaking activities. However, limitations include the small sample size of 30 students and the controlled academic setting, which may affect the generalizability of the findings. Additionally, while AI-CiCi Bot effectively reduces anxiety, it lacks the emotional depth and empathy of human interaction, suggesting that it should complement, rather than replace, human instructors in EFL education (Muthmainnah, 2024).

Youper. Developed by Hamilton (2025), it is an AI-powered mental health app designed to provide self-guided therapy for individuals experiencing anxiety and depression. It is a mental health assistant designed to provide safe, private, and clinically validated support, utilizing evidence-based interventions like CBT to help users manage conditions such as anxiety and depression. With over 2.5 million users, Youper offers instant, personalized conversations to enhance emotional well-being. Youper collaborates with providers, employers, payers, and life science companies to scale mental healthcare services, making them more accessible and effective Hamilton, 2025). The study of Yarrington et al. (2021) involving 4,517 users, Youper received an average rating of 4.36 out of 5 stars, with 42.66% of users continuing engagement through the fourth week. The study observed significant reductions in anxiety (effect size d=0.57) and depression symptoms (effect size d=0.46) within the first two weeks of use; anxiety improvements were maintained, while depression symptoms showed a slight increase in the subsequent two weeks. A higher proportion of successful emotion regulation attempts during app interactions was associated with greater symptom reduction. These findings suggest that Youper is an acceptable and effective low-cost, self-guided treatment option for anxiety and depression, warranting further research through randomized clinical trials.

CBT Techniques Offered by AI Tools. CBT is a structured, goal-oriented talk therapy that helps manage emotional issues and mental health disorders like anxiety and depression (Nakao et al., 2021). It guides individuals in recognizing negative thoughts and behaviors and introducing techniques to address them (Raypole & Marcin, 2024). CBT has been widely researched and proven effective for conditions such as depression, anxiety disorders, eating disorders, substance abuse, and personality disorders (Chand et al., 2023). By addressing negative thought patterns, CBT can alleviate symptoms and improve well-being.

AI-powered CBT tools offer an accessible and cost-effective alternative to traditional therapy (Jang et al., 2021). AI chatbots like Woebot, Wysa, and Youper provide mental health support and have demonstrated effectiveness (Farzan et al., 2024). However, AI chatbots should not replace professional therapy, as they lack the depth of human understanding (Hodson & Williamson, 2024). While they assist with thought reframing and self-reflection, they are best used as supplementary support when therapists are unavailable.

AI Mindfulness Activities. Stress has become a significant issue in modern education due to academic pressure, social expectations, and future concerns (Jamil et al., 2024). Chronic stress impairs cognitive function, reduces academic performance, and contributes to mental health problems (Cooper, 2023). AI-driven mindfulness tools offer a potential solution by integrating guided exercises into daily routines.

Mindfulness involves being fully present and aware without distraction or judgment (Climent, 2024). AI-enhanced mindfulness apps like Headspace and Smiling Mind personalize user experiences by tracking mood and suggesting tailored meditation exercises (Marschall, 2024; Wilson, 2023). These AI-driven platforms provide an accessible, cost-effective way to engage in mindfulness without needing a personal coach or therapist.

AI integrated apps such as Headspace, an app that provides research-based, self-guided tools for improving your mental health (Marschall, 2024); and Smiling Mind, an app that teaches mindfulness and meditation techniques. (Wilson, 2023). Both apps collect data by tracking the user's state or mood, usually by daily check-ins, providing enough data to the AI in order to recommend guided meditation and exercises. Ultimately, the AI is substituting a coach or a therapist, hence being an inexpensive way to engage in mindfulness activities without feeling discouraged.

A systematic review of O'Daffer et al. (2022) evaluated the efficacy, risk of bias, and conflicts of interest (COIs) in randomized controlled trials (RCTs) of the mental health apps Headspace and Calm. Researchers identified 15 RCTs—14 focusing on Headspace and one on Calm—targeting outcomes such as stress, depressive symptoms, and mindfulness. While some studies reported positive effects, the overall evidence was mixed, with many studies being underpowered and exhibiting methodological limitations. Notably, 71% of the studies had at least one domain with a high risk of bias, particularly concerning blinding and incomplete outcome data. Furthermore, 64% of the studies disclosed conflicts of interest, including direct funding from the app companies or authors with financial ties to them. The review highlights the need for more rigorous, independent research to substantiate the effectiveness of these widely used mental health apps. It also underscores the importance of transparency regarding COIs to ensure the reliability of digital mental health intervention studies (O'Daffer et al., 2022).

Development of AI made videos. Generative AI has evolved beyond chatbots, now enabling users to create videos with simple prompts (Zhou et al., 2024). AI-powered video tools enhance efficiency by transforming text into engaging visual content, making information more accessible (Grabb, 2024).

AI is increasingly being utilized to create video-based interventions aimed at improving mental health outcomes. For instance, Olawade et al.'s (2024) study on AI-driven digital therapeutics, such as SHIVA, integrate virtual reality and AI with interventions like SelfHelp+ to provide personalized mental health support. Additionally, AI-enabled virtual assistants, like Alleviate, have been developed to assist patients with mental health challenges by offering personalized care and aiding clinicians in understanding their patients better. These AI-powered video interventions offer scalable and accessible solutions, potentially enhancing engagement and effectiveness in mental health care. However, further research is needed to fully understand their impact and optimize their integration into existing mental health services (Olawade et al., 2024).

In mental health education, AI-generated videos help disseminate knowledge quickly and effectively. Research suggests that mental health-related videos can reduce symptoms of psychological distress (Yang et al., 2023). Schools can leverage AI-generated content to provide guidance and educational materials, improving mental health awareness among students.

AI's Threat to the School Guidance Profession

AI has revolutionized various industries, including telecommunications, entertainment, healthcare, and education (Rashid & Kausik, 2024; Alowais et al., 2023; Olawade et al., 2024; Zhang & Aslan, 2021). While AI enhances efficiency, it also raises concerns about job displacement and the reliability of AI-generated content (Mortaji & Sadeghi, 2024). The field of school guidance is no exception. AI's integration into counseling services has sparked debates about its impact on human professionals and ethical considerations (Nkedishu et al., 2024).

Potential Job Displacement. AI has the potential to automate various job functions, including decision-making and administrative tasks (Farhan, 2023). Highly educated professionals perceive AI as a threat due to its rapid advancements (Wang & Lu, 2024).

School guidance counselors, particularly in the Philippines, face staffing shortages (Lacson et al., 2024). AI chatbots like ChatGPT and Wysa help bridge this gap, offering students career guidance when counselors are unavailable (Suresh et al., 2021). AI improves accessibility and personalization in counseling (Rahman et al., 2024). However, while AI tools provide support, they lack the emotional intelligence essential for effective counseling. A balanced approach—leveraging both human expertise and AI technology—is necessary.

Minimized Human Connection. Despite their ability to mimic natural conversations, AI chatbots cannot match human professionals' emotional intelligence (Rahman et al., 2024). Many people consult AI for sensitive issues due to mental health stigmas (Jemison, 2024; Park, 2025). However, relying solely on AI limits in-depth analysis and human empathy, which are crucial in mental health care.

The article of Brown & Halpern (2021) discusses while chatbots show potential for short-term mental health support, their effectiveness depends on ensuring quality care and equitable access for diverse populations. Relying on self-advocacy in chatbot-based triage poses ethical concerns, particularly for vulnerable individuals whose needs may be overlooked as mental illness can impair self-advocacy, making it difficult for individuals to seek necessary human intervention. They further discussed that chatbots cannot replicate the embodied empathy and non-verbal communication crucial in in-person mental healthcare. In-person interventions offer indirect social benefits that virtual platforms cannot replicate, impacting overall well-being (Brown & Halpern, 2021).

Potential Data Privacy and Ethical Issues. AI raises concerns about privacy, as it requires large datasets for training (Stahl, 2021). Data privacy involves properly handling, storing, and disposing personal information (Devineni, 2024). AI poses risks, including unauthorized data collection and ethical challenges such as algorithmic bias, environmental impact, and misuse for malicious purposes (Gomstyn & Jonker, 2024; Kanungo, 2024; Chen, 2023; Blauth et al., 2022).

Fiske et al. (2019) identified overarching ethical issues and concerns include in the use of AI chatbots in mental health intervention. They identified the issue of harm prevention and various questions of data ethics. They also claimed that there is a lack of guidance on development of AI applications. The clinical integration and training of health professionals have 'gaps' in ethical and regulatory frameworks. There is also a potential for misuse of the technologies to replace established services, thereby potentially exacerbating existing health inequalities. Specific challenges identified and discussed in their research include: matters of risk assessment, referrals, and supervision; the need to respect and protect patient autonomy; the role of non-human therapy; transparency in the use of algorithms; and specific concerns regarding long-term effects of these applications on understandings of illness and the human condition (Fiske et al., 2019).

Errors in Content. Despite advancements, AI-generated content is prone to misinformation (Monteith et al., 2024). Users unfamiliar with a topic may struggle to identify inaccuracies, leading to the spread of false information (Evans & Snead, 2024). In fields like mental health and education, AI-generated misinformation can have serious consequences, making accuracy a critical concern.

CONCLUSIONS: AI AND THE FUTURE OF PHILIPPINE SCHOOL GUIDANCE-RELATED SERVICES

In conclusion, integrating AI into school guidance-related services signifies a transformative shift with profound implications for navigating the complexities of the modern world. In an increasingly VUCAD (volatile, uncertain, complex, ambiguous, and diverse) environment, students confront unprecedented challenges in their academic, personal, and career development. AI provides powerful tools to help tackle these uncertainties by offering personalized support, streamlining access to information, and delivering data-driven insights that can empower students to make informed decisions and build resilience. From AI-powered counseling assistance and personalized career guidance to efficient assessment tools and streamlined referral processes, the intelligent use of these technologies holds the potential to create more responsive and effective guidance programs that can better prepare students for the demands of the future.

However, the successful and ethical implementation of AI in school guidance requires careful consideration of its implications, particularly with respect to the training of guidance counselors. As AI tools become increasingly integrated into their workflows, counselors will need to develop a new set of skills and competencies. This includes understanding the capabilities and limitations of various AI applications, interpreting AI-generated data and insights, and effectively incorporating these tools into their professional practice while maintaining the essential human elements of empathy, ethical judgment, and personalized connections with students. Training programs must adapt to equip counselors with the necessary digital literacy, critical thinking skills, and ethical awareness to leverage AI effectively and responsibly.

While AI has the potential to transform school guidance services through timely interventions, predictive analytics, and accessible mental health support, ethical and privacy concerns must be addressed with urgency. The handling of sensitive student data, including academic records, emotional patterns, and psychological profiles, demands strict safeguards to prevent misuse, breaches, or surveillance, if Philippine schools can adapt AI integration in school guidance services. Without clear national guidelines on data protection regarding AI, these systems risk violating student confidentiality and trust. It is recommended that educational institutions adopt a rights-based framework for integrating AI into guidance systems. This includes crafting ethical policies aligned with the Data Privacy Act, ensuring informed consent from both students and parents, and conducting regular audits to ensure algorithmic fairness. Furthermore, AI should complement, not replace, human counselors—preserving the empathy and cultural sensitivity essential to the well-being of Filipino students. Responsible AI deployment must strike a balance between innovation, care, equity, and ethical integrity in every school context.

On the other hand, students who use open-source AI indeed have an additional source of inquiry for mental health concerns. This lowers costs and promotes innovation. However, their integration in guidance programs must be approached with caution. Many open-source models lack built-in safeguards for privacy, bias detection, or ethical use. This raises concerns when handling sensitive student data. Given this, institutions should critically evaluate open-source AI tools before deployment, ensuring alignment with ethical standards, data privacy laws, and guidance objectives. Open-source AI should not be viewed merely as a cost-saving solution, but as a platform for ethical, inclusive, and culturally grounded innovation in student support systems. Moreover, AI is considered a supplement, not a replacement, for traditional face-to-face guidance services, where the client interacts with a human counselor.

As AI systems increasingly take their place in school guidance offices, an essential yet often overlooked concern is the need for cultural sensitivity and contextual relevance. Many AI platforms are developed using datasets and psychological models that prioritize Western standards, which can obscure the values, communication styles, and emotional expressions typical of Filipino students. Guidance services are deeply personal and rely heavily on cultural nuances such as *pakikisama* (harmonious relationships), *hiya* (a sense of shame or propriety), *utang na loob* (debt of gratitude), and *kapwa* (shared identity). These cultural values play a crucial role in how students express distress, seek help, and respond to authority figures. Ignoring these cultural elements may result in AI systems offering intervention that seems emotionally disconnected or inappropriate.

At times, language use and tone matter. AI that communicates only in English or uses rigid, formal language may alienate students who are more comfortable with Filipino or regional dialects. However, Filipinos are taught English from nursery school to college, so language issues in comprehending English are addressed. However, the warmth and empathy typically offered by Filipino guidance counselors cannot be replicated by AI without careful cultural programming.

To address this, AI tools should be co-developed with local educators, psychologists, and cultural experts to ensure contextual fit in the future, or if funds permit it. Training datasets should include culturally relevant scenarios, and AI responses should reflect Filipino communication patterns. Additionally, guidance counselors and students must be trained not just to use AI, but to evaluate its recommendations through a culturally sensitive lens critically.

AI should serve as a culturally responsive assistant, not a replacement, for human guidance. Emphasizing cultural sensitivity ensures that technology enhances, rather than undermines, the trust and emotional safety that are essential in school counseling.

Ultimately, the future of school guidance in a VUCAD world will be shaped by the collaborative partnership between human expertise and artificial intelligence. AI holds the potential to enhance the reach, efficiency, and personalization of guidance services, enabling counselors to focus on the distinctly human aspects of their roles – building rapport, nurturing emotional well-being, and providing comprehensive support for complex individual needs. By thoughtfully embracing AI and investing in the ongoing training of guidance professionals, schools can develop a more robust and adaptive support system that empowers all students to flourish in an ever-evolving landscape.

Another limitation to the implementation of AI systems in education in the Philippines is the lack of resources, particularly in urban poor, rural and underserved areas. While AI holds promise for enhancing personalized learning, automating administrative tasks, and improving access to quality education, its integration is hindered by stark disparities in digital infrastructure caused by lack of finds. apossible to shell out for most schools. Economically, this investment is necessary for AI adoption, encompassing the procurement of devices, software, educator training, and system maintenance. This poses a heavy burden for local government units and the Department of Education.

For AI to be meaningfully and inclusively implemented, there must be deliberate national investment in infrastructure development, inclusive policymaking, and capacity-building for teachers and school leaders. Without these, the promise of AI risks becoming a tool that benefits only a privileged few, if any, rather than a catalyst for broad educational transformation.

REFERENCES

Adams, C., Pente, P., Lemermeyer, G., & Rockwell, G. (2022). Ethical principles for artificial intelligence in K-12 education. *Computers and Education: Artificial Intelligence*, *4*, 100131. DOI: 10.1016/j.caeai.2023.100131

Ajlouni, A., Almahaireh, A., & Whaba, F. (2023). Students' perception of using ChatGPT in counseling and mental health education: The benefits and challenges. [iJET]. *International Journal of Emerging Technologies in Learning*, *18*(20), 199–218. https://www.learntechlib.org/p/223772/?nl=1. DOI: 10.3991/ijet.v18i20.42075

Akingbola, A., Adeleke, O., Idris, A., Adewole, O., & Adegbesan, A. (2024). Artificial Intelligence and the Dehumanization of Patient Care. *Journal of Medicine, Surgery, and Public Health*, *3*, 100138. DOI: 10.1016/j.glmedi.2024.100138

Al Maqbali, S. B., & Tahir, N. M. (2024, August). AI Opportunities and Risks for Students' Decision-Making Skill. In *2024 IEEE 14th International Conference on Control System, Computing and Engineering (ICCSCE)* (pp. 321-326). IEEE. DOI: 10.1109/ICCSCE61582.2024.10696240

Alfaris, M. M., Sauri, S., & Gaffar, M. A. (2021). Guidance and counseling management on personal, social, learning and career development of SMK 19 Bandung students during COVID-19 pandemics. *Guidance and Counseling*, *2*(2), 2. DOI: 10.52690/jswse.v2i2.244

Alowais, S. A., Alghamdi, S. S., Alsuhebany, N., Alqahtani, T., Alshaya, A. I., Almohareb, S. N., Aldairem, A., Alrashed, M., Saleh, K. B., Badreldin, H. A., Yami, M. S. A., Harbi, S. A., & Albekairy, A. M. (2023). Revolutionizing healthcare: The role of artificial intelligence in clinical practice. *BMC Medical Education*, *23*(1), 689. DOI: 10.1186/s12909-023-04698-z

Anuyah, O., Conrado, A. M., Carlson, C., Gilbride, H., & Metoyer, R. (2023). Exploring the barriers and potential opportunities of technology integration in Community-Based social service organizations. *ACM Journal on Computing and Sustainable Societies*, *1*(1), 1–28. DOI: 10.1145/3610720

Astuti, L. P. (2021). The role of guidance and counseling services in individual counseling during the covid-19 pandemic. *International Journal of Applied Guidance and Counseling*, *2*(1), 25–30. DOI: 10.26486/ijagc.v2i1.1592

Bagunaid, W., Chilamkurti, N., & Veeraraghavan, P. (2022). Aisar: Artificial intelligence-based student assessment and recommendation system for e-learning in big data. *Sustainability (Basel)*, *14*(17), 10551. DOI: 10.3390/su141710551

Blauth, T. F., Gstrein, O. J., & Zwitter, A. (2022). Artificial Intelligence Crime: An overview of Malicious use and abuse of AI. *IEEE Access : Practical Innovations, Open Solutions*, *10*, 77110–77122. DOI: 10.1109/ACCESS.2022.3191790

Brown, K. (2021, June 1). *Something Bothering You? Tell It to Woebot.* The New York Times. https://www.nytimes.com/2021/06/01/health/artificial-intelligence-therapy-woebot.html?smid=url-share

Bulmer, L., Stanley, C., Loffredo, L., Mills, R., & Doyle, L. (2022). Building a foundation in self-awareness: Genetic counseling students' experiences with self-care, reflection, and mindfulness. *Journal of Genetic Counseling*, *31*(3), 722–734. DOI: 10.1002/jgc4.1539

Campo, J., de los Reyes, R & Gomez, MGAG. (October 2022). Challenges Affecting the Well-Being of Filipino Guidance Counselors Amidst the COVID-19 Pandemic. (2). pp.17-28

Carlà, M. M., Gambini, G., Baldascino, A., Boselli, F., Giannuzzi, F., Margollicci, F., & Rizzo, S. (2024). Large language models as assistance for glaucoma surgical cases: A ChatGPT vs. Google Gemini comparison. *Graefe's Archive for Clinical and Experimental Ophthalmology*, *262*(9), 2945–2959. DOI: 10.1007/s00417-024-06470-5

Chaka, C. (2020). Skills, competencies and literacies attributed to 4IR/Industry 4.0: Scoping review. *IFLA Journal*, *46*(4), 369–399. DOI: 10.1177/0340035219896376

Chand, S. P., Kuckel, D. P., & Huecker, M. R. (2023, May 23). *Cognitive Behavior Therapy*. StatPearls - NCBI Bookshelf. https://www.ncbi.nlm.nih.gov/books/NBK470241/

Chen, Z. (2023). Ethics and discrimination in artificial intelligence-enabled recruitment practices. *Humanities & Social Sciences Communications*, *10*(1), 567. Advance online publication. DOI: 10.1057/s41599-023-02079-x

Chiu, T. K. (2021). A holistic approach to the design of artificial intelligence (AI) education for K-12 schools. *TechTrends*, *65*(5), 796–807. https://eric.ed.gov/?id=EJ1309807. DOI: 10.1007/s11528-021-00637-1

Climent, E. F. (2024, March 5). *Embracing Mindfulness in the age of AI: A Path to Inner Peace*. https://www.linkedin.com/pulse/embracing-mindfulness-age-ai-path-inner-peace-edgardo-zih6e#:~:text=Integrating%20AI%20into%20mindfulness%20practices,but%20unsure%20where%20to%20start

Cooper, J. (2023, September 26). *Stress and Depression*. WebMD. https://www.webmd.com/depression/features/stress-depression

Devineni, S. K. (2024). AI in Data Privacy and Security. In *International Journal of Artificial Intelligence & Machine Learning (IJAIML)* (Vol. 3, Issue 1, pp. 35–49) [Journal-article]. https://iaeme.com/MasterAdmin/Journal_uploads/IJAIML/VOLUME_3_ISSUE_1/IJAIML_03_01_004.pdf

Dianovi, A., Siregar, D., Mawaddah, I., & Suryaningsih, S. (2022). Guidance and Counselling in Education. *World Psychology*, *1*(2), 99–107. DOI: 10.55849/wp.v1i2.95

Evans, H., & Snead, D. (2024). Understanding the errors made by artificial intelligence algorithms in histopathology in terms of patient impact. *NPJ Digital Medicine*, *7*(1), 89. Advance online publication. DOI: 10.1038/s41746-024-01093-w

Fadli, R. P., Daharnis, D., & Yusuf, A. M. (2022). How The Implications of Assessment for Guidance and Counseling in Schools? [Jurnal Penelitian Guru Indonesia]. *JPGI*, *7*(1), 148–153. DOI: 10.29210/021875jpgi0005

Farhan, A. (2023). The impact of artificial intelligence on human workers. *Journal Of Communication Education*, *17*(2), 93–104. https://jurnal.unipem.ac.id/index.php/joce-ip/article/view/350. DOI: 10.58217/joce-ip.v17i2.350

Farhud, D. D., & Zokaei, S. (2021, October 27). Ethical Issues of Artificial Intelligence in Medicine and Healthcare. *Iranian Journal of Public Health*, *50*(11), i. DOI: 10.18502/ijph.v50i11.7600

Farrell, I. C., Binkley, E. E., Garcia, M. A., & Jackson, T. N. (2022). Advocacy of School Counselors Working With ELL Students. *Professional School Counseling*, *26*(1), 2156759X221134276. Advance online publication. DOI: 10.1177/2156759X221134276

Farzan, M., Ebrahimi, H., Pourali, M., & Sabeti, F. (2024). Artificial Intelligence-Powered Cognitive Behavioral Therapy Chatbots, A Systematic Review. *Iranian Journal of Psychiatry*. Advance online publication. DOI: 10.18502/ijps.v20i1.17395

Fiske, A., Henningsen, P., & Buyx, A. (2019). Your robot therapist will see you now: Ethical implications of embodied artificial intelligence in psychiatry, psychology, and psychotherapy. *Journal of Medical Internet Research*, *21*(5), e13216. DOI: 10.2196/13216

Gardner, M. M., Hickmott, J., & Ludvik, M. J. B. (2023). *Demonstrating student success: A practical guide to outcomes-based assessment of learning and development in student affairs*. Routledge., DOI: 10.4324/9781003444046

Garza Schuster, J. E. (2022). A phenomenological investigation of the lived experiences of middle school professional school counselors in addressing student mental health, during the COVID-19 pandemic, after a return to in-person instruction. https://tamucc-ir.tdl.org/server/api/core/bitstreams/8b50554a-9c41-4d73-9554-9b5337de03b9/content

Gisonna, N. (2025, February 26). chatbot. Encyclopedia Britannica. https://www.britannica.com/topic/chatbot

Gomstyn, A., & Jonker, A. (2024, November 25). Exploring privacy issues in the age of AI. *IBM*. https://www.ibm.com/think/insights/ai-privacy

Grabb, D. (2024). Text-to-Video AI Is Here To Stay: What It Means for Mental Health. *Psychiatric News, 59*(06), appi.pn.2024.06.6.34. Advance online publication. DOI: 10.1176/appi.pn.2024.06.6.34

Grassini, S. (2023). Shaping the future of education: Exploring the potential and consequences of AI and ChatGPT in educational settings. *Education Sciences, 13*(7), 692. DOI: 10.3390/educsci13070692

Guerra, A. (2023). *The future benefits of artificial intelligence for students*. Urbe University. https://urbeuniversity.edu/blog/the-future-benefits-of-artificial-intelligence-for-students

Habsy, B. A., Apriliya, K., Apriliyana, G. S., Zahra, K. F. A., & Mahendra, W. (2024). Concept of Information Service Management Guidance and Counseling. *Jurnal Multidisiplin Indonesia, 3*(12), 4568–4574. DOI: 10.58344/jmi.v3i12.2075

Hamilton, J. (2025). Youper: Your Emotional Health Assistant. https://www.youper.ai

Himelfarb, I. (2019, October 01). A primer on standardized testing: History, measurement, classical test theory, item response theory, and equating. *The Journal of Chiropractic Education, 33*(2), 151–163. DOI: 10.7899/JCE-18-22

Hodson, N., & Williamson, S. (2024). Can Large Language Models Replace Therapists? Evaluating Performance at Simple Cognitive Behavioral Therapy Tasks. *JMIR AI, 3*, e52500. DOI: 10.2196/52500

Hornstein, S., Lueken, U., Wundrack, R., & Hilbert, K. (2025). Predicting Satisfaction With Chat-Counseling at a 24/7 Chat Hotline for the Youth: Natural Language Processing Study. *JMIR AI, 4*(1), e63701. DOI: 10.2196/63701

Jaiswal, C., Jaiswal, L., Kalia, N., & Sharma, O. P. (2025). Artificial Intelligence in Counseling: Evaluating Its Strengths, Limitations, and Ethical Considerations in Indian Schools. *International Journal of Science and Social Science Research, 2*(4), 328–331. DOI: 10.5281/zenodo.15090441

Jamil, T., Hussain, S., Khan, Z., & Atif, H. (2024). Investigating the Effects of Mindfulness and Meditation on Student Stress Levels and Academic Outcomes with AI. [BBE]. *Bulletin of Business and Economics, 13*(3), 472–479. https://bbejournal.com/BBE/article/view/1036?articlesBySimilarityPage=53

Jang, S., Kim, J., Kim, S., Hong, J., Kim, S., & Kim, E. (2021). Mobile app-based chatbot to deliver cognitive behavioral therapy and psychoeducation for adults with attention deficit: A development and feasibility/usability study. *International Journal of Medical Informatics, 150*, 104440. DOI: 10.1016/j.ijmedinf.2021.104440

Jannah, M., Izzati, U. A., Bachri, B. S., & Wismanadi, H. (2023, January). Guidance and Counseling Referral System Initiative. In *Unima International Conference on Social Sciences and Humanities (UNICSSH 2022)* (pp. 383-387). Atlantis Press. https://www.atlantis-press.com/proceedings/unicssh-22/125984046

Jayabhaduri, R., Vijayaraghavan, A., & Ceralaathan, G. (2024, June). AI Powered Chatbot For Mental Health Treatment. In *2024 First International Conference on Technological Innovations and Advance Computing (TIACOMP)* (pp. 168-172). IEEE. **DOI:** DOI: 10.1109/TIACOMP64125.2024.00037

Jemison, J. (2024, October 15). *Mental illness remains taboo in the Philippines, but technology might just help break the stigma — Medicinal Media*. Medicinal Media. https://www.medicinalmedia.com/explore/tech-helps-break-the-stigma-of-mental-illness-in-the-philippines

Kanungo, A. (2024, March 5). The Green Dilemma: Can AI Fulfil Its Potential Without Harming the Environment? https://earth.org/the-green-dilemma-can-ai-fulfil-its-potential-without-harming-the-environment/

Karaman, M. A., Eşici, H., Tomar, İ. H., & Aliyev, R. (2021). COVID-19: Are school counseling services ready? Students' psychological symptoms, school counselors' views, and solutions. *Frontiers in Psychology, 12*, 647740. DOI: 10.3389/fpsyg.2021.647740

Karan, B., & Angadi, G. R. (2023). Potential Risks of Artificial Intelligence Integration into School Education: A Systematic Review. *Bulletin of Science, Technology & Society, 43*(3-4), 67–85. Advance online publication. DOI: 10.1177/02704676231224705

Krach, S. K., & Corcoran, S. (2024). Will Computers Replace School Psychologists? An Analysis of Tech-Based Tools for Assessment, Consultation, and Counseling. *Contemporary School Psychology*, *28*(4), 496–508. DOI: 10.1007/s40688-023-00455-7

Lacson, J., Kilag, O. K., Sasan, J. M., Groenewald, E., Vidal, E., & Ponte, R. (2024). The Crisis: An In-Depth Analysis of the Shortage of Guidance Counselors and Its Impact on Student Suicide Rates in Philippine Schools. *International Multidisciplinary Journal of Research for Innovation, Sustainability, and Excellence (IMJRISE), 1*(1), 129-135. https://risejournals.org/index.php/imjrise/article/view/15

Leatherman, A. J. (2024). Exploring How Experienced High School Counselors Make Sense of COVID-19's Impact on their Attitudes and Beliefs about Postsecondary Planning, and their Postsecondary Planning Practices: Two Interpretive Phenomenological Analysis Studies. https://ir.library.oregonstate.edu/concern/graduate_thesis_or_dissertations/tb09jf23h?locale=en

Lee, J. (2025). Smart Solutions for Student Well-being: AI-driven Mental Health Support in a Polytechnic. In *The Rise of Intelligent Machines* (pp. 211-242). Chapman and Hall/CRC. https://www.taylorfrancis.com/chapters/edit/10.1201/9781003469551-9/smart-solutions-student-well-being-jeffrey-lee

Li, Y., Ding, X., Chen, Y., Li, Y., & Ma, N. (2025, July). Customizable AI for Depression Care: Improving the User Experience of Large Language Model-Driven Chatbots. In *Proceedings of the 2025 ACM Designing Interactive Systems Conference* (pp. 1844-1866). https://doi.org/DOI: 10.1145/3715336.3735795

Liu, Y., & Wang, H. Digital Development Global Practice, Research Support Team, & World Bank. (2024). Who on Earth is using generative AI? In World Bank, *Policy Research Working Paper*. https://documents1.worldbank.org/curated/en/099720008192430535/pdf/IDU15f321eb5148701472d1a88813ab677be07b0.pdf

Maghsudi, S., Lan, A., Xu, J., & van Der Schaar, M. (2021). Personalized education in the artificial intelligence era: What to expect next. *IEEE Signal Processing Magazine*, *38*(3), 37–50. DOI: 10.1109/MSP.2021.3055032

Majjate, H., Bellarhmouch, Y., Jeghal, A., Yahyaouy, A., Tairi, H., & Zidani, K. A. (2023, December 28). AI-Powered Academic Guidance and Counseling System Based on Student Profile and Interests. *Applied System Innovation*, *7*(1), 6. DOI: 10.3390/asi7010006

Malik, T., Ambrose, A. J., & Sinha, C. (2022). Evaluating user feedback for an artificial intelligence–enabled, cognitive behavioral therapy–based mental health app (Wysa): Qualitative thematic analysis. *JMIR Human Factors*, *9*(2), e35668. DOI: 10.2196/35668

Marschall, A. M. (2024, June 11). I'm a Therapist Who Tried Headspace to Help Conquer My Stress. *Verywell Mind*. https://www.verywellmind.com/i-tried-headspace-review-7562523

Meier, S. T. (2025). Initial evaluation of an AI-augmented progress monitoring and outcome assessment. *Counselling & Psychotherapy Research*, *25*(1), e12869. DOI: 10.1002/capr.12869

Mielgo-Conde, I., Seijas-Santos, S., & Grande-de-Prado, M. (2021). Review about online educational guidance during the COVID-19 pandemic. *Education Sciences*, *11*(8), 411. DOI: 10.3390/educsci11080411

Monteith, S., Glenn, T., Geddes, J. R., Whybrow, P. C., Achtyes, E., & Bauer, M. (2024). Artificial intelligence and increasing misinformation. *The British Journal of Psychiatry*, *224*(2), 33–35. DOI: 10.1192/bjp.2023.136

Mortaji, S. T. H., & Sadeghi, M. E. (2024). Assessing the reliability of artificial intelligence systems: challenges, metrics, and future directions. In Iran University of Science and Technology & University of Tehran, *International Journal of Innovation in Management Economics and Social Sciences* (Vol. 4, Issue 2, pp. 1–13). https://ijimes.ir/index.php/ijimes/article/view/133

Muthmainnah, M. (2024). AI-CiciBot as Conversational Partners in EFL Education, focusing on Intelligent Technology Adoption (ITA) to Mollify Speaking Anxiety. *Journal of English Language Teaching and Applied Linguistics, 6*(4), 76-85. ISSN: 2707-756X

Nakao, M., Shirotsuki, K., & Sugaya, N. (2021). Cognitive–behavioral therapy for management of mental health and stress-related disorders: Recent advances in techniques and technologies. *BioPsychoSocial Medicine*, *15*(1), 16. DOI: 10.1186/s13030-021-00219-w

Ngeno, G. (2022). Students' Perceptions of the Impact of Guidance and Counselling Programs on Academic Needs Satisfaction in Secondary Schools within the Rift Valley Region, Kenya. *Educational Research Review*, *17*(4), 145–151. https://eric.ed.gov/?id=EJ1344846. DOI: 10.5897/ERR2022.4232

Nkedishu, V. C., & Okonta, V. (2024). Unpacking Optimism versus Concern: Tertiary Students' Multidimensional Views on the Rise of Artificial Intelligence (AI). [IRJMS]. *International Research Journal of Multidisciplinary Scope*, *5*(4), 362–37. DOI: 10.47857/irjms.2024.05i04.01261

O'Daffer, A., Colt, S. F., Wasil, A. R., & Lau, N. (2022). Efficacy and conflicts of interest in randomized controlled trials evaluating Headspace and Calm apps: Systematic review. *JMIR Mental Health*, *9*(9), e40924. DOI: 10.2196/40924

Ofem, U. J., Anake, P. M., Abuo, C. B., Ukatu, J. O., & Etta, E. O. (2025). Artificial intelligence application in counselling practices. A multigroup analysis of acceptance and awareness using gender and professional rank. *Frontiers in Digital Health*, *6*, 1414178. DOI: 10.3389/fdgth.2024.1414178

Olawade, D. B., Wada, O. Z., Odetayo, A., David-Olawade, A. C., Asaolu, F., & Eberhardt, J. (2024). Enhancing mental health with Artificial Intelligence: Current trends and future prospects. *Journal of Medicine, Surgery, and Public Health*, *3*, 100099. DOI: 10.1016/j.glmedi.2024.100099

Ouédraogo, I. (2024). *Mobile technology and artificial intelligence for improving health literacy among underserved communities* (Doctoral dissertation, Université de Bordeaux; Université Nazi Boni (Bobo-Dioulasso, Burkina Faso)). https://theses.hal.science/tel-04574957/

Pagliarin, S., La Mendola, S., & Vis, B. (2023). The "qualitative" in qualitative comparative analysis (QCA): Research moves, case-intimacy and face-to-face interviews. *Quality & Quantity*, *57*(1), 489–507. DOI: 10.1007/s11135-022-01358-0

Park, E. (2025). I Trust You, but Let Me Talk to AI: The Role of the Chat Agents, Empathy, and Health Issues in Misinformation Guidance. *International Journal of Strategic Communication*, *19*(2), 1–30. DOI: 10.1080/1553118X.2025.2462087

Pedroso, J. E., Siason, A., Ortizo-Roces, C., & Basbas, J. (2022). Implementation of guidance and counseling services during the COVID-19 Pandemic. *ISSRA Journal of Education, Linguistics and Literature,* *2*(1), 1-12. https://www.researchgate.net/profile/John-Erwin-Pedroso/publication/358395202_Implementation_of_Guidance_and_Counseling_Services_during_the_COVID-19_Pandemic/links/61ffd980870587329e974b7b/Implementation-of-Guidance-and-Counseling-Services-during-the-COVID-19-Pandemic.pdf

Peterson, L. (2019). School Counselors' Lived Experiences Supporting Students with Mental Health Concerns. https://scholarworks.waldenu.edu/cgi/viewcontent.cgi?article=8696&context=dissertations

Ping, Y. (2024). Experience in psychological counseling supported by artificial intelligence technology. *Technology and Health Care, 32*(6), 3871–3888. DOI: 10.3233/THC-230809

Putri, R. A., Mailana, Z., Fadilah, N., Mardenil, F., & Oktarini, I. (2024). The Effectiveness of Artificial Intelligence Technology in Facing the Challenges of Guidance and Counseling in the Digital Age. *BICC Proceedings, 2*, 213-219. https://doi.org/ DOI: 10.30983/bicc.v1i1.130

Rahman, M. Z. (2024). Leveraging Artificial Intelligence for Enhanced Career Guidance and Development in Bangladesh: Addressing Educational and Employment Gaps. *International Journal of Career Development, 13*. https://www.researchgate.net/profile/Albina-Amin/publication/384243013_International_Journal_of_Career_Development/links/66f05e9a97a75a4b48405bf7/International-Journal-of-Career-Development.pdf#page=13

Rezaiee, M., & Kareshki, H. (2024, November). Empowering career pathways: integrating self-regulation strategies with career counseling practices. In *Frontiers in Education* (Vol. 9, p. 1422692). Frontiers Media SA. https://doi.org/DOI: 10.3389/feduc.2024.1422692

Romael Haque, M. D., & Rubya, S. (2023, May 22). An Overview of Chatbot-Based Mobile Mental Health Apps: Insights From App Description and User Reviews. *JMIR mHealth and uHealth, 11*, e44838. DOI: 10.2196/44838

Roubini, N. (2023). The AI threat. *Horizons: Journal of International Relations and Sustainable Development*, (24), 26-45. https://www.cirsd.org/en/horizons/horizons-summer-2023--issue-no24/the-ai-threat

Rubin, M., Arnon, H., Huppert, J. D., & Perry, A. (2024, June 11). Considering the Role of Human Empathy in AI-Driven Therapy. *JMIR Mental Health, 11*, e56529. DOI: 10.2196/56529

Sanni, A. B. (2024). *Social Class Factors, Academic Well-Being And Academic Achievement Of Public Secondary School Students In Ekiti State, Nigeria* (Doctoral dissertation, Doctoral Dissertation, University of Ibadan).

Savitz-Romer, M., Rowan-Kenyon, H. T., Nicola, T. P., Alexander, E., & Carroll, S. (2021). When the kids are not alright: School counseling in the time of COVID-19. *AERA Open, 7*, 23328584211033600. https://eric.ed.gov/?id=EJ1323994. DOI: 10.1177/23328584211033600

Sinha, C., Meheli, S., & Kadaba, M. (2023). Understanding digital mental health needs and usage with an artificial intelligence–led mental health app (Wysa) during the COVID-19 pandemic: Retrospective analysis. *JMIR Formative Research*, *7*(1), e41913. DOI: 10.2196/41913

Stahl, B. C. (2021). Artificial intelligence for a better future. In *SpringerBriefs in research and innovation governance*. https://link.springer.com/book/10.1007/978-3-030-69978-9

Su, S. W., Hung, C. H., Chen, L. X., & Yuan, S. M. (2024). Development of an AI-based system to enhance school counseling models for Asian elementary students with emotional disorders. *IEEE Access*. https://ui.adsabs.harvard.edu/abs/2024IEEEA.12o9121S/abstract

Sun, J. C., & Pratt, T. L. (2024). Navigating AI Integration in Career and Technical Education: Diffusion Challenges, Opportunities, and Decisions. *Education Sciences*, *14*(12), 1285. DOI: 10.3390/educsci14121285

Suresh, N., Mukabe, N., Hashiyana, V., Limbo, A., & Hauwanga, A. (2021). Career Counseling Chatbot on Facebook Messenger using AI. *DSMLAI : Data Science, Machine Learning and Artificial Intelligence*, 65–73. DOI: 10.1145/3484824.3484875

Tewari, A., Chhabria, A., Khalsa, A. S., Chaudhary, S., & Kanal, H. (2021, April). A survey of mental health chatbots using NLP. In *Proceedings of the International Conference on Innovative Computing & Communication (ICICC)*. https://papers.ssrn.com/sol3/papers.cfm?abstract_id=3833914

Tilala, M. H., Chenchala, P. K., Choppadandi, A., Kaur, J., Naguri, S., Saoji, R., & Devaguptapu, B. (2024, June 15). Ethical Considerations in the Use of Artificial Intelligence and Machine Learning in Health Care: A Comprehensive Review. *Cureus*, *16*(6), e62443. DOI: 10.7759/cureus.62443

Tutun, S., Johnson, M. E., Ahmed, A., Albizri, A., Irgil, S., Yesilkaya, I., Ucar, E. N., Sengun, T., & Harfouche, A. (2023). An AI-based decision support system for predicting mental health disorders. *Information Systems Frontiers*, *25*(3), 1261–1276. DOI: 10.1007/s10796-022-10282-5

Wang, K., & Lu, W. (2024). AI-induced job impact: Complementary or substitution? Empirical insights and sustainable technology considerations. *Sustainable Technology and Entrepreneurship, 100085*. Advance online publication. DOI: 10.1016/j.stae.2024.100085

Westman, S., Kauttonen, J., Klemetti, A., Korhonen, N., Manninen, M., Mononen, A., . . . Paananen, H. (2021). Artificial Intelligence for Career Guidance--Current Requirements and Prospects for the Future. *IAFOR Journal of Education, 9*(4), 43-62. https://eric.ed.gov/?id=EJ1318705

Wilson, E. (2023, September 12). I tried the Smiling Mind app to see if it could help me stop worrying constantly. *Verywell Mind*. https://www.verywellmind.com/i-tried-smiling-mind-app-review-7643815

Wong, L. P. (2024). Artificial Intelligence and Job Automation: Challenges for Secondary Students' Career Development and Life Planning. *Merits*, *4*(4), 370–399. DOI: 10.3390/merits4040027

Wong, M. F., Guo, S., Hang, C. N., Ho, S. W., & Tan, C. W. (2023). Natural language generation and understanding of big code for AI-assisted programming: A review. *Entropy (Basel, Switzerland)*, *25*(6), 888. DOI: 10.3390/e25060888

Yarrington, J. S., Lasser, J., Garcia, D., Vargas, J. H., Couto, D. D., Marafon, T., Craske, M. G., & Niles, A. N. (2021). Impact of the COVID-19 Pandemic on Mental Health among 157,213 Americans. *Journal of Affective Disorders*, *286*, 64–70. DOI: 10.1016/j.jad.2021.02.056

Ye, J. (2021). Advancing mental health and psychological support for health care workers using digital technologies and platforms. *JMIR Formative Research*, *5*(6), e22075. DOI: 10.2196/22075

Yeh, P. L., Kuo, W. C., Tseng, B. L., & Sung, Y. H. (2025). Does the AI-driven Chatbot Work? Effectiveness of the Woebot app in reducing anxiety and depression in group counseling courses and student acceptance of technological aids. *Current Psychology (New Brunswick, N.J.)*, *44*(9), 1–13. DOI: 10.1007/s12144-025-07359-0

Yola, R., Azizah, W., Azizah, N., & Sabarrudin. (2024). Implementation of Use Deep Artificial Intelligence (AI) Guidance and Counseling Student Learning Process . *BICC Proceedings, 2*, 138–142. https://doi.org/DOI: 10.30983/bicc.v1i1.118

Zeren, G., Erus, S. M., Amanvermez, Y., Genç, A. B., & Duy, B. (2022). Client's experiences of online counseling: Satisfaction and therapeutic alliance. *Cukurova University Faculty of Education Journal*, *51*(1), 634–658. DOI: 10.14812/cuefd.843542

Zhang, K., & Aslan, A. B. (2021). AI technologies for education: Recent research & future directions. *Computers and Education Artificial Intelligence*, *2*, 100025. DOI: 10.1016/j.caeai.2021.100025

Zhou, P., Wang, L., Liu, Z., Hao, Y., Hui, P., Tarkoma, S., & Kangasharju, J. (2024). A survey on generative AI and LLM for video generation, understanding, and streaming. *arXiv (Cornell University)*. https://doi.org//arxiv.2404.16038DOI: 10.36227/techrxiv.171172801.19993069/v1

Chapter 4
Enhancing Assessment With AI:
Strategies for Complementing Teacher Expertise

Andi Asrifan
https://orcid.org/0000-0002-9934-6129
Universitas Negeri Makassar, Indonesia

Rismawati Sudirman
https://orcid.org/0000-0001-8046-6764
Universitas Muhammadiyah Palopo, Indonesia

Rusdiana Junaid
https://orcid.org/0000-0002-9653-1812
Universitas Cokroaminoto Palopo, Indonesia

Juvrianto Chrissunday Jakob
https://orcid.org/0000-0002-5267-3448
Politeknik Negeri Ambon, Indonesia

ABSTRACT

This chapter examines the revolutionary impact of Artificial Intelligence (AI) on educational evaluation, highlighting how AI tools can enhance, rather than supplant, teacher ability. In response to the changing requirements of 21st-century education, AI provides avenues for individualized learning, immediate feedback, and effective performance monitoring. Grounded in cognitive and constructivist learning theories, the book delineates various AI-driven assessment models, encompassing rule-based grading and adaptive analytics. It emphasizes the pedagogical, ethical, and technical aspects of AI integration by utilizing empirical research and practical

DOI: 10.4018/979-8-3373-0396-3.ch004

case studies. The debate emphasizes promoting a human-centered approach that maintains teacher autonomy, guarantees equity, and fosters inclusivity. The book advocates for a collaborative future where instructors and AI synergistically enhance assessment processes and student results.

INTRODUCTION TO AI-DRIVEN ASSESSMENT IN EDUCATION

1.1 Framing the Shift: From Traditional Assessment to AI-Augmented Evaluation

Assessment has historically been fundamental to educational processes, both as a metric for learning outcomes and a diagnostic instrument for informing instructional tactics (Akintayo et al., 2024; Kılınç, 2024; Swiecki et al., 2022). Historically, evaluation in educational settings has predominantly depended on human assessment via standardized tests, written examinations, and qualitative comments. Although these methods have yielded significant insights into student performance, they are frequently hindered by subjectivity, scalability constraints, and labor-intensive grading procedures. In reaction to the increasing intricacies of contemporary classrooms and the necessity for individualized learning, artificial intelligence (AI) has arisen as a revolutionary influence in redefining the design, delivery, and interpretation of assessments.

The transition to AI-enhanced assessment signifies a wider educational framework that adopts data-driven decision-making and flexible learning settings. AI-driven assessment systems utilize algorithms, machine learning, and natural language processing to measure students' cognitive and behavioral responses with enhanced speed and accuracy. These systems provide real-time feedback, pattern recognition, and predictive analytics that facilitate more dynamic and continuous assessment methods, transitioning from static point-in-time testing to formative, embedded evaluation models (Agu et al., 2024; Caspari-Sadeghi, 2022; Okeleke et al., 2024; Taylor et al., 2021). In contrast to conventional methods, AI systems can scrutinize extensive datasets to discern trends, learning deficiencies, and opportunities for enhancement at both individual and collective levels.

This change is not alone technical but also pedagogical. AI does not supplant educators; rather, it serves as an augmentation of their knowledge, enhancing their ability to engage with a varied array of learners more successfully. When applied judiciously, AI can facilitate customized education, customize tests to meet student requirements, and mitigate assessment bias. It enables the transition from summative assessment to a more comprehensive, process-focused evaluation that aligns with 21st-century educational objectives.

However, the incorporation of AI into evaluation methodologies presents both potential benefits and apprehensions. It requires critical examination of openness, accountability, and ethical data utilization. Educators must retain a pivotal role in the evaluation process, applying professional judgment to contextualize insights offered by AI. This chapter will examine the theoretical, practical, and ethical aspects of AI-enhanced assessment and advocate for a collaborative paradigm where AI supports rather than supplants the human educator (Akintayo et al., 2024; Al-Zahrani, 2024; Badmus et al., 2024). This part establishes a foundation for comprehending how AI might transform assessment frameworks while maintaining the essential principles of human-centered education, by examining this change via technological and pedagogical perspectives.

1.2 Rationale and Objectives of AI Integration in Educational Assessment

The incorporation of artificial intelligence (AI) into educational evaluation is propelled by a synthesis of pedagogical, technological, and systemic necessities. In a period marked by swift digital transition, educational institutions under mounting pressure to provide more personalized, equitable, and efficient learning experiences. Conventional assessment methods, though fundamental, frequently fail to address the increasing diversity of student demographics, the necessity for ongoing learning evaluation, and the scalability needed in both physical and digital educational settings (Caspari-Sadeghi, 2022; Hickey & Harris, 2021; Swiecki et al., 2022). Artificial intelligence, with its ability to analyze extensive datasets, identify trends, and deliver immediate feedback, presents a persuasive alternative and enhancement to traditional assessment methods.

The primary justification for incorporating AI into assessment is its capacity to improve personalization. Students have diverse cognitive styles, speeds, and levels of involvement, which may be disregarded in standardized testing frameworks. AI systems, especially those utilizing adaptive learning technologies, can customize questions and assessment sequences in real-time according on individual student replies. This dynamic interaction promotes more precise evaluations of student comprehension and supports varied instructional tactics tailored to each learner's distinct path.

Secondly, AI facilitates prompt and actionable feedback, an essential element in enhancing learning results. In contrast to conventional examinations that frequently postpone outcomes, AI-driven tools deliver instantaneous diagnostic insights, allowing students to reflect, revise, and self-regulate with greater efficacy. Educators can utilize real-time analytics to modify instruction and interventions with greater responsiveness (Badmus et al., 2024).

A third aim of AI integration is to improve efficiency and scalability. In expansive classrooms or digital platforms, manual assessment and personalized feedback are laborious and resource-demanding. AI automates monotonous evaluation tasks, such as marking multiple-choice examinations, evaluating writing trends, or monitoring participation, liberating educators to concentrate on advanced pedagogical responsibilities such as mentorship, curriculum development, and classroom interaction. Moreover, AI offers potential for fairness in evaluation. AI can enhance equitable evaluation methods by reducing human prejudice and assuring grade consistency, contingent upon the ethical design of its algorithms and training on different datasets.

Notwithstanding these benefits, the use of AI must correspond with explicitly articulated educational objectives. AI solutions must be built to assist and enhance teacher skill rather than replace it. The justification for AI integration is not based on technical determinism, but on the strategic enhancement of human talents to facilitate more profound and inclusive learning assessment methodologies (McKay & Macomber, 2021; Moundridou et al., 2024).

1.3 Scope, Limitations, and Structure of the Chapter

This chapter seeks to thoroughly examine the changing function of artificial intelligence (AI) in educational evaluation, focusing on how AI can enhance, rather than supplant, the professional judgment and pedagogical expertise of educators. It is located within the extensive discourse of AI in education (AIED), where evaluation is one of the most promising yet intricate domains of innovation (AlTwijri & Alghizzi, 2024; Guan et al., 2020; Swiecki et al., 2022). The chapter is both theoretical and practical, providing foundational concepts with methodologies, tools, and case studies that illustrate the integration of AI into assessment processes in many educational settings.

This chapter encompasses an analysis of AI technologies utilized in formative and summative assessments, including automated essay scoring, adaptive testing systems, learning analytics, and intelligent tutoring systems. It also analyzes AI's ability to provide real-time feedback, facilitate differentiated training, and produce predicted insights regarding student performance. The discourse encompasses K-12 and higher education settings, along with mixed and online learning environments. This research focuses on the role of AI as a decision-support tool that augments instructors' interpretative and diagnostic functions, rather than as an independent assessor.

Nonetheless, the chapter recognizes various limits. Firstly, it does not seek to provide a technical manual for AI programming or system architecture. The emphasis is on pedagogy and ethics. Secondly, although the chapter utilizes empirical evidence and case studies, it fails to perform a thorough meta-analysis of current AI assessment techniques. The chapter acknowledges that AI technologies continue to develop, and several implications, particularly ethical and social, are still emerging and context-dependent (Akintayo et al., 2024; Kumar, 2025; Stahl et al., 2023).

The chapter comprises five principal sections. Section 1 covers the context, reasoning, and aims of AI integration in assessment. Section 2 explores theoretical foundations and evaluation models. Section 3 delineates strategic frameworks for the incorporation of AI into pedagogical practices. Section 4 emphasizes practical applications via case studies, while Section 5 rigorously examines ethical implications and prospective trajectories. Together, these sections construct a unified narrative that underlines the value of human-centered AI in education. This chapter delineates its scope and parameters, encouraging readers to critically examine the benefits and problems of AI-enhanced assessment, while envisioning a future where technology and pedagogical knowledge are seamlessly integrated.

THEORETICAL FOUNDATIONS AND MODELS OF AI IN ASSESSMENT

2.1 Cognitive and Constructivist Learning Theories in AI-Supported Assessment

Incorporating artificial intelligence (AI) in educational evaluation must be based on solid pedagogical theory to guarantee that technological advancements facilitate significant learning. Two predominant paradigms—cognitive learning theory and constructivist learning theory—offer critical frameworks for comprehending how AI might synchronize with human learning processes. These theoretical frameworks facilitate the creation and execution of AI assessment systems that are both technologically proficient and pedagogically robust (Booyse & Scheepers, 2023; Minn, 2022; Vieriu & Petrea, 2025).

Cognitive learning theory highlights internal mental processes, including memory, attention, problem-solving, and information processing. This idea emphasizes the necessity of evaluating not just superficial information but also profound cognitive abilities in the realm of AI-assisted evaluation. AI systems can be engineered to monitor students' metacognitive techniques, discern patterns in their responses, and adjust to individual cognitive profiles. Intelligent tutoring systems (ITS) and adaptive testing platforms utilize cognitive diagnostics to customize learning routes and produce formative feedback (Taylor et al., 2021). This personalization is based on the recognition that learners assimilate information differently, and effective evaluation must accommodate these differences.

Constructivist learning theory asserts that learners actively build knowledge through experience, reflection, and social interaction. From this approach, assessment is not simply a measurement instrument but a process integral to the learning experience. Artificial intelligence can enhance constructivist methodologies by enabling authentic assessments, including simulations, project-based assignments, and scenario-based evaluations that mirror real-world complications. Utilizing natural language processing and semantic analysis, AI can assess open-ended responses and facilitate self-directed learning environments in which students participate in inquiry, problem-solving, and collaborative activities (Basha & Thoti, 2024; Shahzad et al., 2024; Swiecki et al., 2022).

The interplay between these two theories facilitates the advancement of formative, ongoing, and contextual assessments. AI technology, grounded in cognitive and constructivist ideas, can transform assessment from a summative conclusion to a dialogic and developmental process. They empower instructors to create feedback-rich environments that promote self-regulation, reflection, and advanced cognitive skills (Kruiper et al., 2021; Milne et al., 2020).

The effective use of these theories in AI evaluation necessitates deliberate instructional design, teacher engagement, and rigorous oversight. Educators must remain pivotal in evaluating AI outputs and ensuring that assessments encompass not only cognitive accomplishments but also learners' socio-emotional growth and contextual comprehension.

2.2 Models of Automated Assessment: From Rule-Based Systems to Machine Learning

The development of automated assessment models has paralleled the overall advancement of artificial intelligence (AI) technology, evolving from deterministic rule-based systems to more adaptable and intelligent machine learning (ML) methodologies. Comprehending this continuum is crucial for assessing AI's capabilities and constraints in educational evaluation and for developing tools that effectively enhance teacher proficiency (BankoleFalaye, 2024; Caspari-Sadeghi, 2022).

Rule-based systems are the initial iteration of automated evaluation. These systems depend on established criteria, algorithms, or scoring rubrics devised by specialists. They are frequently utilized in objective item formats, such as multiple-choice assessments, where grading adheres to a binary correct/incorrect framework. While rule-based systems provide consistency and speed, they are constrained in their ability to comprehend nuance, evaluate higher-order thinking, or handle open-ended responses (Swiecki et al., 2022; Wang et al., 2024). Their inflexibility renders them optimal for standardized testing contexts; however, they are inadequate for dynamic and individualized learning settings.

Due to advancements in computational power and the availability of extensive educational data, machine learning models have emerged as a more adaptable option. Machine learning systems, encompassing supervised, unsupervised, and reinforcement learning models, derive insights from past data to discern patterns and generate predictions or classifications. In evaluative environments, machine learning may examine student essays, identify misconceptions, generate automated feedback, and forecast future performance (Injadat et al., 2021; Janiesch et al., 2021; Zhaı et al., 2020). These models are especially potent in areas like natural language processing (NLP), facilitating the evaluation of free-text replies and the detection of underlying cognitive and emotional tendencies.

An especially transformational application is observed in adaptive assessment platforms that employ real-time machine learning algorithms to modify question difficulty according to student replies. These systems customize the assessment path, providing varied tasks corresponding to a learner's existing degree of comprehension (Taylor et al., 2021; Zhaı et al., 2020). Furthermore, learning analytics dashboards, powered by machine learning models, offer educators detailed insights into student behavior, progress, and risk factors.

Nonetheless, the increasing intricacy of machine learning systems also presents issues with interpretability, transparency, and bias. In contrast to rule-based models, machine learning outcomes are frequently opaque, complicating educators' ability to comprehend or validate the rationale behind a specific score. Consequently, human supervision is essential to guarantee that automated evaluations uphold fairness, validity, and contextual relevance (Badmus et al., 2024; Zhaı et al., 2020).

This section delineates the progression from rule-based logic to intelligent algorithms, establishing a theoretical framework for comprehending the technological environment of AI-assisted evaluation and preparing for strategic and ethical deployment.

2.3 Validity, Reliability, and Fairness in AI-Assisted Evaluation

As artificial intelligence (AI) becomes more integrated into educational evaluation, validity, reliability, and fairness must be thoroughly scrutinized and strictly maintained. The foundational psychometric principles, historically rooted in conventional assessment design, require recontextualization considering the capabilities and limitations of AI. Without these protections, AI-enhanced assessments threaten to compromise the educational objectives they intend to uphold (Akintayo et al., 2024; Badmus et al., 2024; McKay & Macomber, 2021).

Validity denotes the extent to which an evaluation accurately assesses what it claims to assess. In AI-assisted assessment, it is imperative to guarantee validity in both algorithm development and result interpretation. For instance, when AI systems evaluate essays or problem-solving activities, it is imperative to validate the correspondence between the scoring model and the desired learning outcomes (Akintayo et al., 2024; Antwi et al., 2024; Guan et al., 2020; Pack et al., 2024). Underrepresentation and construct-irrelevant variance—prevalent risks to validity—may be exacerbated if AI prioritizes superficial attributes (e.g., word count, grammar) over profound content comprehension. Consequently, educators must validate AI models via expert evaluation, alignment with educational objectives, and continuous empirical assessment.

Reliability, defined as the consistency of assessment results across varying situations and periods, is simultaneously enhanced and undermined by AI. Automated scoring systems, particularly those employing rule-based algorithms or trained machine learning models, generally surpass human evaluators in internal consistency. Nonetheless, their reliability may decline when confronted with unexpected replies or out-of-sample data absent from the training set. Ensuring rigorous model training, cross-validation, and error analysis is crucial for sustaining high dependability.

Fairness constitutes a critically significant ethical dimension of AI-assisted evaluation. Although AI has the potential to mitigate human bias, it may also reinforce or intensify disparities if it is trained on biased datasets or implemented without regard for cultural, linguistic, and contextual diversity. NLP-based grading systems may unjustly disadvantage students from non-dominant linguistic backgrounds (Agu et al., 2024; Liang et al., 2023). Ensuring fairness necessitates proactive bias auditing, inclusive data methodologies, and explainable AI (XAI) techniques to render algorithmic conclusions interpretable and contestable. Ultimately, artificial intelligence in evaluation must adhere to the same norms of educational integrity as conventional instruments. By including validity, reliability, and fairness into the design and execution of AI systems, educators and developers may guarantee that technology enhances, rather than undermines, the quality and equity of learning assessments.

STRATEGIES FOR INTEGRATING AI IN ASSESSMENT PRACTICES

3.1 Complementary Roles of Teachers and AI in Formative Assessment

Formative assessment, as an ongoing and evaluative process, is essential in facilitating student learning by detecting misconceptions, informing instructional modifications, and fostering self-regulation. The incorporation of artificial intelligence (AI) into formative assessment in the era of digital education presents significant prospects for improvement. Instead of supplanting educators, AI need to be regarded as a collaborative ally that enhances instructors' ability to provide prompt, individualized, and pedagogically robust feedback (Çelik et al., 2022; Lampou, 2023).

AI systems can aid educators by automating monotonous chores, such the evaluation of short-answer responses, identifying at-risk kids, or producing learning analytics dashboards. These instruments allow instructors to allocate additional time to reflective discourse, personalized coaching, and instructional strategizing. AI-driven platforms that monitor student involvement and performance trends can facilitate the identification of knowledge deficiencies in real time (Alzahrani et al., 2023; BankoleFalaye, 2024). Educators can subsequently analyze these findings, contextualize them with their own classroom observations, and devise suitable responses.

Notwithstanding these benefits, AI is deficient in the empathic intelligence and contextual awareness intrinsic to human educators. Formative assessment transcends mere data gathering; it is a relationship process rooted in trust, encouragement, and adaptable pedagogy. Educators provide essential interpretative skills to AI-generated data by comprehending student emotions, motives, and external influences on performance (Akintayo et al., 2024; Guan et al., 2020; Ma et al., 2024). Although AI can recognize a deterioration in a student's performance, only the teacher can determine whether the underlying cause is conceptual misunderstanding, disengagement, or personal challenges.

Furthermore, the integration of AI must be governed by teacher agency and ethical awareness. Educators must retain authority in determining the application and timing of AI usage, ensuring that technology corresponds with instructional objectives and learner requirements. Professional development is crucial for enabling educators to assess AI tools and utilize them wisely and critically (Guan et al., 2020; McKay & Macomber, 2021).

A balanced, human-centered model of AI-enhanced formative assessment emerges, wherein AI facilitates immediacy and scalability, while educators provide interpretation, empathy, and adaptation. This synergy enhances educational efficacy while maintaining assessment's ethical and instructional obligations. When executed as a collaborative partnership, AI and educators can jointly develop adaptive learning environments that are informed by data, equitable, and profoundly humanistic.

3.2 Adaptive Learning Systems and Real-Time Feedback Loop

Adaptive learning systems signify a crucial development at the convergence of artificial intelligence (AI) and educational evaluation. These systems are engineered to adaptively modify the learning material, tempo, and complexity based on real-time data derived from student interactions. This strategy is fundamentally based on a real-time feedback loop, a system whereby AI consistently assesses learner performance, analyzes data, and provides instantaneous insights to both students and educators (BankoleFalaye, 2024; Pahi et al., 2024).

In contrast to static evaluations, adaptive learning systems utilize advanced algorithms, frequently powered by machine learning, to discern specific learner profiles. These profiles are developed by the analysis of historical and contemporary data, including response accuracy, response time, content engagement, and error tendencies. The system customizes successive learning assignments to align with the learner's zone of proximal growth, providing suitably challenging content while strengthening areas of deficiency.

The real-time feedback loop is fundamental to the effectiveness of adaptive learning. Instant feedback for students augments metacognition by facilitating the identification of strengths and areas for enhancement, hence promoting self-regulated learning. Real-time analytics dashboards provide teachers with a detailed perspective on classroom performance, facilitating data-informed decisions such as student grouping, instructional adjustments, or targeted assistance. This ongoing stream of actionable insights converts evaluation from a conclusive overview into an engaging learning process (Alzahrani et al., 2023; BankoleFalaye, 2024).

Furthermore, adaptive systems provide scalable customisation across various educational settings, especially in extensive or diverse classrooms. They facilitate differentiated learning without necessitating continual manual adjustments, which are frequently unfeasible for human educators alone. These systems maintain the values of justice and inclusivity in education, offering each student a customized route to mastery (Campbell et al., 2022; Guan et al., 2020).

Nonetheless, dependence on adaptive learning should be considered with careful deliberation. Excessive automation may jeopardize cohesive learning experiences, particularly if AI decision-making lacks transparency. Educators must lead, interpreting AI results within wider educational frameworks and incorporating social-emotional learning indicators that robots cannot detect. Adaptive learning systems and real-time feedback loops illustrate the transformational potential of AI in evaluation. However, their complete potential is only actualized when integrated into pedagogically robust, morally informed, and instructor-led settings, where technology enhances the capabilities of both educators and students in the quest for more profound and adaptive education.

3.3 Leveraging AI for Inclusive and Differentiated Assessment

In modern educational environments, guaranteeing inclusivity and addressing student diversity has become fundamental to policy and practice. Assessment, frequently perceived as a gatekeeping instrument, must transform into a flexible, supporting tool that recognizes and accommodates the diverse cognitive, linguistic, cultural, and physical characteristics of learners. In this context, artificial intelligence (AI) provides significant capabilities to enhance inclusive and differentiated evaluation procedures that are responsive, equitable, and personalized (Ayeni et al., 2024; Cevallos et al., 2024; Guan et al., 2020).

AI-driven assessment systems are equipped to recognize and address specific student requirements instantaneously. Using ongoing data gathering and pattern recognition, these systems identify learning preferences, limitations, or signs of disengagement, enabling prompt and customized interventions. For example, AI can modify assessment modalities—providing auditory, visual, or textual input and output alternatives—to support learners with visual impairments, language obstacles, or neurodiverse characteristics (Agu et al., 2024; Ayeni et al., 2024). This flexibility signifies a substantial shift from standardized testing, frequently disadvantaging kids with atypical learning styles.

Furthermore, AI improves differentiated assessment by dynamically adjusting content complexity and presentation format to align with each learner's developmental stage. Students may be evaluated via methods that align with their strengths, such as visual storytelling, interactive simulations, or structured problem-solving, thereby minimizing cognitive overload and increasing engagement. This capacity corresponds with the concepts of Universal Design for Learning (UDL), which promotes many methods of representation, activity, and expression in educational settings.

Significantly, inclusive evaluation by AI must extend beyond mere accessibility. The incorporation of culturally responsive algorithms trained on varied datasets is necessary to prevent the reinforcement of dominant linguistic or cultural norms. In the absence of ethical design, AI programs may unintentionally perpetuate bias, misread language diversity, or favor specific knowledge systems. Consequently, educators must actively evaluate AI-generated evaluations to guarantee their adherence to content validity and cultural relevance (Ajiga et al., 2024; Foltýnek et al., 2023).

Moreover, inclusive AI assessment promotes student agency, allowing learners to monitor their progress, establish personal objectives, and obtain feedback that empowers rather than stigmatizes. It fosters the development of a growth attitude and acknowledges that learners advance at diverse rates and along distinct pathways (BankoleFalaye, 2024; Guan et al., 2020).

Utilizing AI in assessment design enables educators and institutions to establish more equitable, inclusive, and differentiated learning environments, ensuring that all students, regardless of background or aptitude, can succeed on their own terms.

PRACTICAL APPLICATIONS AND CASE STUDIES

4.1 Case Study 1: AI-Powered Essay Scoring in Secondary Education

A significant application of artificial intelligence (AI) in educational assessment is automated essay scoring (AES). This case study examines the deployment of an AI-driven essay evaluation system inside a secondary education framework in Singapore, where a pilot program was initiated to enhance English language writing assessments for Grade 10 pupils. The aim was to assess the potential of AI in assisting educators to deliver prompt, consistent, and formative feedback while maintaining the educational significance of essay writing (Chen et al., 2023; Kaharuddin et al., 2024; Marzuki et al., 2023).

The trial method employed a commercially available AES tool that leverages natural language processing (NLP) and machine learning algorithms. The system was trained on thousands of pre-scored student essays to create a predictive scoring model that assessed the prompt's coherence, grammar, word richness, structure, and relevance. Student-submitted essays were initially evaluated by AI, subsequently verified by teachers, allowing educators to concentrate on interpretive comments while depending on AI for preliminary assessment and technical adjustments (Akintayo et al., 2024; Pack et al., 2024; Sienes & Sarsale, 2024).

The pilot results indicated numerous advantages. The feedback turnaround time was markedly decreased from 3–5 days to under 24 hours. Students obtained immediate ratings and recommendations for enhancement, which promoted iterative drafting and self-directed learning. Secondly, the method established scoring uniformity over extensive cohorts, reducing discrepancies sometimes caused by human grading due to weariness or subjectivity (Guo et al., 2021; Roshanaei et al., 2023).

Educators indicated that AI grading liberated time for more comprehensive conversations regarding writing quality, enabling a transition from superficial faults to advanced skills such as reasoning, evidence integration, and rhetorical strategy. Furthermore, the system's analytics dashboard facilitated teachers in recognizing overarching writing trends within the class, hence promoting data-driven instruction (Ngubane et al., 2020; Taye & Mengesha, 2024; Veramuthu & Shah, 2020).

Nonetheless, constraints were also noted. The AI occasionally misread subtle phrasing, colloquial idioms, or culturally unique references, underscoring the need for human monitoring. Educators retained authority over final grading determinations, particularly for creative or non-linear writings that posed challenges to computational pattern identification.

This study demonstrates the appropriate integration of AI into secondary writing assessment to augment, rather than supplant, teacher judgment. When ethically planned and jointly implemented, AI-driven essay scoring provides a scalable, responsive tool that enhances instructional objectives and fortifies formative feedback procedures.

4.2 Case Study 2 – AI-Based Learning Analytics in Higher Education

The use of AI-driven learning analytics in higher education has become a vital instrument for real-time monitoring, evaluation, and instructional decision-making. This case study examines a multi-disciplinary implementation at a large public university in the Netherlands, where AI-driven analytics were integrated into a blended learning platform to enhance student performance and provide faculty with insights into learning trajectories among first-year undergraduate students.

The system employed machine learning algorithms to examine data obtained from diverse student activities, such as clickstream activity, quiz performance, forum engagement, and assignment submissions. This ongoing flow of digital footprints was transformed into actionable metrics, including engagement scores, visualizations of learning progression, and early warning alerts for students at risk of academic underachievement (Alzahrani et al., 2023; Fahd et al., 2021; Sghir et al., 2022).

The effort prominently included a dashboard interface for educators. Faculty members got weekly reports that illustrated individual and group-level trends, including comparative analyses between current and previous cohorts. Informed by these insights, instructors modified their formative assessments by providing prompt feedback, tailored follow-up tasks, and intervention strategies for students exhibiting signs of disengagement or cognitive stagnation (Kruiper et al., 2021; Maghsudi et al., 2021; Ole, 2020; Wang & Han, 2020).

A significant result was a pronounced enhancement in student retention in basic scientific courses, which have historically been linked to elevated attrition rates. AI-enhanced feedback methods enabled students to track their progress and receive prompts that encouraged contemplation and motivation. Faculty indicated more efficacy in monitoring learning outcomes and less dependence on mid-term summative assessments.

Nonetheless, the execution revealed significant ethical and pedagogical issues. Several students articulated unease with the extent of surveillance, highlighting the necessity for transparent data governance and informed consent procedures. Moreover, challenges arose in contextualizing analytics, particularly in differentiating between diminished platform engagement attributable to user disengagement and external influences such as internet connectivity problems or part-time employment obligations (Akintayo et al., 2024; Andreotta et al., 2021; Rossi & Lenzini, 2020; Wiertz & Boldt, 2022).

This scenario underscored the significance of teacher autonomy in the interpretation of AI data. Although the learning analytics system offered comprehensive measurements, it was the educators that converted data into instructional judgments via contextual comprehension and relational insight.

In summary, AI-driven learning analytics in higher education provides robust instruments to enhance pedagogical proficiency. When executed with ethical forethought and collaborative design, these technologies improve the responsiveness, personalization, and inclusivity of academic assessment methods.

4.3 Implementation Challenges and Lessons Learned

The incorporation of artificial intelligence (AI) into evaluation methodologies presents significant potential, although the transition from theory to practical application in educational settings is laden with difficulties. This chapter consolidates insights from various real-world initiatives, highlighting the technical, pedagogical, ethical, and institutional obstacles that must be addressed to facilitate the successful integration of AI in assessment (Implementing Artificial Intelligence (AI) in Higher Education: A Narrative Literature Review, 2023; Ocran et al., 2024).

A significant technological difficulty is the integration of AI systems with current learning management platforms and data infrastructure. Numerous institutions lack the digital infrastructure necessary for uninterrupted data flow and instantaneous processing. Moreover, reliability concerns—such as system delays, algorithmic inaccuracies, and restricted adaptability to various subject domains—can erode educator confidence and impede scalability.

Pedagogical resistance constitutes a substantial obstacle. Educators frequently articulate apprehension regarding the perceived erosion of professional autonomy, worrying that AI tools may diminish their roles to mere data interpreters or content facilitators. Furthermore, inadequate training and professional development opportunities restrict instructors' ability to effectively utilize AI tools. In the absence of a comprehensive knowledge of how AI corresponds with educational goals and pedagogical principles, its adoption may be superficial or only symbolic (Cukurova et al., 2023; Lampou, 2023; Ng et al., 2023).

Ethical problems regarding data privacy, algorithmic prejudice, and monitoring are prominent. Many colleges implement AI systems without sufficient transparency concerning the collection, analysis, and utilization of student data. These concerns can undermine student trust and elevate compliance risks under data protection requirements like GDPR. The lack of explainable AI (XAI) exacerbates the situation, as educators may find it challenging to comprehend AI-generated feedback or rationalize automated scoring results (Khosravi et al., 2022; Okeleke et al., 2024; Roshanaei et al., 2023).

Institutionally, policy misalignment and resource constraints often hinder sustainable implementation. Educational institutions may implement AI tools due to modernization pressures, yet fail to create essential support structures, like cross-functional AI ethical committees, inclusive procurement processes, and long-term evaluation frameworks (Agarwal & Vij, 2024; Akintayo et al., 2024).

Notwithstanding these hurdles, numerous crucial lessons have surfaced. Initially, AI should be deployed slowly, commencing with pilot programs that engage educators in co-design and iterative assessment. Secondly, explicit communication regarding the function of AI—as an adjunct rather than a substitute—is essential for cultivating educator support. Third, continuous training, ethical supervision, and adaptive technical assistance must accompany any implementation. The effective deployment of AI in assessment depends not only on the technology's complexity but also on the collaborative involvement of educators, learners, and institutional leaders in developing a unified vision of responsible innovation.

ETHICAL CONSIDERATIONS AND FUTURE IMPLICATIONS

5.1 Teacher Autonomy and Human Judgment in AI-Augmented Classrooms

As artificial intelligence (AI) becomes increasingly integrated into educational institutions, a significant ethical problem is the safeguarding of teacher autonomy and human discernment. Although AI provides unparalleled powers in data processing, pattern recognition, and feedback production, it is inherently constrained in its capacity to grasp the nuanced, compassionate, and context-sensitive aspects of teaching. In AI-enhanced classrooms, educators must maintain a pivotal role in evaluation procedures, serving not only as decision-makers but also as ethical guardians of the learning experience (Ma et al., 2024; Ng et al., 2023; Swiecki et al., 2022).

Teacher autonomy denotes the professional liberty and authority that educators hold to make decisions on pedagogy, evaluation, and relationships. The proliferation of algorithmic technologies threatens to diminish this liberty if educators become excessively reliant on—or restricted by—automated results. For instance, when AI delineates learning trajectories or evaluates student assignments, there exists a risk that instructors may uncritically accept these outcomes, thereby marginalizing their own professional judgments. This issue is particularly pronounced when AI systems operate as “black boxes,” providing findings without clear explanation (Akintayo et al., 2024; McKay & Macomber, 2021; Swiecki et al., 2022).

Preserving human judgment entails acknowledging that educators possess vital interpretative abilities in the classroom. They comprehend student motivations, emotional conditions, social dynamics, and cultural contexts—elements no algorithm can grasp entirely. Human educators also confront ethical dilemmas, including the timing of leniency, the necessity of challenging assumptions, and the equilibrium between fairness and compassion. Such decisions necessitate critical deliberation, ethical discernment, and professional expertise—attributes that ought to inform, rather than be supplanted by, AI recommendations.

Certain criteria must be maintained to preserve teacher autonomy in AI-enhanced settings. AI systems must be collaboratively built with educators to ensure that these tools enhance rather than prescribe instructional practices. Secondly, educators must engage in continuous professional development to critically examine AI technologies and incorporate them effectively into evaluations. Third, policies must ensure that teachers are responsible for grading decisions, interpretation of feedback, and instructional modifications (Akintayo et al., 2024; Ma et al., 2024; McKay & Macomber, 2021).

Ultimately, cultivating a culture of reflective AI utilization, where educators engage in discourse regarding the advantages and constraints of AI, can enhance professional identity and ethical responsibility. When AI is utilized as an intelligent aid rather than an independent assessor, it can enhance the evaluation process while preserving the teacher's ethical and intellectual responsibilities. In the future of education, great learning is defined not by AI, but by the empowered educator, bolstered by ethical and transparent technologies.

5.2 Data Privacy, Consent, and Surveillance Risks

As artificial intelligence (AI) increasingly integrates into assessment inside contemporary classrooms, significant concerns around data privacy, informed consent, and the possibility for monitoring have emerged in the realm of educational ethics. AI-driven assessment systems depend on ongoing data collection, encompassing student answers, behavioral patterns, biological markers, and emotional cues. Although such data can provide essential insights for tailored instruction, its improper use or management presents considerable threats to student rights, autonomy, and psychological safety (Alzahrani et al., 2023; Fischer et al., 2020; Gouseti et al., 2024).

Data privacy denotes the ethical and legal responsibility to safeguard students' personal and academic information from unlawful access, misuse, or exploitation. AI-powered systems frequently utilize cloud-based infrastructures administered by third-party vendors, which raises issues regarding ownership, security, and adherence to privacy regulations such as the General Data Protection Regulation (GDPR) and the Family Educational Rights and Privacy Act (FERPA). The large-scale collection of student data, frequently without their comprehensive awareness of its consequences, poses a risk that assessment instruments may transform into means of data commodification, wherein learning records are monetized or utilized for purposes beyond their educational intent (Akintayo et al., 2024; Campbell & Koffi, 2024; Potgieter, 2020).

Informed consent is equally crucial. Students and parents must be thoroughly informed about the data being gathered, its intended purpose, the individuals with access, and the rights they possess concerning that information. Consent must be unequivocal, retractable, and suitable for the age group—particularly in elementary and secondary educational environments. In reality, consent processes are frequently simplified to generic agreements within terms-of-service forms, so neglecting the ethical principles of transparency and agency.

The increasing prevalence of educational surveillance is particularly concerning. When AI systems track keystrokes, screen duration, facial expressions, or eye movements to evaluate interest or performance, the classroom may transform into an environment of perpetual surveillance rather than genuine learning. This surveillance can result in behavioral conformity, erode trust, and disproportionately impact marginalized students who may already experience scrutiny in educational environments (Guan et al., 2020; Proudfoot, 2021; Swiecki et al., 2022).

To alleviate these concerns, educational institutions must establish comprehensive data governance frameworks, implement stringent vendor accountability, and promote digital literacy among educators and students. AI must be utilized in manners that honor student dignity, sustains democratic principles, and fosters educational settings grounded on liberty, trust, and informed engagement.

5.3 Toward a Collaborative Future: Designing Human-Centered AI Assessment Tools

As artificial intelligence (AI) becomes more integrated into educational practices, the future of assessment should be directed by a collaborative, ethical, and human-centered design philosophy. Instead of framing AI as a replacement for educators, the proposed approach advocates for a collaborative relationship wherein technology enhances human insight, empathy, and professional discernment to promote equitable and significant learning (Badmus et al., 2024; Holstein & Aleven, 2022; Oh & Ahn, 2024).

An approach to AI assessment design focusing on human considerations prioritizes learners' and instructors' needs, situations, and values. This entails engaging educators in the collaborative development of AI tools, guaranteeing that technical systems are informed by pedagogical expertise rather than being externally imposed on educational practices. Co-design frameworks enable educators to define assessment objectives, pinpoint essential learning indicators, and adjust feedback systems that correspond with authentic classroom experiences (Hickey & Harris, 2021; Kohli, 2024; Kühn et al., 2023).

The active involvement of learners in the development of AI systems that influence their educational experience is equally essential. Students should be involved as co-agents rather than simply as data subjects. Human-centered design promotes transparency, user autonomy, and the right to challenge automated judgments. Developers must implement explainable AI (XAI) models that elucidate not only the conclusions of a system but also the rationale behind them, enabling both students and educators to interpret, question, and enhance those outcomes (Ajiga et al., 2024; D'Souza et al., 2024; Khosravi et al., 2022; Warner & Sloan, 2021).

Institutions must develop multidisciplinary alliances among educators, technologists, ethicists, and policymakers to foster a collaborative future. Such cooperation can guarantee that AI technologies are inclusive, culturally attuned, and adaptable to various educational environments. Equity audits, ethical impact evaluations, and inclusive datasets ought to be established as routine practices in the development cycle of educational AI.

Moreover, professional development is essential for maintaining human-centered implementation. Educators must possess AI literacy, ethical reasoning abilities, and pedagogical methodologies to include AI in assessments effectively. Institutions should endorse perpetual learning communities that promote reflective practice, experimentation, and reciprocal support. Ultimately, the creation of human-centered AI assessment tools transcends mere technicality; it is a moral and pedagogical obligation. It envisions a future in which innovation is evaluated not only on efficiency and precision, but also on its ability to enhance human connection, dignity, and educational equity. In this collective future, AI functions not as a substitute for educators but as a reliable collaborator in fostering more adaptive, inclusive, and revolutionary assessment methodologies (Lampou, 2023; Ma et al., 2024; Madigan et al., 2023)

CONCLUSION

The incorporation of artificial intelligence (AI) in educational evaluation signifies a crucial transformation in pedagogical methods and technical advancement. This volume illustrates that AI can improve personalization, efficiency, and responsiveness in assessment processes, complementing educators' nuanced expertise rather than a replacement. AI techniques offer scalable answers to enduring difficulties in various educational environments, ranging from formative diagnostics to adaptive feedback systems.

This transformation has inherent restrictions. Concerns regarding validity, dependability, fairness, and data ethics necessitate meticulous scrutiny. Automated systems must be developed and executed with a keen understanding of cultural, linguistic, and contextual diversity to prevent the perpetuation of current injustices. The opacity of algorithmic processes requires the creation of explainable AI frameworks that enable educators to understand and question machine-generated assessments.

A fundamental principle of this book is the endorsement of teacher autonomy. Although AI demonstrates superiority in pattern recognition and scalability, only human educators can provide empathy, ethical judgment, and contextual comprehension in the evaluation process. Consequently, successful integration relies on framing AI as an intelligent helper that enhances human decision-making instead of supplanting it.

The future success of AI in assessment will depend on collaborative design, continuous professional development, and institutional dedication to transparency and inclusivity. The objective is not solely to automate assessment, but to humanize it—utilizing AI to enhance profound learning, reflective practice, and equal educational results. In conclusion, augmenting assessment using AI necessitates a balanced, ethically informed strategy that integrates the accuracy of computers with the understanding and empathy of educators. Upon achieving this equilibrium, AI can function as a revolutionary partner in re-envisioning assessment for the future of education.

REFERENCES

Agarwal, P., & Vij, A. (2024). Assessing the Challenges and Opportunities of Artificial Intelligence in Indian Education. *International Journal for Global Academic & Scientific Research, 3*(1), 36–44. DOI: 10.55938/ijgasr.v3i1.71

Agu, E. E., Abhulimen, A. O., Obiki-Osafiele, A. N., Osundare, O. S., Adeniran, I. A., & Efunniyi, C. P. (2024). Utilizing AI-driven predictive analytics to reduce credit risk and enhance financial inclusion. *International Journal of Frontline Research in Multidisciplinary Studies, 3*(2), 20. DOI: 10.56355/ijfrms.2024.3.2.0026

Ajiga, D. I., Ndubuisi, N. L., Asuzu, O. F., Owolabi, O. R., Tubokirifuruar, T. S., & Adeleye, R. A. (2024). AI-Driven Predictive Analytics In Retail: A Review Of Emerging Trends And Customer Engagement Strategies [Review Of Ai-Driven Predictive Analytics In Retail: A Review Of Emerging Trends And Customer Engagement Strategies]. International Journal of Management & Entrepreneurship Research, 6(2), 307. Fair East Publishers. https://doi.org/DOI: 10.51594/ijmer.v6i2.772

Akintayo, T. A., Paul, C., Queenet, M. C., Nnadiekwe, O. A., Victoria, S. S., David, F. B., Joel, O. O., Agada, O. I., Ngozi, E. R., Arinze, U. U., Ojemerenvhie, G. A., Oluwadamilola, A. A., Nnamani, C. C., & Olayinka, U. W. (2024). Transforming Data Analytics with AI for Informed Decision-Making. *International Journal of Education Management and Technology, 2*(3), 196–215. DOI: 10.58578/ijemt.v2i3.3812

Al-Zahrani, A. M. (2024). Unveiling the shadows: Beyond the hype of AI in education. *Heliyon, 10*(9), e30696. Advance online publication. DOI: 10.1016/j.heliyon.2024.e30696 PMID: 38737255

AlTwijri, L., & Alghizzi, T. M. (2024). Investigating the integration of artificial intelligence in English as foreign language classes for enhancing learners' affective factors: A systematic review [Review of Investigating the integration of artificial intelligence in English as foreign language classes for enhancing learners' affective factors: A systematic review]. Heliyon, 10(10). Elsevier BV. https://doi.org/DOI: 10.1016/j.heliyon.2024.e31053

Alzahrani, A. S., Tsai, Y., Aljohani, N. R., Whitelock-wainwright, E., & Gašević, D. (2023). Do teaching staff trust stakeholders and tools in learning analytics? A mixed methods study. *Educational Technology Research and Development, 71*(4), 1471–1501. DOI: 10.1007/s11423-023-10229-w PMID: 37359481

Andreotta, A. J., Kirkham, N., & Rizzi, M. (2021). AI, big data, and the future of consent. *AI & Society, 37*(4), 1715–1728. DOI: 10.1007/s00146-021-01262-5 PMID: 34483498

Antwi, B. O., Adelakun, B. O., & Eziefule, A. O.Bernard Owusu AntwiBeatrice Oyinkansola AdelakunAugustine Obinna Eziefule. (2024). Transforming Financial Reporting with AI: Enhancing Accuracy and Timeliness. *International Journal of Advanced Economics, 6*(6), 205–223. DOI: 10.51594/ijae.v6i6.1229

Ayeni, O. O., Hamad, N. M. A., Chisom, O. N., Osawaru, B., & Adewusi, O. E. (2024). AI in education: A review of personalized learning and educational technology [Review of AI in education: A review of personalized learning and educational technology]. *GSC Advanced Research and Reviews, 18*(2), 261–271. DOI: 10.30574/gscarr.2024.18.2.0062

Badmus, O., Rajput, S., Arogundade, J. B., & Williams, M. H. (2024). AI-driven business analytics and decision making. *World Journal of Advanced Research and Reviews, 24*(1), 616–633. DOI: 10.30574/wjarr.2024.24.1.3093

BankoleFalaye, A.BankoleFalaye. (2024). AI-Powered Knowledge Systems for SME Financial Management: A Conceptual Approach. [IJSR]. *International Journal of Science and Research (Raipur, India), 13*(11), 1099–1103. DOI: 10.21275/SR241117060640

Basha, Mrs. N. R. Dr. H. S. A., & Thoti, K. K. (. (2024). AI-powered Recruitment and Employee Selection: Evaluating Bias and Fairness in Hiring Practices. [EEL]. *European Economic Letters, 14*(1), 827. DOI: 10.52783/eel.v14i1.1107

Booyse, D., & Scheepers, C. B. (2023). Barriers to adopting automated organisational decision-making through the use of artificial intelligence. *Management Research Review, 47*(1), 64–85. DOI: 10.1108/MRR-09-2021-0701

Campbell, J., & Koffi, B. A. (2024). The Role of AI-powered financial analytics in shaping economic policy: A new era for risk management and national growth in the United States. *World Journal of Advanced Research and Reviews, 23*(3), 2816–2825. DOI: 10.30574/wjarr.2024.23.3.2963

Campbell, L. O., Howard, C., Lambie, G. W., & Gao, X. (2022). The efficacy of a computer-adaptive reading program on grade 5 students' reading achievement scores. *Education and Information Technologies, 27*(6), 8147–8163. DOI: 10.1007/s10639-022-10953-5

Caspari-Sadeghi, S. (2022a). Artificial Intelligence in Technology-Enhanced Assessment: A Survey of Machine Learning. *Journal of Educational Technology Systems, 51*(3), 372–386. DOI: 10.1177/00472395221138791

Caspari-Sadeghi, S. (2022b). Learning assessment in the age of big data: Learning analytics in higher education. *Cogent Education, 10*(1), 2162697. Advance online publication. DOI: 10.1080/2331186X.2022.2162697

Çelik, İ., Dindar, M., Muukkonen, H., & Järvelä, S. (2022). The Promises and Challenges of Artificial Intelligence for Teachers: a Systematic Review of Research [Review of The Promises and Challenges of Artificial Intelligence for Teachers: a Systematic Review of Research]. TechTrends, 66(4), 616. Springer Science+Business Media. https://doi.org/DOI: 10.1007/s11528-022-00715-y

Cevallos, M. G. O., Jaramillo, G. A. L., Vélez, J. L. B., Zambrano, M. I. U., Montesdeoca, L. D. Z., & Palomeque, M. A. B.Miguel Giancarlo Ormaza CevallosGustavo Alberto Lozano JaramilloJosé Luis Bernardo VélezMaritza Irinuska Ureta Zambrano-Lady Diana Zambrano MontesdeocaManuel Augusto Bermúdez Palomeque. (2024). Implementation of Artificial Intelligence in Quality Management in SMEs: Benefits and Challenges. *Evolutionary Studies in Imaginative Culture, 1489*, 1489–1500. Advance online publication. DOI: 10.70082/esiculture.vi.1590

Chen, B., Wu, Z., & Zhao, R. (2023). From fiction to fact: The growing role of generative AI in business and finance. *Journal of Chinese Economic and Business Studies, 21*(4), 471–496. DOI: 10.1080/14765284.2023.2245279

Cukurova, M., Miao, X., & Brooker, R. A. (2023). Adoption of Artificial Intelligence in Schools: Unveiling Factors Influencing Teachers' Engagement. In Lecture notes in computer science (p. 151). Springer Science+Business Media. https://doi.org/DOI: 10.1007/978-3-031-36272-9_13

D'Souza, R., Mathew, M., Mishra, V., & Surapaneni, K. M. (2024). Twelve tips for addressing ethical concerns in the implementation of artificial intelligence in medical education. *Medical Education Online, 29*(1), 2330250. Advance online publication. DOI: 10.1080/10872981.2024.2330250 PMID: 38566608

Fahd, K., Miah, S. J., & Ahmed, K. (2021). *Predicting student performance in a blended learning environment using learning management system interaction data.* Applied Computing and Informatics., DOI: 10.1108/ACI-06-2021-0150

Fischer, C., Pardos, Z. A., Baker, R. S., Williams, J. J., Smyth, P., Yu, R., Slater, S., Baker, R., & Warschauer, M. (2020). Mining Big Data in Education: Affordances and Challenges. *Review of Research in Education, 44*(1), 130–160. DOI: 10.3102/0091732X20903304

Foltýnek, T., Bjelobaba, S., Glendinning, I., Khan, Z. R., Santos, R., Pavletić, P., & Kravjar, J. (2023). ENAI Recommendations on the ethical use of Artificial Intelligence in Education. *International Journal for Educational Integrity*, *19*(1), 12. Advance online publication. DOI: 10.1007/s40979-023-00133-4

Gouseti, A., James, F., Fallin, L., & Burden, K. (2024). The ethics of using AI in K-12 education: A systematic literature review. *Technology, Pedagogy and Education*, *1*. Advance online publication. DOI: 10.1080/1475939X.2024.2428601

Guan, C., Mou, J., & Jiang, Z. (2020). Artificial intelligence innovation in education: A twenty-year data-driven historical analysis. *International Journal of Innovation Studies*, *4*(4), 134–147. DOI: 10.1016/j.ijis.2020.09.001

Guo, Q., Feng, R., & Hua, Y. (2021). How effectively can EFL students use automated written corrective feedback (AWCF) in research writing? *Computer Assisted Language Learning*, *35*(9), 2312–2331. DOI: 10.1080/09588221.2021.1879161

Hickey, D. T., & Harris, T. (2021). Reimagining online grading, assessment, and testing using situated cognition. *Distance Education*, *42*(2), 290–309. DOI: 10.1080/01587919.2021.1911627

Holstein, K., & Aleven, V. (2022). Designing for human–AI complementarity in K-12 education. *AI Magazine*, *43*(2), 239–248. DOI: 10.1002/aaai.12058

Implementing Artificial Intelligence (AI) in Higher Education. A Narrative Literature Review. (2023). https://www.researchgate.net/publication/376553922_Implementing_Artificial_Intelligence_AI_in_Higher_Education_A_Narrative_Literature_Review

Injadat, M., Moubayed, A., Nassif, A. B., & Shami, A. (2021). Machine learning towards intelligent systems: Applications, challenges, and opportunities. *Artificial Intelligence Review*, *54*(5), 3299–3348. DOI: 10.1007/s10462-020-09948-w

Janiesch, C., Zschech, P., & Heinrich, K. (2021). Machine learning and deep learning. *Electronic Markets*, *31*(3), 685–695. DOI: 10.1007/s12525-021-00475-2

Kaharuddin, K., Ahmad, D., Mardiana, M., Latif, I., Arafah, B., & Suryadi, R. (2024). Defining the Role of Artificial Intelligence in Improving English Writing Skills Among Indonesian Students. *Journal of Language Teaching and Research*, *15*(2), 568–678. DOI: 10.17507/jltr.1502.25

Khosravi, H., Shum, S. B., Chen, G., Conati, C., Tsai, Y., Kay, J., Knight, S., Martínez-Maldonado, R., Sadiq, S., & Gašević, D. (2022). Explainable Artificial Intelligence in education. *Computers and Education Artificial Intelligence*, *3*, 100074. DOI: 10.1016/j.caeai.2022.100074

Kılınç, S. (2024). Comprehensive AI Assessment Framework: Enhancing Educational Evaluation with Ethical AI Integration. Journal of Educational Technology and Online Learning. https://doi.org/DOI: 10.31681/jetol.1492695

Kohli, J. K. (2024). *Impact of Artificial Intelligence on Fashion Education for Future Jobs*. Higher Education for the Future., DOI: 10.1177/23476311241284860

Kruiper, S. M. A., Leenknecht, M. J. M., & Slof, B. (2021). Using scaffolding strategies to improve formative assessment practice in higher education. *Assessment & Evaluation in Higher Education*, *47*(3), 458–476. DOI: 10.1080/02602938.2021.1927981

Kühn, C., Khoo, S., Czerniewicz, L., Lilley, W., Bute, S. J. R., Crean, A., Abegglen, S., Burns, T., Sinfield, S., Jandrić, P., Knox, J., & MacKenzie, A. (2023). Understanding Digital Inequality: A Theoretical Kaleidoscope. *Postdigital Science and Education*, *5*(3), 894–932. DOI: 10.1007/s42438-023-00395-8 PMID: 40479087

Kumar, C. R. (2025). AI-Powered Recruitment: Transforming Talent Acquisition in the Digital Age. *Journal of Informatics Education and Research*, *5*(1). Advance online publication. DOI: 10.52783/jier.v5i1.2166

Lampou, R. (2023). The Integration of Artificial Intelligence in Education: Opportunities and Challenges. *Review of Artificial Intelligence in Education*, *4*(00), e015. Advance online publication. DOI: 10.37497/rev.artif.intell.educ.v4i00.15

Liang, W., Yüksekgönül, M., Mao, Y., Wu, E. Q., & Zou, J. (2023). GPT detectors are biased against non-native English writers. *Patterns (New York, N.Y.)*, *4*(7), 100779. DOI: 10.1016/j.patter.2023.100779 PMID: 37521038

Ma, K., Zhang, Y., & Hui, B.-H. (2024). How Does AI Affect College? The Impact of AI Usage in College Teaching on Students' Innovative Behavior and Well-Being. *Behavioral Sciences (Basel, Switzerland)*, *14*(12), 1223. DOI: 10.3390/bs14121223 PMID: 39767364

Madigan, D. J., Kim, L. E., Glandorf, H. L., & Kavanagh, O. (2023). Teacher burnout and physical health: A systematic review [Review of Teacher burnout and physical health: A systematic review]. International Journal of Educational Research, 119, 102173. Elsevier BV. https://doi.org/DOI: 10.1016/j.ijer.2023.102173

Maghsudi, S., Lan, A., Xu, J., & van der Schaar, M. (2021). Personalized Education in the Artificial Intelligence Era: What to Expect Next. *IEEE Signal Processing Magazine*, *38*(3), 37–50. DOI: 10.1109/MSP.2021.3055032

Marzuki, M., Widiati, U., Rusdin, D., Darwin, D., & Indrawati, I. (2023). The impact of AI writing tools on the content and organization of students' writing: EFL teachers' perspective. *Cogent Education*, *10*(2), 2236469. Advance online publication. DOI: 10.1080/2331186X.2023.2236469

McKay, C., & Macomber, G. (2021). The Importance of Relationships in Education: Reflections of Current Educators. *Journal of Education*, *203*(4), 751–758. DOI: 10.1177/00220574211057044

Milne, L., McCann, J., Bolton, K. A., Savage, J., & Spence, A. C. (2020). Student satisfaction with feedback in a third year Nutrition unit: A strategic approach. *Journal of University Teaching & Learning Practice*, *17*(5). Advance online publication. DOI: 10.53761/1.17.5.5

Minn, S. (2022). AI-assisted knowledge assessment techniques for adaptive learning environments. *Computers and Education Artificial Intelligence*, *3*, 100050. DOI: 10.1016/j.caeai.2022.100050

Moundridou, M., Matzakos, N., & Doukakis, S. (2024). Generative AI tools as educators' assistants: Designing and implementing inquiry-based lesson plans. *Computers and Education Artificial Intelligence*, *7*, 100277. DOI: 10.1016/j.caeai.2024.100277

Ng, D. T. K., Leung, J. K. L., Su, J., Ng, C. W., & Chu, S. K. W. (2023). Teachers' AI digital competencies and twenty-first century skills in the post-pandemic world. *Educational Technology Research and Development*, *71*(1), 137–161. DOI: 10.1007/s11423-023-10203-6 PMID: 36844361

Ngubane, N., Ntombela, B., & Govender, S. (2020). Writing approaches and strategies used by teachers in selected South African English First Additional Language classrooms. *Reading and Writing*, *11*(1). Advance online publication. DOI: 10.4102/rw.v11i1.261

Ocran, G., Yusuf, S. O., Owusu, P., Boateng, E. A., Krampah, S. O., & Paul-Adeleye, A. H. (2024). AI-driven business analytics for SMES: Unlocking value through predictive and prescriptive analytic. *International Journal of Science and Research Archive*, *13*(1), 3009–3022. DOI: 10.30574/ijsra.2024.13.1.2001

Oh, S., & Ahn, Y. (2024). Exploring Teachers' Perception of Artificial Intelligence: The Socio-emotional Deficiency as Opportunities and Challenges in Human-AI Complementarity in K-12 Education. In Lecture notes in computer science (p. 439). Springer Science+Business Media. https://doi.org/DOI: 10.1007/978-3-031-64299-9_41

Okeleke, P. A., Ajiga, D., Folorunsho, S. O., & Ezeigweneme, C. (2024). Predictive analytics for market trends using AI: A study in consumer behavior. *International Journal of Engineering Research Updates*, *7*(1), 36. DOI: 10.53430/ijeru.2024.7.1.0032

Ole, F. C. B. (2020). Development and Validation of Teachers' Practices on Formative Assessment Scale (TPFAS): A Measure Using Feedback Loop Model. *International Journal of Education*, *13*(1), 53–62. DOI: 10.17509/ije.v13i1.24715

Pack, A., Barrett, A., & Escalante, J. (2024). Large language models and automated essay scoring of English language learner writing: Insights into validity and reliability. *Computers and Education Artificial Intelligence*, *6*, 100234. DOI: 10.1016/j.caeai.2024.100234

Pahi, K., Hawlader, S., Hicks, E., Zaman, A., & Phan, V. (2024). Enhancing active learning through collaboration between human teachers and generative AI. *Computers and Education Open*, *6*, 100183. DOI: 10.1016/j.caeo.2024.100183

Potgieter, I. (2020). Privacy concerns in educational data mining and learning analytics. *International Journal of Information Ethics*, *28*. Advance online publication. DOI: 10.29173/irie384

Proudfoot, K. (2021). Panopticism, teacher surveillance and the 'unseen.'. *British Journal of Sociology of Education*, *42*(5-6), 812–827. DOI: 10.1080/01425692.2021.1914549

Roshanaei, M., Olivares, H., & Lopez, R. R. (2023). Harnessing AI to Foster Equity in Education: Opportunities, Challenges, and Emerging Strategies. *Journal of Intelligent Learning Systems and Applications*, *15*(4), 123–143. DOI: 10.4236/jilsa.2023.154009

Rossi, A., & Lenzini, G. (2020). Transparency by design in data-informed research: A collection of information design patterns. *Computer Law & Security Review*, *37*, 105402. DOI: 10.1016/j.clsr.2020.105402

Sghir, N., Adadi, A., & Lahmer, M. (2022). Recent advances in Predictive Learning Analytics: A decade systematic review (2012–2022). *Education and Information Technologies*, *28*(7), 8299–8333. DOI: 10.1007/s10639-022-11536-0 PMID: 36571084

Shahzad, M. F., Xu, S., Lim, W. M., Yang, X., & Khan, Q. (2024). Artificial intelligence and social media on academic performance and mental well-being: Student perceptions of positive impact in the age of smart learning. *Heliyon*, *10*(8), e29523. Advance online publication. DOI: 10.1016/j.heliyon.2024.e29523 PMID: 38665566

Sienes, M. J. V., & Sarsale, J. C. S. (2024). Revisiting AI in an English Classroom. In Atlantis highlights in social sciences, education and humanities/Atlantis Highlights in Social Sciences, Education and Humanities (p. 37). Atlantis Press. https://doi.org/DOI: 10.2991/978-94-6463-396-2_4

Stahl, B. C., Antoniou, J., Bhalla, N., Brooks, L., Jansen, P., Lindqvist, B., Kirichenko, A. S., Marchal, S., Rodrigues, R., Santiago, N., Warso, Z., & Wright, D. (2023). A systematic review of artificial intelligence impact assessments [Review of A systematic review of artificial intelligence impact assessments]. *Artificial Intelligence Review*, *56*(11), 12799–12831. DOI: 10.1007/s10462-023-10420-8 PMID: 37362899

Swiecki, Z., Khosravi, H., Chen, G., Martínez-Maldonado, R., Lodge, J. M., Milligan, S., Selwyn, N., & Gašević, D. (2022). Assessment in the age of artificial intelligence. *Computers and Education Artificial Intelligence*, *3*, 100075. DOI: 10.1016/j.caeai.2022.100075

Taye, T., & Mengesha, M. (2024). Identifying and analyzing common English writing challenges among regular undergraduate students. *Heliyon*, *10*(17), e36876. Advance online publication. DOI: 10.1016/j.heliyon.2024.e36876 PMID: 39263167

Taylor, D. L., Yeung, M., & Bashet, A. Z. (2021). Personalized and Adaptive Learning. In *SpringerBriefs in statistics* (p. 17). Springer International Publishing., DOI: 10.1007/978-3-030-58948-6_2

Veramuthu, P., & Shah, P. (2020). Effectiveness of Collaborative Writing among Secondary School Students in an ESL Classroom. *Creative Education*, *11*(1), 54–67. DOI: 10.4236/ce.2020.111004

Vieriu, A. M., & Petrea, G. (2025). The Impact of Artificial Intelligence (AI) on Students' Academic Development. *Education Sciences*, *15*(3), 343. DOI: 10.3390/educsci15030343

Wang, D., & Han, H. (2020). Applying learning analytics dashboards based on process-oriented feedback to improve students' learning effectiveness. *Journal of Computer Assisted Learning*, *37*(2), 487–499. DOI: 10.1111/jcal.12502

Wang, J., Huang, Y., Chen, C., Liu, Z., Wang, S., & Wang, Q. (2024). Software Testing With Large Language Models: Survey, Landscape, and Vision. *IEEE Transactions on Software Engineering*, *50*(4), 911–936. DOI: 10.1109/TSE.2024.3368208

Warner, R., & Sloan, R. H. (2021). Making Artificial Intelligence Transparent: Fairness and the Problem of Proxy Variables. *Criminal Justice Ethics*, *40*(1), 23–39. DOI: 10.1080/0731129X.2021.1893932

Zhai, X., Yin, Y., Pellegrino, J. W., Haudek, K. C., & Shi, L. (2020). Applying machine learning in science assessment: a systematic review [Review of Applying machine learning in science assessment: a systematic review]. Studies in Science Education, 56(1), 111. Taylor & Francis. https://doi.org/DOI: 10.1080/03057267.2020.1735757

ADDITIONAL READING

Baker, R. S., & Inventado, P. S. (2014). Educational data mining and learning analytics. In Larusson, J. A., & White, B. (Eds.), *Learning analytics: From research to practice* (pp. 61–75). Springer., DOI: 10.1007/978-1-4614-3305-7_4

Shute, V. J., & Ventura, M. (2013). *Stealth assessment: Measuring and supporting learning in video games*. MIT Press.

Williamson, B., & Piattoeva, N. (2021). Objectivity as standardization in data-scientific educational governance: Grasping the global through the local. *Research in Education, 101*(1), 69–91. DOI: 10.1177/0034523721995020

KEY TERMS AND DEFINITIONS

Adaptive Learning: An educational methodology utilizing technology that modifies material, pacing, and learning trajectories according to real-time learner data and performance metrics.

Algorithmic Bias: The systematic and recurrent errors in AI decision-making processes resulting from erroneous data, model design, or assumptions, frequently culminating in unjust or discriminating consequences.

Artificial Intelligence (AI): A domain of computer science dedicated to creating computers that can execute activities usually necessitating human intelligence, including learning, reasoning, and decision-making.

Educational Data Mining (EDM): The application of data analytic methods to investigate patterns in educational environments, frequently employed to improve learning outcomes and facilitate decision-making.

Formative Assessment: A systematic assessment carried out during the learning process to deliver feedback and guide instructional modifications intended to enhance student performance.

Human-in-the-Loop (HITL): An AI design concept that prioritizes human judgment as a fundamental element in decision-making to guarantee ethical oversight and contextual appropriateness.

Intelligent Tutoring System (ITS): An AI-driven computer-based learning environment that provides tailored education and feedback according to a learner's specific requirements.

Learning Analytics: The gathering and examination of data regarding learners and their surroundings, aimed at comprehending and enhancing learning processes and environments.

Pedagogical Expertise: The expertise and competencies that educators employ to enhance learning, encompassing curriculum development, assessment proficiency, and classroom administration.

Stealth Assessment: A discreet approach to assessing learners via their interactions with digital learning environments, completely integrated without disrupting the learning process.

Chapter 5
The Role of AI in Experiential Learning: Balancing Ethics and Expertise

Vaishnavi Balaji
https://orcid.org/0000-0001-5047-4333
International School of Management Excellence, CMR University, India

Sanjit Kumar Ghosh
https://orcid.org/0009-0001-2128-284X
International School of Management Excellence, CMR University, India

ABSTRACT

This work demonstrates that AI offers significant potential for personalizing learning pathways, providing immediate feedback, and increasing educational access. Its effective implementation requires maintaining the irreplaceable human elements of teaching, establishing robust ethical frameworks Integrating Kolb's experiential learning theory with AI and human teachers creates a dynamic educational environment where students engage in hands-on activities, reflect on their experiences, form abstract concepts, and test these concepts in new situations. AI enhances the process by providing personalized learning experiences and immediate feedback, supporting reflective observation with active experimentation. Human teachers complement AI by offering emotional support, mentorship, and imbibing critical thinking, guiding students through reflective observation and encouraging deeper insights. However, ethical considerations are crucial in this integration, ensuring AI systems are fair, protecting privacy, maintaining accountability, prioritizing transparency, and well-being of learners.

DOI: 10.4018/979-8-3373-0396-3.ch005

INTRODUCTION

Today's educational landscape stands at an important crossroads where artificial and human intelligence intersect. It is also undergoing transformative changes in redefining experiential learning in contemporary settings. This transformation introduces sophisticated possibilities for personalized instruction, scenario-based learning, real-time assessment, and democratized access while simultaneously raising foundational questions about authenticity, purpose, and value in experiential learning. As per Kolb's theory of experiential learning, knowledge is created through the transformation of experience, involving a cycle of four stages: Concrete Experience, Reflective Observation, Abstract Conceptualization, and Active Experimentation. Learners continuously navigate through these stages, adapting and applying their understanding in new situations to deepen their learning.

STAGES OF KOLB'S THEORY OF EXPERIENTIAL LEARNING

Experiencing (Concrete Experience): In this stage, learning begins through direct involvement in a new or meaningful situation. The learner actively participates, using their senses such as seeing, hearing, touching, or feeling to fully engage with the present moment. This hands-on experience forms the foundation for deeper reflection and understanding.

Reflective Observation: After an experience, the learner takes time to think about what occurred and how it made them feel. They begin to analyze the situation, considering both emotional reactions and the events themselves. This reflection helps them make sense of the experience and draw meaningful insights. By linking emotions with thoughts, the learner starts to build a deeper understanding of what they went through.

Thinking (Abstract Conceptualization): The learner begins to analyze their experience by thinking critically about what happened. They draw conclusions and start forming ideas or explanations based on their reflections. These ideas often take the shape of theories, concepts, or general rules. Once developed, these can be tested or applied in future situations to see how well they hold onto.

Acting (Active Experimentation): The learner puts their ideas into action by trying them out in real-world situations. This step allows them to see how well their concepts work and gather feedback from the results. Through this process, they refine their understanding and adjust their approach if needed. The outcome of this application becomes the basis for new experiences and continued learning.

Kolb's Experiential Learning Theory shows that people can learn most effectively through real experiences and thoughtful reflection. By integrating AI features with different stages of Kolb's experiential learning theory, we can create realistic digital simulations that allow learners to safely practice new skills or scenarios in a virtual environment or playground. Following these activities, AI analyzes learner's actions, experiences and provides personalized feedback, helping them understand what worked well and what needs improvement. AI tools can also prompt reflection by encouraging learners to think about their experiences or collaborate with others. Furthermore, AI can recommend relevant videos, articles, case studies, or lessons to deepen understanding and connect hands-on activities with theoretical concepts. As the learning path progresses, AI can suggest new cases or challenges where learners can apply what they've learned, adapting tasks to match learning best practices. This combination of Kolb's four-stage learning cycle and AI's adaptability makes learning more engaging, personalized, and effective for learners. This also hints at the usage of AI in educational institutions.

From this worldview, Action Research grew. Instead of standing back and observing, the investigator becomes a co-participant: first diagnosing a problem, then planning an intervention, next putting the plan into practice, and finally observing and reflecting on the results. Each cycle clarifies what works, what doesn't, and why, so the group can launch a sharper follow-up round. The process is iterative, democratic, and firmly rooted in real-world issues, whether it involves boosting factory morale, resolving community conflict, or improving classroom engagement. Lewin's legacy is clear: the surest way to understand a social system is to try to change it while learning from every step along the way.

REVIEW OF LITERATURE

David A. Kolb introduced his Experiential Learning Theory (ELT) in 1984, focusing on how people learn through real experiences. Kolb's work on, "Experiential Learning: Experience as the Source of Learning and Development," explains a four-step learning cycle. The cycle includes concrete experience, reflective observation, abstract conceptualization, and active experimentation and describes four learning styles that show how people prefer different stages of the cycle. The theory is widely used in education and training because it treats learning as an active, ongoing process

Donald Schön (1996) cracked open the black box of professional expertise by distinguishing two types of reflection. Reflection in action happens in the heat of the moment: a surgeon adjusting mid operation, a teacher pivoting when students look confused, a designer sketching a solution as problems emerge. This isn't just quick thinking, it's a conversation with the situation itself, where practitioners notice surprises, reframe problems, and experiment on the fly. Reflection on action comes later, in the quiet moments after work ends. Here, professionals replay their decisions, analyze what worked or failed, and prepare for next time.

Schön's insight was revolutionary because it challenged the old model of professional knowledge. Experts don't simply apply textbook rules to predictable situations; they navigate what he called the "swampy lowlands" of practice, where problems are messy, stakes are high, and no manual provides clear answers. The architect sketching variations, the nurse reading subtle patient cues, the manager sensing team tension all demonstrate knowledge that emerges through reflective practice rather than preceding it. By making this tacit knowledge visible, Schön gave professionals a language for their artistry and educators a method for developing it. His work explains why the best training programs combine rigorous theory with supervised practice: only through repeated cycles of action and reflection do novices develop the improvisational wisdom that marks true expertise.

Flores-Viva et al. (2023) explore how Artificial Intelligence (AI) can contribute to achieving Sustainable Development Goal 4, which centers on ensuring quality education for all. Their study highlights both the promise and the complexity of integrating AI into educational systems. One of the key advantages they mention is AI's ability to tailor learning experiences to individual student needs, making education more inclusive and effective. They also point out that AI can help expand access to learning resources, especially in underserved regions. However, the authors caution that the use of AI in education raises important ethical concerns. Issues such as protecting student data and avoiding bias in algorithms must be carefully managed. They emphasize that successful AI implementation depends on having the right infrastructure in place, including reliable technology and internet access. Teacher training is another critical factor, as educators need to understand and effectively use AI tools. Cultural attitudes toward technology can also influence how AI is received and adopted in different educational contexts. Ultimately, the authors advocate for a thoughtful and balanced approach that maximizes AI's benefits while addressing its risks, aligning with the broader goals of SDG4.

Flores-Boddington, Millican, and Wooldridge (2017) present a special issue that delves into the ethical dimensions of artificial intelligence. They underscore the importance of collaboration between philosophy and computer science in tackling these complex issues. The authors argue that AI raises deep moral questions that cannot be addressed by technical expertise alone. Philosophical approaches to ethics, they suggest, offer essential tools for evaluating the societal impact of AI systems. This work brings together a range of viewpoints, enriching the conversation around AI ethics. As AI continues to evolve, the authors stress that ethical concerns are becoming more pressing and multifaceted. They advocate for ongoing dialogue that bridges disciplinary boundaries to better understand and manage these challenges.

Overall, the issue serves as a platform for thoughtful exploration of how ethical theory can inform responsible AI development.

Baskara (2023) investigates how AI-driven personalized learning can be harmonized with Ignatian pedagogy, showing that modern technology can complement traditional educational values. The study carefully analyzes how artificial intelligence can support key aspects of Ignatian teaching, such as personal reflection, experiential learning, and service-oriented education. It identifies AI tools that resonate with Ignatian principles, while also acknowledging areas where conflicts may arise and need thoughtful resolution. Through empirical findings, the author demonstrates that AI can enrich students' engagement with the humanistic and spiritual dimensions of Ignatian learning. A conceptual model is introduced to guide the integration of AI in ways that uphold the integrity of Ignatian pedagogy. The framework emphasizes maintaining the depth and purpose of traditional methods while embracing technological advancements. Baskara also outlines practical strategies for schools and universities aiming to adopt AI without compromising their core educational identity. The research concludes by encouraging institutions to thoughtfully balance innovation with tradition in their pursuit of meaningful learning experiences.

De Cremer and Kasparov (2022) explore what they call the "ethical AI paradox," emphasizing that as AI becomes more advanced, the need for human oversight actually increases. Drawing from Kasparov's experience as a chess champion who has faced AI opponents, they offer unique insights into the dynamics between humans and intelligent machines. Their work proposes a structured approach to assigning ethical responsibility when deploying AI technologies. They warn that sophisticated AI systems can blur lines of accountability, making it harder to determine who is responsible when things go wrong. The authors present evidence showing that human judgment remains crucial, even in highly automated environments. They argue that ethical decision-making cannot be fully delegated to machines, regardless of their capabilities. Instead, they advocate for a collaborative model where human values and reasoning guide AI development. Their conclusion stresses that responsible innovation must be rooted in clear ethical frameworks and shared accountability among all stakeholders.

Fisher & Fisher (2023) provide a comprehensive examination of ethical perspectives on AI applications, methodically analyzing their potential impacts in workplace environments and on individual well-being. The authors synthesize diverse ethical frameworks including consequentialism, deontology, and virtue ethics to evaluate AI implementations across various professional domains. Their research identifies significant ethical tensions between organizational efficiency and individual autonomy when AI systems are deployed in workplace settings. Fisher and Fisher present empirical evidence demonstrating that effective AI integration requires alignment with stakeholder values and organizational ethical cultures. The authors develop a novel evaluative framework for assessing the ethical dimensions of workplace AI applications. Their conclusions emphasize the necessity of proactive ethical consideration during the design phase of AI systems rather than retrospective ethical analysis.

Milossi, Alexandropoulou-Egyptiadou, and Psannis (2021) explore the conflict between algorithm-driven decision-making and personal autonomy within the context of AI ethics. They use the General Data Protection Regulation (GDPR) as a lens to assess how automated systems can compromise individual freedom through hidden processes and inherent biases. Their study critically evaluates how well GDPR safeguards human agencies, especially in relation to decisions made by algorithms. The authors propose a conceptual framework that seeks to balance the efficiency of AI with the protection of privacy and autonomy. Through real-world examples, they illustrate the difficulties of applying GDPR principles to complex AI technologies. These case studies reveal gaps between regulatory intentions and practical implementation. The authors argue that regulations must be flexible and adaptive to keep pace with rapid technological change. Their conclusion emphasizes the importance of evolving legal structures to ensure that human self-determination remains central in an increasingly automated world.

Akgun and Greenhow (2022) conduct a detailed study on the ethical concerns surrounding the use of AI in K-12 education, with particular attention to fairness, data protection, and openness. They propose a structured framework to assess AI tools in schools, focusing on how these technologies affect students from varied backgrounds. Their findings reveal a noticeable gap between what AI systems can technically achieve and the ethical measures currently in place. The authors caution that without careful oversight; AI may unintentionally worsen educational disparities while appearing to offer solutions. They support their analysis with case studies that showcase ethically sound AI applications in school environments. These examples highlight effective strategies for integrating AI responsibly and equitably. Akgun and Greenhow stress the importance of collaboration among educators, developers, and ethics experts to ensure AI tools are used thoughtfully. Their work concludes with a call for inclusive and transparent development processes that prioritize student well-being and educational justice.

Latif et al. (2023) investigate the growing possibilities of Artificial General Intelligence (AGI) in education, highlighting both its transformative potential and the ethical dilemmas it introduces. They differentiate between today's specialized AI tools and the broader, more adaptable nature of AGI, which could revolutionize teaching methods and learning environments. Their study outlines a conceptual model for how AGI might reshape roles such as instruction, evaluation, and curriculum design. The authors raise concerns about how AGI could affect student autonomy, critical thinking, and the preservation of core human values in education. Drawing from disciplines like cognitive science, educational theory, and AI research, they assess how AGI might influence learners' mental and social development. The paper emphasizes that while AGI could enhance learning, it also poses risks that must be carefully managed. Latif et al. propose a roadmap for future research that addresses the technical, ethical, and instructional challenges of integrating AGI into schools. Their work calls for thoughtful planning to ensure that AGI supports rather than undermines the human-centered goals of education.

Siau and Wang (2020) offer a detailed theoretical exploration of AI ethics, making a clear distinction between creating ethical AI systems and the ethical responsibilities involved in developing them. They examine core ethical principles such as fairness, transparency, doing no harm, and promoting good and how these apply across various AI technologies. Their study reveals a persistent conflict between profit-driven motives and ethical standards in the AI industry. To address this, the authors introduce a layered framework that evaluates ethical concerns from the level of system design to organizational practices and societal consequences. They support their framework with real-world examples that show how ethical failures in AI can disproportionately affect vulnerable groups. These case studies underscore the importance of embedding ethical thinking into every stage of AI development. Siau and Wang conclude by recommending structured methods for ensuring that ethical values are consistently integrated throughout the lifecycle of AI systems.

Khare, Stewart, and Khare (2018) studied how AI is used in colleges and universities. They looked at how AI affects students in both learning and administrative areas. The authors created a model to show how AI works with teaching methods and student needs. They found that AI should match the goals and values of the institution to work well. The study showed that AI can help students, but it can also reduce their control if not used carefully. The authors said schools need good technology, clear rules, and teamwork to use AI properly. They ended by saying that strong leadership and planning are needed to make sure AI improves education and supports students. AI can help teachers by making tasks like grading and planning easier. It can also give students personalized support based on their learning needs. But schools must be careful to use AI in ways that are fair and helpful to everyone.

Krakowski and colleagues (2022) suggest a new way to teach AI and ethics together. They use real-world problems to help students learn how ethics connects to technology. Their method is based on the idea that people learn better by doing and thinking through problems. Instead of just talking about ethics, students work on real AI challenges. This helps them understand how their technical choices can affect people. The authors show that students think more deeply about ethics when they solve real problems. They also found that students got better at spotting ethical issues in AI design. The study shares teaching methods that link technical skills with ethical thinking. The authors believe this kind of learning prepares students for real-life AI work. They say it's important for future AI professionals to understand both the tech and the ethics behind it. Authors also present empirical evidence from classroom implementations showing significant improvements in students' ability to identify ethical implications of technical design choices. The authors identify specific pedagogical strategies that effectively bridge the gap between technical training and ethical reasoning in AI education. Their analysis concludes that socio-technical problem-based learning prepares students to address the complex ethical challenges they will encounter as AI practitioners.

Nguyen and colleagues (2023) created a set of ethical rules for using AI in education. They combined ideas from different ethical traditions and laws to make clear guidelines for schools and developers. Their study points out that AI in education brings special challenges, like protecting student freedom and supporting learning. They also talk about keeping strong relationships between teachers and students. The authors explain how big ethical ideas can be turned into practical steps for using AI. They give examples from real classrooms showing when AI was used well and when it caused problems. Their research shows that ethical rules must be flexible and fit the needs of different schools and age groups. They believe that one-size-fits-all rules don't work well in education. Instead, ethics should be shaped by the learning environment and the students' development. Their work helps educators and developers use AI in ways that are fair, safe, and supportive of learning. The authors stress that AI tools should support learning, not replace human interaction. They believe teachers and developers must work together to make AI more helpful and safe. Students should also be involved in decisions about how AI is used in their education. The study encourages schools to think carefully before using AI, especially with younger learners. Overall, the goal is to use AI in ways that respect students and improve their learning experience.

Holmes and colleagues (2022) suggest a shared approach to solving ethical problems in educational AI. They believe everyone involved, such as students, teachers, parents, and developers, should help make decisions. The authors say current ethical rules often miss the special needs of schools and classrooms. Their study shows that working together over time is better than using fixed rules. They created a model that looks at how AI affects teaching, technology, and social interactions. This model helps people think about all parts of AI in education. The authors also give ideas for how schools can include different voices in decision making. They show that when people work together, AI can be used more fairly. Ethical decisions should not be made by one group alone. Instead, they must reflect the values and concerns of the whole educational community. Holmes et al. argue that ethical frameworks must evolve as technology and classroom needs change. They emphasize that ethical planning should be flexible and open to feedback. Without this, AI might harm rather than help students and teachers.

Hemment and colleagues (2023) introduce a broad framework called Experiential AI that focuses on making AI systems easier to understand and more supportive of human control. They combine ideas from computer science, design, philosophy, and social sciences to create a well-rounded approach to ethical AI. Their study points out that many current ethical models overlook how people actually experience and interact with AI. To address this, they propose new methods that improve how AI systems explain themselves and how users engage with them. Through case studies, they show that when users better understand AI systems, ethical risks can be reduced. The authors argue that ethical AI is not just about technical accuracy but also about how people feel and respond during interactions. Their work concludes that ethical AI design must consider both the system's inner workings and the human experience to truly support responsible use.

Brusseau (2023) suggests that AI ethics should be based on real-world experiences instead of just theories. He argues that top-down methods often miss the details that matter in actual situations. His research shows that ethics built from hands-on work are more useful for guiding AI responsibly. He creates a method to find ethical issues in how AI is made and used. Brusseau shares case studies to show how working with AI in specific areas brings out ethical ideas. These examples prove that ethics can come from doing work, not just thinking about it. He believes that both theory and practice should work together in AI ethics. One should not be more important than the other. Ethics in AI should be a constant conversation between ideas and actions. This balanced approach helps make AI fairer and more responsible.

Dyoub, Costantini, and Lisi (2022) suggest a new way to think about AI ethics by focusing on specific areas and listening to users. They believe that talking to users and watching how they interact with AI can help uncover hidden ethical values. Their method helps find these values from user feedback and behavior in real situations. The study shows that using ethics based on user input works better than using general rules. People trust AI more and feel more satisfied when it follows ethics that match their needs. The authors also build tools to include these user-based ethics in AI systems. This helps make sure the AI respects what users care about. They show that ethics in AI should change depending on the situation. One set of rules doesn't fit all cases. Their work proves that flexible and user-focused ethics are key to building better AI.

Slimi and Carballido (2023) studied seven global AI ethics policies related to higher education. They looked at what these policies have in common and where they differ. Their work focused on key ethical issues like privacy, fairness, openness, and responsibility in using AI for education. They found that some policies aim to support innovation, while others focus more on protecting students. The authors noticed that many policies miss important topics like neurodiversity, cultural differences, and long-term effects on students. They also checked how easy it is to put these policies into action, considering limits in schools and technology. Their study shows that current policies are not always complete or practical. They suggest that future policies should be more flexible and fit the needs of different countries. Ethics in educational AI should be shaped by real-world situations. Their work helps guide better and more useful AI ethics in schools and universities.

Yu and Yu (2023) studied AI ethics in education using advanced tools like VOS viewer and CitNetExplorer. They looked at both numbers and meanings in research papers. Their work found key research groups and important changes in thinking over time. They showed how ethical concerns have shifted as AI in education has grown. The authors found that many studies lack real-world data and ignore cultural differences. They created a detailed list of ethical issues found in the research. This list can help guide future studies in the field. Their findings suggest that AI ethics in education is becoming more focused on specific situations. Ethics now aims to fit the needs of different learning environments. Their study helps build a better understanding of how to handle ethics in educational AI.

Chan and Tsi (2023) explore how AI might change teaching in universities. They ask whether AI will replace teachers or help them do their jobs better. They create a framework to study how humans and AI can work together in different ways. Their research looks at real examples of AI in education to see where it works well and where human skills are still needed. They study teaching tasks like giving lessons, grading, giving feedback, and mentoring. They compare how AI and humans perform in these areas. The authors find that schools face challenges when trying to use AI, such as cultural issues and concerns about teachers' roles. They also mention problems with rules and leadership. Chan and Tsi say that using AI well means rethinking what teaching looks like. Instead of just using AI to copy what teachers do, we should find new ways for AI and humans to work together.

Zawacki-Richter and his team (2019) reviewed 146 studies on how AI is used in higher education. They found that most of the research was done by computer scientists, with little help from educational experts. This shows a major gap in how AI is being studied for teaching and learning. The authors point out that many studies ignore important teaching methods and ethical issues. They grouped AI applications into three main types: *predicting student behavior, grading and feedback, and personalizing learning*. While AI tools are becoming more advanced, studies often miss the point of helping students learn better. The focus seems to be more on showing what AI can do, rather than how it supports education. The authors worry that without strong teaching theories, AI might not meet learning goals. They also highlight the lack of attention to values and ethics in AI use. The paper calls for teamwork between teachers, learning experts, and AI developers. It says that AI should be built with input from people who understand education. This way, AI can truly support students and teachers. The authors believe that combining technical skills with teaching knowledge is key. They stress that AI should not replace good teaching but improve it. Their work supports the idea that education experts must lead AI development. This helps make sure AI tools are useful and fair in classrooms.

Selwyn (2019) takes a critical look at learning analytics and questions the basic ideas behind using data in education. He points out six major problems with how learning analytics is used. These include turning learning into numbers, focusing on prediction instead of understanding, and supporting old teaching methods. He also warns about the risks of surveillance and treating education as a product. Another concern is that learning analytics often help institutions more than students. He also shows that these tools offer technical fixes but ignore deeper social and cultural issues. He explains that learning analytics can limit how we think about learning. They may also strengthen existing power structures in education. His work challenges the overly positive view of technology in schools. He calls for more thoughtful and realistic ways to use learning analytics. The author believes that we need to understand the limits and risks of these tools. He wants educators and researchers to work together and think critically. His ideas support the need for balanced and human-centered approaches in education.

Roll and Wylie (2016) explore how AI has changed education over time. They explain the difference between improving current teaching methods and completely changing how education works. The authors create a framework to study AI tools by looking at their goals, abilities, and how well they match learning theories. Their research shows that most AI tools still follow old teaching styles, even though they claim to be new. They believe AI can do more than just deliver content it can help students learn by working together and building knowledge. The paper argues that to use AI well, humans need to rethink what education is for. It's not enough to just use AI to do what teachers already do. The authors say humans should design AI tools that support deeper learning. They want AI to help students think, explore, and grow. Their study shows that AI should be guided by how people really learn. They suggest that researchers and educators work together to make this happen. The paper also points out that AI should not replace teachers but support them. Roll and Wylie believe that thoughtful use of AI can make learning better. Their work supports the idea that human expertise is key in using AI wisely.

Reich and his team (2017) take a close look at how educational technology affects fairness in education. They challenge the idea that digital tools automatically make learning more equal. Their study shows that technology often helps students who already have advantages, a pattern known as the "Matthew Effect." This means that instead of closing gaps, tech can make them wider. The authors look at real examples to support their claims. They say that to make technology fair, it must be designed with care. This includes being aware of culture, context, and power differences. They stress that technology alone cannot fix inequality. It needs to be built with inclusion in mind. The authors offer clear ideas for how to design better tools. They suggest ways for teachers, developers, and leaders to work together. Their goal is to make digital learning fairer for everyone. They believe that thoughtful design can help them reach this goal. Their work supports the idea that AI and tech should improve access, not create new problems. This fits well with the case study's focus on fairness and inclusion in education.

ADVANTAGES OF USING AI IN EDUCATION

AI can help learners in different stages of experiential learning. On assuming an experiential learning platform is integrated with an AI platform to harness the power of AI.

1. Concrete Experience

In this stage, the learner is engaging in a new experience or activity.
Possible application of AI:

- **Simulations & Virtual Labs**: Simulations can help the learner in this stage. In this stage, different AR/VR tools can also help. AI-powered platforms can be used to simulate real-world use cases like business analytics cases, economic models, and scientific models for hands-on learning.
- **Adaptive Learning Tools**: AI based Adaptive tools can play an important role here. It can personalize content delivery based on the learner's experience; prior knowledge; and it can ensure experience is novel and relevant.
- **Uses of Virtual Assistants**: chat boat or any virtual assistance tool can provide real-time guidance during tasks, like coding, analyzing data sets or use cases.

2. Reflective Observation

Here the learner uses reflection on the experience from different perspectives.
Possible application of AI:

- **AI powered Sentiment Analysis**: AI can play an important role in analyzing written reflections of learners to detect emotional tone or cognitive bias. This will help learners become more self-aware.

- **AI powered meaningful Feedback**: Different available LMS Tools can review your work like case study, session plans or blog drafts and offer constructive suggestions.

3. Abstract Conceptualization

In this stage, the learner uses his "Thinking" ability to form theories or concepts based on reflections in the second stage.

Possible application of AI

- **Concept Mapping**: AI can generate visual maps linking various concepts like responsible AI, ethics, data analysis. This will help the learner in forming theories.
- **In Content Summarization**: AI can help to simplify complex theories into understandable insights which can give conceptual clarity. This will help where experimental outcomes are huge and complicated in nature.
- **In Challenging assumptions and asking contradictory questions**: AI can challenge basic assumptions of learners and deepen understanding through guided inquiry. This will enable the learner to think about contradictions.

4. Active Experimentation

Here learner will "be Applying" ideas and will test new ideas in real-world or simulated settings.

Possible application of AI:

- **Creating Playground:** AI can be used to create a playground to test new ideas with simulated settings.
- **Code Generation & Debugging**: For any code-based experiment different LMS tools can help you prototype code-based solutions for business problems.
- **Scenario-Based Learning**: AI can be used to generate valid case studies or role-play exercises which can tailor the learner's learning goals.
- **In doing Performance Analysis**: AI based apps can track and evaluate learner's application of concepts over time and suggest specific areas for improvement.

Educational AI for Experiential Learning is an evolving concept, and its importance is growing day by day. In addition to experiential learning, we need to study what are the other areas in which AI can help to improvise educational practices.

It is also explored how our traditional model of education delivery by offline or online mode of training through physical presence of teacher is getting challenged by introduction of AI tools and explore what should be the role of AI in education? *Will it eliminate the role of teacher, or it will coexist with human teacher and help its human counterpart in delivering knowledge effectively to learner.*

To begin with the advantages and disadvantages of using educational AI for experimental learning is discussed below:

Personalized Learning

AI can help in personalized learning along with adaptive features. This is a very important now a days and help for most of the leaner, AI can encourage learner through experimental learning so that they can use own experience and hypothesis.

Availability of AI Tutor 24X7

Contrary to instructor based leaning where instructor is available as per routine of the course or session, AI tutor bot can be available anytime. If leaner has doubt, he/she can take help from AI tutor any time. This helps learner who can study as per own convenience, this will also lead to increase the urge for learning since timing is not a constraint anymore.

Contradiction and Synthesis

AI can help in giving different views which may apparently contradicting to learner so that learner can have opposing viewpoints and synthesize knowledge dynamically.

Help in Developing Future Skills

Experimental learning with AI can help student to learn future skills, adaptability, problem solving skills by own. Specifically for future skills getting training from good and experienced trainer may be difficult but getting help from AI based learning can be possible.

Valuable Insights Through Data Analysis

During experiential learning process of learner different data points getting generated regarding learners' performance, areas for improvement, instructional strategies, possible adjacent skills. AI can help in analysing the data and prescribe possible course correction if needed.

Democratization of Learning

By using Dialectic AI, it is possible to reduce the entry barrier for participation of leaner for any training and making it more accessible for diverse learners regardless of their background, location and expertise.

Adaptive Assessment

One of the most effective ways to evaluate learning is though Adaptive assessment. AI can enhance experiential learning by providing real-world problem-solving scenarios and can also help in creating Adaptive assessment.

Mitigating Bias and Ethical Consideration

One of the challenges in using AI in education is, there might chances that AI is biased because of biased data set used for training AI or due biased algorithm. This can lead to gaining wrong information by learner. To mitigate that AI must be trained responsibly by using unbiased data set with ethical considerations in mind.

AI and Human Collaboration

AI should be used to support human teacher in delivering experiential learning, but it should not be used as complete replacement to human tutor. It should emphasize that using AI to facilitate collaboration, critical thinking and reflection rather giving simple automated solution.

Immersive knowledge Platform

By integrating AI with virtual and augmented reality to create interactive, engaging and hands on learning experience. It can also help learner to collaborate with peer learner worldwide.

Though above-mentioned points have shown the various advantages of using AI in education in delivering experimental learning, but few points humans need to consider with respect to ethical challenges, probable bias infusion intentionally and unintentionally. The limitation of AI is discussed below.

LIMITATIONS OF USING AI IN EDUCATION

Ethical Challenges in AI-Based Learning

Now a days AI is transforming education by personalizing learning experiences in all sectors of educations, but we need to also introspect about different ethical dilemmas arise mainly due to student privacy, data security, and the probable impact due to AI replacing human instructors. We should ensure AI supports rather than neglecting the fundamental values of education and ethics.

Bias in AI-Based Learning Models

For effective output from AI model it must be train from historical data, which means they can inherit biases intentionally or unintentionally. If AI trained with biased data, then AI can favour certain results over others, leading to wrong conclusion. It may also generate wrong information or learning content. Organization needs to emphasize strategies to make AI systems bias free through proper validation of test data.

Accountability and Transparency

AI-driven tools can suggest do need analysis and suggest learning pathways, do grading, and even give feedback. However, user don't have any information on underlying algorithms and it's working principal. Transparent AI systems allow user to understand how decisions are made, ensuring accountability when errors or biases occur.

Need Governance Policy in AI Education Ethic

There needs to be a clear governance guideline for ethical use of AI in education system. It should address bias free approach of test data for training Ai models, data protections and responsible use of AI to educational purpose without changing basic learning principal and ethics.

In addition to bias and ethical issues, other areas where human involvement is needed are as follows:

Motivation and encouragement: giving student encouragement and motivation whenever needed can boost their self-worth and intrinsic motivation. Teacher has the power to acknowledge students' effort, offer positive criticism and create a friendly atmosphere in classroom, which AI based system may still need some time to master.

Classroom engagement: Student involvement in classroom generally depends on teachers' excitement, way of teaching and passion for the subject. Teacher engages student by using various instructional techniques, interactive experiments by individual interaction.

Rapport building: Teacher and learner rapport is crucial. By exhibiting respect, empathy towards learner's learning capability, wellbeing's teacher fosters a welcoming environment for learning.

This synergy between experiential learning, AI, and human teachers, underpinned by ethical principles, nurtures a holistic and effective learning experience. Educational institutions must develop clear governance through usage of responsible AI that prioritize student wellbeing, protect privacy, address algorithmic bias, and maintain the relational aspects of education, even as they embrace the transformative potential of AI technologies to enhance teaching and learning.

CONCLUSION

With advent of Artificial intelligence, humans are facing challenges of embracing AI's capabilities in education sector while preserving the irreplaceable human touch of learning. Effective governance frameworks are essential for guiding decisions on integrating technology while keeping traditional educational principles. A well-structured approach must welcome collaborative design potential and be led by individuals who grasp both the possibilities of technology and the importance of human-cantered values. One of the most important approaches leverage AI to handle routine tasks, making personalized learning approach, while creating more space for meaningful human interaction. This can be amplified with the use AI powered data-driven insights to enhance individual learning journeys. The future of experiential learning lies not in artificial intelligence alone, but in thoughtfully integrated systems where technology amplifies human capacity and wisdom. Humans should not use AI to replace human teacher, but we should explore how AI can enhance human capability of delivering meaningful knowledge to intended learners at least in academic level. By proper amalgamation of both AI and human centric approach, we can create learning environments that are simultaneously more personalized, more human, more accessible and transformative.

REFERENCES

Akgun, S., & Greenhow, C. (2022). Artificial intelligence in education: Addressing ethical challenges in K-12 settings. *AI and Ethics*, *2*(3), 431–440.

Baskara, F. R. (2023). Personalised learning with AI: Implications for Ignatian pedagogy. *International Journal of Educational Best Practices*, *7*(1), 1–16.

Boddington, P., Millican, P., & Wooldridge, M. (2017). Minds and machines special issue: Ethics and artificial intelligence. *Minds and Machines*, *27*, 569–574.

Brusseau, J. (2023). From the ground truth up: Doing AI ethics from practice to principles. *AI & Society*, ●●●, 1–7.

Chan, C. K. Y., & Tsi, L. H. (2023). The AI revolution in education: Will AI replace or assist teachers in higher education? *arXiv preprint arXiv:2305.01185.*

De Cremer, D., & Kasparov, G. (2022). The ethical AI—paradox: Why better technology needs more and not less human responsibility. *AI and Ethics*, *2*(1), 1–4.

Dyoub, A., Costantini, S., & Lisi, F. A. (2022). Learning domain ethical principles from interactions with users. *Digital Society : Ethics, Socio-Legal and Governance of Digital Technology*, *1*(3), 28.

Fisher, E. J. P., & Fisher, E. (2023). A fresh look at ethical perspectives on artificial intelligence applications and their potential impacts at work and on people. *Business and Economic Review*, *13*(3), 1–22.

Flores-Viva, J. M., & García-Peñalvo, F. J. (2023). Reflections on the ethics, potential, and challenges of artificial intelligence in the framework of quality education (SDG4). *Comunicar: Media Education Research Journal*, *31*(74), 35–44.

Hemment, D., Murray-Rust, D., Belle, V., Aylett, R., Vidmar, M., & Broz, F. (2023). Experiential AI: A transdisciplinary framework for legibility and agency in AI. *arXiv preprint arXiv:2306.00635.*

Holmes, W., Porayska-Pomsta, K., Holstein, K., Sutherland, E., Baker, T., Shum, S. B., & Koedinger, K. R. (2022). Ethics of AI in education: Towards a community-wide framework. *International Journal of Artificial Intelligence in Education*, ●●●, 1–23.

Khare, K., Stewart, B., & Khare, A. (2018). Artificial intelligence and the student experience: An institutional perspective. *The International Academic Forum (IAFOR).*

Kolb, D. A. (1984). *Experiential learning: Experience as the source of learning and development.*

Krakowski, A., Greenwald, E., Hurt, T., Nonnecke, B., & Cannady, M. (2022, June). Authentic integration of ethics and AI through sociotechnical, problem-based learning. *Proceedings of the AAAI Conference on Artificial Intelligence*, *36*(11), 12774–12782.

Latif, E., Mai, G., Nyaaba, M., Wu, X., Liu, N., Lu, G., . . . Zhai, X. (2023). Artificial general intelligence (AGI) for education. *arXiv preprint arXiv:2304.12479*, 1.

Milossi, M., Alexandropoulou-Egyptiadou, E., & Psannis, K. E. (2021). AI ethics: Algorithmic determinism or self-determination? The GPDR approach. *IEEE Access : Practical Innovations, Open Solutions*, *9*, 58455–58466.

Nguyen, A., Ngo, H. N., Hong, Y., Dang, B., & Nguyen, B. P. T. (2023). Ethical principles for artificial intelligence in education. *Education and Information Technologies*, *28*(4), 4221–4241.

Reich, J., & Ito, M. (2017). *From good intentions to real outcomes: Equity by design in learning technologies*. Digital Media and Learning Research Hub.

Roll, I., & Wylie, R. (2016). Evolution and revolution in artificial intelligence education. *International Journal of Artificial Intelligence in Education*, *26*(2), 582–599.

Selwyn, N. (2019). What's the problem with learning analytics? *Journal of Learning Analytics*, *6*(3), 11–19.

Siau, K., & Wang, W. (2020). Artificial intelligence (AI) ethics: Ethics of AI and ethical AI. [JDM]. *Journal of Database Management*, *31*(2), 74–87.

Slimi, Z., & Carballido, B. V. (2023). Navigating the ethical challenges of artificial intelligence in higher education: An analysis of seven global AI ethics policies. *TEM Journal, 12*(2).

Yu, L., & Yu, Z. (2023). Qualitative and quantitative analyses of artificial intelligence ethics in education using VOSviewer and CitNetExplorer. *Frontiers in Psychology*, *14*, 1061778.

Zawacki-Richter, O., Marín, V. I., Bond, M., & Gouverneur, F. (2019). Systematic review of research on artificial intelligence applications in higher education – Where are the educators? *International Journal of Educational Technology in Higher Education*, *16*(1), 1–27.

Chapter 6
The Role of AI in Education–Challenges and Ethical Implications to Enhance Teachers' Expertise

K. Siva Kumar Gowda
https://orcid.org/0009-0004-8957-0276
Sreenidhi Institute of Science and Technology, India

I. Sowmyasri
Sreenidhi Institute of Science and Technology, India

T. Venkat Narayana Rao
https://orcid.org/0000-0002-1996-1819
Sreenidhi Institute of Science and Technology, India

ABSTRACT

Application of AI in the teaching learning process has raised questions on how it can supplement or supplant part or the entire function of a tutor.. However, the main disadvantage of implementing AI to replace the human-based and context-sensitive sensible judgement of a teacher is a number of ethical and practical consequences. It is evident that AI cannot emulate human emotions, therefore, there remains no empathy and touch, there exists a potential transmission of undesirable algorithmic bias, and, finally, the absence of human touch devaluates the possibilities of creating thinking, imagination, and ethical personality. Moreover, there are questions concerning data privacy. This study has highlighted that AI should support the

DOI: 10.4018/979-8-3373-0396-3.ch006

activities teachers perform; when appropriate, integrated should be ethical and offer the same advantages learners. These are the challenges that future research has to solve to gain the best opportunity for uniting the AI and human values for education. This chapter purpose is to determine if and how AI can replicate and enhance educational processes.

1.INTRODUCTION

The speed of AI progress has generated huge debate in every industry, and education is not an exception. It has attracted a great deal of interest and anxiety as to the possibility of using AI as a substitute or complement in the classroom. Current AI systems can personalize learning, automate administrative tasks, and give real-time feedback, and some have even questioned whether human educators might eventually become obsolete. However, the prospect of AI replacing teachers' expertise raises many more ethical and practical questions. Although AI holds great promise to enhance the educational experience and make learning more efficient and accessible, it also poses critical questions on accountability, empathy, and human interaction in education.

Education is hardly an exception in the context of all discussions sweeping through every industry. Heated debate and excitement, above all, concern over the fast development of AI. Sophistication of AI technologies has made possible, exciting, and a cause for concern the possibility of using AI to replace or complement the role of a teacher in the classroom. Can AI really replace all traditional aspects of teaching? Besides, the ethical concerns in the dissemination of AI applications in education call for proper utilization of such technologies, that is, issues of bias, privacy, and fairness. Thus, this paper debates whether AI shall replace teacher know-how or is it a great tool in which teacher knowhow shall be sidelined. Although excellent, this paper would indicate why teachers exist and how this AI should first be introduced and implemented more so as a supplementary tool rather than a replacement in education.

We analyse the delicate balance between exploiting and mitigating the advantages of AI for useful purposes without losing those human elements characteristic of the teaching profession. And as AI continues to evolve further, people have become curious about its implication for human teachers in the near future. Such is the case as AI serves best to better and enhance the fruit of education since it will easily automate mundane managerial work, the monitoring of all the student grades, and different learning experience offered according to student's special requirement. For instance, adaptive software for learning would ensure the customization of the class by individual pupils; it also means the task burden for educators might ease by a few measures. In this sense, AI is more of an extension of the conventional teaching methodologies; therefore, it ensures better efficiency and specialized support to learners. (Pedro et.al,2019)

2.THE POTENTIAL OF AI IN EDUCATION

Artificial Intelligence is making education more personalized, automated, and accessible. Probably the most important contribution AI can make towards the future of education lies in personalized learning experiences. Traditional classrooms largely fail to meet the individual needs of the student because of the homogenization that occurs in the setting. AI-based models can look at the patterns of performances by the learners and adjust lessons according to those patterns. AI monitors progress, finds out the areas of strength and weakness, and modifies content in real time to ensure that every student learns at his or her own pace. The major beauty of adaptive learning systems like Dream Box and Kenston lies in modifying lesson difficulty based on individual performance, thereby making learning both efficient and engrossing. Automated assessments and feedback are one of the other significant benefits of AI.

The biggest challenge that instructors face is grading assignments and giving feedback, but AI can grade essays, quizzes, and exams in a matter of seconds. Grade scope and Turnitin are tools that use machine learning to grade assignments, detect plagiarism, and give detailed feedback in helping students improve with more interactive teaching. It allows instant feedback and, therefore, can inform students what they are doing wrong so that they learn immediately, hence making learning even more rewarding. Virtual tutors and AI chatbots increasingly are the face of the education sector to bridge academically outstanding gaps outside classrooms. For instance, Google's Socratic and ChatGPT act as AI-powered tutors; that is, they can answer questions, explain concepts, and guide a student through difficult topics at any time. Unlike human teachers, who have to go off-duty at some point, AI tutors work 24/7 without any breaks. Besides that, the incorporation of AI into voice assistants and chatbots increases student participation in learning because they make it more interactive and accessible. Besides individual support, AI is bridging the educational gap and making education more accessible. (Zhai et.al, 2021).

AI-driven education platforms support students from very remote or low-income backgrounds. Platforms such as Google Translate and Duolingo have broken language barriers so that any student, regardless of the background of their mother tongue, can learn perfectly.

Further, AI-based assistive technologies-such as speech-to-text and text-to-speech-applications are helping children with disabilities, and the same learning materials become accessible to them. Such innovations ensure greater inclusion and equity in education. AI is also greatly contributing towards making administrative activities more efficient and to the management of classes. Most instructors have to spend enormous amounts of precious time engaged in very ordinary routine work, including keeping records of attendance, making lesson plans, and producing study material. All such mundane tasks can be automated so that maximum interaction time can be obtained from the instructors on the part of the students. The product will generate lesson plans, quizzes, and guides according to the demand of the curriculum, owing to smart content development. AI predictive analytics may predict a student who probably stumbles or indicates earlier intervention into avoiding losing academic ground.

In reality, AI has been one thing highly influencing education due to the reason that AI could personalize it and make it both efficient and inclusive. However, while AI may help in some fields, it can never replace the critical roles played by human teachers to foster creativity, emotional intelligence, and mentorship. The ideal approach would be an integration of AI as an added support for education while making sure that all human interaction and guidance are at the core of the learning process.

2.1. AI-Powered Teaching Tools

The advancement in teaching tools powered by Artificial Intelligence does change the educational landscape. Improvement in teaching and learning experience comes as an aid to all teachers. Probably, the most exciting development of AI education is the virtual tutor. Such intelligent systems deliver immediate feedback, answer students' doubts, and guide students stepwise through multipart topics with explanations. Some programs, such as Socratic by Google and Khan Academy's Khan Migo, use AI in analysing the questions of students so that individual learning resources can be provided to assist learners at their own pace. Another development is the adaptive learning systems, where the content would be personalized for a given student's needs. These systems assess the strength and weakness of the student constantly, adapting to change the lesson difficulty as needed. This type of learning has witnessed rapid adoption within platforms such as Dream Box and Century Tech. Within these, AI is used to generate personalized learning paths, meaning that there would be more engagement and efficacy within the field of education.

In this way, students will gain work on just the right level of challenge, keeping them from being either frustrated or bored (Pokrivcakova et.al,2019).

Also, Artificial Intelligence assists in another aspect of the curriculum design by providing help to teachers during lesson planning based on student performance data and particular educational standards. Platforms like Squirrel AI will analyse the trends of learning and suggest changes to teaching strategies, allowing educators to make the best use of their methodologies. Further, the AI-enabled grading tools like Grade scope and Turnitin can automate the assessment process, thus saving educational time while giving students personalized feedback on their assignments. Automation allows teachers extra time to engage in interactive teaching and student engagement rather than doing logistical assessments.

2.2 Automating Administrative Tasks

Artificial Intelligence changes education by doing away with the tiring clerical work so that teachers can do more teaching and interacting with their students. In fact, AI has found great application in automatic grading and marking. For example, grade scope and Turnitin are AI-enabled tools that help grade multiple-choice quizzes, short answers, or even essays; the student then receives instant feedback. These tools also reduce the workload of teachers but ensure that marking is fair and unbiased since there is no scope for human errors and inconsistencies.

Another key area in which AI ensures efficiency is in attendance tracking and classroom management. Conventional attendance tracking methods are tedious, but AI facial recognition and biometric systems simplify the process to ensure accurate and trouble-free attendance recording. Many schools and universities use AI-driven systems that automatically track students' attendance through facial recognition or smart ID cards. It eliminates the cumbersome roll calls and minimizes interruptions during class sessions.

AI is also transforming the game of student progress monitoring through analysing learning patterns and performance data. Some platforms, like IBM Watson Education, are using AI to give educators real-time insights into their students' strengths and weaknesses. This automatically aids educators to reach the children who are going to fall behind early and intervene with strategies that are more individualized to each child. Such predictive analytics tools support teachers to make data-driven decisions, which will enable a reduction in overall dropout rates and improve student outcomes (Willis et.al,2020).

AI also made it easier to communicate as well as schedule through intelligent chatbots and virtual assistants. Most learning institutions have integrated AI chatbots that regularly receive routine questions from the students and parents concerning their schedules, deadlines, and coursework among others. These AI assistants provide instant answers compared to human administrators. They enable seamless communication between students, teachers, and parents as visible on university portals.

More broadly, AI automation of administrative work in schools means that these educational institutions are now more efficient in their operation. It saves unnecessary work, improves accuracy, and takes teachers out of repetitive and mundane work to spend quality time with students. The human factor cannot be replaced by AI in education, but its ability to make the management of administrative work more efficient is a very crucial tool for modernizing and optimizing learning.

2.3 Enhancing Student Engagement

Artificial intelligence can really bring significant benefits in terms of more student engagement since it takes advantage of a more personalized, dynamic, and interactive experience in learning. The traditional approach tends to fail to engage learners as it takes the monolithic approaches, non-interactional, or unresponsive to learners' diverse needs. AI is able to overcome these challenges by creating learning environments responsive, adaptive, and relevant to individual interests and abilities. When used thoughtfully, AI tools can spark curiosity, keep students engaged, and make them an active participant in the learning process. The first way AI increases student engagement is through personalized learning experiences.

Content-adaptive learning platforms adapt and evolve based on a student's pace, progression, and style of learning, such as Kenton or Smart Sparrow. They evaluate and alter the level of difficulty for lessons in real-time according to performance analysis and provide specific personalized feedback when needed. For instance, in the process of trying to make sense of any given concept, it may encounter challenges and the AI system can suggest another source or change the teaching methodology of the course work making it more palatable and digestible. Personal! Learning allows the student to be challenged but not overwhelmed. The learner remains interested and always motivated to continue the process. AI supports active learning through gamification and other interactive tools. Learning platforms like Kahoot! This would include features like scorekeeping, levels, and leaderboards added to the learning content in Quizlet and Duolingo. If done well, this can increase engagement since it introduces natural elements of competition, rewards, and fun into learning. This can possibly mean that AI can track a student's game experience and provide learning opportunities that will be at an appropriate level of difficulty as students will not get bored or frustrated with their products. Further, AI-based chatbots and virtual assistants, such as Mind spark or Class craft, offer instant interactions that allow students to ask questions, get individual hints, and remain engaged throughout the learning process without waiting for a teacher's intervention. Another powerful tool is AI-based simulations and virtual environments that immerse students in interactive learning scenarios. For example, in science class, students can use AI to conduct virtual experiments through simulated environments and test hypotheses against outcomes without any physical labs around (Peters.et.al,2019) .

AI-based tools enable students to collaborate in real time, irrespective of the distance between places. For example, AI-based virtual classrooms and discussion forums will be enabled automatically, where AI will group students, find resources for discussion, and even facilitate discussions. Other widely used platforms include Google Classroom and Edmodo. The former enables instant idea sharing among students and provides instant feedback. It further connects students with the larger online learning communities. AI can analyse the dynamics of each group interaction and suggest appropriate tasks according to each individual's strengths, and make everyone contribute to the collaborative process in such a way that brings about teamwork and makes the students feel they are active participants in learning together, hence achieving greater engagement. Last but certainly not least, AI-Content Creation Tool can allow a student to creatively create and connect content through creative production tools. During the learning process, tools might include video or podcasting; or interaction in Socrative or Synthesis, among many others.

Through participative involvement in creating learning resources, AI creates critical thinking over the application of knowledge with a greater engagement over the subject material. This approach towards participation is not only going to enhance the sense of engagement but also of the skills related to critical thinking and problem-solving abilities. Hence, AI is stated to change the learning of a student into customized, participative, and dynamic processes. With AI, the possibilities of adaptation, gamification, collaboration, and creativity become accessible so that students will stay engaged and inquisitive during their process of learning. The use of AI enhances the experience in relation to learning but at the same time keeps it clear that the importance of human guidance, mentorship, and connection is never compromised within the educational process. Thus, AI would make learning more engaging, enjoyable, and accessible for all students when properly integrated (Leach et.al,2016).

3. LIMITATIONS AND CHALLENGES OF AI IN TEACHING

Figure 1. Limitations and Challenges of AI in Teaching

Though AI holds immense promise for better education, simultaneously there is so much more that AI does not do well and thus cannot replace a human teacher.

Education encompasses far more than knowledge, like emotional intelligence, critical thinking, creativity, and interaction, for which AI lags.

Perhaps one of the biggest challenges of AI in teaching is that it has no emotional quotient and empathy. A teacher, apart from delivering content, understands a student's feelings, struggles, and motivations. Human teachers offer encouragement, non-verbal cue recognition, and emotional support that are all significant for the successful completion of student learning. The other reason is since AI is entirely data-driven and can never capture the human quotient; hence it cannot be successful in handling student emotional and psychological needs.

Another critical weakness is that AI does not make the student any more creative or critical thinking. Indeed, whereas AI might be able to give some form of controlled learning experience, it is not an open-ended discussion, debate, and innovative problem-solving. Human teachers encourage the student to get beyond textbooks, think more creatively, and cultivate ability in critical thinking—capacities AI cannot nurture to the same degree. Facts and solutions can be provided by AI, but that cannot reach the breadth of human reasoning and contextual understanding for independent thought.

The most considerable challenge to AI-driven education has been classroom management and student motivation. A teacher always plays a significant role in setting discipline, captivating the attentions of students, or adjusting the process of teaching for a class contingent on classroom conditions. An advanced AI system still cannot manage students as a team, resolve student conflicts, and develop the "we-feeling" of joint activity, as any ordinary human teacher can. Education is a social process, and so user-friendly learning will never come from a machine, without any really interesting and meaningful communication between the machine and the learner.

In addition, greater reliance on AI in education also raises the issue of digital divide and accessibility. Not all students have equal access to AI-based learning tools, especially in underprivileged regions with limited technological infrastructure. If AI-based education becomes the norm, students without access to advanced technology could face disadvantages, further widening the educational gap between privileged and marginalized communities.

Bias and fairness are two other critical problems with AI. AI models get trained based on existing data that is likely to carry biases; hence, learning becomes unfair or even inaccurate at times. This can lead to reinforcing stereotypes with AI algorithms, or favouring certain groups of students, hence creating inequalities in education. Unbiasing AI and providing opportunities to all learners is a gigantic challenge for the implementation of AI in education (et.al,2023).

There is also the aspect of data privacy and security in AI integration into education. Big amounts of student data are collected in AI systems for personalization purposes, but that increases data breach and unauthorized access risks. Protecting students' personal information and ensuring ethical use of AI is important to the trust displayed by learners in AI-driven education.

4. ETHICAL CONSIDERATIONS IN AI-DRIVEN EDUCATION

Except for the above-mentioned ethical issues, there are a few other very significant considerations to be kept in mind before implementing AI in the education sector. Relationship between teacher and student: Undeniably AI can aid in the betterment of personalization in learning but cannot replace human teachers with emotional and social support systems. It gives an interest to the minds of students through mentors, appreciation, and guidance by teachers who are humans only. Human relations in education provide a base of trust and well-understood, subtle needs for students. Heavy reliance on AI may risk minimizing the significance of these crucial interpersonal bonds, thus harming the motivation of students to perform.

Access to Technology and Digital Literacy: AI in education relies heavily on technology, which raises access concerns, especially for students in underprivileged or rural areas where access to devices or high-speed internet may be limited.

Role of AI in Assessments and Grading: AI-based grading and assessment systems allow for greater efficiency, but accuracy and equity need to be established. The AI grading systems will not so smoothly work when dealing with the interpretation of subjective work such as essays or a creative project and could thus be missing the real deep sense the student had acquired. Additionally, it might withdraw the all-rounded educational approach that is generally depicted by teachers and find convenience in human judgment to an algorithmic outcome (Klimova et.al,2023).

Long-term impacts on the cognitive skills of learners: There are always debates regarding how AI-based education technologies affect the cognitive capabilities of students, particularly their critical thinking and problem-solving capabilities. Immediate access to ready-made solutions via AI along with personalized content adaptation according to individual learning styles do not foster a spirit of grit and independent thought that would come into play while dealing with deep, ill-defined problems. It is thus important that AI in education focus on output improvement, but in some skills such as creativity, resilience, and critical inquiry, which will be harder to learn through an automated system.

Global Standards and Regulation: Since the application of AI cuts across all educational systems around the world, each has a unique approach to applying it. This will make it hard to set international standards on how AI should be used and legislation that applies to education. This is because differences in quality of education may emerge based on variations in the usage of AI from one country or region to another. This suggests a need for adequate statutory protection to establish universal ethical standards of AI technologies as well as using them responsibly and ethically for education globally through regulatory bodies.

Ultimately, while the potential for AI to transform learning is so great, all these ethical considerations must be given clear thought while developing and implementing it. Making sure that any education approach will always be human-centred means ensuring that the technology used will augment rather than supplant the very elements of teaching and learning that are so critical. Now it is in that context that artificial intelligence becomes something that can push the force shaping more personalized equitable, and ultimately effective educational experiences for all learners (Zaman et.al,2023).

4.1 Data Privacy and Security

As the artificial intelligence factor is introduced in education, privacy and security concerns have shot into the stratosphere. Data-related cyber and security issues consist of AI-based learning platforms, virtual tutors, and even monitoring systems for students that collect huge chunks of information about their personal data, academic records, and even patterns of behaviour. Although the data can be the key to personalizing education or improving student outcomes, it shows more serious issues regarding ethics and security.

Data collection and storage are also among the top concerns. AI systems rely on large datasets to operate properly, but the way this information is handled raises significant privacy issues. If student data is not kept in secure, encrypted servers, it may become vulnerable to hacking, unauthorized access, and misuse. Cybercriminals can sell this information for identity theft, phishing attacks, or other nefarious activities on the dark web. Strict data security measures, for example, encryption, multi-factor authentication, and secure cloud storage, should be in place to prevent breaches in educational institutions. Another important issue is student surveillance and consent(salomon et.al,2012).

Many educational application tools with AI tracking online student activities and engagement levels, from even facial expressions, of on-task behaviours, and performance. Despite their presumed benefit in promoting an efficient learning process, they also raise ethical issues concerning the limits of surveillance on students' autonomy. Sometimes, a child or a parent is not told how much data is already being collected. Transparency is essential—schools and AI providers must clearly communicate what data is being gathered, how it will be used, and who will have access to it. Thirdly, there is the risk of sharing third-party data. Most learning institutions outsource grading, tutoring, and administration to external AI service providers.

If student information distributed by these firms to marketers, research companies, and other businesses is not overseen by their guardians, then exploitation and a loss of student information control are the end results. Strict guidelines also include regulations like the GDPR in Europe and COPPA in the United States, which set guidelines for dealing with student data, but this does not easily translate into real-world enforcement or compliance.

It must also be guided by AI governance ethics to ensure responsible usage of student data. Therefore, schools, policymakers, and others must have a joint engagement in establishing responsible AI frameworks to govern education: prioritizing privacy while harnessing the benefits that AI technology affords. With regular audits and AI transparency reports, stronger cyber security measures are expected to abate risks as well as bolster trust in these AI-powered systems of learning. While education and learning are broad fields that AI can transform, data privacy and security should take precedence. Without proper security in place, the risk of misuse and other data breaches could be worse compared to the benefits. In doing so, this risks the violation of various dimensions of ethics by students. And innovation and responsibility in balance with each other provide safety and security for an AI-driven educational environment (salomon et.al,2012).

4.2 Fairness and Equity in AI-Driven Education

Artificial intelligence is the future of education: It will keep education more personalized and efficient, yet it raises serious questions about fairness and equity. AI-driven education relies upon algorithms and data-driven decision-making and ends up, very frequently, reinforcing biases, creating disparities, and limiting access for marginalized student. So, ensuring that AI-based educational tools keep it fair and inclusive is a necessity to equity in learning. For instance, face recognition technologies used in attendance tracking or behavioural analysis misclassify many students from their racial or ethnic groups with higher error rates, and thus are wrongly identified with such groups where they are also discriminated. Developers must teach the AI models with diversified and inclusive datasets to help minimize bias and offer equal opportunity to be fairly assessed among students.

Another challenge is the digital divide in the access of AI-based education to the students. This also means that AI-based learning tools usually demand a fast internet, new devices, and digital literacy skills. Learners who come from disadvantaged families or stay in remote areas or in schools with a low budget face

This would pose even more difficulties for access to these resources. As a consequence, education would become more polarized than more inclusive in nature. Governance must incur infrastructure investment, make affordable technology an avenue, and ensure every student enjoys AI-driven education beyond geographical backgrounds.

AI-driven assessments and recommendations limit students' potential at some points by making very rigid predictions regarding their abilities. The best suggestion that an AI system provides from analysing a student's performance for a career or an academic path will be mostly with limited data that does not count personal interest, creativity, and growth capacity. If an AI system miscalculates the potential of the student, then it can hamper that child's development from exploring different aspects of learning. This can be avoided by designing AI as a supporting tool rather than a decision-making tool, while human oversight would ensure that the students are not unfairly categorized or restricted in their learning choices.

Ethical AI governance and transparency is also necessary for fairness. Educational institutions and policymakers must be able to make clear guidelines for how AI systems are designed, tested, and implemented. It would be important for the students, parents, and the educators to be informed of how decisions are made by AI-based decisions. There should always be the provision for challenging or appealing an unfair AI assessment. AI can be responsibly used to better education without creating inequalities through the inclusion of transparency, accountability, and human supervision (Chinta et.al,2024).

While AI is capable of shifting the learning outcomes and efficiency, it has to be centred within fairness and equity in its development and application. In order to deal with the issues of bias, accessibility, and ethical oversight, AI-driven education can prove to be the most powerful instrument for inclusion, rather than a further accelerator of educational disparities.

4.3 Teacher-Student Ethical Boundaries with AI

With more deployment of artificial intelligence in schools, obviously comes the demand for more evident demarcations of where the teacher ceases and the student begins, and where the AI tool begins. This technology that enhances learning, automates clerical work, even personalizes education for individuals inspires anxieties around accountability, use of technology, and ethical choices by teachers and students within the interaction process. Unless regulated, AI would blur the roles of the more traditional functions. It could further compromise academic integrity and raise concerns about ethics in education.

The biggest concern is that reliance on AI becomes so extreme in teaching and assessment that AI would supplant the role of the teacher in critical thinking, mentorship, and emotional support. If the students rely highly on AI explanations, then there are chances to miss deeper discussions, creative problem-solving, and valuable insights from teachers. Additionally, feedback generated by AI lacks the emotional intelligence and subtle nature that a teacher provides in assessing students' work.

A teacher must always be an active guide to his or her students in such a manner that AI does not become the only teacher for him or her. The third ethical dilemma is the transparency of the AI-based decisions about grading and assessment. AI-based grading tools, for instance, automated essay grading tools scanning the patterns of the text to grade assignments; however, such systems fail to understand contexts, creativity, or subtle reasoning. If the student is wrongly graded by this AI because of an error caused by it, then who will take responsibility? Is it going to be the teacher's, developers', or the institutions? Human judgment needs to balance AI in grading. Schools should create policies allowing the appeal of assessments conducted by AI and also ensure teachers check and validate final grades for the students (Airaj, 2024).

The student-teacher relationship, too, will have to be treaded extremely carefully in the AI-based classroom. There cannot be a personal touch of communication if all communications are by AI-based tools such as chatbots or virtual assistants. Though AI will promptly answer the questions asked by the students instantly, AI cannot replace supportive mentorship, empathy, or encouragement that a human being is capable of rendering. Besides, once the same students will be interacting more with AI than with their teachers, then this traditional backbone of the support system in education is going to take a dent. Schools should be sure that the AI increases without substituting major interactions between their teachers and the students.

Finally, the greatest challenge is to maintain academic integrity in AI-supported learning. With help from homework assistants and AI-based writing tools, students may misuse technology to hand in assignments dishonestly. That call upon teachers to educate students on the ethical use of AI, encouraging them to use AI as a learning aid instead of cheating for their homework. Institutions should have policies involving AI-supported work, including honesty, originality, and responsible use of AI for education.

Achieving ethical bounds between the two in AI-led learning environments depends on how teachers and learners interact with the environment by bringing along technology as assistance, not substituting. That there must also be clarity through policies concerning how fair and open and responsibly made decisions will keep the essence, trust, and personal relationship alive in good-quality education (Guilherme, 2019).

5.THE FUTURE OF AI AND HUMAN TEACHERS

The future of AI and human teachers is cooperation, not competition. They would be working together in concert to produce better educational results. AI would be able to act as an auxiliary for the human teacher, thereby lessening some of the challenges of the traditional model. Human teachers will continue to play the emotional and mentoring role that guides critical thinking and creativity within the experience.

Perhaps one of the greatest advantages AI can provide for education is the delivery of personalized learning at scale. AI learns the strengths, weaknesses, learning pace, and preferences of students and delivers content that has been modified to fit their needs best. This enables human teachers to focus more on giving individualized support or intervention to certain students who may have specific needs for that process. In the future, AI can carry out repetitive and clerical work-like grading which, subsequently, will allow teachers to spend more time with direct interaction with students.

Data-Driven Insights: AI will collect and analyse large amounts of data to generate real-time insights into student performance and behaviour. Teachers can, therefore, look for patterns and track the development of each student to make informed decisions about what to do with each one. For instance, if a particular concept is posing a challenge for a student, AI can propose additional resources while the teacher may offer one-on-one guidance to better support that student in getting over the difficulty.

Improve teacher effectiveness: AI frees the human teacher from much administrative burden, which can be allocated to preparing better lessons, learning paths, and resources for every student. In a classroom, teachers will focus on building emotional and social skills, but AI can ease all the administrative hassles related to lesson planning and grading assessments to free up their time for imagination and interpersonal relationships.

Lifelong learning and teacher development: AI will support teachers in their professional development. AI may be used for tracking teachers' progress and making them aware of new methods of teaching, insights related to pedagogy, and more. AI-driven platforms can help teachers keep track of the latest trends in education and methodologies of learning, enabling them better to cope with an ever-changing educational environment.

Human-AI Collaboration: The future would most probably bring a combination and complementation of roles by AI and human teachers. Despite the fact that AI may do most of the work, there would always be human interaction to inspire the students. The role of a teacher in terms of fostering relationships, maintaining a good learning environment, and giving moral direction will always remain intact. AI will collaborate with them in accomplishing this, providing tools to make teaching more efficient and effective. This human-AI partnership can drive better outcomes for the students through combining the best of both worlds to deliver more personalized and engaging learning experiences that are comprehensive(Felix, 2020).

This might be crucial in regions that lack quality teaching or resources to support students to succeed academically. AI can fill such gaps by providing quality educational material as well as immediate feedback. However, such integration into the education sector must be done fairly; this is to ensure that all students, with any background or location, get equal and fair access to such facilities.

5.1 AI as a Supportive Tool Rather Than a Replacement

Artificial intelligence is revolutionizing education by making learning more personalized, automatically performing routine administrative tasks, and engaging students in higher numbers. AI must be viewed as a facilitator and not a replacement for human teachers because AI excels in processing data, recognizing patterns, and automating repetitive tasks but fails to deliver emotional intelligence, creativity, and mentorship, all of which are qualities provided by human teachers. Human-AI partnership is the best way to approach AI in education, where technology complements teaching but does not replace it.

The personalization of learning experience is perhaps one of the most significant contributions of AI towards education. AI-driven platforms analyse student performance and adapt content for individual learning needs. All such automation enables educators to focus more on the meat of education-to mentor students, foster creativity, and discuss meaningful topics. AI grading tools like Grade scope can grade multiple-choice quizzes and even written responses but cannot appreciate the subjective elements such as creativity, argumentation, and emotional depth in the student's work. Teachers need to stay involved in the assessment to ensure fairness and provide personalized feedback.

While AI grows in pace, human-to-human interaction is always a necessity in learning. Teachers are a lot more than the mere transfer of content; they encourage curiosity and emotional support sometimes; students lack motivation or anxiety/ anxiety issues that impact the act of learning. An AI system might be able to grasp a lapse in performance, but it cannot give the encouragement, mentorship, or empathetic response of a teacher, which is a requirement to ensure a student's sense of confidence, resilience, and well-being.

Moreover, AI systems do not have freedom from bias or error. As AI learns from history, there might be a chance of reaffirming the already available bias, resulting in biased reviews or recommendation. For instance, an AI career advice tool will propose all those professions that are popular based on historical trends, and not based on the potentials and desires of the student. Teachers are surely the only ones who can guarantee that all conclusions based on AI are fair. They base their judgment calls purely on experience and context. Hence, AI should act like information only, directing or informing the choice rather than actually deciding (Huang & Rust, 2018).

This must always be in a balance wherein the potential benefits of AI are maximized and education is not compromised. Schools and policymakers need to set up some guidelines on ethical use of AI, protection of the privacy of learners, and ensuring AI becomes a tool meant to supplement teachers, not replace them. This training for effective use of AI in teaching methods will be very essential for the future of education.

In conclusion, AI is so powerful for the betterment of education; however, it shouldn't replace the teacher instead complement him. The best educational system is the one where AI takes over the data-driven work, and teachers inspire, motivate, and connect personally with students in such a way that learning becomes meaningful, ethical, and student-centred.

5.2 Hybrid Models of Education

Blended learning is also known as hybrid education; it combines the classroom face-to-face instructions with AI-based digital tools to better facilitate, personalise, and effectively more flexibly carry on the learning process. This will enable students to retain the best of both human instruction and artificial intelligence worlds so that students have meaningful teacher-student interaction benefits from technology. Hybrid education is not a replacement but an enhancement of traditional ways to enable learning through AI-based platforms, virtual classrooms, and actual classrooms.

Another advantage of hybrid education is that it can offer the practice of tailoring learning according to a student's needs. Discussing the cycle of learning, AI-based learning platforms keep track of the performance of each student and tailor up the lessons to the student because every student would have learnt at her or his own pace. For instance, the adaptive learning systems are Dream Box, Coursera, and Edmodo. These provide the students with exercises based on their strength and weakness. This creates the opportunity for mentors and more effective guidance to teachers, but AI takes on routine assessments and the delivery of the content. Hybrid models make sure that students who need individualized guidance are given more, while advanced learners learn more challenging material.

Hybrid education has other advantages in terms of flexibility and accessibility. The students can access e-learning materials, recorded lectures, and AI tutoring at any moment from anywhere on earth. Especially for the students who live far away, those with a disability, or for people whose education takes place along with other responsibilities. For example, using Google Classroom, Microsoft Teams, and AI chatbots, students can communicate with their teacher, upload assignments, and receive feedback. In this manner, learning is not confined to the physical classroom and opportunities for continuous engagement exist.

Hybrid models also make learning collaborative and interactive. AI can allow for a group of students to take up a group project, simulations, or even virtual experiments and ensure that the class is active all the time. Kahoot! and Quizlet are some of the AI systems that turn learning into fun activities. AI language models are supportive in group discussions, and support students on whatever questions they pose, making things clear to students instantly. As such, with large classes, students will never disengage.

But with hybrid education, there is always a challenge, for instance, equal access to technology. The digital divide is still an issue because most students do not have access to high-speed internet or modern devices. Schools and governments must invest in digital infrastructure to prevent such disparities in education. This must be taught to teachers to employ AI tools with effectiveness in teaching their subjects not to be automation-dependent. Triumph of hybrid learning is in the importance of instruction driven by AI and human mentorship.

Hybrid education is the future of learning. It presents a balanced approach combining the efficiency of technology with the human touch of traditional teaching. AI is considered an augmentative tool rather than a replacement of it, and thus allows for an interesting, inclusive, and personalized educational experience in a hybrid model. Success will lie in using AI to enhance and expand the central, basic role of teachers such that students have both technological innovation and meaningful human interaction as a part of learning (Shenet.al,2022).

Figure 2. Moving to a Hybrid Learning Model

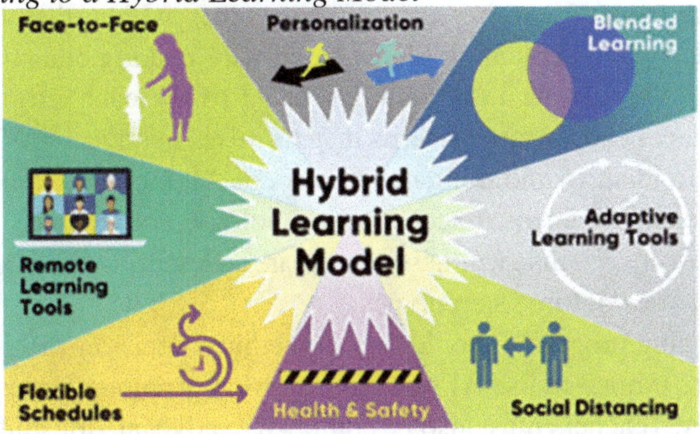

5.3 Training the Next Generation of AI-Ready Teachers

As artificial intelligence sets the future scene of education in place, this also raises greater needs for developing teachers who become ready to operate and use modern advanced technologies at a teaching skill level. For AI to positively impact the classroom, teachers need to be ready not only to use these tools but also to understand their implications, manage their ethical use, and find a balance between AI-driven instruction and human interaction. The preparation of the next generation of educators requires a shift in teacher training programs to include AI literacy, technology integration, and ethical considerations. One of the first steps in training AI-ready teachers is to build AI literacy.

Teachers need to understand the capabilities, limitations, and ethical concerns of AI technologies. This includes familiarizing themselves with how AI tools can assist with grading, personalizing learning, automating administrative tasks, and enhancing student engagement. In terms of AI basics, future teachers should receive some courses or workshops on it to learn about the nature and design of the system, the possible applications and tools in their own classrooms, and how these could be best applied to their own teaching practice. Building the necessary AI literacy for teachers is empowering them with making informed judgments when and how they should effectively utilize AI. Besides technical skills, teachers must develop digital fluency that is, the ability to use digital tools and AI-driven systems efficiently in teaching. This also means familiarity with online learning platforms, adaptive learning technologies, and AI-powered tools like virtual assistants or intelligent tutoring systems.

Programs include practical experience or the time they can take using these tools while teaching and other experiences with one's peers by designing lessons through AI, determining student learning as well using other AI-based techniques. They ought to troubleshoot technical problems along with making ethical, efficient and unbiased use of AI tools. An important part of AI-ready teacher training is understanding the ethical and equity concerns that AI raises in education. Teachers need to be prepared to identify and mitigate the risks of AI, including algorithmic bias, privacy violations, and unequal access to technology. For instance, AI tools may inadvertently Favor certain learning styles, create accessibility barriers for students with disabilities, or reinforce stereotypes.

Teacher training programs should focus on ethical decision-making and ensure that teachers are trained to use AI tools in ways that promote fairness, inclusivity, and data privacy. Teachers must also be equipped to advocate for student rights and privacy, ensuring that AI systems adhere to ethical standards and protect student information. Collaboration between AI experts, educators, and policymakers is essential for a sustainable model of AI integration in education. It should also give teachers an opportunity to join ongoing professional development programs. Such programs help them to interact with the developers of AI

tools and provide immediate feedback on how to improve AI. They keep them updated about educational technology trends. Through these, the designers of AI tools will be aware of the educators needs and should consider their opinions when implementing AI in classrooms. Another essential emphasis in preparing AI-ready teachers is to establish the ability to retain the human touch of learning.

Even though AI can assist with administrative tasks and personalized learning, the social-emotional skills that help teach, mentor, empathize, and improve well-being cannot be substituted by AI. Teachers should be trained to use AI tools in ways that advance their roles as mentors and guides, through emotional support, critical thinking development, and creativity in students. In other words, AI should not compete with the teacher's role but supplement it. Finally, training AI-ready teachers is the surest way to ensure that artificial intelligence is effectively used responsibly and ethically (Guan et al, 2025).

Equipping teachers with the skills, knowledge, and ethical frameworks will allow us to build a future where AI is a powerful ally in the classroom—enhancing, rather than replacing, the human connection that is at the heart of education. Schools, teacher training institutions, and policymakers must work together to provide comprehensive professional development that prepares teachers for the AI-driven classroom of tomorrow.

6.CONCLUSION

AI teachers will at least change the face of education, but definitely, they won't replace human teachers in the near future. The AI system may offer more customized learning and adaptive feedback; it is also available 24/7. However, the human teacher owns emotional intelligence, creativity, and the capacity for social and emotional development. Indeed, AI can be a great supplement to traditional methods of teaching, for example, in administrations, personalized instruction, or analysing data, yet the role of human teachers remains vital and indispensable for building connections, developing critical thinking skills, and mentorship.

Therefore, it would be appropriate to conclude that AI teachers would supplement and strengthen the education system instead of replacing the human educator totally, especially in areas that are concerned with empathy, finer judgment, and development of interpersonal skills. AI has much future in revolutionizing education for personalized learning, adaptive feedback, and constant availability; definitely, it cannot replace the role of a human teacher indispensable to the future.

AI is good at providing administrative support, data analysis and providing individualized learning but weak in emotional intelligence, creativity and social and emotional development, all of which human teachers inherently have. Teachers play a significant role in connecting students to themselves, taking them through problem areas, and teaching essential skills in a classroom as important as critical thinking and empathy. It is possible that AI may increase learning in any other specific field apart from the supplementation of meaningful teaching. Still, at last, the human element of teaching remains paramount for the formation of an environment that is intellectual as well as one of personal growth. This is why AI should complement the human teacher rather than replace the human teacher for technology to illuminate the human sense of education rather than darken it. The potential of AI has thus far been measured in contrast to the uniqueness that human trainers give to the future of education.

REFERENCES

Airaj, M. (2024). Ethical artificial intelligence for teaching-learning in higher education. *Education and Information Technologies*, ●●●, 1–23.

Chinta, S. V., Wang, Z., Yin, Z., Hoang, N., Gonzalez, M., Quy, T. L., & Zhang, W. (2024). FairAIED: Navigating fairness, bias, and ethics in educational AI applications. *arXiv preprint arXiv:2407.18745*.

Felix, C. V. (2020). The role of the teacher and AI in education. In *International perspectives on the role of technology in humanizing higher education* (pp. 33–48). Emerald Publishing Limited.

Guan, L., Zhang, Y., & Gu, M. M. (2025). Pre-service teachers preparedness for AI-integrated education: An investigation from perceptions, capabilities, and teachers' identity changes. *Computers and Education: Artificial Intelligence*, *8*, 100341.

Guilherme, A. (2019). AI and education: The importance of teacher and student relations. *AI & Society*, *34*, 47–54.

Huang, M. H., & Rust, R. T. (2018). Artificial intelligence in service. *Journal of Service Research*, *21*(2), 155–172.

Klimova, B., Pikhart, M., & Kacetl, J. (2023). Ethical issues of the use of AI-driven mobile apps for education. *Frontiers in Public Health*, *10*, 1118116.

Leach, L. (2016). Enhancing student engagement in one institution. *Journal of Further and Higher Education*, *40*(1), 23–47.

Pedro, F., Subosa, M., Rivas, A., & Valverde, P. (2019). Artificial intelligence in education: Challenges and opportunities for sustainable development.

Peters, H., Zdravkovic, M., João Costa, M., Celenza, A., Ghias, K., Klamen, D., & Weggemans, M. (2019). Twelve tips for enhancing student engagement. *Medical Teacher*, *41*(6), 632–637.

Pokrivcakova, S. (2019). Preparing teachers for the application of AI-powered technologies in foreign language education. *Journal of Language and Cultural Education*, *7*(3), 135–153.

Salomon, D. (2012). *Data privacy and security*. Springer Science & Business Media.

Shen, Y., & Shao, W. (2022). Influence of hybrid pedagogical models on learning outcomes in physical education: A systematic literature review. *International Journal of Environmental Research and Public Health*, *19*(15), 9673.

Tian, Y. (2023). Limitations and Advancements of AI Teachers in Classroom Instruction. *Education and Teaching Research*, *3*, 66–72.

Willis, M., Duckworth, P., Coulter, A., Meyer, E. T., & Osborne, M. (2020). Qualitative and quantitative approach to assess the potential for automating administrative tasks in general practice. *BMJ Open*, *10*(6), e032412.

Zaman, B. U. (2023). Transforming education through ai, benefits, risks, and ethical considerations. *Authorea Preprints*.

Zhai, X., Chu, X., Chai, C. S., Jong, M. S. Y., Istenic, A., Spector, M., & Li, Y. (2021). A Review of Artificial Intelligence (AI) in Education from 2010 to 2020. *Complexity*, *2021*(1), 8812542.

Chapter 7
Artificial Intelligence (AI) Integration and Higher Education Faculty:
Tools, Ethics, Challenges, and Pedagogical Insights

Joshua Williams
https://orcid.org/0000-0002-6525-1607
Saint Peter's University, USA

Nicole Luongo
https://orcid.org/0000-0002-1225-8426
Saint Peter's University, USA

Michael Finetti
Saint Peter's University, USA

Jay Garrels
https://orcid.org/0009-0002-5213-6949
Saint Peter's University, USA

ABSTRACT

This chapter examines the increasing role of Artificial Intelligence (AI) in higher education, focusing on its integration, implementation strategies, and the ethical challenges that arise. It provides insights into how generative AI (GenAI) tools and large language models (LLMs) can be used effectively in classrooms, offering educators and administrators practical guidance for navigating this evolving landscape. The chapter also highlights potential future developments of AI in higher education

DOI: 10.4018/979-8-3373-0396-3.ch007

and explores professional development opportunities to help institutions adapt. By addressing both the benefits and challenges of AI, the chapter aims to empower higher education professionals with the knowledge and tools needed to use AI to enhance teaching, learning, and overall educational experiences. Ultimately, it provides a guide for effectively incorporating AI to support and transform educational practices.

INTRODUCTION

Do not surrender to the robot overlords just yet. Keep in mind that for all the hype and buzz, these AI tools are just computer systems. They can go wrong. They are created by humans. Their values are shaped by companies and institutions. Their data is not neutral but is defined by the historical patterns. Be cautious and thoughtful about what you are doing with artificial intelligence, and remember: it's not magic (Zeide, 2019, p. 39).

Recently, the use of Artificial Intelligence (AI) tools and applications has become more prevalent in higher education. This chapter focuses on the background of artificial intelligence (AI), emphasizing implementation strategies while addressing the ethical considerations and current challenges associated with its integration in the higher education classroom. GenAI creates unique outputs through algorithms that frequently resemble human interaction. Large Language Models (LLMs), such as ChatGPT, which are intended to comprehend and produce human language, are also covered in this chapter.

The use of computer systems that can execute tasks that typically require human intelligence is referred to as artificial intelligence (AI). Users can produce personalized content with GenAI tools such as Gemini (Google), Copilot (Microsoft), and ChatGPT (OpenAI). Large Language Models (LLMs), which produce logical text and carry out intricate language-based tasks, power many of these tools. ChatGPT, Bard (Google), Llama (Meta), and Copilot are a few examples that provide educators with effective tools to improve instruction and learning.

In this chapter, there is a discussion of the possible future directions of AI tools in higher education settings. Professional development options for higher education institutions are introduced. Furthermore, the chapter aims to provide information that helps higher education instructors and administrators navigate the landscape of AI in their courses. The discussion includes how project-based and experiential learning, rooted in constructivism, can enable students to actively build knowledge through real-world problem-solving and application. The mission of this chapter is to provide an overview of AI in higher education by presenting background information, ethical considerations, and current challenges, while emphasizing practical strategies for its classroom implementation.

This chapter's main goal is to investigate the use of AI tools in higher education and how they affect teaching strategies, faculty duties, and student learning outcomes. AI-driven technologies are being used more often to improve administrative workflows, boost instructional effectiveness, and give students individualized support. Faculty must adjust to new pedagogical approaches as a result of these innovations, which mark a paradigm shift in education. As GenAI takes on more responsibility for automating administrative tasks and content delivery, the traditional roles of educators are changing, and faculty members must concentrate on honing their critical thinking abilities, ethical considerations, and the human elements of learning that AI cannot replace (Kim et al., 2025).

BACKGROUND

Artificial intelligence (AI) has transitioned from a theoretical concept to a transformative force, altering the way labor and reasoning are conducted across multiple industries, including higher education. Recent developments in AI have drastically altered the way teachers and students interact by enabling personalized learning experiences across a variety of academic domains. Newer AI applications involve machine learning, adaptive learning models, natural language processing, and immersive educational technologies (Zhang & Aslan, 2021). In addition to giving students a more individualized education, this evolution is also simplifying faculty preparation and administrative tasks. AI is now a key component of institutional digital transformation initiatives, which affects how education is communicated and evaluated.

Yet, AI is different from other technology tools as it is impossible to ignore. The seamless integration of AI into everyone's lives is demonstrated by the fact that virtual assistants driven by AI, such as Siri and Alexa, have become an essential part of everyday routines, helping with everything from reminders to managing smart home appliances. The same is true in higher education, where AI is increasingly becoming a fundamental part of daily life. Hodges and Ocak (2023) asserted,

Higher education institutions—recently rocked by the COVID-19 pandemic and fearing the effects of the enrollment cliff—are now faced with a new disruption: generative AI. Colleges and universities have generally been slow to adopt change. In the not-so-distant past, other technological tools have been met with consternation in the classroom setting. For example, calculators were banned from classrooms, and Wikipedia was considered an unreliable source to avoid. And while calculators and Wikipedia may not be fully integrated into every classroom, they do not draw the same ire as they did in the past. Generative AI is different from these innovations. AI is not a device that can be banned, it is not a source that students can be instructed not to use, and its use cannot be discovered with crude plagiarism detection tools. This new technology will be difficult to avoid (para. 5).

The recently released EDUCAUSE AI Landscape Study (Robert, 2024) offered an in-depth analysis of how higher education institutions are adapting to the swift adoption and integration of AI tools. The preliminary study highlighted the vital need for ethical and transparent AI practices in all applications, based on responses from participants in almost 900 schools. According to the study, AI is most significantly affecting laws pertaining to technology, cybersecurity, data privacy, and teaching and learning. 95% of respondents specifically stated that AI has "already impacted" or is "soon to be impacted" in policies related to teaching and learning, compared to 79% for technology policies and 72% for cybersecurity and data privacy policies.

AI's capacity to process vast volumes of data, automate repetitive tasks, and give instructors and students immediate feedback is what is propelling its development in higher education. Course management, academic advising, learning analytics, and curriculum design are just a few of the specific fields that are rapidly using AI-powered solutions (Southworth et al., 2023). This technological advancement can enable faculty members to devote more of their time to research and pedagogical innovation, and institutions can use AI-driven decision-making processes to improve administrative and operational procedures. Furthermore, AI also makes academic resources more accessible, allowing institutions to take a closer look at how prepared they are to support their growing role in higher education.

Institutional Readiness

Institutional readiness is a current motivator for AI-related strategic planning in higher education, according to the EDUCAUSE AI Landscape Study (Robert, 2024). Due to students' increasing use of AI, educational institutions are concentrating on their capacity to successfully implement AI tools. In particular, 73% of the EDUCAUSE AI Landscape Study participants cited the growing use of AI in the classroom as a primary motivator to learn more, 68% expressed concern about the dangers of improper AI use, and 59% expressed concern about falling behind in the adoption of AI. These findings highlight the importance of institutions being ready to integrate AI to stay competitive and promote effective use of AI in instruction.

The adoption of AI in higher education warrants strong institutional governance and faculty support. Universities that successfully implement AI-based solutions improve their operational efficiencies, strengthen their student engagement strategies, and become more globally competitive (Kim et al., 2025). AI-powered chatbots, for example, are making student support services easier to use, allowing educational institutions to assist students while freeing up teachers and staff from administrative tasks. A chatbot is AI software created to help users engage with content through conversational interfaces. It can offer explanations, respond to questions, provide summaries, guide users through processes, and facilitate interactive learning experiences. Some examples of chatbots in higher education could enhance student support, provide personalized learning, assist with academic advising, and automate registration. Institutions can set up AI governance frameworks that provide precise guidelines for academic integrity, data privacy, and AI deployment. To guarantee compatibility with institutional goals and best practices in education, faculty involvement should be incorporated into these frameworks (Castillo-Martínez et al., 2024).

Student Support Systems

Another role of GenAI among students is its application to virtually support them throughout their academic pursuits. Virtual chatbots and AI assistants can provide real-time academic guidance to students, helping guide them through course registration and career advising. For students who desire immediate answers and do not have easy access to instructors or administration, these solutions offer accessibility. AI-powered mental health applications are being developed to help students with their mental health by providing personalized coping mechanisms and directing them to the university counseling office (Southworth et al., 2023).

A NEW LANDSCAPE IN HIGHER EDUCATION

As institutions adapt to rapid technological change, AI is reshaping the core structures of higher education. This section explores the evolution of AI in higher education.

Evolution of AI in Higher Education

Through the introduction of new teaching methods that promote interactive and data-driven learning environments, AI is transforming higher education. The use of AI in education should be based on effective teaching methodologies, such as project-based learning (PBL). Zheng et al. (2024) defined project-based learning (PBL) as a student-centered approach grounded in constructivist theory and assuring that knowledge is actively constructed by students via practical experiences. PBL students work on AI-enhanced projects, producing tangible products, as opposed to passively absorbing knowledge. AI in PBL is also beneficial for learning general skills and for promoting self-directed and adaptive learning (Ruiz Viruel et al., 2025).

Institutions are able to provide students with a more personalized educational experience because of AI-driven course suggestion systems, intelligent tutoring programs, and automated evaluation tools (Zhang & Aslan, 2021). While guaranteeing that students accomplish the required learning objectives, AI-based educational models can design adaptive learning pathways that let them understand difficult subjects at their own pace. Salinas-Navarro et al. (2024) explained that higher education supports pedagogical approaches that take into account real-world situations and create experiential learning opportunities for their future professional careers. AI can provide targeted feedback during this process by identifying areas for development and suggested learning techniques, assisting students in recognizing their strengths and shortcomings, and creating productive study habits (Alqahtani et al., 2023).

Evidence from a systematic review by Lin et al. (2023) suggests that blended learning environments, which combine traditional instruction with AI-driven virtual assistants, have demonstrated encouraging outcomes in terms of increased student involvement and comprehension. To make learning more engaging and accessible, AI chatbots and discussion facilitators are being utilized to respond to student questions and provide immediate feedback. Furthermore, AI-generated analytics help educators assess which teaching strategies are most effective, allowing them to revise and elevate their approaches based on real-time data (Southworth et al., 2023).

Impact on Faculty Workload

Within the context of this chapter, reducing faculty workload is one of the most important uses of GenAI in higher education. According to Rahman et al. (2024), faculty burnout and stress have increased in the post-COVID-19 environment, leading to educators seeking technological solutions that enhance productivity. AI-powered tools facilitate task automation, including grading, content generation, and curriculum adaptation, enabling instructors to allocate more time to student engagement and mentorship.

GenAI platforms for grading cut down on the amount of time needed to evaluate tests, especially in big classes with demanding schedules. AI-generated feedback systems, plagiarism detection software, and automated essay scoring tools give students answers while freeing up teachers to concentrate on individualized interventions. Additionally, by examining patterns in student performance and anticipating areas in which students could struggle, AI-driven curriculum design tools help teachers produce more interesting and pertinent coursework (Castillo-Martínez et al., 2024).

Despite these benefits, faculty members may initially be reluctant to embrace AI because they fear it would depersonalize instruction. To make sure that AI complements faculty contributions rather than takes their place, a balanced strategy that incorporates AI while maintaining the human element of training is required. Institutions ought to actively assist teachers by offering instruction on how to successfully integrate AI tools without sacrificing pedagogical objectives and academic integrity (Al-Zahrani, 2024; Kim et al., 2022).

Enhancing Student Learning Outcomes

Students can obtain individualized educational experiences based on their unique needs because of GenAI's capacity to personalize training. Analytics powered by AI monitors students' development and modifies course materials to accommodate their varying learning styles. This enables educators to use research-proven teaching techniques that improve comprehension, retention, and student engagement (Lin et al., 2023; Kim et al., 2025). However, the capacity and willingness of the faculty to successfully incorporate AI tools into their teaching techniques will determine how beneficial these strategies are.

While pushing higher-achieving students through increasingly difficult content, AI-powered personalized learning platforms can suggest extra resources for students who are having difficulty. By giving them access to automated tutoring, AI-generated explanations, and real-time feedback on their academic achievement, these intelligent solutions also empower students to take charge of their education (Southworth et al., 2023). In higher education, AI-supported gamification strategies have also become popular, improving student engagement and making learning sessions more interesting (Kim et al., 2022).

GenAI and LLMs have also improved accessibility and language acquisition in higher education. International students and others with disabilities can now access education more easily thanks to AI-powered translation tools and speech recognition software. While AI-generated transcripts and captions make online courses more inclusive, voice-assisted AI can help students who are visually impaired. Universities can increase their reach and guarantee fair educational opportunities for all students by utilizing AI-driven accessibility solutions (Zhang & Aslan, 2021).

ARTIFICIAL INTELLIGENCE (AI) TOOL INTEGRATION IN HIGHER EDUCATION

With its impact on almost every facet of teaching, learning, and administration, AI has emerged as a crucial element of contemporary higher education. Both virtual and physical classrooms are rapidly incorporating AI techniques to boost student engagement, optimize staff workload, and improve the quality of instruction. AI is offering creative solutions that enable educational institutions to scale individualized education while preserving instructional efficacy, ranging from AI-powered grading systems to intelligent tutoring platforms and predictive analytics (Castillo-

Martínez et al., 2024; Heaps, 2024; Lin et al., 2023). There are many GenAI tools available that educators can use in the classroom. The use of AI tools in teaching and assessment will be the focal point of this section.

Current AI Tools (General)

While there is a growing landscape of AI tools tailored specifically for higher education, this chapter will focus on a few general AI chatbots and LLMs that are adaptable, multifunctional, and have valuable applications in a variety of academic contexts. Table 1 provides a comprehensive overview of all AI tools covered in this chapter for easy reference. Important features, such as the tool's primary educational purposes and its main application in teaching and learning, are highlighted in this table. For educators looking to make well-informed decisions about incorporating AI into their teaching practices, Table 1 provides a solid framework.

Table 1. Common Artificial Intelligence Tools and Their Applications

Tool Name	Primary Educational Function	Primary Use in Teaching & Learning	Primary Use(s)
ChatGPT https://chatgpt.com/	Content generation and tutoring	Generates human-like responses to questions; assists with writing, brainstorming, and summarization	Educators, Learners
Gemini https://gemini.google.com/	Personalized instruction and multimedia interaction	Identifies learning gaps; customizes instruction using text, image, audio, and video inputs	Educators, Learners
Grok https://x.ai	Conversational learning and engagement	Summarizes material, answers queries, and promotes informal learning through dialogue	Learners, Educators
Copilot https://copilot.microsoft.com/	Coding and productivity enhancement	Offers code suggestions, generates documentation, integrates with Microsoft Office tools	Educators, Administrators, Learners (especially in STEM fields)
Perplexity https://www.perplexity.ai/	Information literacy and research	Provides accurate, cited responses; supports source evaluation and research synthesis	Educators, Learners

Note. This table summarizes popular artificial intelligence tools and their educational uses. Tool websites are included beneath the tool names.

Current AI Tools (Instruction & Assessment)

In addition to general generative AI tools and LLMs, a range of AI-driven instructional and assessment tools are reshaping how instructors in higher education evaluate student performance. These tools provide capabilities such as automated grading, personalized feedback, and data-driven insights, all of which enhance the assessment process and enable more efficient monitoring of student progress. A thorough summary of various AI assessment tools and their real-world uses in higher education is provided in Table 2. It describes the main objective of each tool, its noteworthy characteristics and capabilities, and the advantages and drawbacks for users.

Table 2. Artificial Intelligence Assessment Tools and Their Practical Applications in Higher Education

AI Tool	Primary Use	Key Features & Functions	User Benefits	Limitations / Notes
Gradescope https://www.gradescope.com	Grading & Assessment Management	Assists grading, rubric development, detailed analytics for grading consistency and accuracy	Significantly reduces grading time; helps maintain grading consistency and accuracy	Requires initial setup time and learning to use all features effectively
Grammarly https://www.grammarly.com	Writing Improvement	Grammar checks, tone adjustments, plagiarism detection, broad language tools	Improves writing clarity and effectiveness for academic, professional, and personal use	Free version offers basic grammar; paid subscription needed for advanced features like tone detection and plagiarism
Magic School AI https://www.magicschool.ai	Lesson Planning & Student Assessment	Rubric generators, automated report card comments, test/quiz design, worksheet creation, instant assessment analysis	Saves teachers' time; supports student personalized feedback, customized practice worksheets	Basic version free; full features require paid plan
Khanmigo (Khan Academy) https://www.khanmigo.ai/	AI Teaching Assistant & Tutor	Supports student problem-solving, integrated with Khan Academy content library (math, coding, humanities, social studies)	Engages students efficiently; lightens teacher workload by aiding differentiation, lesson planning	Developed by nonprofit Khan Academy; unique full content integration

continued on following page

Table 2. Continued

AI Tool	Primary Use	Key Features & Functions	User Benefits	Limitations / Notes
Notebook LM https://notebooklm.google/	Research & Note-Taking	Uploads PDFs, websites, videos; auto-generates summaries, FAQs, timelines, mind maps, briefing docs, citation-backed insights; podcast-style audio overviews	Facilitates rapid info processing; ideal for auditory learners; organizes large data efficiently	Requires document uploads; audio overview is downloadable
Brisk Teaching https://www.briskteaching.com/	Curriculum & Instruction Automation	Creates curriculum materials, tailors feedback, analyzes student writing, plans lessons; modifies reading levels for differentiation	Automates instructional tasks; reduces teacher admin burden; supports individualized learning	Integrates 30+ AI technologies; practical for modern teaching
Turnitin https://www.turnitin.com/	Plagiarism & AI Content Detection	Detects plagiarism via large database; AI-generated content detection (ChatGPT); introduced "Turnitin Clarity" for responsible AI use	Widely used in higher ed; supports academic integrity; helps faculty monitor AI usage	AI detection accuracy <80%; some false positives possible; concerns about reliability remain

Note. This table summarizes popular artificial intelligence assessment tools and their practical applications in higher education. Assessment tool websites are included beneath the tool names.

With the use of these AI-powered tools, teachers may create student-centered courses that integrate data-driven decision-making and real-time feedback (Kim et al., 2022). In order to improve course content depending on student performance indicators, faculty can use AI-driven analytics to identify the most successful teaching tactics, such as designing quizzes, evaluations, or recommending course objectives that align with learning outcomes. Furthermore, instructors are increasingly utilizing AI technologies such as ChatGPT, Copilot, Gemini, Perplexity, and Grok to generate content and instructional tasks. Due to their sophisticated natural language processing and content production features, ChatGPT-4 and Gemini are the most popular of these, and ChatGPT-4 is regarded as the most well-known LLM (Imran & Almusharraf, 2024). At one point, Gemini and Perplexity had an advantage and higher efficiency in generating audio, visual, and video data simultaneously; however, today, ChatGPT-4o is among the most capable of the LLMs using a multi-modal model (Imran & Almusharraf, 2024)

Faculty Support

Although student learning is the main topic of conversation when it comes to AI in education, faculty support is also greatly impacted by AI. Virtual assistants with GenAI capabilities aid teachers with administrative duties like setting up office hours, answering questions from students, and arranging course materials (Ofosu-Ampong, 2024). AI frees up faculty time for research, mentoring, and one-on-one student interaction by automating these time-consuming tasks.

Academic Advising

Another area of increasing interest is academic guidance enhanced by AI. In order to deliver tailored suggestions, AI-powered advising systems examine students' academic records, course histories, and career objectives. By identifying students who could be at risk of slipping behind, these technologies can notify academic advisors before problems get out of hand. Institutions can improve student retention rates and overall academic success by using predictive analytics to help them create focused intervention plans (Castillo-Martínez et al., 2024).

Research and Data Analytics

AI is transforming academic research outside of the classroom, too. Researchers can process massive information, spot trends, and produce insights at previously unheard-of speeds with the use of AI-powered data analytics tools (Lin et al., 2023). Semantic search engines and other AI-driven literature review tools make it possible for researchers to quickly uncover and compile pertinent research findings. For instance, Gemini and Perplexity improve research efficiency by highlighting scholarly articles, locating important details, and even recommending related studies.

Institutional Integration with Learning Management Systems

AI is improving LMS functionality in a number of areas, and they are essential to contemporary higher education. Machine learning is used by AI-powered LMS platforms to automate administrative activities, forecast student success, and improve course delivery. Faculty can identify at-risk students and modify their teaching methods by using these systems, which give them real-time data on student engagement levels (Southworth et al., 2023; Mallik & Gangopadhyay, 2023).

Intelligent chatbot integration is one of the most exciting GenAI developments in LMS platforms. These chatbots help students by resolving common queries, assisting them with course materials, and resolving technical difficulties. AI-driven chatbots reduce the workload for faculty while increasing students' access to course materials (Zhang & Aslan, 2021). Additionally, every new AI model is being incorporated into LMS to provide students with contextual support in real time based on ongoing class discussions and tasks.

ADVANTAGES OF IMPLEMENTING AI IN HIGHER EDUCATION

AI integration in higher education offers several advantages, including personalizing teaching and learning experiences and enhancing assessment practices, along with assisting instructors and administrators with administrative tasks. In fact,

A recent EDUCAUSE QuickPoll survey of higher education stakeholders provides insights into the interest and perhaps inevitability of AI integration in day-to-day institutional work. Most of the respondents (83%) believe that "generative AI will profoundly change higher education in the next three to five years," and 65 percent believe "the use of generative AI in higher ed has more benefits than drawbacks" (Hodges & Ocak, 2023, para. 5).

The use of AI tools in higher education can enhance teaching and learning by supporting the creation of instructional materials, providing personalized feedback, aiding student assessment, and improving communication (Trust et al., 2023).

Personalized Teaching and Learning Uses

One of AI's most important contributions to higher education is personalized learning. AI uses adaptive learning platforms to tailor learning experiences according to students' skill levels, learning styles, and pace (Lin et al., 2023). Lesson plans and recommended resources are adjusted as needed by these AI-powered systems, which collect and analyze data on student performance to inform their updates. Alqahtani et al. (2023) assert that, "AI helps develop individualized learning plans, taking into consideration each student's learning style, interests, and objectives, which keeps students motivated and engaged, leading to better academic results" (p. 1237).

For instance, outside of the classroom, students can receive tailored teaching from AI-powered intelligent tutoring systems. These systems respond to inquiries from students, produce explanations, and offer detailed instructions in challenging areas like physics and math using natural language processing. AI-based tutors, in contrast to traditional tutors, are accessible around the clock, guaranteeing that pupils get prompt academic assistance when they require it (Lin et al., 2023). For instance, Perplexity enables students to investigate ideas with referenced citations for increased accuracy and depth, while ChatGPT-4 and Grok function as AI tutors that can produce explanations across disciplines. According to research, ChatGPT continues to be the most popular AI tool among instructors and students, offering a wide range of features for both autonomous and coursework learning (Ofosu-Ampong, 2024).

Instructors can use GenAI tools and LLMs to design content and adapt instructional methods to meet the individual needs of students. This tailored approach benefits all facets of learning outcomes, student engagement, and different learning styles. For example, Celik et al. (2022) explained that, "AI can enable teachers to select or adapt the optimum learning activity based on AI feedback" (p. 622). Furthermore, teachers can use AI to decide on the suitability of learning content when deciding on students' proficiency and needs. The authors provided an example where teachers decided to implement exercises such as writing letters and numbers for students with a low graphomotor level based on the feedback they received from AI. AI may improve the adaptability of resources to students' strengths and needs. They also discovered that AI may provide support and improve teaching jobs using automated assistants or other AI tools. Plus, AI can enable teachers to extend the support they offer to students when they run out of time. Finally, AI can enable greater customizability of curricular resources to meet specific teacher and student needs.

Zheng et al. (2024) disclosed that students suggested ways they would like to incorporate AI into their PBL-based learning. The study's participants favored the use of AI for learning guidance, feedback, automation of repetitive tasks, and creative thinking. Students' views on the function of AI were also noted by Zheng et al., and each of these had a major impact on how participants interpreted and framed data on AI usage. These included AI as an expert, AI as a teammate, and AI as a tool. Similarly, Ruiz Viruel et al. (2025) found that educators have a favorable opinion of AI in the context of PBL, as they perceive its potential to enhance productivity and facilitate the development of pedagogical models optimized for AI.

Additionally, AI makes competency-based education possible, which lets students complete assignments at their own speed. This approach aligns with experiential learning theory, which emphasizes learning through direct experience and reflection, as it gives students the flexibility to revisit and master foundational concepts before advancing to more complex topics (Salinas-Navarro et al., 2024). This paradigm is especially helpful for non-traditional learners who might need more flexible learning schedules, such as working professionals and adult learners (Rahman et al., 2024). AI-generated learning pathways offer tailored suggestions to make sure students grasp the fundamentals before moving on to more difficult subjects.

Bates (2022) explained that AI could generate courses and programs on a wide range of topics in a wide range of subject disciplines as effectively, if not more effectively, than human teachers. Also, AI applications have the ability to provide guidance to learners through chatbots and automated feedback, as well as to assess students. Heaps (2024) added that AI can be used to produce custom images or videos for courses or lessons; it can aid in converting text or audio content into a format such as a comic or animation. According to Celik et al. (2022), AI can also make the process more interesting for teachers. They found that AI-tutors facilitated enjoyable teaching experiences for them by breaking the monotony in the classroom. In addition to providing personalized learning options for students, AI in higher education can provide instructors with access to teaching and learning resources they may not have had in the past.

Research has shown that GenAI and LLMs can be valuable tools for instructors when planning course activities. By using AI, educators gain access to a wider range of resources and materials that may have previously been unavailable to them. Trust et al. (2023) claimed that AI tools such as Chat GPT can help instructors with writing course syllabi, lesson plans, classroom rules and policies, learning objectives, directions for learning activities, discussion prompts, mini-lecture presentation scripts, and tips for classroom management. AI can also help with student assessments, including creating test questions and quizzes, grading rubrics, and student progress reports.

Assessment and Feedback Mechanisms

Balanced assessment is another significant benefit of AI-driven systems. Conventional assessment techniques often employ static, one-size-fits-all exams that fail to account for students' diverse learning needs. This is being transformed by AI-driven assessment models, which enable dynamic, real-time assessments that adapt to each student's individual development. These artificial intelligence grading tools are able to evaluate student responses, spot trends in their mistakes, and offer quick, tailored feedback (Ofosu-Ampong, 2024; Southworth et al., 2023). Alqahtani et al. (2023) described,

Several advantages could be associated with using these technologies in grading and assessment. First, it can save educators significant time and effort compared to traditional manual grading. Second, AI grading can be more consistent and systematic, with no impact of fatigue, unlike human grading, thus, helping to reduce subjectivity and bias. Third, AI grading is much faster than manual grading, which can help educators to provide feedback to students more quickly, allowing them to spend more time on other important tasks. Fourth, AI can analyze data on student performance and provide insights into areas where students may be struggling or excelling (p. 1237).

AI is improving formative assessment methods beyond grading by examining how students engage with traditional learning management systems (LMS), such as Blackboard, Brightspace, and Canvas. AI is able to identify when pupils are having trouble with particular ideas and offer suggestions for further resources or focused interventions in real time. With the use of this technology, teachers may start assessing students proactively rather than reactively, spotting knowledge gaps before they become serious obstacles to learning (Mallik & Gangopadhyay, 2023).

Efficiency in Administrative Tasks

Another possible advantage of GenAI relates to increased efficiency in completing administrative tasks, such as grading and communication. AI can assist in reducing administrative workloads, freeing up faculty time to concentrate on teaching and simultaneously enabling students to receive real-time feedback. "AI helps teachers in exam automation and essay scoring and in decision-making on student performance. It has been found that an automated essay scoring system can not only significantly advance the effectiveness of essay scoring but also make scoring more objective" (Celik, 2022, p. 622).

AI can assist with complex tasks for administrators as well via data entry, tracking applicant progress and budgets, and assisting in decision-making based on pre-programmed criteria (Bates, 2022). For administrators, this assistance not only saves time but also ensures better resource utilization and reduces human error.

Lastly, lest we forget, AI tools can be a dependable crutch in everyday, simple tasks such as revising emails, templates, meeting agendas, and meeting minutes (Heaps, 2024). AI can also assess the results of meetings and assemblies and provide advice on how these can be improved or adjusted to better fit each faculty member's schedule. By shifting these tasks to be completed through AI-automation, instructors can focus on the aspects of their work they find most critical and necessary.

CHALLENGES AND OBSTACLES FOR IMPLEMENTING AI IN HIGHER EDUCATION

Although AI has many positive aspects, there are some significant challenges that higher education faculty and administrators may face when integrating AI into educational practices. This section describes the challenges and obstacles to implementing AI in higher education.

Adoption in Academia

Barriers exist in the way of AI's ability to revolutionize higher education. Bates (2022) noted that expectations for AI in education are increasing due to developments in generative AI models such as ChatGPT, Gemini, and DALL-E. However, ethical concerns, a lack of technological expertise, and faculty concerns about job displacement significantly impede effective AI integration (Ofosu-Ampong, 2024). Concerns regarding the increasing usage of AI are often expressed by faculty members, who fear that automation may reduce the value of traditional teaching techniques or lead to staff layoffs. Additionally, there are concerns about AI bias, data privacy, and institutional readiness, further complicating the integration of AI into curricula and administrative processes (Castillo-Martínez et al., 2024).

Technological Proficiency Issues

Higher education instructors should be technologically literate enough to use AI applications in order to use them effectively. However, because faculty frequently lack the necessary AI-based knowledge, many instructors struggle in this area. The effective integration of AI in higher education classrooms may be impeded by this disparity in technological proficiency. Additionally, there may be a lack of interest among some educators, with some perceiving AI as unappealing or potentially hazardous to traditional teaching methods. Celik et al. (2022) stressed that the lack of technological knowledge of teachers and the lack of technical infrastructure in schools are the main challenges in integrating AI into education.

Faculty Readiness

One of the primary concerns with AI deployment is still faculty readiness. The necessity for thorough professional development programs is highlighted by the fact that many educators lack the AI literacy required to successfully integrate these tools. Higher education institutions can proactively manage AI's complexities as it continues to change the educational landscape in order to optimize its advantages and minimize the potential drawbacks (Southworth et al., 2023). It is imperative that faculty development programs be adapted to AI capability. Institutions should offer practical training and AI certification programs so that faculty members can comfortably use AI tools in ways that complement human instruction rather than replace it. According to recent studies by Kim et al. (2022) and Ofosu-Ampong (2024), faculty members' opinions about AI are significantly influenced by how familiar they are with AI tools. Faculty who receive AI training tend to be more receptive to AI integration, while those who have had little to no exposure to it view it as a threat to conventional teaching methods.

Job Displacement Concerns

There is a concern among educators that AI might threaten their job security. In 2018, Ma and Siau (2018) explained that the future job market and required skill sets will be significantly different since jobs that involve tasks that are routine and structured are easier to automate and will most likely be replaced by AI. Conversely, job tasks that involve managing and interacting with people are less likely to be replaced by AI. Faculty members may view themselves as part of this category, given that their knowledge and expertise have been essential for many years in educating students. However, the growing prevalence of automated and online courses fueled by AI-related research raises questions about whether this need will continue in the future. Ma and Siau suggest that as AI advances and becomes more common in higher education, higher education must be flexible and willing to evolve.

Saaida (2023) recently brought attention to critical issues with AI integration in higher education, specifically the possibility of job displacement. Higher education teachers fear being replaced or having their jobs become less relevant as AI tools get better at giving lectures, marking homework, and creating individualized learning experiences. This cultural shift and concern within the educational landscape raises questions about the future of teaching jobs in higher education and the need for faculty to adapt to new technologies while maintaining their professional value.

Privacy and Security Issues

Finding a balance between AI's effectiveness and the need to address privacy and security concerns is one of the main obstacles to its integration. According to Hepler et al. (2023), using AI systems in educational settings frequently necessitates a large amount of personal data, which raises serious concerns about the possibility of abuse or unauthorized access. Higher education institutions must proactively identify and mitigate these risks as AI naturally becomes increasingly integrated into teaching and learning activities (Saaida, 2023). For both privacy protection and upholding confidence in AI technologies, it is imperative to enforce cybersecurity measures, obtain informed consent, and ensure strong data governance. In 2023, Trust et al. voiced a concern over AI's use of data and information,

Additional risks of using ChatGPT include giving away personal data and sensitive information and violating the terms of use. OpenAI's privacy policy for ChatGPT indicates that the company collects a lot of information from the user, including log data, usage data, cookies, device information, IP address, interactions with the site, and date and time of use. The policy states that this information may be shared with vendors and service providers, law enforcement, affiliates, and other users. While users can request to have their data deleted, OpenAI will not delete any prompts a user inputs. So, if a user inputs a sensitive prompt (like asking about a medical condition or mental health issue), OpenAI keeps a permanent record of that input (para. 23).

Ethical Concerns

Research has shown the need for higher education instructors to be clear about their AI policies as they talk to students about ethics, including academic integrity and plagiarism. McDonald et al. (2025) collected policy documents and guidelines from 116 higher education institutions (HEIs) to understand how institutions are guiding faculty in their AI use. The findings demonstrate that institutions are adopting AI but frequently doing so without considering full ethical implications, which places an unclear onus on both faculty and students. The researchers advised that faculty discuss issues such as biases and inaccuracies in AI outputs, increasing AI dependency, and concerns about data privacy with students.

In 2019, Zawacki-Richter et al. conducted a review of the literature on AI in education. The review began with 2,656 papers, which were narrowed down to 145 relevant, peer-reviewed articles published between 2007 and 2018. The researchers then classified the articles into different uses of AI in education. They found, "a stunning result of this review is the dramatic lack of critical reflection of the pedagogical and ethical implications as well as risks of implementing AI applications in higher education." (p. 21).

The use of AI itself presents an ethical challenge in the practical use of AI applications. For example, when it comes to appropriately giving credit to the source from where the information came from, AI tools, such as ChatGPT are often given credit (McDonald et al., 2025). There are sources directing the generative creation of information that are unknown and uncredited. This could prevent college students from being able to use information derived from AI in research papers, for example, because they are unable to appropriately give credit where credit is due. This issue is leading to litigation as sources are suing generative AI platforms for copyright infringement. It would not be surprising if colleges, universities, and their faculty and researchers sue for their work being used without permission and compensation.

There is also an ethical issue when it comes to equity among historically disadvantaged populations. The hope is that AI will enhance the learning environment rather than hinder it. However, an argument can be made that access and understanding of AI tools would benefit those students already flourishing in well-supported and well-financed academic institutions (McDonald et al., 2025).

The most contentious component of AI is likely its ethical implications. Consequently, it is recommended that institutions set explicit criteria for responsible AI use. AI bias is a particular concern, as algorithms trained on insufficient or unrepresentative information may perpetuate already-existing educational inequities. Transparency in AI decision-making is crucial, especially for grading and evaluation systems that affect academic results, according to research by Al-Zahrani (2024). The layers and nuances of ethical considerations are explored more thoroughly later in this chapter.

SOLUTIONS AND RECOMMENDATIONS

Several solutions and recommendations can support higher education instructors in effectively using AI in their teaching. These include integrating AI through data-driven decision-making, policy considerations, strategic implementation, and aligning AI with existing pedagogical methods. Additional solutions involve professional development opportunities, training programs, and exploring AI's role in research and innovation. As was discussed in previous sections of this chapter, AI can be used for personalized learning of both faculty and students (Chadha, 2024). Personalized learning, supported by artificial intelligence (AI), adaptive learning technologies, and gamification, can offer customized educational experiences that enhance engagement and improve performance. At the same time, immersive learning environments powered by virtual and augmented reality (VR/AR) provide students with interactive, hands-on experiences. It is important to acknowledge that gamification can also play a significant role in AI training of both faculty and students, integrating interactive elements that enhance engagement and make the learning process more accessible.

Data-Driven Decision-Making in Higher Education

By evaluating enormous volumes of student performance data to offer insights into learning practices, engagement levels, and at-risk students, AI is transforming data-driven decision-making in higher education. Teachers can put in place timely assistance methods by using predictive analytics technologies to identify kids who might require academic intervention before they fall behind (Castillo-Martínez et al., 2024).

By matching programs to student interests and labor market demands, AI-powered recommendation engines assist educational institutions in optimizing their course offerings (Kim et al., 2025). Universities can also monitor student attrition rates and proactively apply retention tactics that raise graduation rates thanks to AI-driven retention models. AI's contribution to data-driven decision-making is crucial for organizations looking to establish effective, adaptable, and student-focused learning environments.

Institutional Policy Considerations

Policy considerations are necessary for AI adoption and application. Higher education institutions may consider adopting student and faculty policies on the use of AI in the classroom and establishing ongoing evaluation processes regarding AI use. Moreover, institutions may set standards for the application of AI to maintain the openness and equity of AI-driven decision-making. Particularly in areas like grading and admissions procedures, AI systems can be surveilled for bias, ensuring they do not provide an advantage to certain groups (Al-Zahrani, 2024).

When considering AI-related policy, Robert (2024) suggested that institutions conduct a thorough review of existing policies, such as those related to data governance, cybersecurity, data privacy, and academic integrity, to determine whether new policies need to be created or if existing ones are sufficient. Additionally, it is recommended that institutions communicate with all stakeholders about how existing policies apply to emerging AI-related issues.

Strategic Integration in Higher Education

Higher education is facing a sudden realization that it can adapt to survive in the AI world. The recent EDUCAUSE report (Robert, 2024) highlighted that the primary goals of AI-related strategic planning are focused on supporting students. The three top-ranking goals identified are preparing students for the future workforce, exploring new methods of teaching and learning, and improving higher education for the greater good, with 64%, 63%, and 41% of respondents selecting these, respectively. Additionally, the majority of respondents (76%) indicated that their AI-related strategy is somewhat or largely aimed at enhancing educational experiences and student services. Hence, many institutions have abruptly accepted AI use as a contemporary and long-lasting change within their institutional procedures, faculty productivity, and teaching strategies. AI-driven automation improves research, expedites administrative work, and facilitates individualized learning, all of which elevate academic performance and student engagement. Nonetheless, implementing AI successfully calls for a calculated strategy that strikes a balance between faculty readiness, ethical considerations, and technology breakthroughs. Institutions can invest in professional development programs that equip educators with the skills needed to leverage AI responsibly while maintaining academic integrity (Al-Zahrani & Alasmari, 2024).

Higher education institutions can place a strong priority on human-centered teaching methods, data privacy measures, and ethical AI governance in order to completely incorporate AI into traditional pedagogy. AI tools can assist in curriculum design, grading automation, and predictive analytics for student retention, but their effectiveness depends on institutional support and faculty readiness. Higher education institutions may consider adopting proactive strategies that assist educators in using AI, rather than looking at AI to replace them (Chien-Chang et al., 2023; Kim et al., 2022; Ofosu-Ampong, 2024). Institutions can maximize instructional efficiency while maintaining the core values of higher education by creating an adaptable learning environment that combines AI and human knowledge (Southworth et al., 2023).

Professional Development Options

In the EDUCAUSE report, Robert (2024) highlighted that training is the most prevalent element in AI-related strategies across educational institutions. The study revealed that 56% of faculty, 49% of staff, and 39% of students identified training as the most crucial aspect of their institution's AI strategy. This suggests a clear emphasis on training to better integrate and adapt to emerging AI technologies. The results reveal the recognition of AI's growing influence in higher education and the need for continuous learning to keep pace with technological advancements. By prioritizing training, institutions are equipping their faculty, staff, and students with the necessary tools and knowledge to navigate the evolving AI landscape effectively.

Through various forms of professional development and training, higher education individuals can be better equipped to navigate and mitigate interactions with AI tools (Southworth et al., 2023). Robert and Muscanell (2023) suggest providing easily accessible resources to support the learning and integration of AI concepts. These resources should include a variety of formats, such as online courses, instructional tutorials, webinars, and interactive workshops. In addition, educational materials like handbooks, guides, and case studies should be made available to introduce faculty, staff, and students to the fundamental principles of AI, its practical applications, and established best practices. Furthermore, establishing a community of practice, also known as AI sandbox, and creating AI facilitator roles can enhance the learning process.

According to Robert and Muscanell (2023), establishing a community of practice is essential to creating a culture of collaboration and continuous learning around AI. This can be achieved by creating a safe, controlled environment, often referred to as an AI sandbox. This is where faculty, staff, and students can come together to explore and experiment with AI tools and applications. An AI sandbox allows participants to interact with various AI technologies, test out new ideas, and develop skills in a low-risk setting.

In this community, members can share knowledge, discuss challenges, and learn from one another, ultimately enhancing their understanding of AI's potential (Robert & Muscanell, 2023). The sandbox also offers a hands-on approach to learning, where individuals can apply theoretical knowledge to real-world scenarios, gaining practical experience with AI models. Regular workshops, meetups, and collaborative projects within the sandbox can further build relationships, promote innovation, and create a shared sense of ownership over AI initiatives. This kind of collaborative environment allows for the exchange of best practices and creates a network of AI learners who promote responsible AI use.

Robert and Muscanell (2023) also suggested establishing AI facilitator roles on campuses. Facilitators can help faculty and staff navigate their identity as AI users and educators. They can implement professional development opportunities and resources such as training, workshops, coaching and mentoring programs, peer learning communities, and educational materials to help faculty and staff become facilitators. Additionally, AI facilitators can supply educators with critical educational resources that promote ongoing learning, helping them effectively integrate AI into their teaching practices. According to Burton et al. (2017), a common approach to AI training for teachers is through case studies that are based on either real-world events or hypothetical scenarios. Case studies provide in-depth analyses of situations where educators, students, or the education system face challenges related to AI implementation. By examining these cases, teachers can explore how AI tools and technologies impact teaching and learning, while identifying strategies to support diverse needs and improve educational outcomes. This approach allows educators to develop best practices and gain insights into effectively integrating AI into their classrooms.

Institutions can offer faculty members specialized training programs that cover AI ethics, technical skills, and pedagogical applications in order to successfully integrate AI. Workshops, certification courses, and multidisciplinary AI training programs can enable teachers to safely use AI. Faculty who receive structured AI training are more comfortable utilizing AI to improve their teaching strategies while reducing the ethical risks related to AI bias and data privacy issues, according to research by Al-Zahrani (2024) and Ofosu-Ampong (2024).

Moreover, cultivating a collaborative culture among educators and AI experts can improve AI deployment tactics. To enable ongoing learning and adaptation to AI breakthroughs, universities should support faculty participation in transdisciplinary AI conversations, AI research initiatives, and shared best practices (Southworth et al., 2023). Institutions that proactively invest in AI professional development will be better positioned to prepare their educators for the evolving demands of higher education.

PRACTICAL IMPLICATIONS AND STRATEGIES

Having explored various facets of AI use in higher education in this chapter, attention will now turn to the practical implications and strategies concerning the technology application. In chapter 9 of his textbook, Bates (2022) asked, "The key question then is whether technology should aim to replace teachers and instructors through automation, or whether technology should be used to empower not only teachers but also learners" (para. 75). Hepler et al. (2024) asserted that while some faculty are still responding (or not responding) to generative AI tools by hoping they will go away, others, believe that with the advent of generative artificial intelligence, we are now living in what some may call a "postplagiarism" world. If used properly, AI can be a powerful tool to help instructors personalize lessons, track student progress, and create more engaging, interactive classrooms. Ultimately, rather than replacing teachers, AI should be used to enhance teaching and learning, making education more accessible, personalized, and equitable, while still keeping the human touch.

Institutional Policies and Guidelines

Another practical implication of using AI is the need to establish strong institutional policies for the implementation of these tools that rely on analytics and data collection (Robert, 2024; Zeide, 2019). The EDUCAUSE 2024 study revealed notable gaps in AI-related policies and guidelines across higher education institutions (Robert & McCormack, 2024). It also uncovered that only 23% of respondents reported having AI-related acceptable use policies in place at their institution, while nearly half (48%) disagreed or strongly disagreed that their institution had appropriate policies and guidelines to support ethical and effective decision-making regarding AI use.

Higher education institutions need to establish clear, comprehensive guidelines that outline how AI will be used across departments. Robert and McCormack (2024) suggested that institutions should take action to integrate AI tools and policies across campuses. First, ensuring equitable access to AI tools is crucial, as departments may have varying budgets and staff capabilities. Additionally, hiring leadership and staff specifically tasked with leading AI initiatives will be important for developing training opportunities, raising awareness, and establishing policies, governance, and guidelines. A high-level AI governance structure, separate from IT, should also be created, including regular audits, to promote a culture of ethical and responsible AI use.

Additionally, there is a need for clear guidelines on how AI can be used responsibly to support meeting pedagogical goals and promoting ethical decision-making. UNESCO, which is the United Nations Educational, Scientific and Cultural Organization, published the first-ever global ethical AI standards in 2021 along with a detailed recommendation (UNESCO, 2021). Even though a lot has changed in the AI space since the release of the UNESCO publication, many of the ethical recommendations made in 2021 still hold true today. In September 2023, UNESCO released the updated "Guidance for Generative AI in Education and Research". In their updated guidelines, UNESCO specifically stressed the institutional implementation of ethical principles, emphasizing the importance of making certain that researchers, teachers, and learners use generative AI tools responsibly and ethically. It also highlighted the need for individuals to critically assess the accuracy and validity of the outputs generated by AI tools.

Professional Development Options

As was discussed earlier in this chapter, professional development plays a key role in making sure that educators are not only able to use AI tools but also understand their benefits, limitations, and ethical considerations. As Zeide (2019) emphasized, it is essential to train those who will implement and use these tools, providing them with an understanding of the advantages and shortcomings of AI systems. Several options are available, including resources from organizations that offer strategies that can help educators use AI tools effectively in their teaching.

Table 3. Professional Development Programs & Courses

Organization	Program/Course Name	Key Features	Primary User(s)
Google https://grow.google/ai-essentials	Google AI Essentials	Courses and tools to integrate AI into curricula; promotes AI literacy across disciplines; professional development for educators.	Educators, Learners
ISTE (International Society for Technology in Education) https://iste.org/ai	Artificial Intelligence in Education AI Explorations for Educators Next Level AI Skills for Educators	Foundational to advanced AI skills; prompt engineering; ethical and societal AI issues; develop GPT-based tools; student-driven learning integration.	Educators (All Levels)
Auburn University https://biggio.auburn.edu/programs/professional-development-programs/teaching-with-ai-auburn	Teaching with AI	Focus on academic integrity and AI's impact on learning; AI-infused course redesign; collaborative reflection; exposure to AI research.	Higher Education Faculty, Graduate Students, Professional Staff
Khan Academy https://www.khanacademy.org/khan-for-educators/khanmigo-for-educators	Khanmigo for Educators	Training in using Khanmigo AI tools for lesson planning, content creation, rubric generation, and differentiated instruction; practical classroom applications.	K-12 Teachers

continued on following page

Table 3. Continued

Organization	Program/Course Name	Key Features	Primary User(s)
Coursera https://www.coursera.org/campus/generative-ai-courses	Introduction to Generative AI	Basics of Generative AI; differences from traditional ML; intro to Google tools for developing AI applications.	Beginners (General Audience)
Code.org https://code.org/curriculum/generative-ai	Exploring Generative AI	Covers text-based generative AI models, bias, and language representation; prompt engineering; chatbot development; practical teaching applications.	Educators

Note. This table summarizes available professional development programs and courses designed to enhance educators' knowledge and skills in integrating AI into teaching and learning. Program/Course websites are included beneath the organization.

FUTURE RESEARCH DIRECTIONS

This chapter has explored various aspects of AI integration in education, including its impact on teaching methodologies, administrative processes, and professional development opportunities. Numerous studies, such as the recent EDUCAUSE study (Robert, 2024) cited in this chapter, have contributed valuable insights to the field. However, significant research remains to be done to fully understand the future of AI in higher education and its long-term implications for teaching, learning, and institutional operations.

Additionally, AI is becoming increasingly important as a tool for academic research. By automating certain time-consuming processes such as research planning and data categorization, AI enables researchers to focus on higher-level analysis and the generation of new insights, ultimately advancing academic research. Researchers can swiftly find pertinent studies and produce fresh insights based on current knowledge bases thanks to AI tools such as natural language processing models (Lin et al., 2023). These developments could increase multidisciplinary cooperation in higher education institutions and speed up intellectual output.

Zawacki-Richter et al. (2019) emphasized the need for further research by educators on integrating AI applications across the student lifecycle to fully see the potential they offer for developing learning and teaching systems. There are several potential future directions for research on AI in higher education. Some future research directions include a focus on institutional efficiency, professional development and training, AI development, and addressing the ethical implications of AI use in academic settings.

Improving Institutional Efficiency

As Hodges and Ocak (2023) noted, "Making predictions about technology and education is tricky at best, but considering the possible futures of generative AI in education may help educators and campus leaders develop a future-oriented mindset" (para. 10). Chadha (2024) agreed,

AI holds tremendous promise for transforming higher education by enabling personalized learning, enhancing student support, and improving institutional efficiency. To realize this potential fully, stakeholders must engage in ongoing dialogue and collaboration, focusing on ethical implementation, inclusive policies, and research-driven practices (p. 64).

More research is needed on how AI can improve institutional effectiveness, particularly in areas like administrative processes, academic advising, decision-making, and resource management. Research can be done through case studies, pilot programs, and data analysis.

Professional Development and Training

Additional research is needed in areas of professional development (PD) opportunities for AI in higher education. One key area of focus is assessing whether AI PD initiatives successfully prepare teachers to incorporate AI tools into their pedagogy and curriculum and how the tools impact student outcomes. According to Ouyang et al. (2022), there is a need for empirical research to assess the practical implications of AI applications in higher education. This requires conducting studies that test the effectiveness of AI tools in real-world online learning settings, evaluating how they affect student outcomes, teaching practices, and the entire learning process.

Al-Zahrani and Alasmari (2024) conducted an in-depth study examining the impact of AI on higher education, with a particular focus on its ethical and social implications. This study revealed the significant role that chatbots can play in enhancing student motivation and improving teaching practices. Therefore, further research should be required to examine how ethical issues involving AI can be included in PD programs for faculty, such that teachers are prepared to address the issues in their classrooms and research.

Application and Tool Development

Another research initiative that should be addressed is the future development of AI. Specifically, who is developing the GenAI applications and tools that higher education students and faculty are using? Since AI seems to be developed by computer scientists with no background in higher education, they tend to use models of learning based on how computers or computer networks work (Bates, 2022). Similarly, Zawacki-Richter et al. (2019) agreed that most AI developments for teaching and learning are by computer scientists, not educators. Hence, this implication needs to be acknowledged when discussing AI use in higher education.

Ethical Implications

Institutions can also explore areas of research pertaining to the ownership of AI-generated material and data privacy. Universities need to establish explicit policies about academic integrity and intellectual property rights as AI tools become more widely used in content creation. To avoid an over-reliance on AI-generated content that could undermine academic work's originality and critical thinking, faculty members can be trained on the ethical use of AI (Al-Zahrani, 2024; Kim et al., 2022). UNESCO (2023) emphasized that while generative AI can benefit education and research, it may also disrupt existing systems. And, any changes it triggers should be carefully reviewed and guided by a human-centered approach..

CONCLUSION

Depending on one's perspective, higher education has not yet reached a point where humanoid robot teachers are standing at the front of classrooms. The use of AI in education today remains disembodied, as roboticists describe it. This chapter can serve as a practical guide for higher education instructors, administrators, and curriculum developers who are exploring the use of AI in teaching and learning and seeking effective integration strategies for their higher education settings.

This chapter offers actionable insights and frameworks to help educators navigate ethical issues and challenges of integrating GenAI tools and LLMs while maximizing their potential to enhance student learning. By addressing both current and future possibilities, the chapter aims to equip higher educational professionals with the knowledge needed to make informed decisions about using AI tools at their institutions.

ACKNOWLEDGMENT

This research received no specific grant from any funding agency in the public, commercial, or not-for-profit sectors.

DECLARATION OF GENERATIVE AI AND AI-ASSISTED TECHNOLOGIES IN THE WRITING PROCESS: During the preparation of this work, the authors used generative AI tools in order to edit and format the chapter.

REFERENCES

Al-Zahrani, A. M. (2024). Unveiling the shadows: Beyond the hype of AI in education. *Heliyon*, *10*(9), e30696. DOI: 10.1016/j.heliyon.2024.e30696 PMID: 38737255

Al-Zahrani, A. M., & Alasmari, T. M. (2024). Exploring the impact of artificial intelligence on higher education: The dynamics of ethical, social, and educational implications. *Humanities & Social Sciences Communications*, *11*(1), 912. DOI: 10.1057/s41599-024-03432-4

Alqahtani, T., Badreldin, H. A., Alrashed, M., Alshaya, A. I., Alghamdi, S. S., Bin Saleh, K., & Albekairy, A. M. (2023). The emergent role of artificial intelligence, natural learning processing, and large language models in higher education and research. *Research in Social & Administrative Pharmacy*, *19*(8), 1236–1242. DOI: 10.1016/j.sapharm.2023.05.016 PMID: 37321925

Bates, A. W. (2022). *Teaching in a digital age: Guidelines for designing teaching and learning* (3rd ed.). Tony Bates Associates Ltd., https://pressbooks.bccampus.ca/teachinginadigitalagev3m/

Biggio Center for the Enhancement of Teaching and Learning. (n.d.). *Teaching with AI: Auburn University*. Auburn University. https://biggio.auburn.edu/programs/professional-development-programs/teaching-with-ai-auburn

Brisk Teaching. (n.d.). *Brisk Teaching*. Brisk Teaching. https://www.briskteaching.com/

Burton, E., Goldsmith, J., Koenig, S., Kuipers, B., Mattei, N., & Walsh, T. (2017). Ethical considerations in artificial intelligence courses. *AI Magazine*, *38*(2), 22–34. DOI: 10.1609/aimag.v38i2.2731

Castillo-Martínez, I., Fernández-Segovia, I., & Rodríguez-López, C. (2024). The impact of AI on academic research practices: Opportunities and challenges. *Frontiers in Education*, *9*, 1391485. DOI: 10.3389/feduc.2024.1391485

Celik, I., Dindar, M., Muukkonen, H., & Järvelä, S. (2022). The promises and challenges of artificial intelligence for teachers: A systematic review of research. *TechTrends*, *66*(4), 616–630. DOI: 10.1007/s11528-022-00715-y

Chadha, A. (2024). Transforming higher education for the digital age: Examining emerging technologies and pedagogical innovations. *Journal of Interdisciplinary Studies in Education*, *13*(S1), 53–70. DOI: 10.32674/em2qsn46

Code.org. (n.d.). *Exploring generative AI.* Code.org. https://code.org/curriculum/generative-ai

Coursera. (n.d.). *Generative AI courses.* Coursera. https://www.coursera.org/campus/generative-ai-courses

Google. (n.d.-a). *Gemini.* Google. https://gemini.google.com/app

Google. (n.d.-b). *Google AI essentials.* Grow with Google. https://grow.google/ai-essentials

Google. (n.d.-c) *Notebook LM*. Google. https://notebooklm.google

Gradescope. (n.d.). *Gradescope*. Gradescope. https://www.gradescope.com

Grammarly. (n.d.). *Grammarly.* Grammarly. https://www.grammarly.com

Heaps, T. (2024). *Generative artificial intelligence: Practical uses in education.* The Manitoba Open Education Initiative. https://pressbooks.openedmb.ca/aiineducation/

Hepler, R. C., Vecchione, A., Hensley, R., Fensie, A., Sinha, S., Otero, L., Riechers, D., Long, L., Liang, L., Randall, R., & Gladd, J. (2024). Introduction to AI and Ethics in Higher Education. https://edtechbooks.org/introduction_to_ai_and_ethics_in_higher_education

Hodges, C., & Ocak, C. (2023, August 30). *Integrating generative AI into higher education: Considerations.* https://er.educause.edu/articles/2023/8/integrating-generative-ai-into-higher-education-considerations

Imran, M., & Almusharraf, N. (2024). Google Gemini as a next generation AI educational tool: A review of emerging educational technology. *Smart Learning Environments*, *11*(1), 22. Advance online publication. DOI: 10.1186/s40561-024-00310-z

International Society for Technology in Education (ISTE). (n.d.). *Artificial intelligence in education.* ISTE. https://iste.org/ai

Khan Academy. (n.d.-a). *Khanmigo: AI-powered teaching assistant.* Khan Academy. https://www.khanmigo.ai/

Khan Academy. (n.d.-b). *Khanmigo for educators.* Khan Academy. https://www.khanacademy.org/khan-for-educators/khanmigo-for-educators

Kim, J., Klopfer, M., Grohs, J. R., Eldardiry, H., Weichert, J., Cox, L. A.II, & Pike, D. (2025). Examining faculty and student perceptions of generative AI in university courses. *Innovative Higher Education*, *50*(4), 1281–1313. Advance online publication. DOI: 10.1007/s10755-024-09774-w

Kim, J., Lee, H., & Cho, Y. H. (2022). Learning design to support student-AI collaboration: Perspectives of leading teachers for AI in education. *Education and Information Technologies*, *27*(5), 6069–6104. DOI: 10.1007/s10639-021-10831-6

Lin, C. C., Huang, A. Y. Q., & Lu, O. H. T. (2023). Artificial intelligence in intelligent tutoring systems toward sustainable education: A systematic review. *Smart Learning Environments*, *10*(1), 41. DOI: 10.1186/s40561-023-00260-y

Lu, J. (n.d.). *Artificial intelligence (AI) LibGuide.* Purdue University Libraries. https://guides.lib.purdue.edu/c.php?g=1371380&p=10135065

Ma, Y., & Siau, K. L. (2018). *Artificial intelligence impacts on higher education.* MWAIS 2018 Proceedings, 42. https://aisel.aisnet.org/mwais2018/42

Magic School AI. (n.d.). *Magic School AI: Automated lesson planning and assessments*. Magic School AI. https://www.magicschool.ai

Mallik, S., & Gangopadhyay, A. (2023). Proactive and reactive engagement of artificial intelligence methods for education: A review. *Frontiers in Artificial Intelligence*, *6*, 1151391. DOI: 10.3389/frai.2023.1151391 PMID: 37215064

McDonald, N., Johri, A., Ali, A., & Collier, A. H. (2025). Generative artificial intelligence in higher education: Evidence from an analysis of institutional policies and guidelines. *Computers in Human Behavior: Artificial Humans, 3*. https://doi.org//arXiv.2402.01659DOI: 10.48550

Meli, K., Taouki, J., & Pantazatos, D. (2024). Empowering educators with generative AI: The GenAI education frontier initiative. In *EDULEARN24 Proceedings* (pp. 4289-4299). IATED. https://doi: DOI: 10.21125/edulearn.2024.1077

Microsoft. (n.d.). *Copilot.* Microsoft. https://www.microsoft.com/en-us/microsoft-copilot

Ofosu-Ampong, K. (2024). Beyond the hype: Exploring faculty perceptions and acceptability of AI in teaching practices. *Discover Education*, *3*(1), 38. Advance online publication. DOI: 10.1007/s44217-024-00128-4

Open, A. I. (n.d.). *ChatGPT.* OpenAI. https://chat.openai.com

Ouyang, F., Zheng, L., & Jiao, P. (2022). Artificial intelligence in online higher education: A systematic review of empirical research from 2011 to 2020. *Education and Information Technologies*, *27*(8), 7893–7925. DOI: 10.1007/s10639-022-10925-9

Perplexity. (n.d.). *Perplexity*. Perplexity AI. https://www.perplexity.ai/

Rahman, M. A., Das, P., Lam, L., Alif, S. M., Sultana, F., Salehin, M., Banik, B., Joseph, B., Parul, P., Lewis, A., Statham, D., Porter, J., Foster, K., Islam, S. M. S., Cross, W., Jacob, A., Hua, S., Wang, Q., Chair, S. Y., & Polman, R. (2024). Health and wellbeing of staff working at higher education institutions globally during the post-COVID-19 pandemic period: Evidence from a cross-sectional study. *BMC Public Health*, *24*(1), 1848. DOI: 10.1186/s12889-024-19365-1 PMID: 38992680

Robert, J. (2024). *EDUCAUSE AI landscape study* [Research report]. EDUCAUSE. https://www.educause.edu/ecar/research-publications/2024/2024-educause-ai-landscape-study/introduction-and-key-findings

Robert, J., & McCormack, M. (2024). *EDUCAUSE action plan: AI policies and guidelines*. EDUCAUSE. https://www.educause.edu/research/2024/2024-educause-action-plan-ai-policies-and-guidelines

Robert, J., & Muscanell, N. (2023). Horizon action plan: Generative AI. EDUCAUSE. https://www.educause.edu

Ruiz Viruel, S., Sánchez Rivas, E., & Ruiz Palmero, J. (2025). The role of artificial intelligence in project-based learning: Teacher perceptions and pedagogical implications. *Education Sciences*, *15*(2), 150. DOI: 10.3390/educsci15020150

Saaida, M. B. (2023). AI-driven transformations in higher education: Opportunities and challenges. *International Journal of Educational Research and Studies*, *5*(1), 29–36. DOI: 10.5281/zenodo.8164414

Salinas-Navarro, D. E., Vilalta-Perdomo, E., Michel-Villarreal, R., & Montesinos, L. (2024). Using generative artificial intelligence tools to explain and enhance experiential learning for authentic assessment. *Education Sciences*, *14*(1), 83. DOI: 10.3390/educsci14010083

Southworth, J., Migliaccio, K., Glover, J., Glover, J., Reed, D., McCarty, C., Brendemuhl, J., & Thomas, A. (2023). Developing a model for AI across the curriculum: Transforming the higher education landscape via innovation in AI literacy. *Computers & Education: Artificial Intelligence*, *4*, 100127. DOI: 10.1016/j.caeai.2023.100127

Strielkowski, W., Grebennikova, V., Lisovskiy, A., Rakhimova, G., & Vasileva, T. (2024). AI-driven adaptive learning for sustainable educational transformation. *Sustainable Development*, •••, 1–27. DOI: 10.1002/sd.3221

Trust, T., Whalen, J., & Mouza, C. (2023). ChatGPT: Challenges, opportunities, and implications for teacher education. *Contemporary Issues in Technology & Teacher Education, 23*(1), 1–23. https://citejournal.org/volume-23/issue-1-23/editorial/editorial-chatgpt-challenges-opportunities-and-implications-for-teacher-education

Turnitin. (n.d.). *Turnitin.* Turnitin. https://www.turnitin.com/

United Nations Educational, Scientific and Cultural Organization (UNESCO). (2021). *Recommendation on the Ethics of Artificial Intelligence.* United Nations Educational, Scientific and Cultural Organization. https://www.unesco.org/en/artificial-intelligence/recommendation-ethics

United Nations Educational, Scientific and Cultural Organization (UNESCO). (2023). *Guidance for generative AI in education and research.* United Nations Educational, Scientific and Cultural Organization., DOI: 10.54675/EWZM9535

Weber-Wulff, D., Anohina-Naumeca, A., Bjelobaba, S., Foltýnek, T., Guerrero-Dib, J., Popoola, O., Šigut, P., & Waddington, L. (2023). Testing of detection tools for AI-generated text. *International Journal for Educational Integrity, 19*(1), 26. Advance online publication. DOI: 10.1007/s40979-023-00146-z

Zawacki-Richter, O., Marín, V. I., Bond, M., & Gouverneur, F. (2019). Systematic review of research on artificial intelligence applications in higher education–where are the educators? *International Journal of Educational Technology in Higher Education, 16*(1), 1–27. DOI: 10.1186/s41239-019-0171-0

Zeide, E. (2019, August 26). Artificial intelligence in higher education: Applications, promise and perils, and ethical questions. *EDUCAUSE Review, 54*(3), 31–39. https://ssrn.com/abstract=4320049

Zhang, K., & Aslan, A. B. (2021). AI technologies for education: Recent research & future directions. *Computers and Education: Artificial Intelligence, 2*, 100025. DOI: 10.1016/j.caeai.2021.100025

Zheng, C., Yuan, K., Guo, B., Hadi Mogavi, R., Peng, Z., Ma, S., & Ma, X. (2024, May). Charting the future of AI in project-based learning: a Co-design exploration with students. In *Proceedings of the 2024 CHI Conference on Human Factors in Computing Systems* (pp. 1-19). DOI: 10.1145/3613904.3642807

ADDITIONAL READING

Chen, L., Chen, P., & Lin, Z. (2020). Artificial intelligence in education: A review. *IEEE Access : Practical Innovations, Open Solutions*, *8*, 75264–75278. DOI: 10.1109/ACCESS.2020.2988510

Crompton, H., & Burke, D. (2023). Artificial intelligence in higher education: The state of the field. *International Journal of Educational Technology in Higher Education*, *20*(1), 22. DOI: 10.1186/s41239-023-00392-8

Ouyang, F., Zheng, L., & Jiao, P. (2022). Artificial intelligence in online higher education: A systematic review of empirical research from 2011–2020. *Education and Information Technologies*, *27*(6), 7893–7925. DOI: 10.1007/s10639-022-10925-9

KEY TERMS AND DEFINITIONS

Adaptive Learning: An educational method that uses AI to deliver real-time, personalized content based on individual needs, preferences, and performance, allowing each learner to progress at their own pace.

Artificial Intelligence (AI): The theory and development of computer systems able to perform tasks that normally require human intelligence, such as visual perception, speech recognition, decision-making, and translation between languages.

Ethics: Moral principles and societal implications surrounding the development and use of artificial intelligence technologies, ensuring they align with human values and well-being in a higher education environment.

Higher Education: Institutions providing study beyond the level of secondary education, such as colleges and universities, community colleges, and vocational and technical schools.

Generative AI (GenAI): Type of artificial intelligence that is designed to create new content, such as text, images, music, or other forms of media, by learning patterns from existing data.

Large Language Models (LLMs): Type of generative artificial intelligence that focuses on understanding and generating human language.

Machine Learning (ML): Machine learning is an application of AI that provides systems the ability to automatically learn and improve from experience without being explicitly programmed.

Natural Language Processing (NLP): Natural Language Processing is a form of AI that gives machines the ability to interpret human language and perform tasks including speech recognition, sentiment analysis, and automatic text summarization.

Pedagogy: Integration of tools and techniques to enhance teaching, learning, and curriculum development.

Personalized Learning: Use of educational tools and techniques to match educational content, pacing, and assessments to the individual needs, preferences, and learning styles of students, enhancing their academic experience and outcomes.

Professional Development: Training educators and administrators to effectively integrate tools and techniques into teaching, research, and administrative practices to enhance institutional effectiveness and student success.

Chapter 8
The Role of AI in Education:
Complementing or Competing With Teachers?

Sally D. Abualgasim
https://orcid.org/0000-0003-4154-8112
University of Gezira, Sudan

Zeinab E. Ahmed
https://orcid.org/0000-0002-6144-8533
University of Gezira, Sudan

ABSTRACT

The learning process, a fundamental component of educational achievement, has been significantly enhanced by the rapid advancement and proliferation of Artificial Intelligence (AI) technologies. These developments play a crucial role in addressing complex challenges in the educational system. Educators, as the cornerstone of this system, possess extensive expertise cultivated through years of dedicated practice, continuous professional development, and commitment to their profession. This chapter provides a comprehensive examination of AI's role in education, illustrating how it can complement and enhance the instructional functions performed by teachers. The discussion critically evaluates the advantages AI brings to diverse educational settings while also acknowledging its limitations in fully replicating human instruction. By highlighting the unique and irreplaceable aspects of human teaching, this analysis underscores the indispensable role of educators in the learning process. Subsequent sections will explore AI as a supplementary tool within traditional educational frameworks.

DOI: 10.4018/979-8-3373-0396-3.ch008

1. INTRODUCTION

The combination of artificial intelligence (AI) and education has sparked both excitement and debate. As AI machineries, such as adaptive learning platform- automated grading systems, and predictive analytics- increasingly permeate classrooms, they promise to revolutionize how students learn and educators teach. These tools can personalize instruction, identify learning gaps, and streamline administrative tasks, potentially freeing teachers to focus on fostering creativity and critical thinking. Yet this shift also raises pressing questions: Is AI poised to complement teachers, enhancing their capabilities, or could it eventually compete with them, overshadowing the human elements central to education?

AI's potential lies in its ability to handle data-driven tasks efficiently. For instance, adaptive software tailors content to individual student needs, while chatbots provide instant academic support. Predictive systems flag at-risk students, enabling timely intervention. Such innovations suggest a future where AI alleviates administrative burdens, allowing educators to prioritize mentorship and emotional support roles deeply rooted in human connection. However, concerns persist. Could over-reliance on AI undermine the teacher-student relationship, a cornerstone of effective learning? Ethical challenges, including data privacy and algorithmic bias, further complicate its adoption. Moreover, while AI exceeds at pattern identification, it suffer of the sympathy unavailability, cultural sensitivity, and improvisational skills that teachers bring to dynamic classroom environments. The discourse is not merely technological but philosophical: How can education balance efficiency with humanity? Current research underscores AI's effectiveness in boosting engagement and outcomes, yet emphasizes its role as a tool, not a replacement. Developing nations are leveraging AI to bridge systemic educational disparities, utilizing its capacity to analyze student competencies and customize instructional content, thereby creating a supportive framework for overburdened teaching staff rather than displacing them. In more affluent educational systems, AI adoption focuses on automating administrative functions including assessment grading and performance feedback, prompting teachers to devote more attention to student engagement and the development of their higher-order skills.

1.1. Outline of AI Tools in Education

AI is reshaping education by both augmenting traditional teaching methods and prompting critical discussions about its evolving relationship with human educators. This dual dynamic presents for modern learning environments a lot of chances and many challenges. As a supportive tool, AI enhances educational delivery through personalized learning algorithms that adjust content and speed according to each student's requirements, enabling differentiated instruction at scale (Kim, 2024). It streamlines administrative burdens by automating routine tasks like evaluating performance and tracking attendance, allowing teachers to focus on higher-value interactions. AI also expands accessibility through assistive technologies that support diverse learners, while intelligent tutoring systems provide supplemental instruction beyond classroom hours. Research demonstrates these benefits, with studies showing how structured AI literacy programs can effectively build technical understanding across student populations with varying academic backgrounds (Ahmed, Hashim, et al., 2024). However, AI's growing sophistication raises legitimate concerns about potential displacement of teaching functions. Automated instruction systems and cost-effective digital solutions may tempt institutions to substitute human educators in certain contexts. Moreover, AI's inherent limitations in fostering creativity, emotional intelligence, and adaptive teaching approaches highlight the irreplaceable value of human educators (Srinivasan, 2022).

The most promising educational paradigm leverages the complementary strengths of both. AI excels in data processing, personalization, and operational efficiency, while teachers provide mentorship, critical thinking guidance, and emotional support (Al-Zawqari et al., 2022). This synergistic approach, where educators utilize AI-generated insights to inform their pedagogy while maintaining their central role in fostering meaningful learning experiences, represents the optimal path forward. By viewing AI as an enhancement rather than a replacement, education systems can harness technological advancements while preserving the human elements essential for holistic student development (Saeed et al., 2024). The future of education lies not in competition between man and machine, but in their strategic collaboration to create more effective, inclusive, and adaptive learning ecosystems (Bryant et al., 2020). AI tools are increasingly being integrated into educational settings to enhance learning experiences, streamline administrative tasks, and provide personalized learning opportunities. There are various AI tools in education, such as:

- Intelligent Tutoring Systems (ITS).
- Learning Management Systems (LMS) with AI capabilities.
- AI-Powered Educational Games and Simulations.
- Natural Language Processing (NLP) Tools.
- Adaptive Learning Platforms.
- AI for Special Education.
- Automated Essay Scoring (AES).
- Chatbots and Virtual Assistants.
- Data Analytics and Predictive Modeling.
- Language Learning Applications

AI tools are revolutionizing education by increasing teaching efficiency, personalizing instruction, and delivering immediate feedback through advanced technologies like natural language processing, machine learning, and automated assessment systems(Luo et al., 2025). These innovations support both teachers and learners across multiple applications. Automated writing evaluation tools such as Grammarly and DeepL Write provide grammar corrections and writing suggestions while reducing teacher workload, though they struggle with higher-order writing skills like coherence and argument development. Intelligent tutoring systems like Carnegie Learning adapt to individual student needs through personalized learning paths and interactive exercises, enhancing knowledge retention. AI learning assistants including Google's Socratic offer real-time academic support through natural language queries and multilingual translation capabilities (Osman & Ahmed, 2024). For assessment, platforms like Turnitin automate grading and plagiarism detection while facing challenges regarding evaluation nuance and algorithmic bias. Special education benefits from AI through accessibility tools like Microsoft's Immersive Reader that assist students with disabilities via speech/text conversion and predictive analytics. Classroom management systems such as ClassDojo track student engagement and generate automated progress reports. Looking ahead, the education sector is moving toward hybrid AI-teacher models where machines handle administrative tasks while educators focus on critical thinking development, though concerns remain about data privacy, over-reliance on technology, and maintaining academic integrity with generative AI tools (Toyokawa et al., 2023) .While these technologies significantly improve educational efficiency and accessibility, they serve best as complements to - rather than replacements for - human teachers, with successful implementation depending on thoughtful integration that leverages both artificial and human intelligence to optimize learning outcomes. The key insight remains that AI's educational potential lies not in substitution but in strategic collaboration with skilled educators (Schiff, 2021).

1.2. The Rise of AI in Education

The rise of AI in education has been a transformative development, reshaping how educators teach, and students learn. AI's integration into educational systems has been driven by its potential to personalize learning, automate administrative tasks, and provide actionable insights through data analytics(Hwang et al., 2020). The rise of AI in education could be in many areas like personalized learning, automation of administrative tasks, enhanced engagement through gamification, data-driven insights and expansion of access to education. Key Developments in AI Education:

1. AI Literacy Initiatives: Efforts like the AI literacy course described in Hong Kong aim to equip students from diverse academic backgrounds with foundational AI knowledge. These courses focus on concepts such as machine learning, supervised and unsupervised learning, regression, and clustering, without requiring prior programming expertise. By using a flipped classroom approach, learners experience flexible and interactive learning environments (Molefi et al., 2024).
2. Empowerment Through AI Education: AI literacy courses are designed not only to teach technical concepts but also to empower individuals. Empowerment includes fostering self-efficacy, meaningfulness, societal impact awareness, and creative problem-solving skills. This enables learners to interact confidently with AI systems and apply their knowledge to real-world challenges (Karataş et al., 2025).
3. Inclusion and Accessibility: AI education initiatives prioritize inclusivity by targeting participants from various study backgrounds and genders. For example, efforts in Hong Kong aim to narrow the digital gender gap and ensure equal opportunities for all learners to engage with AI technologies. Such inclusivity aligns with global trends that emphasize diversity in tech-related fields (Al-khresheh, 2024).
4. Inclusion and Accessibility: AI education initiatives prioritize inclusivity by targeting participants from various study backgrounds and genders. For example, efforts in Hong Kong aim to narrow the digital gender gap and ensure equal opportunities for all learners to engage with AI technologies. Such inclusivity aligns with global trends that emphasize diversity in tech-related fields (Feigerlova et al., 2025) .
5. Bridging Knowledge Gaps: By targeting non-technical audiences, these initiatives democratize access to AI knowledge.

The integration of AI in education presents several challenges that must be addressed to ensure its effective and ethical use. One key concern is the potential for biases inherent in AI systems, which can perpetuate existing inequalities if not properly managed (Ding et al., 2024). Additionally, data privacy and security are critical issues, as the vast amount of personal and academic information processed by AI tools must be safeguarded to protect students' rights and privacy. Furthermore, there is a need to strike a balance between the role of human educators and the increasing use of automated teaching tools. While AI can enhance the learning experience by providing personalized support, it cannot replace the essential mentorship, emotional guidance, and nuanced understanding that human educators offer. Therefore, careful consideration is required to integrate AI in a way that complements, rather than undermines, the invaluable contributions of educators in the classroom. The rise of AI in education represents a shift towards more inclusive, empowered, and technologically integrated learning environments. By fostering literacy and critical engagement with AI concepts, educational institutions can prepare students for a rapidly evolving digital society (Bryant et al., 2020).

2. THE STRENGTHS OF AI IN EDUCATION

AI has several strengths in education that can enhance learning experiences, improve efficiency, and provide personalized support. Main strengths of AI in education are discuss in the following points:

- Personalization: One of the key advantages of AI in education lies in its ability to deliver personalized learning experiences tailored to individual students' needs, preferences, and learning paces. AI-powered tools can adapt in real time, providing personalized feedback and resources that foster student engagement and improve outcomes. For instance, adaptive learning algorithms analyze student performance, adjusting task difficulty, recommending targeted exercises, and offering additional explanations to ensure learners progress optimally (Bhutoria, 2022). Furthermore, AI enables immediate, customized feedback, as exemplified by tools like DeepL Write, which provide continuous, iterative corrections on grammar, vocabulary, and syntax, contrasting with the time delay of traditional teacher feedback. AI also supports diverse learning styles, offering content in various formats (e.g., interactive simulations, videos, quizzes), thereby catering to visual, auditory, or kinesthetic learners. Additionally, AI enhances scalability and accessibility, delivering personalized support to large groups, thus addressing gaps in under-resourced classrooms. By tracking long-term progress, AI generates valuable data-driven insights, helping both students and teachers identify trends and areas for improvement. However, while AI excels in personalizing mechanical aspects of learning, it remains limited in fostering higher-order skills such as argumentation and creativity, areas where human educators are indispensable. The most effective approach combines the efficiency of AI with the mentorship and critical guidance provided by human educators, ensuring a balanced educational experience that nurtures both technical proficiency and higher-order thinking. Future advancements in AI should aim to enhance contextual understanding, while maintaining the irreplaceable value of human interaction in the learning process (Holmes et al., 2019).
- Efficiency: AI significantly enhances the efficiency of educational institutions by automating repetitive administrative tasks such as grading, attendance tracking, and scheduling. This automation allows educators to allo-

cate more time to teaching and mentoring. For instance, AI-powered tools like Gradescope expedite the grading of objective assignments and exams, ensuring both accuracy and efficiency. Additionally, AI facilitates the management of administrative processes by streamlining tasks such as scheduling, attendance monitoring, and resource allocation. AI chatbots, such as AdmitHub, support universities in managing student inquiries and streamlining admissions processes, improving response times and operational efficiency. By reducing the administrative burden, AI enables educators to focus on higher-level pedagogical tasks, ultimately enhancing the overall educational experience for both students and instructors (Zawacki-Richter et al., 2019)

- Accessibility and Inclusivity: AI enhances educational accessibility for students with disabilities and those facing language barriers through a variety of supportive tools. For students with disabilities, AI-powered features such as text-to-speech and speech-to-text facilitate learning by providing real-time assistance and improving comprehension (Ng et al., 2021). Additionally, AI-driven language translation tools break down language barriers, enabling non-native speakers to access educational content in multiple languages. For instance, Microsoft Immersive Reader supports students with dyslexia by reading text aloud and highlighting words, while Google Translate provides real-time translation of educational materials. These technologies contribute to a more inclusive learning environment, ensuring that students, regardless of their challenges, can fully engage with and benefit from educational content. By offering personalized support, AI plays a vital role in making education more accessible to a diverse global audience (Chiu et al., 2022).
- Enhanced Engagement: AI-powered tools, such as gamified learning platforms, virtual tutors, and interactive simulations, significantly enhance student engagement by making learning more interactive and enjoyable. These technologies offer immersive experiences through virtual reality (VR) and augmented reality (AR), which help simplify complex concepts and increase understanding. For example, Duolingo leverages gamification to make language learning both fun and interactive, while Kahoot! transforms quizzes into competitive games, fostering engagement through a dynamic, AI-driven platform. These tools not only increase student motivation but also cater to diverse learning styles, enhancing the overall educational experience by providing personalized and interactive content that maintains students' interest. Through such innovations, AI plays a pivotal role in creating a more engaging and effective learning environment (Su et al., 2023).
- Data-Driven Insights: AI leverages large datasets to analyze student performance, identify trends, and generate actionable insights for educators. In the context of learning analytics, AI platforms, such as Knewton, process exten-

sive student data to recommend personalized learning resources, tailoring the educational experience to individual needs. One of AI's key strengths lies in its ability to detect at-risk students early by analyzing various metrics, including attendance, grades, and engagement levels. This early identification enables educators to implement targeted interventions that can improve student outcomes. By providing real-time, data-driven insights, AI supports a proactive approach to education, enhancing the ability to address challenges before they impact academic achievement. While AI offers valuable support in personalizing learning and facilitating early intervention, it is essential that its use be integrated with human judgment to ensure that students receive the most appropriate and effective support.

- Scalability: AI-driven educational platforms enhance the scalability and cost-effectiveness of education by enabling access to quality learning for a vast number of students across diverse geographical locations. By automating repetitive tasks and offering scalable solutions, AI significantly reduces the cost of education. Platforms such as Massive Open Online Courses (MOOCs), including Coursera and edX, leverage AI to deliver courses to millions of learners globally, while AI-powered tutoring tools like Squirrel AI provide personalized support to thousands of students simultaneously. These advancements allow for the broad dissemination of educational resources, making high-quality learning more accessible and efficient, regardless of location or institutional constraints. As AI continues to evolve, its capacity to expand the reach of education and deliver tailored learning experiences will further enhance its role in democratizing education worldwide (Blommerde et al., 2024) .
- 24/7 Availability: AI-powered tools, such as chatbots and virtual tutors, enable on-demand learning by providing students with continuous access to support, allowing them to seek assistance whenever necessary. This facilitates self-paced learning, as students can engage with AI-driven resources at their convenience and progress at their own speed. For instance, Georgia State University's chatbot, Pounce, offers round-the-clock responses to student inquiries, while IBM Watson Tutor delivers instant, accessible help to learners anytime and from anywhere. These AI technologies significantly enhance flexibility in learning, providing personalized support tailored to individual needs and ensuring that students can access educational resources outside of traditional classroom hours. Such innovations promote a more autonomous and personalized approach to education, fostering a learning environment that adapts to the unique pace and timing preferences of each student (Gašević et al., 2023).

- Innovative Teaching Tools: AI offers innovative tools that significantly enhance teaching by enabling the creation of customized lesson plans, quizzes, and educational materials. Platforms such as Canva for Education utilize AI to assist teachers in designing visually engaging and effective teaching resources, thereby improving lesson delivery. Additionally, AI facilitates the development of virtual labs and simulations, providing students with the opportunity to engage in practical education knowledges without the need for physical resources. For instance, Labster provides AI-powered virtual science labs, it enables learners to perform in a virtual environment thus expanding access to practical learning opportunities, particularly in under-resourced settings. These AI-driven tools not only enhance the efficiency of content creation but also foster interactive and immersive learning experiences, enabling students to explore complex concepts in a dynamic, accessible manner (Wu et al., 2024) .
- Lifelong Learning: AI plays a crucial role in supporting lifelong learning by providing personalized recommendations for upskilling and reskilling opportunities. By analyzing individual strengths, interests, and career goals, AI can suggest relevant courses and resources to help professionals develop new skills and advance in their careers. For example, platforms like LinkedIn Learning leverage AI to recommend courses tailored to career aspirations and skill gaps, while Coursera offers personalized course suggestions to facilitate continuous learning. Additionally, AI can offer personalized career guidance, helping individuals identify suitable career paths and educational opportunities. By supporting the ongoing development of skills, AI enhances professional growth, enabling individuals to adapt to evolving job markets and stay competitive in their respective fields. As a result, AI-driven platforms foster continuous learning, empowering individuals to take charge of their career development (Selwyn, 2019).
- Global Collaboration: AI-powered platforms are instrumental in connecting learners and educators across the globe, fostering cross-cultural collaboration and knowledge exchange. These platforms facilitate interactions among students and educators from diverse geographical and cultural backgrounds, promoting global learning opportunities. For example, platforms such as Flipgrid enable students from various countries to collaborate on projects, enhancing their understanding of different perspectives. Additionally, AI-driven translation tools like Microsoft Translator help overcome language barriers, ensuring effective communication and participation in international classrooms. This technological integration not only enriches the learning experience but also contributes to the development of a more inclusive and interconnected global educational community (Holmes et al., 2019).

AI has the ability to revolutionize education by utilizing these advantages, rendering it more effective, individualized, and accessible for students of all ages and backgrounds. Nonetheless, it is crucial to tackle challenges such as data protection, ethical dilemmas, and the digital divide to guarantee fair access to education powered by AI.

3. THE LIMITATIONS OF AI IN REPLACING TEACHERS

While AI has made considerable advancements in education, its ability to fully replace human teachers remains limited due to the complex, nuanced, and deeply interpersonal nature of teaching and learning. Education is not solely a process of information delivery; it involves emotional intelligence, personalized mentorship, and the cultivation of critical thinking and social skills, areas were AI lacks proficiency. Teachers are capable of building meaningful relationships with students, recognizing individual emotional and cognitive needs, and providing tailored guidance that fosters not only academic success but also personal growth. Additionally, human educators are adept at adapting to dynamic classroom environments, offering context-driven insights, and nurturing creativity and higher-order skills. While AI can enhance and support educational practices, its role is best seen as a complementary tool rather than a substitute for the invaluable, transformative influence of human teachers.

1. Emotional Intelligence (EI) is the ability to recognize, understand, and manage emotions both in oneself and in others AI systems lack the emotional intelligence and empathy that human teachers bring to the classroom. Teaching often involves understanding students' emotional states, providing moral support, and fostering a sense of belonging tasks that require human intuition and compassion. AI lacks the ability to perceive and respond to emotions in a meaningful way, which limits its effectiveness in fostering student well-being (Jain et al., 2024) . Looking ahead, advances in emotional AI could narrow the competence gap in empathetic tasks, and teacher training programs will be essential to ensure educators can effectively harness AI tools, fostering synergy rather than competition in the classroom. Ultimately, the future of education lies in a balanced partnership where AI enhances efficiency and personalization, while teachers continue to nurture creativity, critical thinking, and emotional growth (Kim, 2024).
2. Creativity: Limited ability to foster critical thinking and creativity. Creativity is a cornerstone of effective teaching. Teachers design innovative lessons, adapt to unexpected classroom situations, and inspire students to think critically and creatively (Molefi et al., 2024). AI, on the other hand, operates within predefined

algorithms and lacks the ability to think outside the box or generate truly original ideas. While AI can assist in delivering content and assessing rote learning, it struggles to foster critical thinking, creativity, and higher-order cognitive skills. These skills often require open-ended discussions, debates, and mentorship areas where human teachers excel (Duan et al., 2019).

3. The Role of Mentorship and Inspiration and Human Connection: Teachers provide irreplaceable mentorship and motivation. The human connection between teachers and students is a critical component of effective education. Teachers build trust, inspire confidence, and serve as role models for their students. These relationships are built on mutual respect, shared experiences, and genuine care qualities that AI cannot replicate. Teachers serve as role models for students, demonstrating values such as perseverance, integrity, and empathy. AI cannot replicate the inspirational and mentoring role that human teachers play in students' lives (Gobara & Ahmed, 2024). Teachers provide mentorship, guidance, and moral support, helping students navigate both academic and personal challenges. AI lacks the ability to form authentic relationships or understand the cultural, social, and emotional contexts that shape students' lives. Therefore, despite its potential as a supplementary tool, AI cannot substitute the transformative influence and mentorship provided by human educators.

AI can assist teachers by automating administrative tasks, personalizing learning, and providing data-driven insights. However, it cannot replace the emotional intelligence, creativity, and human connection that teachers bring to the classroom. These qualities are essential for fostering a supportive, engaging, and inspiring learning environment. As such, the role of teachers remains irreplaceable, and AI should be viewed as a tool to enhance, rather than replace, human educators.

4. LITERATURE REVIEW

The following section presents a series of case studies that illustrate the diverse applications of AI as a complementary tool in education, spanning multiple disciplines and educational levels. These empirical examples demonstrate how AI can enhance teaching and learning while addressing sector-specific challenges and opportunities. The selected studies highlight innovative implementations of AI technologies, from literacy development in higher education to specialized applications in health professions, design, and early childhood education. Each case study examines AI's role in supporting pedagogical objectives, including personalized learning, inclusive education, skill development, and ethical governance. Collectively, they reveal how AI can augment educators' capabilities when thoughtfully integrated into curricula, while also underscoring persistent challenges related to data accuracy, algorithmic bias, and the preservation of critical thinking skills. By analyzing these real-world applications, this section provides insights into best practices for leveraging AI's potential while maintaining the irreplaceable human elements of teaching and learning. The cases are organized thematically to showcase both the breadth of AI's educational applications and the common principles that emerge across contexts, offering a comprehensive perspective on AI's evolving role as a pedagogical partner.

In order to assess the current status of the literature, a comprehensive literature review was performed to identify significant topics and contemporary research trends concerning AI literacy in adult education and higher learning. Laupichler and others were analyzed ten research databases resulting in 902 initial records. Thirty of these were selected for analysis based on pre-defined eligibility requirements. Concerning the definition of AI literacy in adult education and the instructional resources suitable for non-experts, the findings indicated that research in this domain remains promising and requires further development (Laupichler et al., 2022). A systematic review of 19 peer-reviewed journal articles highlights advancements in AI literacy education across various disciplines. The study emphasizes the importance of critical thinking, ethical reasoning, and practical skills in managing AI-driven complexities. It introduces the AI literacy framework, which includes four dimensions: knowledge and understanding of AI, use and application of AI, evaluation and creation of AI, and AI ethics. The study also explores the Gen-AI literacy framework, designed specifically for generative AI, and provides recommendations for integrating it into curricula. A course designed as application for pre-service teachers integrates AI literacy across disciplines using the TPACK framework and social learning theory. The course equips educators with skills to develop AI-enhanced lesson plans, evaluate AI tools, and address ethical considerations (Smith, 2024). A study at a university in Hong Kong evaluated the impact of an AI literacy course on business students. The course combined self-paced materials, hands-on activities, and case study discussions to develop students' understanding of AI concepts, ethical use, and critical analysis of AI systems. Students used generative AI tools to complete assignments, with a focus on ethical considerations and data-driven decision-making (S.-C. Kong et al., 2023).

A study in Japan investigates the use of AI in inclusive education, focusing on students with mild disabilities. The Learning and Evidence Analysis Framework (LEAF) was used to analyze learning logs and detect specific behaviors. The study highlights the potential of AI to personalize learning and support diverse learners, while also addressing challenges such as data accuracy and human involvement in orchestrating inclusive practices. AI tools like digital e-book readers (e.g., BookRoll) were used to identify students' strengths and stumbling points, providing tailored support for learners with special needs (Toyokawa et al., 2023).A study at a UK university integrated generative AI tools into a module to enhance student employability skills. Students were encouraged to use AI tools ethically and responsibly, with a focus on critical analysis and prompt engineering. The study found that hands-on experiential learning sessions significantly improved students' proficiency and engagement with AI. Generative AI tools like ChatGPT were used to support academic writing, with students comparing AI-generated responses to textbook content. This approach fostered critical thinking and ethical considerations (Blommerde et al., 2024) . A study of 14 prestigious universities in the U.S. examined strategies for responsible AI governance. The findings highlight the importance of multi-unit governance, role-specific guidelines, and academic policies to address ethical and integrity concerns related to AI usage. Universities developed guidelines to balance the benefits of AI (e.g., personalized learning) with challenges like academic integrity and data privacy (Wu et al., 2024) . A qualitative study of 11 design educators explored how AI could support assessment and feedback in project-based learning contexts. The study proposed "situating analytics," a methodology that aligns AI tools with human practices to provide on-demand, learning objectives-based feedback. AI tools were used to analyze design creativity metrics like fluency, flexibility, and visual consistency, helping instructors provide targeted feedback to students (Jain et al., 2024). A systematic review of AI applications in health professions education found that AI tools can enhance personalized learning and performance assessment. However, the study also identified challenges, such as variable accuracy of AI models and potential over-reliance on AI-generated responses, which may hinder critical thinking. AI-powered tools like virtual reality simulations and natural language processing (NLP) were used to track student progress and improve communication skills in clinical settings (Feigerlova et al., 2025) . A case study on AI in supply chain education demonstrated that integrating generative AI tools enhanced student engagement and satisfaction. Students with prior AI exposure found the activities more beneficial, indicating the importance of foundational AI literacy before domain-specific applications. Generative AI was used to simulate supply chain scenarios, helping students develop skills in logistics, forecasting, and customer service (Shalpegin & Nguyen, 2024) .

AI-powered toys and apps are being developed to support early learning and cognitive development. These tools use adaptive learning algorithms to tailor content to individual children's needs. AI tools like speech to-text and text-to-speech technologies are used to support language development in young learners. The integration of AI in learning environments raises important ethical considerations, particularly concerning algorithmic bias and data privacy protections (Ahmed, Hassan, et al., 2024). AI excels in structured, repetitive tasks such as grading, drills, and personalized practice, allowing teachers to dedicate more time to higher order activities like mentoring and creative instruction. Additionally, AI's ability to analyze student performance data helps identify learning gaps, enabling teachers to tailor interventions more effectively. However, human educators remain indispensable for tasks requiring empathy, motivation, and innovative thinking, such as providing essay feedback or fostering critical thinking, as parents and students trust humans to navigate ambiguity and inspire learning(Lan, 2024). Teachers also play a crucial role in building relationships, modelling social skills, and addressing ethical dilemmas, areas where AI currently falls short. For AI to gain broader acceptance, providers must demonstrate its efficacy in niche areas, such as language pronunciation tools, while acknowledging human superiority in holistic education. To maximize benefits, AI should be strategically integrated as an assistant rather than a substitute, with hybrid models leveraging AI for administrative tasks and personalized learning while teachers focus on discussions and project-based learning (Sanusi et al., 2022).

These case studies demonstrate the transformative potential of AI in education, from personalized learning and inclusive education to ethical governance and skill development. However, challenges such as data privacy, bias, and over-reliance on AI must be addressed to ensure equitable and effective implementation. Current research suggests that AI's most effective role in education is as a complementary resource that enhances, rather than replaces, the irreplaceable human dimensions of teaching, maintaining educators' central role in fostering meaningful learning experiences while leveraging technological efficiencies.

5. POTENTIAL RISKS OF OVER-RELIANCE ON AI IN EDUCATION

While the integration of AI in education offers numerous benefits that can enhance the learning experience, it is essential to acknowledge the potential risks associated with excessive reliance on AI systems. Overdependence on these technologies may inadvertently introduce challenges that could undermine the fundamental educational objectives they are intended to support (Ding et al., 2024). Among these risks are various ethical dilemmas, the deterioration of essential human interactions, and the possibility of adverse effects on the overall learning processes and developmental trajectories of students. The potential risks associated with an over-dependence on artificial intelligence within the realm of education are multifaceted and complex:

- Loss of Human Connection and Emotional Support: A critical drawback of excessive AI integration in education is the potential weakening of meaningful teacher-student connections, which are essential for nurturing emotional well-being and interpersonal growth (Li et al., 2024). Unlike AI, educators provide irreplaceable human qualities, such as empathy, personalized mentorship, and ethical guidance, that foster student motivation and psychological resilience. AI's inherent lack of emotional intelligence renders it incapable of perceiving or responding to the complex emotional and psychological needs of learners. Consequently, an over-automated learning environment risks leaving students feeling disconnected, unsupported, and disengaged, particularly in moments requiring nuanced human understanding or encouragement(Leino et al., 2024).

- Bias and Inequality in AI Systems: The efficacy and impartiality of artificial intelligence systems are fundamentally contingent upon the quality and neutrality of the data upon which they are trained; thus, if such training data is imbued with inherent biases, the resulting AI may not only perpetuate existing inequalities but may also exacerbate them, thereby placing certain groups of students at a distinct disadvantage (Quiroz-Martinez & Rushton, 2024). The algorithms employed by AI technologies have the potential to reinforce pre-existing racial, gender, or socioeconomic biases inherent in the data, leading to a scenario in which students from underrepresented or marginalized backgrounds may receive recommendations that are less accurate or equitable, consequently hindering their educational opportunities and outcomes (Dai et al., 2024).
- Privacy and Data Security Concerns: The operational framework of many AI systems frequently involves the extensive collection and analysis of vast quantities of student data, which inevitably raises significant concerns regarding the privacy rights of individuals and the security of sensitive data (Espartinez, 2024). The increasing reliance on AI solutions not only amplifies the risk of potential data breaches but also raises the possibility of the misuse of sensitive information, as the data accumulated by AI systems may fall prey to unauthorized access or hacking attempts. Moreover, there exists a substantive risk that the data collected for educational purposes could be repurposed for activities beyond the educational sphere, such as commercial profiling or targeted advertising, thereby compromising student privacy (Fundi et al., 2024).
- Reduction in Critical Thinking and Creativity: An excessive dependence on AI for decision-making processes and problem-solving tasks has the potential to dissuade students from cultivating essential skills, such as critical thinking and creativity, which are fundamental to their cognitive development (Alwaqdani, 2024). AI systems tend to offer standardized, predefined answers, which may inadvertently limit opportunities for students to engage in open-ended exploration and innovative thought. Consequently, students may develop an over-reliance on AI tools for obtaining answers, which could diminish their capacity to think independently and critically. Furthermore, it

is imperative to recognize that AI lacks the ability to replicate the creative and improvisational dimensions that characterize human teaching and mentorship (Jiang et al., 2024).

- Erosion of Teacher Autonomy and Expertise: The over-reliance on AI technologies in educational settings can significantly undermine the pivotal role of teachers by eroding their autonomy and diminishing their decision-making authority within the classroom (Balasooriya, 2024). Educators may experience pressure to conform to recommendations generated by AI systems, even in instances where such recommendations are at odds with their professional expertise and judgment. Furthermore, AI systems often prioritize operational efficiency over pedagogical effectiveness, which can lead to a homogenized "one-size-fits-all" approach to education that fails to accommodate diverse learner needs. If AI assumes control over a multitude of instructional tasks, teachers may lose valuable opportunities to hone their skills and develop their professional expertise in a dynamic educational environment (Chanda et al., 2025).
- Digital Divide and Inequitable Access: The pervasive over-reliance on AI technologies has the potential to exacerbate the existing digital divide, as not all students possess equal access to the requisite technological resources necessary for engaging in AI-driven educational experiences (Cooper et al., 2025). This digital inequity can serve to widen pre-existing disparities in educational outcomes, particularly affecting students located in under-resourced or rural areas who may lack the necessary internet connectivity, or devices required for effective utilization of AI tools. Consequently, an over-dependence on AI may disproportionately disadvantage students who are less technologically literate or familiar with digital tools, thereby perpetuating cycles of inequality in educational achievement (Duan et al., 2019).
- Overemphasis on Standardization: AI systems frequently operate based on standardized metrics and assessments, which may fail to capture the comprehensive spectrum of student abilities and diverse learning styles that exist within a typical classroom environment (Shalpegin & Nguyen, 2024). An excessive reliance on AI in educational contexts can lead to a constricted focus on test scores and quantifiable outcomes, thereby neglecting the development of essential skills that, while less easily measurable, are equally important, such as creativity, emotional intelligence, and collaboration. Students who exhibit unique or non-traditional learning styles may be overlooked or inadequately supported within an AI-driven educational framework that prioritizes standardization over individualization.
- Ethical Concerns About AI Decision-Making: The decision-making processes of AI systems are predicated on complex algorithms, which may not

consistently align with ethical principles or educational values that are foundational to effective teaching and learning (Petersson et al., 2023). The overreliance on AI technologies raises critical concerns regarding accountability and transparency in educational decision-making processes, as it can be exceedingly challenging to discern the rationale behind the decisions made by AI systems, leading to a pervasive lack of clarity and openness. Furthermore, there exists a tangible risk that AI may make decisions that do not serve the best interests of either students or educators, thereby undermining the ethical fabric of the educational landscape (Laupichler et al., 2022).

AI holds great promise for transforming education through personalized learning, efficiency, and accessibility, but its unchecked use risks compromising essential educational values. Key challenges include weakened teacher-student relationships, reduced educator autonomy, perpetuated biases, privacy concerns, and diminished creativity, highlighting a paradox where AI's strengths (standardization, scalability) may also be its limitations. Beyond technical issues, these concerns touch on deeper pedagogical and ethical questions, as AI lacks human empathy and may prioritize quantifiable outcomes over holistic growth. Disparities in access and opaque decision-making further complicate its adoption(S. C. Kong et al., 2023). The solution lies in a balanced approach: AI should augment, not replace, teachers, supporting their role in nurturing critical thinking and emotional development. This requires ethical oversight, teacher-centered design, and hybrid models that leverage AI's efficiency while preserving human connection and judgment.

These challenges underscore the continued necessity for teacher oversight in implementing educational technologies responsibly. AI's role in education is complementary rather than competitive, serving as a powerful support tool rather than a replacement for human educators (Shao et al., 2025).

6. STRIKING THE BALANCE: AI AND TEACHER COLLABORATION

Striking a balance between AI and teacher collaboration is essential for maximizing the benefits of technology while preserving the irreplaceable human elements of education. When AI is used as a complementary tool rather than a replacement, it can enhance teaching effectiveness, personalize learning, and reduce administrative burdens. Below is a discussion of how to achieve this balance:

- AI as a Tool for Personalized Learning: AI can analyze student data to identify individual learning needs and provide tailored resources, allowing teachers to focus on delivering personalized instruction. This collaboration ensures that students receive both the benefits of technology and the guidance of a human teacher. Platforms like DreamBox and Knewton use AI to adapt learning materials to student performance, while teachers use the insights to provide targeted support (S. C. Kong et al., 2021).

- Automating Administrative Tasks: AI can handle time-consuming administrative tasks, such as grading and attendance tracking, freeing up teachers to focus on instruction and student interaction. Tools like Gradescope use AI to automate grading, allowing teachers to spend more time on lesson p(Okonkwo & Ade-Ibijola, 2021)t (Okonkwo & Ade-Ibijola, 2021).
- Enhancing Teacher Professional Development: AI can provide teachers with data-driven insights into their teaching practices, helping them refine their strategies and improve student outcomes. Platforms like Edthena use AI to analyze classroom videos and provide feedback to teachers, supporting their professional growth (Sanusi et al., 2022).
- Fostering Collaborative Learning Environments: AI can facilitate collaborative learning by grouping students based on their strengths and weaknesses, while teachers guide the process and provide mentorship. Tools like Schoology and Google Classroom use AI to recommend group activities and resources, while teachers oversee the collaborative process.
- Supporting Inclusive Education: AI can help identify students who need additional support, such as those with learning disabilities or language barriers, while teachers provide the necessary interventions. Tools like Brain Power use AI to support students with autism, while teachers adapt their instruction to meet individual needs (Holmes et al., 2019).
- Balancing AI and Human Judgment: Teachers play a critical role in interpreting AI-generated data and making informed decisions. AI should provide recommendations, but teachers should retain the final say in instructional strategies. Platforms like Century Tech offer AI-driven insights, but teachers use their professional judgment to implement the recommendations (Selwyn, 201(K.
- Ethical and Responsible Use of AI: Teachers and policymakers must ensure that AI is used ethically, with transparency, fairness, and accountability. This includes addressing biases in AI algorithms and protecting student privacy. Schools using AI tools like Turnitin must ensure that data is used responsibly and that students understand how their information is being used.
- Professional Development for AI Integration: Teachers need training to effectively integrate AI into their classrooms. Professional development programs can help educators understand how to use AI tools and interpret the data

they provide. Programs like ISTE's AI Explorations provide teachers with resources and training on AI integration.

Striking a balance between AI and teacher collaboration requires a thoughtful approach that leverages the strengths of both. AI can enhance education by personalizing learning, automating tasks, and providing data-driven insights, but teachers remain essential for providing emotional support, fostering creativity, and making ethical decisions. By working together, AI and teachers can create a more effective and inclusive learning environment.

7. CONCLUSION

The integration of artificial intelligence (AI) in educational settings has sparked considerable scholarly debate regarding its potential role as either a complementary tool or a competitive force in relation to human educators. While AI holds significant promise in revolutionizing pedagogical methods through personalized learning systems, automation of administrative tasks, and data-driven instructional insights, it remains fundamentally unable to replicate the essential human qualities that define quality teaching. Contemporary research suggests that AI should not be viewed as a replacement for educators, but rather as a supportive mechanism to enhance teaching effectiveness and optimize learning outcomes. Empirical evidence highlights AI's ability to facilitate differentiated instruction through advanced learning analytics, reduce educator workload through automated assessments, and identify at-risk students early, enabling teachers to concentrate on higher-order mentoring and individualized support. However, AI lacks emotional intelligence, creative pedagogical judgment, and the ability to provide ethical guidance, key competencies of human educators. The emerging consensus advocates for a synergistic model where AI enhances operational efficiency and personalized learning while preserving the human elements critical for socio-emotional development, critical thinking, and moral reasoning. To implement this balanced approach, educational institutions must prioritize ethical AI frameworks, comprehensive educator professional development, and human-centered pedagogical design. The ideal educational paradigm envisions AI as an augmentative rather than a substitutive technology, working alongside human educators to create more adaptive, inclusive, and effective learning environments.

REFERENCES

Ahmed, Z. E., Hashim, A. H. A., Saeed, R. A., & Saeed, M. M. A. (2024). AI-enhanced education: Bridging educational disparities. In *AI-Enhanced Teaching Methods* (pp. 88–107). IGI Global., DOI: 10.4018/979-8-3693-2728-9.ch004

Ahmed, Z. E., Hassan, A. A., & Saeed, R. A. (2024). *AI-Enhanced Teaching Methods* (Ahmed, Z. E., Hassan, A. A., & Saeed, R. A., Eds.). IGI Global., DOI: 10.4018/979-8-3693-2728-9

Al-khresheh, M. H. (2024). Bridging technology and pedagogy from a global lens: Teachers' perspectives on integrating ChatGPT in English language teaching. *Computers and Education: Artificial Intelligence*, *6*, 100218. Advance online publication. DOI: 10.1016/j.caeai.2024.100218

Al-Zawqari, A., Peumans, D., & Vandersteen, G. (2022). A flexible feature selection approach for predicting students' academic performance in online courses. *Computers and Education: Artificial Intelligence*, *3*, 100103. Advance online publication. DOI: 10.1016/j.caeai.2022.100103

Alwaqdani, M. (2024). Investigating teachers' perceptions of artificial intelligence tools in education: Potential and difficulties. *Education and Information Technologies*. Advance online publication. DOI: 10.1007/s10639-024-12903-9

Balasooriya, C. (2024). AI in education: A futuristic vision. *Medical Teacher*, *46*(7), 986–988. DOI: 10.1080/0142159X.2024.2352160 PMID: 38725359

Bhutoria, A. (2022). Personalized education and Artificial Intelligence in the United States, China, and India: A systematic review using a Human-In-The-Loop model. *Computers and Education: Artificial Intelligence*, *3*, 100068. Advance online publication. DOI: 10.1016/j.caeai.2022.100068

Blommerde, T., Charalambous, E., Bright, W., Musgrave, E., Ueno, L., & Magee, T. (2024). Integrating Generative Artificial Intelligence into Teaching and Assessment: A Case Study from a University in the UK. In O'Dea, X., & Ng, D. T. K. (Eds.), *Effective Practices in AI Literacy Education: Case Studies and Reflections* (pp. 119–129). Emerald Publishing Limited., DOI: 10.1108/978-1-83608-852-320241013

Bryant, J., Heitz, C., Sanghvi, S., & Wagle, D. (2020). *How artificial intelligence will impact K-12 teachers.*

Chanda, R. C., Vafaei-Zadeh, A., Hanifah, H., & Ramayah, T. (2025). Artificial intelligence teaching assistant adoption in university education: Key drivers through the ability, motivation and opportunity framework. *Education and Information Technologies*, *30*(10), 14123–14164. Advance online publication. DOI: 10.1007/s10639-025-13360-8

Chiu, T. K. F., Meng, H., Chai, C. S., King, I., Wong, S., & Yam, Y. (2022). Creation and Evaluation of a Pretertiary Artificial Intelligence (AI) Curriculum. *IEEE Transactions on Education*, *65*(1), 30–39. DOI: 10.1109/TE.2021.3085878

Cooper, G., Tang, K. S., & Fitzgerald, A. (2025). Intersections of Mind and Machine: Navigating the Nexus of Artificial Intelligence, Science Education, and the Preparation of Pre-service Teachers. *Journal of Science Education and Technology*. Advance online publication. DOI: 10.1007/s10956-025-10200-9

Dai, R., Thomas, M. K. E., & Rawolle, S. (2024). The roles of AI and educational leaders in AI-assisted administrative decision-making: A proposed framework for symbiotic collaboration. *Australian Educational Researcher*. Advance online publication. DOI: 10.1007/s13384-024-00771-8

Ding, A.-C. E., Shi, L., Yang, H., & Choi, I. (2024). Enhancing teacher AI literacy and integration through different types of cases in teacher professional development. *Computers and Education Open*, *6*, 100178. DOI: 10.1016/j.caeo.2024.100178

Duan, Y., Edwards, J. S., & Dwivedi, Y. K. (2019). Artificial intelligence for decision making in the era of Big Data – evolution, challenges and research agenda. *International Journal of Information Management*, *48*, 63–71. DOI: 10.1016/j.ijinfomgt.2019.01.021

Espartinez, A. S. (2024). Exploring student and teacher perceptions of ChatGPT use in higher education: A Q-Methodology study. *Computers and Education: Artificial Intelligence*, *7*, 100264. Advance online publication. DOI: 10.1016/j.caeai.2024.100264

Feigerlova, E., Hani, H., & Hothersall-Davies, E. (2025). A systematic review of the impact of artificial intelligence on educational outcomes in health professions education. *BMC Medical Education*, *25*(1), 129. DOI: 10.1186/s12909-025-06719-5 PMID: 39871336

Fundi, M., Sanusi, I. T., Oyelere, S. S., & Ayere, M. (2024). Advancing AI education: Assessing Kenyan in-service teachers' preparedness for integrating artificial intelligence in competence-based curriculum. *Computers in Human Behavior Reports*, *14*, 100412. Advance online publication. DOI: 10.1016/j.chbr.2024.100412

Gašević, D., Siemens, G., & Sadiq, S. (2023). Empowering learners for the age of artificial intelligence. In *Computers and Education: Artificial Intelligence* (Vol. 4). Elsevier B.V. DOI: 10.1016/j.caeai.2023.100130

Gobara, R. E. G. E., & Ahmed, Z. E. (2024). Preparing students for an AI-enhanced future. In *AI-Enhanced Teaching Methods* (pp. 286–304). IGI Global., DOI: 10.4018/979-8-3693-2728-9.ch013

Holmes, W., Bialik, M., & Fadel, C. (2019). Artificial Intelligence. In *Education Promises and Implications for Teaching and Learning*. Center for Curriculum Redesign.

Hwang, G. J., Xie, H., Wah, B. W., & Gašević, D. (2020). Vision, challenges, roles and research issues of Artificial Intelligence in Education. In *Computers and Education: Artificial Intelligence* (Vol. 1). Elsevier B.V. DOI: 10.1016/j.caeai.2020.100001

Jain, A., Kerne, A., Fowler, H., Seo, J., Newman, G., Lupfer, N., & Perrine, A. (2024). *How Could AI Support Design Education? A Study Across Fields Fuels Situating Analytics.*

Jiang, J., Vetter, M. A., & Lucia, B. (2024). *Toward a 'More-Than-Digital' AI Literacy: Reimagining Agency and Authorship in the Postdigital Era with ChatGPT.* Postdigital Science and Education., DOI: 10.1007/s42438-024-00477-1

Karataş, F., Eriçok, B., & Tanrikulu, L. (2025). Reshaping curriculum adaptation in the age of artificial intelligence: Mapping teachers' <scp>AI</scp> -driven curriculum adaptation patterns. *British Educational Research Journal, 51*(1), 154–180. DOI: 10.1002/berj.4068

Kim, J. (2024). Leading teachers' perspective on teacher-AI collaboration in education. *Education and Information Technologies, 29*(7), 8693–8724. DOI: 10.1007/s10639-023-12109-5

Kong, S. C., Cheung, W. M. Y., & Tsang, O. (2023). Evaluating an artificial intelligence literacy programme for empowering and developing concepts, literacy and ethical awareness in senior secondary students. *Education and Information Technologies*, *28*(4), 4703–4724. DOI: 10.1007/s10639-022-11408-7

Kong, S.-C., Cheung, W. M.-Y., & Zhang, G. (2023). Evaluating an Artificial Intelligence Literacy Programme for Developing University Students' Conceptual Understanding, Literacy, Empowerment and Ethical Awareness. *Journal of Educational Technology & Society*, *26*, 16–30.

Kong, S. C., Man-Yin Cheung, W., & Zhang, G. (2021). Evaluation of an artificial intelligence literacy course for university students with diverse study backgrounds. *Computers and Education: Artificial Intelligence*, *2*, 100026. Advance online publication. DOI: 10.1016/j.caeai.2021.100026

Lan, Y. (2024). Through tensions to identity-based motivations: Exploring teacher professional identity in Artificial Intelligence-enhanced teacher training. *Teaching and Teacher Education*, *151*, 104736. DOI: 10.1016/j.tate.2024.104736

Laupichler, M. C., Aster, A., Schirch, J., & Raupach, T. (2022). Artificial intelligence literacy in higher and adult education: A scoping literature review. *Computers and Education: Artificial Intelligence*. DOI: 10.1016/j.caeai.2022.100101

Leino, R. K., Kaqinari, T., Makarova, E., & Döring, A. K. (2024). Connectedness with students as a key factor in online teaching self-efficacy. *Computers and Education Open*, *6*, 100192. DOI: 10.1016/j.caeo.2024.100192

Li, B., Lowell, V. L., Wang, C., & Li, X. (2024). A systematic review of the first year of publications on ChatGPT and language education: Examining research on ChatGPT's use in language learning and teaching. In *Computers and Education: Artificial Intelligence* (Vol. 7). Elsevier B.V. DOI: 10.1016/j.caeai.2024.100266

Luo, M., Hu, X., & Zhong, C. (2025). The collaboration of AI and teacher in feedback provision and its impact on EFL learner's argumentative writing. *Education and Information Technologies*, *30*(12), 17695–17715. Advance online publication. DOI: 10.1007/s10639-025-13488-7

Molefi, R. R., Ayanwale, M. A., Kurata, L., & Chere-Masopha, J. (2024). Do in-service teachers accept artificial intelligence-driven technology? The mediating role of school support and resources. *Computers and Education Open*, *6*, 100191. DOI: 10.1016/j.caeo.2024.100191

Ng, D. T. K., Leung, J. K. L., Chu, S. K. W., & Qiao, M. S. (2021). Conceptualizing AI literacy: An exploratory review. *Computers and Education: Artificial Intelligence*, *2*, 100041. Advance online publication. DOI: 10.1016/j.caeai.2021.100041

Okonkwo, C. W., & Ade-Ibijola, A. (2021). Chatbots applications in education: A systematic review. In *Computers and Education: Artificial Intelligence* (Vol. 2). Elsevier B.V. DOI: 10.1016/j.caeai.2021.100033

Osman, S. A., & Ahmed, Z. E. (2024). Navigating AI integration: Case studies and best practices in educational transformation. In *AI-Enhanced Teaching Methods* (pp. 240–267). IGI Global., DOI: 10.4018/979-8-3693-2728-9.ch011

Petersson, L., Vincent, K., Svedberg, P., Nygren, J. M., & Larsson, I. (2023). Ethical Perspectives on Implementing AI to Predict Mortality Risk in Emergency Department Patients: A Qualitative Study. *Studies in Health Technology and Informatics*, *302*, 676–677. DOI: 10.3233/SHTI230234 PMID: 37203776

Quiroz-Martinez, D., & Rushton, E. A. C. (2024). Exploring strategies to sustain teacher agency in the context of 'hyper-accountability': Reflections from ten experienced chemistry school teachers in Chile. *Teaching and Teacher Education*, *152*, 104787. Advance online publication. DOI: 10.1016/j.tate.2024.104787

Saeed, M. M. A., Saeed, R. A., Ahmed, Z. E., Gaid, A. G. S. A., & Mokhtar, R. A. (2024). AI technologies in engineering education. In *AI-Enhanced Teaching Methods* (pp. 61–87). IGI Global., DOI: 10.4018/979-8-3693-2728-9.ch003

Sanusi, I. T., Oyelere, S. S., & Omidiora, J. O. (2022). Exploring teachers' preconceptions of teaching machine learning in high school: A preliminary insight from Africa. *Computers and Education Open*, *3*, 100072. DOI: 10.1016/j.caeo.2021.100072

Schiff, D. (2021). Out of the laboratory and into the classroom: The future of artificial intelligence in education. *AI & Society*, *36*(1), 331–348. DOI: 10.1007/s00146-020-01033-8 PMID: 32836908

Selwyn, N. (2019). *Should robots replace teachers?: AI and the future of education*. John Wiley & Sons.

Shalpegin, T., & Nguyen, A. (2024). AI in Supply Chain Education. In O'Dea, X., & Ng, D. T. K. (Eds.), *Effective Practices in AI Literacy Education: Case Studies and Reflections* (pp. 71–79). Emerald Publishing Limited., DOI: 10.1108/978-1-83608-852-320241008

Smith, C. (2024). Effective Practices in AI Literacy Education: A Legal Education Perspective. In O'Dea, X., & Ng, D. T. K. (Eds.), *Effective Practices in AI Literacy Education: Case Studies and Reflections* (pp. 127–137). Emerald Publishing Limited., DOI: 10.1108/978-1-83608-852-320241014

Srinivasan, V. (2022). AI & learning: A preferred future. *Computers and Education: Artificial Intelligence*, *3*, 100062. Advance online publication. DOI: 10.1016/j.caeai.2022.100062

Su, J., Ng, D. T. K., & Chu, S. K. W. (2023). Artificial Intelligence (AI) Literacy in Early Childhood Education: The Challenges and Opportunities. In *Computers and Education: Artificial Intelligence* (Vol. 4). Elsevier B.V. DOI: 10.1016/j.caeai.2023.100124

Toyokawa, Y., Horikoshi, I., Majumdar, R., & Ogata, H. (2023). Challenges and opportunities of AI in inclusive education: A case study of data-enhanced active reading in Japan. *Smart Learning Environments*, *10*(1), 67. Advance online publication. DOI: 10.1186/s40561-023-00286-2

Wu, C., Zhang, H., & Carroll, J. M. (2024). AI Governance in Higher Education: Case Studies of Guidance at Big Ten Universities. *Future Internet*, *16*(10), 354. DOI: 10.3390/fi16100354

Zawacki-Richter, O., Marín, V. I., Bond, M., & Gouverneur, F. (2019). Systematic review of research on artificial intelligence applications in higher education – where are the educators? *International Journal of Educational Technology in Higher Education*, *16*(1), 39. DOI: 10.1186/s41239-019-0171-0

Chapter 9
Redefining the Role of Educators, Not Replacing Them:
Strategies for Creating Content With AI

Joe Terantino
https://orcid.org/0000-0002-3552-4993
Oklahoma State University, USA

Sidra Zaheer
https://orcid.org/0009-0003-8082-7867
Oklahoma State University, USA

Yimeng Zhu
https://orcid.org/0009-0000-8888-9040
Oklahoma State University, USA

ABSTRACT

This chapter discusses the evolving relationship between artificial intelligence and education by arguing that AI should empower educators rather than replace them. While AI offers significant benefits such as personalized instruction, improved lesson planning, and enhanced assessment capabilities, education fundamentally requires human connection, empathy, and adaptive instruction that AI cannot replicate. We suggest a five-pronged model that redefines educators' roles in light of AI advancements and in conjunction with the Technological Pedagogical Content Knowledge (TPACK) technology integration framework. Our model posits the role of educators with AI integration as Innovators, Instructional Designers, Facilitators of Critical

DOI: 10.4018/979-8-3373-0396-3.ch009

Thinking, Ethical and Moral Guides, and Social-Emotional Mentors. The chapter explores practical applications of AI for content creation across curriculum planning, presentational instruction, interactions, and assessment, and offers guidance for educators to effectively integrate AI while maintaining pedagogical oversight and the human element of teaching.

The role of educators worldwide is rapidly evolving in the face of ongoing technological advancements, especially with artificial intelligence (AI) recently emerging as a disruptive tool in many facets of the educational landscape. We now live in a world where educators have real concerns about the potential impacts of AI on education, including benefits and unintended consequences. Some have documented threats to teaching and learning, such as academic integrity concerns (Perkins, 2023), that prompt maintaining a cautious and balanced approach to AI integration. Yet, AI can also be a powerful tool to transform how teachers design, deliver, and adapt their curriculum (Adıgüzel et al., 2023). As our classrooms grow increasingly more diverse, AI offers educators the ability to create tailored materials that cater to individual learning needs (Kolluru et al., 2018), streamline lesson planning (Bucchiarone, 2024), and enrich the overall learning experience (Barrios-Beltran, 2024). AI's potential to enhance education is also linked to several positive learning outcomes, including enhanced engagement, motivation, and skill development (Xu, 2024).

Furthermore, this growing body of research serves to highlight several important impacts on education. First, there is a need for educational stakeholders to better prepare students and teachers for the appropriate use of AI. AI competencies need to be integrated into content curricula to assist learners in developing such skills and appropriate uses, and we need to provide more AI professional development for educators at all levels. Second, the role educators play in terms of shaping the use of AI is still evolving. Notably, the presence of AI in education has significantly increased the imperative for educators to better understand AI tools, their uses and misuses, and to leverage them in their teaching and learning practices. As Velander et al. (2024, p. 4086) note, "This 'new normality' requires teachers to be able to teach about different aspects of AI related to different subject topics as well as different age groups." We argue here that the role of educators should be redefined to empower them to harness the potential of AI, rather than be replaced by it.

By integrating AI-driven methods, teachers can not only save time (Fitria, 2023) but also unlock new creative possibilities in the classroom (Habib et al., 2024) that have the potential to empower them to meet the unique challenges of modern education. To further illustrate these opportunities, this chapter explores how educators must transform their roles as educators to successfully integrate AI into their instructional practices. Whether you are a veteran educator or new to teaching, this chapter will provide actionable insights and examples to help you integrate AI into your educational practices.

AN INTRODUCTION TO AI IN EDUCATION

The implementation of AI in education began in the 1960s and 1970s with rule-based tutoring systems like SCHOLAR and PLATO, which offered basic, programmed instruction (Nwana, 1990). This form of instruction was intended to simulate one-on-one instruction and consisted of delivering educational content in small, sequential steps, followed by the learner receiving immediate feedback on their responses. In the 1980s and 1990s, researchers expanded their work on intelligent tutoring systems by utilizing AI to further replicate aspects of one-on-one human tutoring, including adapting to the learner's pace and level of understanding, providing immediate and personalized feedback, asking guiding questions, and adjusting instructional strategies based on the learner's responses (Nwana, 1990). Although the early forms of intelligent tutoring systems could not fully match the flexibility and intuition of a human tutor, they marked an important step toward the creation of more personalized, AI-based learning experiences.

As technologies continued to evolve, and computing power and data availability grew in the 2000s, AI applications expanded to include adaptive learning platforms, automated grading, and predictive analytics (Zhai et al., 2021). More recently, advancements in machine learning and natural language processing have enabled the development of sophisticated tools such as chatbots, virtual teaching assistants, and personalized learning environments. These technologies allow systems to analyze vast amounts of data, recognize patterns in student behavior, and understand human language with increasing accuracy. As a result, chatbots and virtual teaching assistants have become more effective in providing real-time support, answering student queries, and offering explanations in natural, conversational language (Davar et al., 2025). Overall, these advancements have positioned AI as a driving force in reshaping how we conceptualize and implement modern education.

Key Benefits of AI for Teachers

While research to date has highlighted the benefits of AI for learners (Barrios-Beltran, 2024; Bucchiarone, 2024; Kolluru et al., 2018; Xu, 2024), it is equally important to note the potential for AI to benefit teachers and enhance their teaching practices. Based on their capacity for natural language processing and intelligent content creation, AI tools offer several advantages for teachers, including but not limited to improved lesson planning and content creation for more personalized instruction (Baidoo-Anu & Ansah, 2023; Wang & Li, 2024).

Effective teaching begins with well-structured lesson plans and high-quality instructional materials. Arguably, the potential for AI to improve lesson planning and content creation is the most significant benefit to teachers and learners, because it has the most direct impact on the quality of learning (Iqbal et al., 2021). AI can generate materials quickly and in a variety of formats such as lesson plans, worksheets, assessments, images, and videos. This increased efficiency for teachers affords them opportunities to attend to other aspects of teaching and learning, especially to focus more on developing students' critical thinking and problem-solving skills (van den Berg & du Plessis, 2023). AI can also customize this content for varied learning levels and diverse students' needs to support more inclusive and equitable instruction (Song et al., 2024). For example, AI can increase language and accessibility support for multilingual learners by generating enrichment activities, providing real-time captions, or modifying the comprehensibility of texts. Thus, AI allows teachers to personalize instruction and learning activities to meet the diverse needs of their students by differentiating content and providing targeted support, ensuring that all students receive the resources and guidance necessary for academic success.

Argument for AI Not Replacing Teachers

As discussed, the advancement of AI tools in recent years has rapidly transformed education. However, let us get directly to the point. AI cannot replace teachers, because education is not just about delivering content. While research related to AI has demonstrated its ability to enhance learning experiences, reshape teaching methodologies, and optimize administrative tasks (Onesi-Ozigagun et al., 2024), effective teaching requires critical thinking, empathy, and adaptability (Akbarovna; 2024). Our argument against AI replacing teachers relies on three principal points: the importance of teacher-student relationships, the complexity of teaching, and the role of teachers in fostering students' social and emotional development.

First, at the heart of effective teaching is the human relationship between students and teachers, which cannot be replicated by AI. Researchers have consistently documented the positive impacts of strong and meaningful teacher-student relationships on students' academic outcomes (Jadoon et al., 2022; Zee et al., 2021), motivation (Timms, 2016; Zee et al., 2021), and overall well-being (Goetz et al., 2021). In a longitudinal study with 10th and 11th grade students, Goetz et al. (2021) found that higher teacher-student relationship quality was associated with stronger positive emotions such as enjoyment and pride and weaker negative emotions including anxiety, anger, boredom, and shame. This type of research demonstrates the human nature of teaching and potential impact that teachers may have on their students.

While AI may simulate empathetic responses when interacting with student users, it does not genuinely understand or connect with students on a personal level, and students still value and respect human teachers more than AI (Chan & Tsi, 2023).

Second, teaching involves much more than just delivering content. Teachers manage the dynamic and constantly evolving classroom, foster students' critical thinking, and adapt to diverse learning styles. To achieve this, teachers employ a variety of pedagogical strategies and cultural responsiveness to meet students' unique needs. For example, teachers who practice Culturally Relevant Pedagogy emphasize the importance of connecting academic content to students' cultural backgrounds, experiences, and identities (Ladson-Billings, 1995). This approach not only helps students feel seen and valued but also enhances their engagement and comprehension by linking new concepts to their lived realities. From a Vygotskian sociocultural perspective, students need this type of social interaction in their learning process, particularly through scaffolding, where teachers guide students within their zone of proximal development (Vygotsky, 1978). Moreover, teaching is an art as much as a science (Marzano, 2017), which integrates human characteristics including creativity, humor, storytelling, and adaptability. Teachers must respond to varying student needs, unexpected challenges, and evolving educational demands with flexibility and resilience. This may involve adjusting lesson plans on the spot, incorporating alternative teaching methods, or addressing social and emotional dynamics that arise during instruction. By remaining adaptable, teachers ensure that learning remains relevant, engaging, and accessible to foster a supportive environment where students can thrive despite any obstacles. AI, however, operates within the boundaries of programmed algorithms and cannot adapt, innovate, or think outside these predefined parameters.

Third, teaching is about building connections, inspiring curiosity, and nurturing the whole learner. "The emotional bond and interpersonal skills that teachers have are essential for students' personal growth and development. Teachers can understand, empathize, and motivate students in a way that AI cannot" (Chan & Tsi, 2023). As such, teachers play a critical role in fostering students' social and emotional development, foundational for long-term success in both academic and personal endeavors (Schonert-Reichl, 2017). Personal interactions in real-world contexts, between adult teachers and students, enable the teachers to serve as mentors and role models, thus cultivating their students' social and emotional skills, such as empathy, collaboration, and resilience (Xiang et al., 2022). Teachers also possess emotional intelligence, empathy, and cultural awareness, which enable them to adapt to the diverse needs of their students and reinforce positive behaviors in ways that AI cannot replicate. Thus, a teacher's role in navigating ethical, emotional, and social challenges is irreplaceable in the educational journey.

In conclusion, while AI has the potential to transform education and teaching, it cannot and should not replace teachers. The human connection, complex artistry of teaching, and the teacher's role in fostering social and emotional growth are essential elements of the teacher that AI cannot replicate successfully. Teachers are not merely disseminators of knowledge; they are human beings that live, breathe, and constantly evolve.

Carving Out New Roles for Teachers

In this evolving educational landscape, teachers remain irreplaceable, but we need to shift our conceptualization of educators' roles to prioritize human-centric aspects of teaching, such as mentorship, empathy, and creativity, while collaborating with AI to enrich the learning experience. As educators ourselves, we have come to realize that our roles extend far beyond simply delivering content; they constantly evolve to meet the changing needs of our students. Therefore, integrating AI into education does not replace the teacher but rather transforms our responsibilities, requiring us to adapt and take on multiple roles to ensure meaningful and effective learning experiences. As Koehler and Mishra (2009) explain, "teaching is a complicated practice that requires an interweaving of many kinds of specialized knowledge." Their Technological Pedagogical Content Knowledge (TPACK) framework outlines an approach for integrating technology into content area teaching, which connects these various forms of teacher knowledge in a meaningful way. In Figure 1, we extend this line of thinking to further illustrate the emerging roles of educators with AI integration embedded in the TPACK model. Our goal is to highlight the complex nature of AI integration, and the interconnection of the educator roles and various forms of knowledge required for successful integration.

Figure 1. Educator Roles with AI Embedded in the TPACK Framework

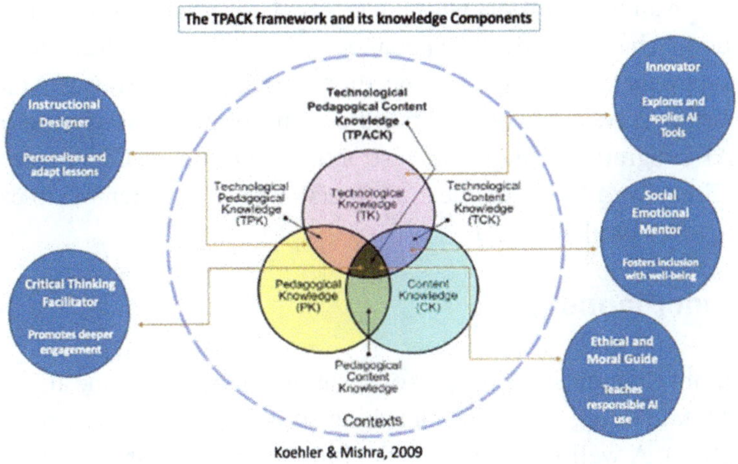

Figure 1 demonstrates how teachers remain at the core of education by adapting their roles and building on TPACK to integrate AI technology effectively. As an Innovator, educators explore and make key decisions around the adoption of cutting-edge technologies, including AI tools, that drive innovation in teaching practices and classroom dynamics. As an Instructional Designer, they leverage AI tools to create and adapt personalized, engaging lesson plans that cater to diverse learners. Educators adapt strategies, assess progress, and modify instruction accordingly. In addition, as a Facilitator of Critical Thinking, they extend their role as instructional designers to encourage students to think deeply and apply knowledge to complex, real-world problems. They encourage inquiry, problem-solving, and independent thought. In their role as an Ethical and Moral Guide, teachers educate students on ethical AI use, data privacy, and the societal impact of technology. In this capacity, teachers also critically review AI outputs. Last, as a Social-Emotional Mentor, educators support students' well-being by fostering a safe and inclusive learning environment, building interpersonal relationships, and addressing students' social and emotional needs. Later in this chapter, we will expand on these initial explanations to discuss how these roles apply directly to AI integration.

AI INTEGRATION

The following sections of this chapter serve to elaborate on the roles that educators will need to assume to be successful with the integration of AI in education. First, we conceptualize AI integration within four instructional areas: curriculum planning, presentational instruction, interactions, and assessment. Next, we delineate the nature of available AI tools within each mode of use, including discussions of their functional characteristics and pedagogical affordances. These discussions are intended to provide an overview, not be all inclusive, as the array of AI tools is vast and constantly evolving. Lastly, we build on our previous description of teachers' roles for AI integration (Innovator, Instructional Designer, Facilitator of Critical Thinking, Ethics and Moral Guide, and Social-Emotional Mentor) to explore how best to adopt and implement AI.

Curriculum Planning

Curriculum planning is the process of designing, organizing, and aligning instructional content, learning objectives, teaching strategies, and assessments (Martone & Sireci, 2009). A well-structured curriculum integrates best practices in teaching supported by content area standards and research, and aims to increase academic achievement, promote critical thinking, and prepare students for real-world challenges. Wiggins & McTighe (2005) put forward the backward design approach to achieving curriculum alignment, which includes starting with the desired learning outcomes and working backwards to develop instructional activities and assessments. By using backward design, educators design curriculum based on providing meaningful and coherent learning experiences that ensure students achieve deep understanding rather than just rote memorization.

Curriculum planning adheres to a structured process that begins with defining learning objectives aligned with educational standards and student needs. Bloom's taxonomy (Krathwohl, 2002) is a widely used hierarchical framework that categorizes learning objectives across six cognitive skills levels: Remember, Understand, Apply, Analyze, Evaluate, and Create. Starting with sound objectives enables teachers to gradually develop students' critical thinking skills. Next, teachers design or identify assessments to measure student progress toward achieving the objectives through formative and summative evaluations of their learning. Then, teachers fill in the instructional gaps between objectives and assessments by selecting and organizing instructional content in a logical sequence. At this point, teachers also choose their instructional strategies and learning materials, including texts and multimedia, to cater activities to diverse learners. If done successfully, the result of curriculum planning should be a structured learning experience that aligns with educational standards, meets diverse student needs, and fosters meaningful academic growth.

AI TOOLS FOR CURRICULUM PLANNING.

AI-powered tools assist educators in various aspects of curriculum planning. For lesson and unit planning, it is important to distinguish between task specific vs. prompt-based AI tools. Popular task-specific AI tools for education, such as MagicSchool.ai and Diffit for Teachers, offer predetermined and specific curriculum planning options available at the user's click of a button. These include built-in tools for generating lesson plans and unit plans to streamline curriculum planning. MagicSchool.ai also provides more targeted curriculum options including an Individualized Education Program Generator, 5E Model Lesson Plan for science, Project Based Learning, Social Emotional Learning Lesson Plan, Accommodation Suggestions, Advanced Learning Plan, and a 504 Plan Generator. These options allow educators to generate plans differentiated with students' diverse needs in mind. Other built-in options allow educators to enhance specific components of lessons by generating writing exercises, assessments, and scaffolding strategies. Figure 2 displays the graphic interface for MagicSchool.ai's Lesson Plan Generator.

Figure 2. MagicSchool.ai Lesson Plan Generator

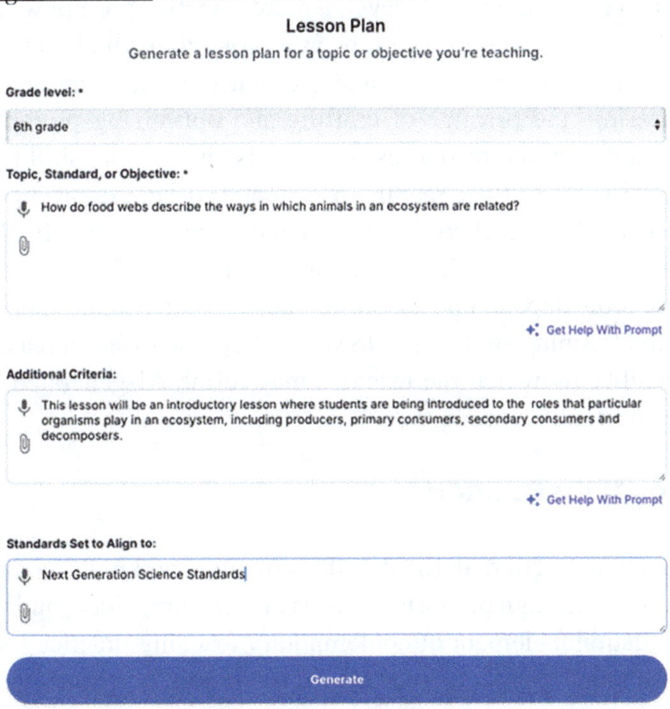

As displayed, educators utilize the generator by selecting the targeted grade level and inputting the topic or learning objective for the lesson. They also have an option to provide further details and select specific standards to assist with alignment. The example depicted in Figure 2 relates to food webs and ecosystems within the field of science. Appendix A displays the output generated by MagicSchool.ai, which organizes the lesson plan in a bulleted outline form. Key components of the AI-generated lesson plan include a step-by-step guide to opening and teaching new content, guided and independent learner practice, and extension and homework activities. Aligned with the standards indicated, the lesson plan also includes samples for suggested worksheets and learning activities, and specific guidance for the teacher related to providing constructive feedback, prompting classroom discussion, and developing critical thinking.

While task-specific AI tools are designed intentionally for K-12 educators, with predetermined, structured tools for curriculum planning, prompt-based AI tools (e.g., ChatGPT and Gemini) require more user input to achieve the same purpose. More detailed prompts typically yield better outputs generated by prompt-based tools. For example, to continue with the science example provided previously based on food webs and ecosystems, one might prompt ChatGPT, “Create a lesson plan on food webs and ecosystems.” However, a more effective prompt would be, “Create a 6th grade lesson plan on food webs and ecosystems, including an engaging warm-up activity, a hands-on activity, and a formative assessment.” In this manner, prompt engineering, the practice of crafting and optimizing prompts to get the most effective and accurate responses from AI, is an essential skill for leveraging prompt-based AI tools to their maximum potential. Because prompt-based tools are not pre-formatted for teachers, the lesson plans generated will likely need additional formatting and organization that require more manual adjustments made by teachers. These tools depend on teacher guidance to determine specific standards, grade levels, and teaching strategies. However, they also offer increased flexibility and customizability by which the teachers may refine AI-generated lesson plans through cycles of iterative prompts.

Presentational Instruction

Presentational instruction, defined as the structured and multimodal delivery of educational content through platforms such as PowerPoint, video, and infographics, remains a foundational element of contemporary teaching practice (Altinay et al., 2024). A multimodal approach to instruction, one that combines visual, textual, and auditory elements, serves to enhance both comprehension and engagement by addressing diverse learner preferences and needs (Nouri & Shahid, 2005).

The central aim of presentational instruction is to communicate complex ideas in clear and accessible ways, all while sustaining learners' interests. Effective presentational instruction draws on cognitive learning approaches for multimedia learning, which advocate for streamlined and well-integrated content delivery (Christina & Panagiotidis, 2024). By focusing on essential content and avoiding distractions, educators can help students achieve a deeper understanding of the material. For example, the assertion-evidence model, where slides present a clear main idea supported by concise and relevant visual evidence, has been shown to enhance both comprehension and retention (Garner & Alley, 2013). This approach attempts to align related text and visuals to ensure that students can easily connect the two without confusion or cognitive strain (Moundridou et al., 2024).

The benefits of presentational instruction extend beyond structural clarity and content delivery. When implemented with pedagogical intent, it becomes a powerful means of promoting active learning and student engagement (Chiu & Chai, 2020). Rather than positioning learners as passive recipients of information, well-designed presentations invite them to interact meaningfully with content and to analyze, question, and connect ideas across different sources. This process not only encourages higher-order thinking, but also supports the development of self-regulated learning practices, as students learn to monitor their understanding and take greater ownership of their learning journey (Kosmala et al., 2024). Additionally, research highlights how multimedia presentations that include videos create visually rich and immersive environments that help students stay engaged and develop a deeper understanding of the content (Christina & Panagiotidis, 2024). Beyond engagement, video-based instruction encourages self-paced learning, giving students the space to revisit complex topics as needed—ultimately promoting greater autonomy and confidence in their learning process (Moundridou et al., 2024).

AI TOOLS FOR PRESENTATIONAL INSTRUCTION.

AI has introduced new possibilities for teachers in designing, delivering, and refining instructional materials, particularly in presentational instruction. Traditionally, educators have dedicated significant time to creating and structuring content, selecting visuals, and ensuring clarity in their delivery. While these efforts remain essential, AI-powered tools now serve as assistive technologies that streamline these processes. They allow teachers to focus more on student engagement, inquiry-driven learning, and conceptual reinforcement. Table 1, while not all inclusive, offers a comprehensive look at the types of products that various AI tools can generate in relation to presentational instruction. This overview also details specific AI tools within each category and their key functions.

Table 1. AI Tools for Presentational Instruction

Category and AI Tools	AI Function
Text and Written Content ChatGPT, Diffit for Teachers, Gemini, QuillBot, Scholarcy	Summarize texts, articles, or chapters, highlighting key points to make learning more efficient.
ChatGPT, Diffit for Teachers, Gemini, Synthesia, VideoScribe	Generate step-by-step explanations of complex concepts, adapting to different proficiency levels.
ChatGPT, Gemini, Jasper, Writesonic	Write original texts of various genres, such as essays, research papers, or blog posts on given topics.
Multimedia Content Murf.ai, NaturalReader	Convert text-based materials into audio.
Canva, Diffit for Teachers, Piktochart	Generate educational images, diagrams, and infographics to visually explain difficult concepts.
VideoScribe, Synthesia	Create video content by converting text-based content into voiceovers and adding visual aids.
Synthesia	Generate voiceovers or personalized audio summaries for instructional videos or podcasts.
Prezi	Build non-linear, story-driven, interactive presentations
Learning or Practice Materials ChatGPT, Diffit for Teachers, Gemini, QuillBot, Scholarcy	Summarize texts, articles, or chapters.
ChatGPT, Gemini, Jenni.ai	Generate reading materials such as stories, case studies, or articles tailored to subject matter.
ChatGPT, Gemini) PowerPoint with Copilot	Create personalized study guides based on student needs, focusing on specific topics or concepts.
Kahoot (as quiz format)	Generate flashcards for vocabulary, formulas, or key concepts.
Kahoot, Mentimeter	Provide personalized feedback on students' work based on their performance.
MagicSchool.ai, PowerPoint with Copilot	Adjust content to match the pace and learning style of individual students, ensuring they remain engaged.
ChatGPT, Diffit for Teachers, Gemini, MagicSchool.ai, Rewordify, Wordtune Read	Generate customized vocabulary lists according to topics or learners' needs.
Eduaide.ai, Grammarly, QuillBot	Create grammar exercises targeting specific language points like sentence structure or syntax.

These AI tools extend beyond basic content creation to enhance how educators structure, deliver, and adapt instructional materials to meet the needs of diverse learners. While each tool has a primary function, their versatility allows teachers to leverage them in innovative ways. For example, PowerPoint with Copilot assists with slide design and helps educators from diverse academic disciplines to organize information effectively. Similarly, Synthesia and VideoScribe while commonly used for video production, promote accessibility and comprehensibility through multilingual narration and animated visualizations. In addition, tools like Mentimeter and Kahoot foster active learning by turning traditional presentations into interactive experiences and encouraging real-time student participation through polls, quizzes, and discussions.

Although many of these tools are designed for broad instructional use, several of the tools exhibit distinctive features that make them particularly valuable in specific content areas. For example, Piktochart is particularly effective in STEM education where the creation of data-driven infographics helps students visualize and interpret complex scientific or statistical information. Figure 3 depicts an infographic of the water cycle as generated by Piktochart.

Figure 3. The Water Cycle: Nature's Recycling System Using Piktochart

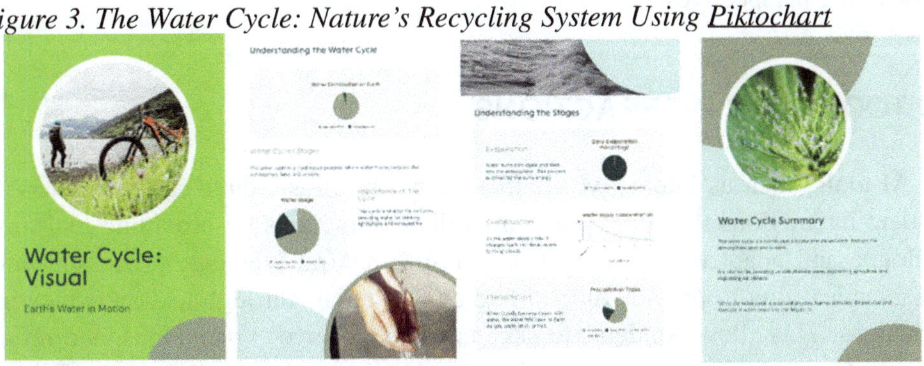

Interactions

Interactions in education refer to various forms of communication and engagement that occur between students and teachers and students with other students. Based on Vygotsky's (1978) theory of social constructivism, which emphasizes the importance of social interactions and guided learning experiences for knowledge development, classroom interactions are an essential component of the teaching and learning process that help to foster active learning and learner engagement. Teacher-student interactions typically consist of direct instruction, questioning or discussions, and cycles of feedback, whether oral or written. Teachers often use these interactions to guide students' understanding of content material. On the other hand, student-student interactions in the classroom tend to be more collaborative in nature, such as projects, peer discussions, and think-pair-share activities. These types of interactions, often implemented as a form of project-based learning in which students research solutions to real-world problems (Boss & Krauss, 2022), encourage students to co-construct understanding of new content through negotiation of meaning with others and exposure to different perspectives.

Meaningful interactions are important for the teaching and learning process, because they support cognitive and social development (Tenebaum et al., 2020). When students engage in meaningful conversations with teachers or their classmates, they have opportunities to co-construct knowledge, rather than just memorize discrete facts. This form of learning allows them to develop higher order thinking skills, advancing them further on Bloom's taxonomy. Similarly, interactions within problem-based learning have notable effects on students' communication skills, collaboration, empathy, and self-confidence (Rafli et al., 2018). Through well-designed and structured interaction in the classroom, students learn to express their own thoughts and opinions, listen actively and discerningly, and respond appropriately to differing perspectives.

AI TOOLS FOR INTERACTIONS

AI tools, such as interactive chatbots and virtual assistants can facilitate AI-student interactions that simulate human-like interactions by providing real-time dialogue and adaptive feedback. Chatbots use natural language processing and machine learning to provide human-like conversations through text and voice interactions. This allows students to ask questions, receive explanations, and refine their understanding through interactive conversations with AI. Within the field of language education, Duolingo Chatbot, depicted in Figure 4, allows learners to engage in role play conversations in a variety of languages, which helps improve speaking and listening skills (Handini et al., 2022). In the following example, the Duolingo Chatbot engages the user in Spanish to navigate the use of various colors in artistic presentation.

Figure 4. Interaction with Duolingo Chatbot in Spanish

More broadly, AI-based virtual assistants, including Siri, Alexa, Google Assistant, and ChatGPT, have the capacity to generate personalized tutoring sessions in which students can initiate interactions by asking targeted questions from their content area of study. Other uses of AI chatbots and virtual assistants include various simulations or role plays that allow students to engage in practical learning experiences such as a virtual lab or an historical reenactment.

The most immediate benefits of these AI-supported learner interactions include personalized responses and adaptive feedback (Baidoo-Anu & Ansah, 2023; Wang & Li, 2024). However, human-AI interactions have also been linked to improvements in learning outcomes, reduced cognitive overload, and increased retention of new material (Zawacki-Richter et al., 2019). Furthermore, because AI chatbots and virtual assistants provide 24-hour availability for students, they can engage in various forms of self-directed learning at any time and any place. Enhanced intrinsic motivation within specific content areas, for example in language (Moybeka et al., 2023) and science education (Deveci Topal et al., 2021).

Assessment

Assessment, a fundamental aspect of the educational process, serves to measure student learning, provide feedback, and inform instructional decisions (Johnson, 2013). It involves the systematic collection and review of information about student progress and achievement (Sokhanvar et al., 2021). Assessment can take various forms, including formative assessments that monitor learning during instruction and summative assessments that evaluate learning at the end of a unit or course (Owan et al., 2023). These complementary approaches serve different purposes in the learning cycle, with formative assessment guiding ongoing instruction and summative assessment providing comprehensive evaluation of achievement (Black & Wiliam, 2009). According to Boud and Soler (2016), assessment practices should prepare students for immediate learning goals and future learning needs throughout their academic and personal lives.

Digital technologies have transformed traditional assessment methods by enabling more personalized, immediate feedback and adaptive evaluation techniques (Gikandi et al., 2011). The integration of technology in assessment has opened new possibilities for measuring complex skills and competencies that were previously difficult to evaluate (Redecker & Johannessen, 2013). Researchers have also emphasized the importance of involving students in the assessment process through self and peer assessment to foster metacognitive skills and deeper engagement with learning material (Panadero et al., 2019). Additionally, Gulikers et al. (2008) highlight the value of authentic assessment practices that mirror real-world applications of knowledge, which help bridge the gap between theoretical understanding and practical implementation. Effective assessment is critical for supporting student success, ensuring educational accountability, and improving the quality of teaching and learning.

AI TOOLS FOR ASSESSMENT

AI has emerged as a transformative technology with the potential to revolutionize educational assessment by automatically scoring student work, providing instant feedback, adapting to individual needs, and generating data-driven insights (Miserandino, 2024). Furthermore, AI enhances design and delivery by streamlining the creation of varied and adaptive assessment instruments. Table 2 provides an overview of various AI-powered educational tools, highlighting their key features, applicable content areas, and primary users.

Table 2. Overview of AI-Powered Assessment Tools

AI Tool	AI Function	Field of Application	Primary User
Socrative	Generates questions and monitors student progress in real-time. Adjusts instruction accordingly.	General Education	Teacher
AutoCrit	Provides feedback on writing for grammar, style, and content.	Writing, Language Arts	Student
Cognii	Creates individualized learning paths based on student needs.	General Education	Student and Teacher
GradeScope	Streamlines grading of written texts by comparing submission with assignment details.	STEM, Humanities	Teacher
Khan Academy	Creates personalized learning paths with targeted practice exercises.	Math, Science, Humanities	Student
Quizlet	Offers adaptive learning paths.	General Education	Student

Table 2 serves as a guide to understanding which tools are best suited for different educational needs. This table showcases a selection of AI-powered educational tools, each with unique features designed to enhance learning and teaching experiences in assessment by offering real-time progress monitoring, personalized learning paths, writing evaluation, and automated grading. For instance, Socrative is particularly beneficial for teachers who need to create and administer quizzes and polls, while AutoCrit excels in offering detailed feedback on writing, making it ideal for students looking to improve their grammar, style, and content.

AI tools also offer the power to generate practice problems or quizzes tailored to specific topics, difficulty levels, and individual student needs. Figure 5 shows a set of reading comprehension questions and sample answers generated by the AI tool Khan Academy based on an article about the voyage of the Mayflower during the early colonization of North America.

Figure 5. Assessment Questions Generated by Khan Academy

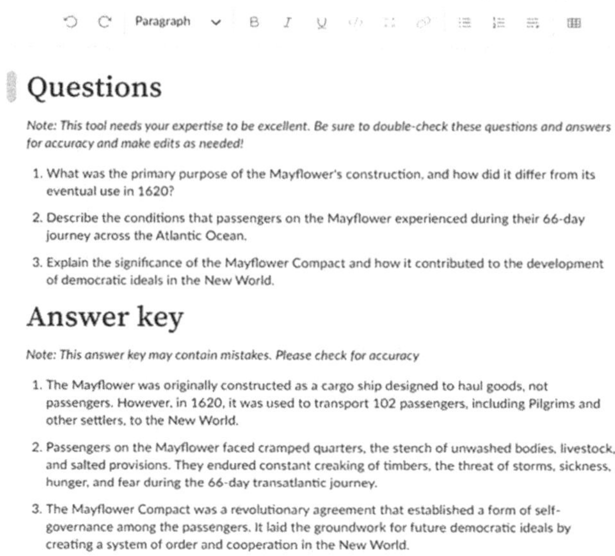

Paragraph

Questions

Note: This tool needs your expertise to be excellent. Be sure to double-check these questions and answers for accuracy and make edits as needed!

1. What was the primary purpose of the Mayflower's construction, and how did it differ from its eventual use in 1620?
2. Describe the conditions that passengers on the Mayflower experienced during their 66-day journey across the Atlantic Ocean.
3. Explain the significance of the Mayflower Compact and how it contributed to the development of democratic ideals in the New World.

Answer key

Note: This answer key may contain mistakes. Please check for accuracy

1. The Mayflower was originally constructed as a cargo ship designed to haul goods, not passengers. However, in 1620, it was used to transport 102 passengers, including Pilgrims and other settlers, to the New World.
2. Passengers on the Mayflower faced cramped quarters, the stench of unwashed bodies, livestock, and salted provisions. They endured constant creaking of timbers, the threat of storms, sickness, hunger, and fear during the 66-day transatlantic journey.
3. The Mayflower Compact was a revolutionary agreement that established a form of self-governance among the passengers. It laid the groundwork for future democratic ideals by creating a system of order and cooperation in the New World.

Our example depicted in Figure 5 demonstrates that AI tools can produce diverse question sets for history content; however, this function also applies to other subjects like math, science, and language arts, and the questions can be tailored to cater to a range of skill levels. In addition, Khan Academy includes sample answers for the teacher's convenience.

One of the primary advantages of AI assessment tools is their ability to provide immediate, consistent, and detailed feedback to students (Sokhanvar et al., 2021). Automated scoring systems can quickly evaluate student responses and offer targeted suggestions for improvement. For example, AI-powered writing evaluation tools can assess the quality of student essays in terms of grammar, structure, and content, and provide specific recommendations for revision (Owan et al., 2023). This real-time feedback can help students identify their strengths and weaknesses and take corrective action to enhance their learning. AI tools such as AutoCrit provide student authors with explicit feedback on various aspects of their writing including word choice and sentence structure. It will even generate an evaluative score based on the criterion provided by the teacher.

Through such automated scoring, AI assessment tools also have the potential to reduce teacher workload and save time spent on grading (Miserandino, 2024). This shift allows teachers to attend to other facets of their work such as providing individualized support. In addition, unlike traditional grading, where students might have to wait days or even weeks for feedback, AI-generated evaluations can offer instant insights that allow learners to reflect on their work and make necessary adjustments in real time. This form of immediate feedback encourages students to take more ownership of their learning experiences. Moreover, AI enables students and teachers to track performance and progress over time, identify patterns and trends, and make data-informed decisions (Sokhanvar et al., 2021) about next steps.

Redefining the Role of Educators

Educators play an essential role in integrating AI tools into academic content creation. As presented in Table 1, these roles vary from instructional designer to ethics and moral guide to navigate the components of academic content creation, including curriculum planning, presentational instruction, interactions, and assessment. This section highlights these varying roles so that teachers may maintain pedagogical oversight to ensure teaching and learning with AI are meaningful and student-centered, attend to diverse student needs, and foster critical thinking.

Educator as Innovator with AI Integration

Often as innovators in education, educators are the first to experiment with and critically review available technology-based tools to determine which is best suited for their teaching context and learning objectives. The same evaluative process applies to AI integration, and Figure 6 displays a cycle of steps for adopting AI that we have created to guide the process of selecting and implementing an AI tool for educational purposes.

Figure 6. Steps for AI Integration

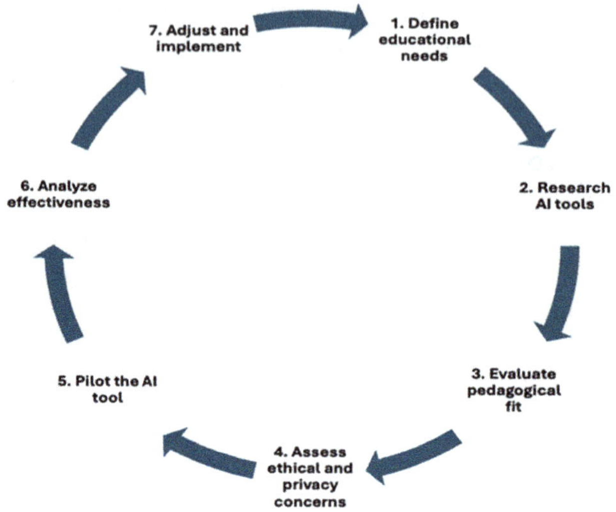

With these steps in mind, as innovators, teachers typically pilot test AI tools within a specific educational context before full-scale implementation. Depending on their familiarity with AI tools and proficiency in prompting, they may select a task-specific tool or prompt-based tool. Educators should first consider their instructional objectives and the most effective way to enhance student comprehension.

By experimenting with and reflecting on AI use, educators play an active role in shaping how it enhances educational content creation. In curriculum planning, for example, teachers leverage AI tools creatively and strategically to enhance learning experiences. In presentational instruction, is the focus on structuring content with clarity and coherence? PowerPoint with Copilot enables teachers to refine slide organization to make sure that key information is sequenced logically and that each slide is balanced visually. Does the material involve complex data or abstract concepts? Tools like VideoScribe and Piktochart generate structured diagrams, infographics, and animations that make it easier to illustrate scientific processes, financial trends, or mathematical models. To develop innovative interactions with AI, teachers may rely on AI-driven simulations based in virtual environments using chatbots and virtual assistants. Will interactivity help reinforce learning? Mentimeter and Kahoot introduce live quizzes, polling, and discussion prompts that transform static presentations into dynamic learning experiences and include components that teachers may utilize to assess student progress.

Educator as Instructional Designer with AI Integration

The role of educators when attempting to integrate AI also goes beyond simply adopting AI; it includes shaping its use in ways that align with pedagogical best practices, academic standards, and student needs. As instructional designers, teachers ensure the AI-generated lesson plans, activities, and assessments present a cohesive curriculum that aligns with the educational objectives and standards. While AI can enhance efficiency and personalization in curriculum planning, the teacher remains at the center, ensuring that curriculum is relevant and of high quality. When integrating AI into presentational design, teachers work to maintain the quality of the instructional materials through their expertise, adaptability, and creativity. AI is a cognitive partner that enhances efficiency, content quality, and accessibility; however, it leaves pedagogical decision-making firmly in the hands of educators (Yang & Kyun, 2022).

For example, a history instructor covering World War II events may opt for creating an AI-based Prezi, such as this one https://prezi.com/p/edit/soptqj8nqpsw/ based on a non-linear storytelling approach. However, AI-generated historical overviews alone may lack critical perspectives and contextual depth. The teacher's role as instructional designer remains essential in integrating primary sources, promoting discussion-based analysis, and encouraging students to critically assess AI-generated narratives (Moundridou et al., 2024). Other AI-powered tools such as PowerPoint with Copilot assist in automating slide formatting, optimizing text-image balance, and suggesting layouts that enhance clarity and readability. However, AI lacks the ability to understand student needs, scaffold content appropriately, or provide explanations tailored to different learning levels. These responsibilities remain with the educator. Similarly, in the humanities and social sciences, a literature teacher may generate a thematic outline using ChatGPT to help analyze key discussion points from a novel. While this can offer a useful starting point, educators must refine AI-generated outlines, integrate critical perspectives, and guide students in constructing deeper literary interpretations. Research suggests that students demonstrate stronger reasoning and argumentation skills when AI-assisted structuring is combined with teacher-led discussions and inquiry-based learning (Altinay et al., 2024).

In relation to AI-based interactions, teachers' roles as instructional designers includes curating AI prompts, scenarios, and conversations that encourage students to think critically. Teachers should design such interactions to be inquiry and problem-based. This might include structuring chatbot interactions for language proactive, STEM-based problem-solving, or role plays with historical characters. In addition, educators should determine how AI best fits within the broader learning experience by deciding when and how students will engage with AI. Teachers should strive to achieve the same purpose when integrating AI for assessment by ensuring that

AI-driven assessments are pedagogically sound, balanced and fair, and beneficial for student learning.

Educator as Facilitator of Critical Thinking with AI Integration

Beyond content development, teachers act as facilitators of critical thinking to guide students in analyzing AI-generated information, questioning biases, and developing higher-order cognitive skills. They help students engage critically with AI outputs, ensuring that learning is not reduced to passive consumption or memorization. In presentational instruction, AI tools such as PowerPoint with Copilot and VideoScribe assist in structuring content, but teachers make pedagogical decisions regarding clarity, coherence, and the effectiveness of instructional delivery. Similarly, AI-generated materials in mathematics or the humanities require teacher intervention to ensure accuracy, appropriate scaffolding, and meaningful application.

AI-powered tools allow educators to integrate multimedia elements that enhance engagement and information retention. By incorporating audio, video, and interactive components, teachers can transform passive presentations into dynamic, multimodal learning experiences. However, AI-generated content alone does not guarantee engagement—teachers must strategically determine how and when to integrate these elements to maximize learning effectiveness. For instance, in language arts and ESL instruction, AI-powered narration in tools like Synthesia has been used to improve tone recognition and contextual comprehension. However, educators must reinforce these AI-generated resources with discussion exercises, role-playing activities, and guided listening tasks to ensure that students internalize linguistic patterns meaningfully (Yang & Kyun, 2022).

AI also enables real-time audience engagement through tools like Mentimeter and Kahoot, which embed interactive quizzes, polling, and formative assessments into presentations. However, the effectiveness of these tools depends on how educators analyze student responses, adapt instruction based on real-time feedback, and facilitate deeper discussion. Studies suggest that students retain information more effectively when interactive AI-driven recall exercises are combined with guided instructor feedback and personalized reinforcement strategies (Schussler et al., 2018).

Additionally, teachers foster student engagement by incorporating AI-generated multimedia elements, interactive quizzes, and discussion prompts into lessons. While AI tools such as Mentimeter and Kahoot facilitate real-time engagement, their effectiveness depends on how teachers analyze student responses, adapt instruction, and foster deeper discussion. In language instruction, AI-powered narration tools such as Synthesia support tone recognition and contextual comprehension, but teachers must complement these with discussion exercises and guided listening tasks.

Despite the advantages of AI assessment tools, it is important to recognize that they should complement rather than replace teacher judgment entirely. There are certain aspects of student learning that may be difficult for AI to capture, such as creativity, critical thinking, collaboration, and socio-emotional skills (Miserandino, 2024). Teachers are uniquely positioned to evaluate these complex competencies through observation, interaction, and professional insight. Moreover, AI assessment tools are not infallible and may have limitations or blind spots. For example, automated essay scoring systems may prioritize surface-level features such as word count or sentence structure over deeper aspects of writing quality such as argumentation or originality (Owan et al., 2023). As such, it is important for teachers to review AI-generated scores and feedback, and to exercise their own judgment in interpreting and applying the results.

The most effective assessment systems will likely involve a combination of AI and human input, leveraging the strengths of each approach. AI tools can provide efficient, consistent, and data-rich feedback at scale, while teachers can offer nuanced, contextualized, and student-centered insights (Sokhanvar et al., 2021). By working together, AI and teachers can create a more comprehensive, reliable, and actionable assessment system that supports student learning and success.

Educator as Ethical and Moral Guide with AI Integration

Teachers also serve as ethical and moral guides in AI-integrated classrooms. They ensure that AI is used ethically and critically in their classrooms, helping students recognize the limitations of AI-generated content. Since AI tools rely on pre-existing datasets, they can sometimes generate biased, incomplete, or misleading information. Teachers must guide students in analyzing AI-generated outputs critically, cross-checking sources, and questioning the assumptions behind AI responses. This is particularly important in fields such as history and social sciences, where AI-generated narratives may oversimplify complex topics or lack multiple perspectives. As ethical and moral guides, teachers encourage students to compare AI responses with scholarly sources and discuss credibility and algorithmic bias. Such work fosters students' digital literacy and responsible AI engagement (Chiu & Chai, 2020).

Educator as Socio-Emotional Mentor with AI Integration

While AI can support content creation in various capacities, it cannot replace the human connection and emotional intelligence that educators provide. The teacher's role as a socio-emotional guide when integrating AI tools is crucial to ensure that students feel supported. Teachers help students to navigate technological challenges to engage meaningfully with AI and to develop critical thinking skills while doing so. They also help learners to understand and manage emotions when interacting with AI.

From a perspective of culturally responsive pedagogy, teachers support students to develop interpersonal skills such as collaboration, conflict resolution, and empathy. Teachers employ elements of culturally responsive teaching to bridge cultural gaps and to build relationships and community within the classroom. They also connect students, teachers, parents, and the school and broader communities to establish supportive learning environments. When integrating AI in education, teachers work to ensure a social and emotional balance that prepares learners to avoid over reliance on AI. By playing this role as socio-emotional guide, teachers maintain education as a human-centered and emotionally supportive experience and help students to develop both cognitive and emotional intelligence.

PRACTICAL IMPLICATIONS

As we have described here, integrating AI into instructional practices brings significant promise; however, it also presents a range of challenges, especially ethical, pedagogical, technical, and institutional. Before concluding this chapter, we will offer a detailed look at several practical implications to address these key challenges.

First, AI uses algorithms to identify patterns and make predictions based on historical data, and the potential for AI to amplify existing biases is well known (Ferrara, 2023). Therefore, educators must conduct bias audits whenever implementing AI to support their instructional practices, whether it be reviewing educational outputs or any automated review of student work. Second, as educators increase their use of AI-based tools, it is possible that they will begin to over rely on AI (Khlaif et al., 2025). This may restrict teachers' professional and pedagogical agency and their ability to implement creative and flexible teaching approaches. It will be imperative that educators maintain discretionary oversight and continue to practice critical approaches to teaching that prioritize human judgment, adapt to the unique needs of learners, and foster reflective, inclusive, and context-sensitive pedagogy beyond what AI can offer. Third, pedagogically speaking, many educators lack training with AI and its integration in education. As a result, teachers may underutilize or misuse AI and its outputs. This potential for a skill gap among educators necessitates ongoing professional development for educators to build their digital literacy skills. Last, from a technical viewpoint, underfunded institutions may lack the infrastructure needed to support the use of AI tools in the classroom. Such institutions will need to implement equitable technology policies to ensure all educators and students can benefit from AI-enhanced learning environments.

CONCLUSION

In conclusion, as we look towards the future of education, one thing is clear; the role of the teacher is not fading, it is transforming. Rather than replacing or displacing educators, AI provokes us to reimagine our roles as educators at the center of an adaptive, responsive, and learner-driven system. This chapter has explored how AI can enrich, not replace, educators' instructional practices by offering new ways to design content, differentiate instruction, and build more engaging learning environments in our classrooms. Through multimodal tools, real-time feedback, and accessible learning formats, AI can extend what is possible in the classroom, while also reaffirming the irreplaceable value of the teacher's human judgement, care, and connection.

Teachers play a pivotal role in shaping AI use in education by promoting learners' agency, autonomy, and creativity. They ensure AI tools are used to enhance—not replace—meaningful learning experiences. By maintaining pedagogical oversight, adapting AI-generated materials for clarity and accessibility, and fostering critical engagement, educators ensure that AI supports high-quality, inclusive, and student-centered instruction.

Our contribution lies in redefining what it means to be a teacher in this evolving landscape. We have proposed a model that positions educators not as technicians of AI, but as Innovators, Instructional Designers, Facilitators of Critical Thinking, Ethical and Moral Guides, and Social-Emotional Mentors that reflect the depth and complexity of teaching in the AI area. By grounding the work in the TPACK framework, this model bridges the technological possibility with pedagogical purpose. In doing so, we shift the conversation from one of replacement to empowerment, where educators shape the direction of AI integration with intention and humanity. At its heart, this vision affirms that the future of education is not about choosing between humans and machines; it is about leveraging both to better serve all learners.

Publisher's Note

Correction Notice: A correction to this manuscript has been published
Reason: Figures were replaced

It was brought to our attention after being published that the images in this chapter were unreadable. We have replaced the images with better quality files.

Correction Date: March 30, 2026

REFERENCES

Adıgüzel, T., Kaya, M. H., & Cansu, F. K. (2023). Revolutionizing education with AI: Exploring the transformative potential of ChatGPT. *Contemporary Educational Technology*, *15*(3), ep429. DOI: 10.30935/cedtech/13152

Akbarovna, I. S. (2024). Professional skills of the teacher. *World of Science*, *7*(8), 1–7.

Altinay, Z., Altinay, F., Sharma, R. C., Dagli, G., Shadiev, R., Yikici, B., & Altinay, M. (2024). Capacity building for student teachers in learning, teaching artificial intelligence for quality of education. *Societies (Basel, Switzerland)*, *14*(8), 148. DOI: 10.3390/soc14080148

Baidoo-Anu, D., & Ansah, L. O. (2023). Education in the era of generative artificial intelligence (AI): Understanding the potential benefits of ChatGPT in promoting teaching and learning. *Journal of AI*, *7*(1), 52–62. DOI: 10.61969/jai.1337500

Barrios-Beltran, D. (2024). Enriching the Teaching-Learning Experience by Using AI Tools in the L2 Classroom. In *AI in Language Teaching, Learning, and Assessment* (pp. 61-77). IGI Global. DOI: 10.4018/979-8-3693-0872-1.ch004

Black, P., & Wiliam, D. (2009). Developing the theory of formative assessment. *Educational Assessment, Evaluation and Accountability*, *21*(1), 5–31. DOI: 10.1007/s11092-008-9068-5

Boss, S., & Krauss, J. (2022). *Reinventing project-based learning: Your field guide to real-world projects in the digital age*. International Society for Technology in Education.

Boud, D., & Soler, R. (2016). Sustainable assessment revisited. *Assessment & Evaluation in Higher Education*, *41*(3), 400–413. DOI: 10.1080/02602938.2015.1018133

Bucchiarone, A., Cicchetti, A., Vázquez-Ingelmo, A., Adami, F., Schiavo, G., García-Holgado, A., & García-Peñalvo, F. J. (2024, September). Designing and generating lesson plans combining open educational content and generative AI. In *Proceedings of the ACM/IEEE 27th International Conference on Model Driven Engineering Languages and Systems* (pp. 78-86). DOI: 10.1145/3652620.3687773

Chan, C. K. Y., & Tsi, L. H. (2023). The AI revolution in education: Will AI replace or assist teachers in higher education? *arXiv preprint arXiv:2305.01185*.

Chiu, T. K. F., & Chai, C. S. (2020). Sustainable curriculum planning for artificial intelligence education: A self-determination theory perspective. *Sustainability (Basel)*, *12*(14), 5568. DOI: 10.3390/su12145568

Christina, R., & Panagiotidis, P. (2024). Teachers' attitudes towards AI integration in foreign language learning: Supporting differentiated instruction and flipped classroom. *European Journal of Education*, *7*(2), 88–104. DOI: 10.26417/171oob60e

Davar, N. F., Dewan, M. A. A., & Zhang, X. (2025). AI chatbots in education: Challenges and opportunities. *Information (Basel)*, *16*(3), 1–25. DOI: 10.3390/info16030235

Deveci Topal, A., Dilek Eren, C., & Kolburan Geçer, A. (2021). Chatbot application in a 5th grade science course. *Education and Information Technologies*, *26*(5), 6241–6265. DOI: 10.1007/s10639-021-10627-8

Ferrara, E. (2023). Fairness and bias in artificial intelligence: A brief survey of sources, impacts, and mitigation strategies. *Sci*, *6*(1), 1–15. DOI: 10.3390/sci6010003

Fitria, T. N. (2023). The Use of Artificial Intelligence in Education: Can AI replace the teacher's role? *EPIGRAM (e-Journal)*, *20*(2), 165-187. DOI: 10.32722/epi.v20i2.5711

Garner, J., & Alley, M. (2013). How the design of presentation slides affects audience comprehension: A case for the assertion-evidence approach. *International Journal of Engineering Education*, *29*(6), 1564–1579.

Gikandi, J. W., Morrow, D., & Davis, N. E. (2011). Online formative assessment in higher education: A review of the literature. *Computers & Education*, *57*(4), 2333–2351. DOI: 10.1016/j.compedu.2011.06.004

Goetz, T., Bieleke, M., Gogol, K., van Tartwijk, J., Mainhard, T., Lipnevich, A. A., & Pekrun, R. (2021). Getting along and feeling good: Reciprocal associations between student-teacher relationship quality and students' emotions. *Learning and Instruction*, *71*, 101349. DOI: 10.1016/j.learninstruc.2020.101349

Gulikers, J. T., Bastiaens, T. J., & Kirschner, P. A. (2008). Authentic assessment, student and teacher perceptions: The practical value of the five-dimensional framework. *Journal of Vocational Education and Training*, *60*(4), 401–412. DOI: 10.1080/13636820802591830

Habib, S., Vogel, T., Anli, X., & Thorne, E. (2024). How does generative artificial intelligence impact student creativity? *Journal of Creativity*, *34*(1), 1–7. DOI: 10.1016/j.yjoc.2023.100072

Handini, B. S., Nurhasanah, N., & Panly, F. I. (2022). The effect of artificial intelligent technology used (Duolingo application) to enhance English learning. *ELLITE: Journal of English Language, Literature, and Teaching*, *7*(2), 86–94. DOI: 10.32528/ellite.v7i2.8354

Iqbal, M. H., Siddiqie, S. A., & Mazid, M. A. (2021). Rethinking theories of lesson plan for effective teaching and learning. *Social Sciences & Humanities Open*, *4*(1), 100172. DOI: 10.1016/j.ssaho.2021.100172

Jadoon, A. I., Khan, F., Syeda Tehmina Naz Bukhari, N. T. S., Gilani, S. Z., Ishfaq, U., & Ullah, M. (2022). Effect of teacher-student relationship on pro-social behavior and academic achievement of secondary school students. *Indian Journal of Economics and Business*, *21*(1), 331–337.

Johnson, S. (2013). On the reliability of high-stakes teacher assessment. *Research Papers in Education*, *28*(1), 91–105. DOI: 10.1080/02671522.2012.754229

Khlaif, Z. N., Hamamra, B., & Hussein, E. T. (2025). AI paradox in higher education: Understanding over-reliance, its impact, and sustainable integration. Preprint (Version 1) available at Research Square. DOI: 10.21203/rs.3.rs-6127885/v1

Koehler, M., & Mishra, P. (2009). What is technological pedagogical content knowledge (TPACK)? *Contemporary Issues in Technology & Teacher Education*, *9*(1), 60–70. DOI: 10.1177/002205741319300303

Kolluru, V., Mungara, S., & Chintakunta, A. N. (2018). Adaptive learning systems: Harnessing AI for customized educational experiences. [IJCSITY]. *International Journal of Computer Science and Information Technologies*, *6*(1), 13–26. DOI: 10.5121/ijcsity.2018.6302

Kosmala, K., Marszałek, A., & Rudawska, E. (2024). Communication in project team management: Identification of research gaps and direction for future research. *European Research Studies*, *27*(Special Issue A, S2), 732–751. DOI: 10.35808/ersj/3746

Krathwohl, D. R. (2002). A revision of Bloom's taxonomy: An overview. *Theory into Practice*, *41*(4), 212–218. DOI: 10.1207/s15430421tip4104_2

Ladson-Billings, G. (1995). Toward a theory of culturally relevant pedagogy. *American Educational Research Journal*, *32*(3), 465–491. DOI: 10.3102/00028312032003465

Martone, A., & Sireci, S. G. (2009). Evaluating alignment between curriculum, assessment, and instruction. *Review of Educational Research*, *79*(4), 1332–1361. DOI: 10.3102/0034654309341375

Marzano, R. J. (2017). *The new art and science of teaching*. Solution Tree Press.

Miserandino, M. (2024). Authentic and creative assessment in a world with AI. *Teaching of Psychology*, •••, 1–6. DOI: 10.1177/00986283241260370

Moundridou, M., Matzakos, N., & Doukakis, S. (2024). Generative AI tools as educators' assistants: Designing and implementing inquiry-based lesson plans. *Computers and Education: Artificial Intelligence*, *5*, 100277. DOI: 10.1016/j.caeai.2024.100277

Moybeka, A. M., Syariatin, N., Tatipang, D. P., Mushthoza, D. A., Dewi, N. P. J. L., & Tineh, S. (2023). Artificial intelligence and English classroom: The implications of AI toward EFL students' motivation. *Edumaspul: Jurnal Pendidikan*, *7*(2), 2444–2454. DOI: 10.33487/edumaspul.v7i2.6669

Nouri, H., & Shahid, A. (2005). The effect of PowerPoint presentations on student learning and attitudes. *Global Perspectives on Accounting Education*, *2*(1), 53–73.

Nwana, H. S. (1990). Intelligent tutoring systems: An overview. *Artificial Intelligence Review*, *4*(4), 251–277. DOI: 10.1007/BF00168958

Onesi-Ozigagun, O., Ololade, Y. J., Eyo-Udo, N. L., & Ogundipe, D. O. (2024). Revolutionizing education through AI: A comprehensive review of enhancing learning experiences. *International Journal of Applied Research in Social Sciences*, *6*(4), 589–607. DOI: 10.51594/ijarss.v6i4.1011

Owan, V. J., Abang, K. B., Idika, D. O., Etta, E. O., & Bassey, B. A. (2023). Exploring the potential of artificial intelligence tools in educational measurement and assessment. *Eurasia Journal of Mathematics, Science and Technology Education*, *19*(8), em2307. Advance online publication. DOI: 10.29333/ejmste/13428

Panadero, E., Broadbent, J., Boud, D., & Lodge, J. M. (2019). Using formative assessment to influence self-and co-regulated learning: The role of evaluative judgement. *European Journal of Psychology of Education*, *34*(3), 535–557. DOI: 10.1007/s10212-018-0407-8

Perkins, M. (2023). Academic integrity considerations of AI large language models in the post-pandemic era: ChatGPT and beyond. *Journal of University Teaching & Learning Practice*, *20*(2), 1–24. DOI: 10.53761/1.20.02.07

Rafli, M. F., Syahputra, E., & Yusnadi, Y. (2018). Influence of problem based learning model and early mathematics ability to mathematical communication skills and self-confidence in junior high school. *American Journal of Educational Research*, *6*(11), 1539–1545. DOI: 10.12691/education-6-11-12

Redecker, C., & Johannessen, Ø. (2013). Changing assessment—Towards a new assessment paradigm using ICT. *European Journal of Education*, *48*(1), 79–96. DOI: 10.1111/ejed.12018

Schonert-Reichl, K. A. (2017). Social and emotional learning and teachers. *The Future of Children*, *27*(1), 137–155. http://www.jstor.org/stable/44219025. DOI: 10.1353/foc.2017.0007

Schussler, E. E., Bautista, N. U., Link-Pérez, M. A., Solomon, N. G., & Steinly, B. A. (2018). Implementing scientific practices in an introductory biology laboratory class: A mixed-methods evaluation. *Journal of College Science Teaching*, *47*(5), 74–81.

Sokhanvar, Z., Salehi, K., & Sokhanvar, F. (2021). Advantages of authentic assessment for improving the learning experience and employability skills of higher education students: A systematic literature review. *Studies in Educational Evaluation*, *70*, 1–10. DOI: 10.1016/j.stueduc.2021.101030

Song, Y., Weisberg, L. R., Zhang, S., Tian, X., Boyer, K. E., & Israel, M. (2024). A framework for inclusive AI learning design for diverse learners. *Computers and Education: Artificial Intelligence*, *100212*, 100212. Advance online publication. DOI: 10.1016/j.caeai.2024.100212

Timms, M. J. (2016). Letting artificial intelligence in education out of the box: Educational cobots and smart classrooms. *International Journal of Artificial Intelligence in Education*, *26*(2), 701–712. DOI: 10.1007/s40593-016-0095-y

van den Berg, G., & du Plessis, E. (2023). ChatGPT and generative AI: Possibilities for its contribution to lesson planning, critical thinking and openness in teacher education. *Education Sciences*, *13*(10), 998. DOI: 10.3390/educsci13100998

Velander, J., Taiye, M. A., Otero, N., & Milrad, M. (2024). Artificial Intelligence in K-12 Education: Eliciting and reflecting on Swedish teachers' understanding of AI and its implications for teaching & learning. *Education and Information Technologies*, *29*(4), 4085–4105. DOI: 10.1007/s10639-023-11990-4

Vygotsky, L. S. (1978). *Mind in society: The development of higher psychological processes*. Harvard University Press., DOI: 10.2307/j.ctvjf9vz4

Wang, N., & Li, M. (2024). Teachers' perceptions of the risks and benefits of AI in higher education: A case study of ERNIE Bot. *Innovations in Education and Teaching International*, •••, 1–13. DOI: 10.1080/14703297.2024.2432429

Wiggins, G., & McTighe, J. (2005). *Understanding by design*. Association for Supervision and Curriculum Development.

Xiang, D., Qin, G., & Zheng, X. (2022). The influence of student-teacher relationship on school-age Children's empathy: The mediating role of emotional intelligence. *Psychology Research and Behavior Management*, *15*, 2735–2744. DOI: 10.2147/PRBM.S380689

Xu, Z. (2024). AI in education: Enhancing learning experiences and student outcomes. *Applied and Computational Engineering*, *51*(1), 104–111. DOI: 10.54254/2755-2721/51/20241187

Yang, H., & Kyun, S. (2022). The current research trend of artificial intelligence in language learning: A systematic empirical literature review from an activity theory perspective. *Australasian Journal of Educational Technology*, *38*(5), 180–210. DOI: 10.14742/ajet.7492

Zawacki-Richter, O., Marín, V. I., Bond, M., & Gouverneur, F. (2019). Systematic review of research on artificial intelligence applications in higher education–where are the educators? *International Journal of Educational Technology in Higher Education*, *16*(1), 1–27. DOI: 10.1186/s41239-019-0171-0

Zee, M., Rudasill, K. M., & Bosman, R. J. (2021). A cross-lagged study of students' motivation, academic achievement, and relationships with teachers from kindergarten to 6th grade. *Journal of Educational Psychology*, *113*(6), 1208–1226. DOI: 10.1037/edu0000574

Zhai, X., Chu, X., Chai, C. S., Jong, M. S. Y., Istenic, A., Spector, M., Liu, J., Yuan, J., & Li, Y. (2021). A Review of Artificial Intelligence (AI) in Education from 2010 to 2020. *Complexity*, *2021*(1), 1–18. DOI: 10.1155/2021/8812542

ADDITIONAL READING

Bowen, J. A., & Watson, C. E. (2024). *Teaching with AI: A practical guide to a new era of human learning*. JHU Press. DOI: 10.56021/9781421449227

Bower, M., Torrington, J., Lai, J. W. M., Petocz, P., & Alfano, M. (2024). How should we change teaching and assessment in response to increasingly powerful generative Artificial Intelligence? Outcomes of the ChatGPT teacher survey. *Education and Information Technologies*, *29*, 15403–15439. DOI: 10.1007/s10639-023-12405-0

Chan, C. K. Y., & Tsi, L. H. (2024). Will generative AI replace teachers in higher education? A study of teacher and student perceptions. *Studies in Educational Evaluation*, *83*, 101395. DOI: 10.1016/j.stueduc.2024.101395

Faggiano, E., Clark-Wilson, A., Tabach, M., & Weigand, H.-G. (Eds.). *(2024). Mathematics education in the digital age: Proceedings of the 17th ERME Topic Conference MEDA 4*. University of Bari Aldo Moro. https://www.dm.uniba.it/meda4

Gentile, M., Città, G., Perna, S., & Allegra, M. (2023, March). Do we still need teachers? Navigating the paradigm shift of the teacher's role in the AI era. In *Frontiers in Education* (Vol. 8, p. 1161777). Frontiers Media SA. DOI: 10.3389/feduc.2023.1161777

Grassini, S. (2023). Shaping the future of education: Exploring the potential and consequences of AI and ChatGPT in educational settings. *Education Sciences, 13*(7), 692. DOI: 10.3390/educsci13070692

Jamal, A. (2023). The role of artificial intelligence (AI) in teacher education: Opportunities & challenges. *International Journal of Research and Analytical Reviews, 10*(1), 139–146.

Luo, J. (2024). A critical review of GenAI policies in higher education assessment: A call to reconsider the "originality" of students' work. *Assessment & Evaluation in Higher Education, 49*(5), 651–664. DOI: 10.1080/02602938.2024.2309963

Ng, D. T. K., Lee, M., Tan, R. J. Y., Hu, X., Downie, J. S., & Chu, S. K. W. (2023). A review of AI teaching and learning from 2000 to 2020. *Education and Information Technologies, 28*(7), 8445–8501. DOI: 10.1007/s10639-022-11491-w

Wang, X., Li, L., Tan, S. C., Yang, L., & Lei, J. (2023). Preparing for AI-enhanced education: Conceptualizing and empirically examining teachers' AI readiness. *Computers in Human Behavior, 146*, 107798. DOI: 10.1016/j.chb.2023.107798

KEY TERMS AND DEFINITIONS

Artificial intelligence: A technology that uses algorithms and machine learning to perform tasks traditionally requiring human intelligence, enhancing educational practices through content creation, personalized learning, and automated assessment.

Assessment: A process by which teachers measure students' understanding and application of content knowledge.

Chatbot: An AI-based conversational tool that simulates human-like dialogue through text and voice interactions, providing students with real-time responses, explanations, and personalized learning assistance.

Curriculum planning: The structured process of designing and organizing instructional content, learning objectives, and assessments to create cohesive educational experiences.

Interactions: Various forms of communication between teachers, students, and educational content that foster active learning and engagement.

Presentational instruction: The structured delivery of educational content through multiple modalities (visual, textual, auditory) designed to enhance comprehension and engagement.

Prompt-based artificial intelligence: AI systems requiring detailed user input to generate tailored educational content, offering flexibility and customization through iterative refinement based on teacher guidance.

Task-specific artificial intelligence: Specialized AI tools designed for specific educational purposes with predefined functions and structured outputs, such as lesson plan generators or assessment creators.

Virtual assistant / agent: AI-powered digital tools that respond to voice or text commands to provide personalized tutoring, content explanations, and learning support across various content areas and educational contexts.

APPENDIX A

MagicSchool.ai Output for Lesson Plan Generator

Exploring Food Webs in Ecosystems

Objective: Students will be able to describe how food webs depict the relationships between animals in an ecosystem, including the roles of producers, primary consumers, secondary consumers, and decomposers.

Assessment: At the end of the lesson, students will complete a worksheet where they identify the different organisms in a food web and label them as producers, primary consumers, secondary consumers, or decomposers.

Key Points:

- Food webs are diagrams that show the feeding relationships between organisms in an ecosystem.
- Producers, such as plants, use sunlight to make their own food through photosynthesis.
- Primary consumers, such as herbivores, eat the producers.
- Secondary consumers, such as carnivores, eat the primary consumers.
- Decomposers, such as bacteria and fungi, break down dead organisms and waste, returning nutrients to the ecosystem.

Opening:

- Begin the lesson by showing students a picture of a food web and ask them to identify the different organisms in the web.
- Engage students in a discussion about how they think the organisms in the web are related to each other.

Introduction to New Material:

- Provide students with a definition of a food web and explain its purpose in representing the relationships between organisms in an ecosystem.
- Show examples of different organisms and ask students to identify whether they are producers, primary consumers, secondary consumers, or decomposers.
- Address the misconception that animals can only be part of one food chain and emphasize the interconnectedness of organisms in a food web.

Guided Practice:

- Divide students into small groups and provide them with food web diagrams.
- Ask students to identify the different organisms in the food web and label them according to their roles as producers, primary consumers, secondary consumers, or decomposers.
- Circulate throughout the classroom, monitoring student performance and providing guidance and support as needed.

Independent Practice:

- Distribute the worksheet to each student.
- Instruct students to identify and label the organisms in the given food web diagram.
- Encourage students to refer back to the key points discussed earlier in the lesson.
- Set clear behavioral expectations for the independent practice time.

Closing:

- Have students share their labeled food web diagrams with the class, discussing the organisms and their roles.
- Summarize the key points of the lesson and highlight the importance of understanding food webs in studying ecosystems.

Extension Activity:

- For students who finish early, provide them with additional food web diagrams to analyze and identify the organisms and their roles.
- Challenge them to create their own food web diagram using organisms from a specific ecosystem.

Homework:

- As a homework activity, ask students to research and find examples of different ecosystems and the organisms that inhabit them. They can draw or describe the food webs for these ecosystems.

Standards Addressed:

- NGSS Standard: MS-LS2-3 - Develop a model to describe the cycling of matter and flow of energy among living and nonliving parts of an ecosystem.
- NGSS Standard: MS-LS2-4 - Construct an argument supported by empirical evidence that changes to physical or biological components of an ecosystem affect populations.

In the lesson above, build me all the worksheets and resources in detail. Sure! Here are the worksheets and resources for the lesson:

1. Food Web Diagram Worksheet:
    - Description: This worksheet will provide students with a food web diagram where they will need to identify and label the different organisms according to their roles as producers, primary consumers, secondary consumers, or decomposers.
    - Instructions: Instruct students to carefully study the food web diagram and use the key points discussed in the lesson to correctly identify and label each organism.
    - Example Question: Label the organism "Rabbit" as a producer, primary consumer, secondary consumer, or decomposer.
    - Answer Key: Provide an answer key that includes the correct labels for each organism in the food web diagram.
2. Extension Activity - Analyzing Food Webs Worksheet:
    - Description: This worksheet will provide additional food web diagrams for students to analyze and identify the organisms and their roles.
    - Instructions: Instruct students to carefully study each food web diagram and use their knowledge from the lesson to correctly identify and label each organism.
    - Example Question: Label the organism "Snake" as a producer, primary consumer, secondary consumer, or decomposer in the given food web diagram.
    - Answer Key: Provide an answer key that includes the correct labels for each organism in the food web diagrams.
3. Extension Activity - Creating a Food Web Worksheet:
    - Description: This worksheet will challenge students to create their own food web diagram using organisms from a specific ecosystem.
    - Instructions: Instruct students to choose an ecosystem (e.g., forest, ocean, grassland) and select organisms that inhabit that ecosystem. They should then create a food web diagram that accurately depicts the relationships between the organisms, labeling them as producers, primary consumers, secondary consumers, or decomposers.

- Example Question: Create a food web diagram for a forest ecosystem using at least four organisms. Label each organism as a producer, primary consumer, secondary consumer, or decomposer.
- Answer Key: Since this is a creative activity, there is no specific answer key. Instead, assess students' diagrams based on the accuracy of the relationships depicted and the appropriate labeling of organisms.

4. Homework - Researching Ecosystems Worksheet:
    - Description: This worksheet will serve as a homework activity where students research and find examples of different ecosystems and the organisms that inhabit them.
    - Instructions: Instruct students to choose a specific ecosystem (e.g., desert, tundra, coral reef) and research the organisms that live in that ecosystem. They should then draw or describe the food web for that ecosystem, including the organisms and their roles.
    - Example Question: Research the coral reef ecosystem and draw a food web diagram that includes at least four organisms. Label each organism as a producer, primary consumer, secondary consumer, or decomposer.
    - Answer Key: Since this is a research-based activity, there is no specific answer key. Instead, assess students' diagrams based on the accuracy of the relationships depicted and the appropriate labeling of organisms.

Remember to include clear instructions, examples, and answer keys where applicable for each worksheet.

How can I effectively provide constructive feedback to students?

Providing constructive feedback is an essential part of the teaching and learning process.

Here are some strategies to effectively provide constructive feedback to students:

1. Be specific and objective: When giving feedback, be specific about what the student did well and what needs improvement. Use objective criteria or rubrics to provide clear expectations and benchmarks for performance.
2. Focus on the task, not the student: Frame your feedback in a way that separates the student's performance on a task from their personal worth. For example, instead of saying "You're not good at this," say "Your response could be improved by including more evidence."
3. Use a balance of positive and constructive feedback: Highlight the strengths and successes of the student's work, as well as areas for improvement. This helps maintain motivation and confidence while also guiding their growth.

4. Give feedback in a timely manner: Provide feedback as soon as possible after the completion of a task or assignment. This ensures that students can make connections between their work and the feedback received.
5. Use a feedback sandwich: Start with positive feedback, then provide constructive feedback, and end with positive feedback again. This approach helps to soften any criticism and keeps the focus on growth and improvement.
6. Be specific about what needs improvement: Instead of vague statements like "Good job!" or "Needs work," provide specific feedback on what aspects of their work need improvement. For example, instead of saying "Your writing is unclear," say "Your writing could be clearer if you provide more examples or explanations."
7. Encourage self-reflection and self-correction: Prompt students to reflect on their own work and identify areas for improvement. Encourage them to think critically about their strengths and weaknesses and develop strategies for self-correction.
8. Provide actionable steps for improvement: Instead of simply pointing out errors or weaknesses, offer specific suggestions or strategies for improvement. This helps students understand how to address the feedback and make progress.
9. Offer opportunities for revision: Whenever possible, provide students with the chance to revise their work based on the feedback received. This allows them to apply the feedback and make improvements, reinforcing the learning process.
10. Maintain a positive and supportive tone: Ensure that your feedback is delivered in a positive and supportive manner. Use encouraging language and acknowledge the effort students put into their work.

Remember, the goal of constructive feedback is to guide students' growth and improvement. By providing specific, timely, and actionable feedback, you can help students understand their strengths, identify areas for growth, and ultimately achieve their learning goals.

What strategies can I use to maintain a positive and supportive tone when giving feedback?

Maintaining a positive and supportive tone when giving feedback is crucial for creating a safe and encouraging learning environment. Here are some strategies to help you maintain a positive and supportive tone:

1. Start with a positive comment: Begin your feedback by acknowledging the student's effort, strengths, or any improvements they have made. This sets a positive tone and helps the student feel valued and appreciated.
2. Use encouraging language: Choose words that convey support, encouragement, and belief in the student's abilities. Phrases such as "I appreciate your effort,"

"You're on the right track," or "I believe in your potential" can uplift the student and motivate them to continue improving.

3. Focus on growth and improvement: Frame feedback as an opportunity for growth and learning rather than as criticism. Emphasize that feedback is meant to help the student improve and reach their goals.
4. Be specific and constructive: Provide specific feedback that highlights areas for improvement or suggests alternative strategies. Instead of using general statements like "You did a good job," provide specific examples and suggestions for how the student can enhance their work.
5. Use the "I" language: When giving feedback, use "I" statements to express your observations and opinions. This helps avoid sounding judgmental or personal. For example, say "I noticed that you could include more evidence to support your argument" instead of "You didn't include enough evidence."
6. Ask open-ended questions: Encourage self-reflection and critical thinking by asking open-ended questions that prompt the student to consider their work and potential improvements. This helps them take ownership of their learning and fosters a positive mindset.
7. Provide specific praise: When acknowledging the student's strengths or improvements, be specific about what they did well. Instead of saying "Good job," say "Your use of descriptive language really brought your writing to life."
8. Offer support and resources: If a student is struggling with a particular concept or skill, offer additional support or resources to help them improve. This can include suggesting extra practice activities, providing additional examples, or recommending relevant online resources.
9. Be approachable and open to discussion: Create an open and safe space for students to ask questions or seek clarification on feedback. Encourage them to approach you if they need further assistance or have concerns.
10. End with positive reinforcement: Conclude your feedback with a positive and encouraging statement that reinforces the student's potential and growth. This leaves the student with a sense of accomplishment and motivation to continue striving for improvement.

Remember, the way feedback is delivered greatly impacts how it is received. By adopting a positive and supportive tone, you can help students feel valued, motivated, and confident in their ability to grow and learn.

What are some specific examples of open-ended questions to ask students?

When giving feedback, asking open-ended questions can stimulate critical thinking and encourage students to reflect on their work. Here are some specific examples of open-ended questions you can ask students:

1. Content Understanding:
    - What evidence or examples could you provide to support your argument?
    - How could you extend or deepen your analysis of the topic?
    - What connections can you make between this concept and other ideas we have studied?
    - Can you think of any real-life situations where this concept applies?
2. Problem-Solving:
    - What alternative strategies could you use to approach this problem?
    - How did you decide on your solution? Can you explain your reasoning?
    - What other factors or variables could affect the outcome?
    - Can you think of any similar problems or scenarios where this strategy could be applied?
3. Writing and Communication:
    - How could you make your writing more engaging or persuasive?
    - What additional details or examples could you include to support your main points?
    - Are there any parts of your writing that may be unclear to the reader? How could you clarify them?
    - What impact do you want your writing to have on the reader? How can you achieve that?
4. Creativity and Innovation:
    - What other ideas or perspectives could you explore to enhance your project?
    - How might you incorporate different media or materials to make your work more visually appealing or interactive?
    - Can you think of any ways to take your project to the next level and make it even more unique or innovative?
    - What feedback or suggestions do you have for your peers' projects? How could they improve or expand their ideas?
5. Reflective Thinking:
    - What challenges or obstacles did you encounter during this task? How did you overcome them?
    - How has your understanding or approach to this topic changed throughout this project?
    - What skills or knowledge have you gained from this experience?
    - What would you do differently if you were to tackle a similar task in the future?

These open-ended questions encourage students to think critically, reflect on their work, and consider different perspectives. They also provide opportunities for students to demonstrate their understanding, generate ideas, and engage in deeper discussions.

Are there any strategies to help students develop critical thinking skills through open-ended questions?

Absolutely! Open-ended questions can be powerful tools for developing critical thinking skills in students. Here are some strategies to help students develop critical thinking skills through open-ended questions:

1. Model Critical Thinking: Demonstrate critical thinking yourself by asking open-ended questions and engaging in thoughtful discussions. Model the process of analyzing information, considering different perspectives, and making informed judgments.
2. Encourage Evidence-Based Reasoning: Prompt students to provide evidence or reasoning to support their answers and opinions. Encourage them to use facts, examples, or logical arguments to justify their thinking.
3. Promote Multiple Perspectives: Encourage students to consider alternative viewpoints and explore different angles of a topic. Ask questions that prompt them to think from different perspectives or challenge their existing ideas.
4. Ask "Why" and "How" Questions: Instead of focusing on "what" questions that have a single correct answer, ask questions that require students to explain the reasoning behind their answers or describe the process they used to arrive at their conclusions.
5. Encourage Problem-Solving: Pose open-ended questions that present real-world problems or challenges for students to solve. Encourage them to think critically and develop creative solutions, considering different approaches and potential consequences.
6. Facilitate Socratic Questioning: Use the Socratic method of questioning to guide students' thinking. Ask probing questions that prompt them to analyze assumptions, evaluate evidence, and consider the implications of their answers.
7. Provide Time for Reflection: Allow students sufficient time to reflect on the questions before responding. This gives them an opportunity to think deeply and consider multiple perspectives before sharing their thoughts.
8. Create a Collaborative Learning Environment: Encourage students to discuss open-ended questions with their peers. Foster a classroom culture that values diverse opinions, active listening, and respectful debate.
9. Support Metacognition: Help students develop metacognitive skills by asking questions that prompt them to reflect on their thinking process. Ask questions like, "What strategies did you use to solve this problem?" or "How did your thinking change as you worked through this task?"

10. Provide Feedback: Give constructive feedback on students' answers to open-ended questions. Highlight strengths in their reasoning, encourage further exploration, and guide them to consider additional angles or evidence.

By employing these strategies, you can foster a classroom environment that nurtures critical thinking skills through open-ended questions. Encourage students to engage in thoughtful discussions, consider multiple perspectives, and develop their analytical and problem-solving abilities.

Can you provide more examples of food webs for different ecosystems?

Certainly! Here are some examples of food webs in different ecosystems:

1. Forest Ecosystem Food Web:
    - Producers: Trees, plants, mosses, ferns
    - Primary Consumers: Deer, rabbits, squirrels, insects
    - Secondary Consumers: Hawks, owls, snakes, foxes
    - Tertiary Consumers: Wolves, bears, mountain lions
    - Decomposers: Fungi, bacteria, earthworms
2. Grassland Ecosystem Food Web:
    - Producers: Grass, wildflowers, shrubs
    - Primary Consumers: Grazing animals like zebras, bison, and antelopes
    - Secondary Consumers: Lions, cheetahs, wolves, jackals
    - Tertiary Consumers: Eagles, hawks
    - Decomposers: Beetles, earthworms, fungi
3. Freshwater Pond Ecosystem Food Web:
    - Producers: Algae, aquatic plants
    - Primary Consumers: Zooplankton, small fish, tadpoles
    - Secondary Consumers: Larger fish, frogs, turtles
    - Tertiary Consumers: Snakes, herons, otters
    - Decomposers: Bacteria, fungi
4. Ocean Ecosystem Food Web:
    - Producers: Phytoplankton, seaweed, kelp
    - Primary Consumers: Zooplankton, small fish, shrimp
    - Secondary Consumers: Squid, larger fish, seals
    - Tertiary Consumers: Sharks, dolphins, killer whales
    - Decomposers: Bacteria, sea cucumbers
5. Desert Ecosystem Food Web:
    - Producers: Cacti, desert grasses, shrubs
    - Primary Consumers: Small rodents like kangaroo rats, mice, insects
    - Secondary Consumers: Snakes, lizards, birds of prey
    - Tertiary Consumers: Coyotes, foxes

- Decomposers: Beetles, bacteria, fungi

Remember, these food web examples are simplified representations of complex ecosystems, and the actual relationships and organisms within each ecosystem can vary. Encourage students to research specific ecosystems in more detail to discover the unique organisms and interactions that exist in each food web.

Chapter 10
Artificial Intelligence in Education:
Partner or Replacement for Teachers?

Sally Dafaalla Awadalkreim Abualgasim
https://orcid.org/0000-0003-4154-8112
University of Gezira, Sudan

Zeinab E. Ahmed
https://orcid.org/0000-0002-6144-8533
University of Gezira, Sudan

ABSTRACT

The learning process is an essential element of educational achievement, and after the spread of artificial intelligence techniques (AI), these technologies had to be used to develop the learning process. In this time, important question appear, is using AI in Education: Partner or Replacement for Teacher? This paper provides a comprehensive study of AI's role in education, illustrating how it can complement and enhance the instructional functions performed by teachers. The discussion critically evaluates the advantages AI brings to diverse educational settings while also acknowledging its limitations in fully replicating human instruction. As a conclusion this paper highlighting the unique and irreplaceable aspects of human teaching, this analysis underscores the indispensable role of educators in the learning process. Subsequent sections will explore AI as a supplementary tool within traditional educational frameworks.

DOI: 10.4018/979-8-3373-0396-3.ch010

I. INTRODUCTION

The rapid advancement of artificial intelligence (AI) in education has sparked intense debate about whether these technologies will serve as collaborative tools for teachers or ultimately replace human educators. As AI systems become increasingly sophisticated capable of tutoring students, grading assignments, and even generating lesson plans the educational landscape faces profound transformation. This paper examines the current state of AI in education, analyzing empirical research on implementation models, teacher and student perceptions, and the evolving relationship between human educators and intelligent systems. Drawing from recent studies and expert analyses, we explore the nuanced reality that AI is more likely to transform teaching than replace it, while acknowledging legitimate concerns about job displacement and the erosion of human connection in learning environments.

The integration of AI in education presents several challenges that must be addressed to ensure its effective and ethical use. One key concern is the potential for biases inherent in AI systems, which can perpetuate existing inequalities if not properly managed (Ding et al., 2024). Additionally, data privacy and security are critical issues, as the vast amount of personal and academic information processed by AI tools must be safeguarded to protect students' rights and privacy. Furthermore, there is a need to strike a balance between the role of human educators and the increasing use of automated teaching tools. While AI can enhance the learning experience by providing personalized support, it cannot replace the essential mentorship, emotional guidance, and nuanced understanding that human educators offer. Therefore, careful consideration is required to integrate AI in a way that complements, rather than undermines, the invaluable contributions of educators in the classroom. The rise of AI in education represents a shift towards more inclusive, empowered, and technologically integrated learning environments. By fostering literacy and critical engagement with AI concepts, educational institutions can prepare students for a rapidly evolving digital society (Bryant et al., 2020) (Rayhan et al., 2023)

II. AI AS A PARTNER IN EDUCATION

The majority of research suggests AI serves education best as a partner rather than replacement for teachers. Several key benefits emerge from this collaborative model:

1. Personalization at Scale: AI systems excel at providing individualized instruction tailored to each student's needs, learning pace, and style (Kim & Kim, 2022) [2] (Marr, 2022). This personalization extends to supporting students with learning differences and providing accommodations that increase accessibility

(Hamilton, 2024) (Seo et al., 2021). Adaptive platforms can modify content difficulty, provide multilingual support, and offer alternative presentation formats capabilities difficult for a single teacher managing a diverse classroom to match (Marr, 2022) .

2. Augmenting Teacher Capabilities: AI amplifies teacher effectiveness by automating time-consuming tasks. Automated grading and administrative work free educators to focus on meaningful student interactions[2] (Hamilton, 2024) (Marr, 2022). AI can also provide teachers with real-time feedback about classroom dynamics and student engagement and areas needing attention (Marr, 2022) (Spencer, 2024) (Karmakar & Das, 2024). For instance, AI systems can analyze classroom discussions and generate post-lesson reports summarizing participation patterns (Spencer, 2024).
3. Supporting Teacher Development: AI offers innovative ways to enhance teacher training and professional growth. New teachers can practice with AI-simulated students that demonstrate confusion and ask adaptive follow-up questions. AI systems can help experienced teachers stay current with developments in their field, suggesting curriculum updates based on the latest research (Spencer, 2024) (Karmakar & Das, 2024) . John Spencer's work shows how AI can assist with lesson planning by serving as a "co-creation" tool that teachers then refine based on their expertise (Spencer, 2024).
4. Enhancing Student Engagement: AI interfaces create low-stakes environments where students feel comfortable making mistakes and asking questions without fear of judgment from peers (Karmakar & Das, 2024). This proves particularly valuable for students who perceive themselves as behind classmates and might otherwise hesitate to participate (Karmakar & Das, 2024). Educational games powered by AI, the most commonly used AI tool in classrooms according to a Forbes survey, demonstrate this engagement potential (Hamilton, 2024).

III. CAN AI REPLACE TEACHERS? LIMITS AND CHALLENGES

Despite these benefits, concerns persist about AI potentially replacing human teachers. A Pew Research Center survey found that 25% of U.S. teachers believe AI tools do more harm than good in K-12 education, with high school teachers being particularly skeptical (35%) [10]. Several factors contribute to this apprehension:

1. Loss of Human Connection: Teachers and researchers worry that increased reliance on AI may reduce valuable human interaction in education (Jern, 2024) (Spencer, 2024). The social-emotional competencies developed through teacher-student relationships are difficult for AI to replicate (Jern, 2024) (Ka

Yuk Chan & Tsi, 2023). As Chan (2023) notes, human teachers possess unique qualities like critical thinking, creativity, and emotional intelligence that current AI cannot match (Spencer, 2024) (Ka Yuk Chan & Tsi, 2023) (Rebecchi et al., 2024).

2. Questionable Pedagogical Effectiveness: While AI can provide answers quickly, these responses aren't always optimized for learning. As Liang observes, the speed at which AI models deliver information often conflicts with pedagogically sound practices that encourage deeper exploration [2] . There are also concerns that AI-generated content may be coherent but incorrect, potentially misleading students. Forbes' survey found 60% of educators have observed students using generative AI to cheat, with academic dishonesty topping teachers' concerns about the technology (Hamilton, 2024).
3. Equity and Access Issues: With over 2.6 billion people lacking basic internet access, AI could exacerbate existing educational inequalities (Spencer, 2024). Edwards warns of a future where privileged students enjoy human teachers while others "sit in rooms with a chatbot," lacking meaningful mentorship and support (Spencer, 2024). Algorithmic bias in AI systems also raises concerns about equitable treatment of diverse student populations (Hamilton, 2024).
4. Job Security Fears: The Goldman Sachs report predicting AI could replace 300 million jobs fuels anxiety among educators [2] . While most experts believe teaching will transform rather than disappear, the profession faces significant changes that require careful management (Spencer, 2024) (Marr, 2022).

IV. THE FUTURE: COLLABORATIVE CLASSROOMS

The Future of Teaching in an AI Era, rather than replacement, the likely future involves transformation of teaching roles:

- From Deliverers to Designers: Teachers will increasingly shift from content delivery to learning experience design. AI handles information transmission while educators focus on crafting meaningful activities, assessments, and environments that promote deep learning (Spencer, 2024).
- From Graders to Guides: With AI automating assessment, teachers can devote more energy to mentoring students and providing the human connection machines cannot replicate (Jern, 2024) (Marr, 2022). As Bernard Marr notes, "Motivating students to learn, practice, and grow is a skill that is currently beyond the scope of artificial intelligence" (Marr, 2022).
- From Generalists to Specialists: Educators may specialize in areas where human strengths shine social emotional learning, ethical reasoning, creativity,

and complex problem-solving (Gimbert et al., 2023) (Bennett & Abusalem, 2024) (Goodall, 2024) (Rebecchi et al., 2024). Chris Goodall predicts teachers will become "guardians, mentors and guides" focusing on standards related to student wellbeing and behavior while AI handles academic content delivery (Goodall, 2024).

- From Solo Practitioners to Collaborators: Teachers will work alongside AI systems, learning to effectively integrate these tools while maintaining human oversight (Spencer, 2024). John Spencer's framework for AI-assisted lesson planning where teachers serve as both creators and curators exemplifies this collaborative approach (Spencer, 2024).

V. CONCLUSION

The question of whether AI will replace teachers stems from a false dichotomy. As current research demonstrates, artificial intelligence serves best as a powerful partner to human educators rather than their replacement. While AI excels at personalizing instruction, automating administrative tasks, and providing data-driven insights, it cannot replicate the mentorship, ethical modeling, and inspirational role that teachers provide. The future of education lies not in choosing between humans and machines, but in thoughtfully integrating their complementary strengths. As we navigate this transformation, maintaining focus on education's ultimate purpose—developing not just skilled workers but thoughtful citizens and fulfilled human beings—will ensure AI enhances rather than diminishes the learning experience. The most effective classrooms of tomorrow will likely feature AI handling what it does best (information processing and personalized practice) while teachers focus on what they do best (inspiring, mentoring, and guiding holistic human development). In this partnership, both human and artificial intelligence can work synergistically to create educational experiences more effective and meaningful than either could achieve alone.

REFERENCES

Bennett, L., & Abusalem, A. (2024). Artificial Intelligence (AI) and its Potential Impact on the Future of Higher Education. *Athens Journal of Education, 11*(3), 195–212. DOI: 10.30958/aje.11-3-2

Bryant, J., Heitz, C., Sanghvi, S., & Wagle, D. (2020). *How artificial intelligence will impact K-12 teachers.*

Ding, A.-C. E., Shi, L., Yang, H., & Choi, I. (2024). Enhancing teacher AI literacy and integration through different types of cases in teacher professional development. *Computers and Education Open, 6*, 100178. DOI: 10.1016/j.caeo.2024.100178

Gimbert, B. G., Miller, D., Herman, E., Breedlove, M., & Molina, C. E. (2023). Social Emotional Learning in Schools: The Importance of Educator Competence. *Journal of Research on Leadership Education, 18*(1), 3–39. DOI: 10.1177/19427751211014920

Goodall, C. (2024, February 11). *Will AI Replace Teachers?* https://www.ai-in-education.co.uk/resources/will-ai-replace-teachers

Hamilton, I. (2024). *Artificial Intelligence In Education: Teachers' Opinions On AI In The Classroom.* https://www.forbes.com/advisor/education/it-and-tech/artificial-intelligence-in-school/

Jern, K. (2024). *Can AI Replace Teachers?* We Finally Know the Answer.

Ka Yuk Chan, C., & Tsi, L. H. (2023). The AI Revolution in Education: Will AI Replace or Assist Teachers in Higher Education? https://arxiv.org/abs/2305.01185

Karmakar, S., & Das, T. (2024). *Optimization and Computing using Intelligent Data-Driven Approaches for Decision-Making* (1st ed.). CRC Press.

Kim, N. J., & Kim, M. K. (2022). Teacher's Perceptions of Using an Artificial Intelligence-Based Educational Tool for Scientific Writing. *Frontiers in Education, 7*, 755914. Advance online publication. DOI: 10.3389/feduc.2022.755914

Marr, B. (2022). *Will Artificial Intelligence Replace Teachers?* Rayhan, A., Rayhan, R., & Rayhan, S. (2023). *Revolutionizing Education: The Power of Artificial Intelligence (AI).* DOI: 10.13140/RG.2.2.10716.97924

Rebecchi, K., Todd, L., & Hagège, H. (2024). Teaching responsible creativity: A path to ethical innovation. *Discover Education, 3*(1), 103. DOI: 10.1007/s44217-024-00164-0

Seo, K., Tang, J., Roll, I., Fels, S., & Yoon, D. (2021). The impact of artificial intelligence on learner–instructor interaction in online learning. *International Journal of Educational Technology in Higher Education*, *18*(1), 54. Advance online publication. DOI: 10.1186/s41239-021-00292-9 PMID: 34778540

Spencer, J. (2024, September 5). *AI Won't Replace Teachers But It Will Transform Nearly Every Aspect of the Job*.

Compilation of References

Aad, S., & Hardey, M. (2025). Generative AI: Hopes, controversies and the future of faculty roles in education. *Quality Assurance in Education*, *33*(2), 267–282. DOI: 10.1108/QAE-02-2024-0043

Aalto University. (2021, March 29). Participatory research to improve artificial intelligence-based public sector services and empower citizens. https://shorturl.at/LO2zm

Abdelwahab, H. R., Rauf, A., & Chen, D. (2023). Business students' perceptions of Dutch higher educational institutions in preparing them for artificial intelligence work environments. *Industry and Higher Education*, *37*(1), 22–34. DOI: 10.1177/09504222221087614

Adams, C., Pente, P., Lemermeyer, G., & Rockwell, G. (2022). Ethical principles for artificial intelligence in K-12 education. *Computers and Education: Artificial Intelligence*, *4*, 100131. DOI: 10.1016/j.caeai.2023.100131

Adelaide Now. (2025, May 26). More efficient and easier: How AI can help teachers spend less time on things other than teaching. *Adelaide Now*. https://shorturl.at/DUSBv

Adıgüzel, T., Kaya, M. H., & Cansu, F. K. (2023). Revolutionizing education with AI: Exploring the transformative potential of ChatGPT. *Contemporary Educational Technology*, *15*(3), ep429. DOI: 10.30935/cedtech/13152

Agarwal, P., & Vij, A. (2024). Assessing the Challenges and Opportunities of Artificial Intelligence in Indian Education. *International Journal for Global Academic & Scientific Research*, *3*(1), 36–44. DOI: 10.55938/ijgasr.v3i1.71

Agu, E. E., Abhulimen, A. O., Obiki-Osafiele, A. N., Osundare, O. S., Adeniran, I. A., & Efunniyi, C. P. (2024). Utilizing AI-driven predictive analytics to reduce credit risk and enhance financial inclusion. *International Journal of Frontline Research in Multidisciplinary Studies*, *3*(2), 20. DOI: 10.56355/ijfrms.2024.3.2.0026

Ahmed, Z. E., Hashim, A. H. A., Saeed, R. A., & Saeed, M. M. A. (2024). AI-enhanced education: Bridging educational disparities. In *AI-Enhanced Teaching Methods* (pp. 88–107). IGI Global., DOI: 10.4018/979-8-3693-2728-9.ch004

Airaj, M. (2024). Ethical artificial intelligence for teaching-learning in higher education. *Education and Information Technologies*, •••, 1–23.

Ajiga, D. I., Ndubuisi, N. L., Asuzu, O. F., Owolabi, O. R., Tubokirifuruar, T. S., & Adeleye, R. A. (2024). AI-Driven Predictive Analytics In Retail: A Review Of Emerging Trends And Customer Engagement Strategies [Review Of Ai-Driven Predictive Analytics In Retail: A Review Of Emerging Trends And Customer Engagement Strategies]. International Journal of Management & Entrepreneurship Research, 6(2), 307. Fair East Publishers. https://doi.org/DOI: 10.51594/ijmer.v6i2.772

Ajlouni, A., Almahaireh, A., & Whaba, F. (2023). Students' perception of using ChatGPT in counseling and mental health education: The benefits and challenges. [iJET]. *International Journal of Emerging Technologies in Learning*, *18*(20), 199–218. https://www.learntechlib.org/p/223772/?nl=1. DOI: 10.3991/ijet.v18i20.42075

Akbarovna, I. S. (2024). Professional skills of the teacher. *World of Science*, *7*(8), 1–7.

Akgun, S., & Greenhow, C. (2021). Artificial intelligence in education: Addressing ethical challenges in K-12 settings. *AI and Ethics*, *2*(3), 431–440. DOI: 10.1007/s43681-021-00096-7 PMID: 34790956

Akingbola, A., Adeleke, O., Idris, A., Adewole, O., & Adegbesan, A. (2024). Artificial Intelligence and the Dehumanization of Patient Care. *Journal of Medicine, Surgery, and Public Health*, *3*, 100138. DOI: 10.1016/j.glmedi.2024.100138

Akintayo, T. A., Paul, C., Queenet, M. C., Nnadiekwe, O. A., Victoria, S. S., David, F. B., Joel, O. O., Agada, O. I., Ngozi, E. R., Arinze, U. U., Ojemerenvhie, G. A., Oluwadamilola, A. A., Nnamani, C. C., & Olayinka, U. W. (2024). Transforming Data Analytics with AI for Informed Decision-Making. *International Journal of Education Management and Technology*, *2*(3), 196–215. DOI: 10.58578/ijemt.v2i3.3812

Al Maqbali, S. B., & Tahir, N. M. (2024, August). AI Opportunities and Risks for Students' Decision-Making Skill. In *2024 IEEE 14th International Conference on Control System, Computing and Engineering (ICCSCE)* (pp. 321-326). IEEE. DOI: 10.1109/ICCSCE61582.2024.10696240

Alba, D. (2024, February 4). Cal State is bringing ChatGPT to all of its campuses. *Axios*. https://www.axios.com/2025/02/04/california-state-university-chatgpt-openai

Alfaris, M. M., Sauri, S., & Gaffar, M. A. (2021). Guidance and counseling management on personal, social, learning and career development of SMK 19 Bandung students during COVID-19 pandemics. *Guidance and Counseling*, *2*(2), 2. DOI: 10.52690/jswse.v2i2.244

Al-khresheh, M. H. (2024). Bridging technology and pedagogy from a global lens: Teachers' perspectives on integrating ChatGPT in English language teaching. *Computers and Education: Artificial Intelligence*, *6*, 100218. Advance online publication. DOI: 10.1016/j.caeai.2024.100218

Alowais, S. A., Alghamdi, S. S., Alsuhebany, N., Alqahtani, T., Alshaya, A. I., Almohareb, S. N., Aldairem, A., Alrashed, M., Saleh, K. B., Badreldin, H. A., Yami, M. S. A., Harbi, S. A., & Albekairy, A. M. (2023). Revolutionizing healthcare: The role of artificial intelligence in clinical practice. *BMC Medical Education*, *23*(1), 689. DOI: 10.1186/s12909-023-04698-z

Alqahtani, T., Badreldin, H. A., Alrashed, M., Alshaya, A. I., Alghamdi, S. S., Bin Saleh, K., & Albekairy, A. M. (2023). The emergent role of artificial intelligence, natural learning processing, and large language models in higher education and research. *Research in Social & Administrative Pharmacy*, *19*(8), 1236–1242. DOI: 10.1016/j.sapharm.2023.05.016 PMID: 37321925

Altinay, Z., Altinay, F., Sharma, R. C., Dagli, G., Shadiev, R., Yikici, B., & Altinay, M. (2024). Capacity building for student teachers in learning, teaching artificial intelligence for quality of education. *Societies (Basel, Switzerland)*, *14*(8), 148. DOI: 10.3390/soc14080148

AlTwijri, L., & Alghizzi, T. M. (2024). Investigating the integration of artificial intelligence in English as foreign language classes for enhancing learners' affective factors: A systematic review [Review of Investigating the integration of artificial intelligence in English as foreign language classes for enhancing learners' affective factors: A systematic review]. Heliyon, 10(10). Elsevier BV. https://doi.org/DOI: 10.1016/j.heliyon.2024.e31053

Alwaqdani, M. (2025). Investigating teachers' perceptions of artificial intelligence tools in education: Potential and difficulties. *Education and Information Technologies*, *30*(3), 2737–2755. DOI: 10.1007/s10639-024-12903-9

Al-Zahrani, A. M. (2024). Unveiling the shadows: Beyond the hype of AI in education. *Heliyon*, *10*(9), e30696. Advance online publication. DOI: 10.1016/j.heliyon.2024.e30696 PMID: 38737255

Al-Zahrani, A. M., & Alasmari, T. M. (2024). Exploring the impact of artificial intelligence on higher education: The dynamics of ethical, social, and educational implications. *Humanities & Social Sciences Communications*, *11*(1), 912. DOI: 10.1057/s41599-024-03432-4

Alzahrani, A. S., Tsai, Y., Aljohani, N. R., Whitelock-wainwright, E., & Gašević, D. (2023). Do teaching staff trust stakeholders and tools in learning analytics? A mixed methods study. *Educational Technology Research and Development*, *71*(4), 1471–1501. DOI: 10.1007/s11423-023-10229-w PMID: 37359481

Al-Zawqari, A., Peumans, D., & Vandersteen, G. (2022). A flexible feature selection approach for predicting students' academic performance in online courses. *Computers and Education: Artificial Intelligence*, *3*, 100103. Advance online publication. DOI: 10.1016/j.caeai.2022.100103

Andreotta, A. J., Kirkham, N., & Rizzi, M. (2021). AI, big data, and the future of consent. *AI & Society*, *37*(4), 1715–1728. DOI: 10.1007/s00146-021-01262-5 PMID: 34483498

Antwi, B. O., Adelakun, B. O., & Eziefule, A. O.Bernard Owusu AntwiBeatrice Oyinkansola AdelakunAugustine Obinna Eziefule. (2024). Transforming Financial Reporting with AI: Enhancing Accuracy and Timeliness. *International Journal of Advanced Economics*, *6*(6), 205–223. DOI: 10.51594/ijae.v6i6.1229

Anuyah, O., Conrado, A. M., Carlson, C., Gilbride, H., & Metoyer, R. (2023). Exploring the barriers and potential opportunities of technology integration in Community-Based social service organizations. *ACM Journal on Computing and Sustainable Societies*, *1*(1), 1–28. DOI: 10.1145/3610720

Aristanto, A., Supriatna, E., Panggabean, H. M., Apriyanti, E., Hartini, H., Sari, N. I., & Kurniawati, W. (2023). The role of Artificial Intelligence (AI) at school learning. *Consilium: Education and Counseling Journal*, *3*(2), 2. Advance online publication. DOI: 10.36841/consilium.v3i2.3437

Astuti, L. P. (2021). The role of guidance and counseling services in individual counseling during the covid-19 pandemic. *International Journal of Applied Guidance and Counseling*, *2*(1), 25–30. DOI: 10.26486/ijagc.v2i1.1592

Ayeni, O. O., Hamad, N. M. A., Chisom, O. N., Osawaru, B., & Adewusi, O. E. (2024). AI in education: A review of personalized learning and educational technology [Review of AI in education: A review of personalized learning and educational technology]. *GSC Advanced Research and Reviews*, *18*(2), 261–271. DOI: 10.30574/gscarr.2024.18.2.0062

Badmus, O., Rajput, S., Arogundade, J. B., & Williams, M. H. (2024). AI-driven business analytics and decision making. *World Journal of Advanced Research and Reviews*, *24*(1), 616–633. DOI: 10.30574/wjarr.2024.24.1.3093

Bagunaid, W., Chilamkurti, N., & Veeraraghavan, P. (2022). Aisar: Artificial intelligence-based student assessment and recommendation system for e-learning in big data. *Sustainability (Basel)*, *14*(17), 10551. DOI: 10.3390/su141710551

Baidoo-Anu, D., & Ansah, L. O. (2023). Education in the era of generative artificial intelligence (AI): Understanding the potential benefits of ChatGPT in promoting teaching and learning. *Journal of AI*, *7*(1), 52–62. DOI: 10.61969/jai.1337500

Baker, T., Smith, L., & Anissa, N. (2019, February 20). *Educ-AI-tion rebooted? Exploring the future of artificial intelligence in schools and colleges*. Nesta. https://www.nesta.org.uk/report/education-rebooted/

Balasooriya, C. (2024). AI in education: A futuristic vision. *Medical Teacher*, *46*(7), 986–988. DOI: 10.1080/0142159X.2024.2352160 PMID: 38725359

BankoleFalaye, A.BankoleFalaye. (2024). AI-Powered Knowledge Systems for SME Financial Management: A Conceptual Approach. [IJSR]. *International Journal of Science and Research (Raipur, India)*, *13*(11), 1099–1103. DOI: 10.21275/SR241117060640

Barrios-Beltran, D. (2024). Enriching the Teaching-Learning Experience by Using AI Tools in the L2 Classroom. In *AI in Language Teaching, Learning, and Assessment* (pp. 61-77). IGI Global. DOI: 10.4018/979-8-3693-0872-1.ch004

Basha, Mrs. N. R. Dr. H. S. A., & Thoti, K. K. (. (2024). AI-powered Recruitment and Employee Selection: Evaluating Bias and Fairness in Hiring Practices. [EEL]. *European Economic Letters*, *14*(1), 827. DOI: 10.52783/eel.v14i1.1107

Baskara, F. R. (2023). Personalised learning with AI: Implications for Ignatian pedagogy. *International Journal of Educational Best Practices*, *7*(1), 1–16.

Bates, A. W. (2022). *Teaching in a digital age: Guidelines for designing teaching and learning* (3rd ed.). Tony Bates Associates Ltd., https://pressbooks.bccampus.ca/teachinginadigitalagev3m/

Bennett, L., & Abusalem, A. (2024). Artificial Intelligence (AI) and its Potential Impact on the Future of Higher Education. *Athens Journal of Education*, *11*(3), 195–212. DOI: 10.30958/aje.11-3-2

Bhutoria, A. (2022). Personalized education and Artificial Intelligence in the United States, China, and India: A systematic review using a Human-In-The-Loop model. *Computers and Education: Artificial Intelligence*, *3*, 100068. Advance online publication. DOI: 10.1016/j.caeai.2022.100068

Biggio Center for the Enhancement of Teaching and Learning. (n.d.). *Teaching with AI: Auburn University*. Auburn University. https://biggio.auburn.edu/programs/professional-development-programs/teaching-with-ai-auburn

Bishop, L. (2007). A Reflexive Account of Reusing Qualitative Data: Beyond Primary/Secondary Dualism. *Sociological Research Online*, *12*(3), 43–56. DOI: 10.5153/sro.1553

Black, P., & Wiliam, D. (2009). Developing the theory of formative assessment. *Educational Assessment, Evaluation and Accountability*, *21*(1), 5–31. DOI: 10.1007/s11092-008-9068-5

Blauth, T. F., Gstrein, O. J., & Zwitter, A. (2022). Artificial Intelligence Crime: An overview of Malicious use and abuse of AI. *IEEE Access : Practical Innovations, Open Solutions*, *10*, 77110–77122. DOI: 10.1109/ACCESS.2022.3191790

Blommerde, T., Charalambous, E., Bright, W., Musgrave, E., Ueno, L., & Magee, T. (2024). Integrating Generative Artificial Intelligence into Teaching and Assessment: A Case Study from a University in the UK. In O'Dea, X., & Ng, D. T. K. (Eds.), *Effective Practices in AI Literacy Education: Case Studies and Reflections* (pp. 119–129). Emerald Publishing Limited., DOI: 10.1108/978-1-83608-852-320241013

Bloomberg Editorial Board. (2025, May 27). *Does college still have a purpose in the age of ChatGPT?* Bloomberg. https://www.bloomberg.com/opinion/articles/2025-05-27/does-college-still-have-a-purpose-in-the-age-of-chatgpt

Boddington, P., Millican, P., & Wooldridge, M. (2017). Minds and machines special issue: Ethics and artificial intelligence. *Minds and Machines*, *27*, 569–574.

Booyse, D., & Scheepers, C. B. (2023). Barriers to adopting automated organisational decision-making through the use of artificial intelligence. *Management Research Review*, *47*(1), 64–85. DOI: 10.1108/MRR-09-2021-0701

Boss, S., & Krauss, J. (2022). *Reinventing project-based learning: Your field guide to real-world projects in the digital age*. International Society for Technology in Education.

Boud, D., & Soler, R. (2016). Sustainable assessment revisited. *Assessment & Evaluation in Higher Education*, *41*(3), 400–413. DOI: 10.1080/02602938.2015.1018133

Bournemouth University. (2023, August 2). Using artificial intelligence to support assignments or assessments. https://www.bournemouth.ac.uk/news/2023-08-02/using-artificial-intelligence-support-assignments-or-assessments

Brisk Teaching. (n.d.). *Brisk Teaching*. Brisk Teaching. https://www.briskteaching.com/

Brown, K. (2021, June 1). *Something Bothering You? Tell It to Woebot.* The New York Times. https://www.nytimes.com/2021/06/01/health/artificial-intelligence-therapy-woebot.html?smid=url-share

Brusseau, J. (2023). From the ground truth up: Doing AI ethics from practice to principles. *AI & Society*, •••, 1–7.

Bryant, J., Heitz, C., Sanghvi, S., & Wagle, D. (2020). *How artificial intelligence will impact K-12 teachers.*

Bucchiarone, A., Cicchetti, A., Vázquez-Ingelmo, A., Adami, F., Schiavo, G., García-Holgado, A., & García-Peñalvo, F. J. (2024, September). Designing and generating lesson plans combining open educational content and generative AI. In *Proceedings of the ACM/IEEE 27th International Conference on Model Driven Engineering Languages and Systems* (pp. 78-86). DOI: 10.1145/3652620.3687773

Bulmer, L., Stanley, C., Loffredo, L., Mills, R., & Doyle, L. (2022). Building a foundation in self-awareness: Genetic counseling students' experiences with self-care, reflection, and mindfulness. *Journal of Genetic Counseling*, *31*(3), 722–734. DOI: 10.1002/jgc4.1539

Burton, E., Goldsmith, J., Koenig, S., Kuipers, B., Mattei, N., & Walsh, T. (2017). Ethical considerations in artificial intelligence courses. *AI Magazine*, *38*(2), 22–34. DOI: 10.1609/aimag.v38i2.2731

Campbell, J., & Koffi, B. A. (2024). The Role of AI-powered financial analytics in shaping economic policy: A new era for risk management and national growth in the United States. *World Journal of Advanced Research and Reviews*, *23*(3), 2816–2825. DOI: 10.30574/wjarr.2024.23.3.2963

Campbell, L. O., Howard, C., Lambie, G. W., & Gao, X. (2022). The efficacy of a computer-adaptive reading program on grade 5 students' reading achievement scores. *Education and Information Technologies*, *27*(6), 8147–8163. DOI: 10.1007/s10639-022-10953-5

Campo, J., de los Reyes, R & Gomez, MGAG. (October 2022). Challenges Affecting the Well-Being of Filipino Guidance Counselors Amidst the COVID-19 Pandemic. (2). pp.17-28

Carlà, M. M., Gambini, G., Baldascino, A., Boselli, F., Giannuzzi, F., Margollicci, F., & Rizzo, S. (2024). Large language models as assistance for glaucoma surgical cases: A ChatGPT vs. Google Gemini comparison. *Graefe's Archive for Clinical and Experimental Ophthalmology*, *262*(9), 2945–2959. DOI: 10.1007/s00417-024-06470-5

Caspari-Sadeghi, S. (2022a). Artificial Intelligence in Technology-Enhanced Assessment: A Survey of Machine Learning. *Journal of Educational Technology Systems*, *51*(3), 372–386. DOI: 10.1177/00472395221138791

Caspari-Sadeghi, S. (2022b). Learning assessment in the age of big data: Learning analytics in higher education. *Cogent Education*, *10*(1), 2162697. Advance online publication. DOI: 10.1080/2331186X.2022.2162697

Castillo-Martínez, I., Fernández-Segovia, I., & Rodríguez-López, C. (2024). The impact of AI on academic research practices: Opportunities and challenges. *Frontiers in Education*, *9*, 1391485. DOI: 10.3389/feduc.2024.1391485

Çelik, İ., Dindar, M., Muukkonen, H., & Järvelä, S. (2022). The Promises and Challenges of Artificial Intelligence for Teachers: a Systematic Review of Research [Review of The Promises and Challenges of Artificial Intelligence for Teachers: a Systematic Review of Research]. TechTrends, 66(4), 616. Springer Science+Business Media. https://doi.org/DOI: 10.1007/s11528-022-00715-y

Celik, I. (2023). Towards intelligent-TPACK: An empirical study on teachers' professional knowledge to ethically integrate artificial intelligence (AI)-based tools into education. *Computers in Human Behavior*, *138*, 107468. Advance online publication. DOI: 10.1016/j.chb.2022.107468

Cevallos, M. G. O., Jaramillo, G. A. L., Vélez, J. L. B., Zambrano, M. I. U., Montesdeoca, L. D. Z., & Palomeque, M. A. B.Miguel Giancarlo Ormaza CevallosGustavo Alberto Lozano JaramilloJosé Luis Bernardo VélezMaritza Irinuska Ureta Zambrano-Lady Diana Zambrano MontesdeocaManuel Augusto Bermúdez Palomeque. (2024). Implementation of Artificial Intelligence in Quality Management in SMEs: Benefits and Challenges. *Evolutionary Studies in Imaginative Culture*, *1489*, 1489–1500. Advance online publication. DOI: 10.70082/esiculture.vi.1590

Chadha, A. (2024). Transforming higher education for the digital age: Examining emerging technologies and pedagogical innovations. *Journal of Interdisciplinary Studies in Education*, *13*(S1), 53–70. DOI: 10.32674/em2qsn46

Chaka, C. (2020). Skills, competencies and literacies attributed to 4IR/Industry 4.0: Scoping review. *IFLA Journal*, *46*(4), 369–399. DOI: 10.1177/0340035219896376

Chan, C. K. Y., & Tsi, L. H. (2023). The AI revolution in education: Will AI replace or assist teachers in higher education? *arXiv preprint arXiv:2305.01185*.

Chand, S. P., Kuckel, D. P., & Huecker, M. R. (2023, May 23). *Cognitive Behavior Therapy*. StatPearls - NCBI Bookshelf. https://www.ncbi.nlm.nih.gov/books/NBK470241/

Chanda, R. C., Vafaei-Zadeh, A., Hanifah, H., & Ramayah, T. (2025). Artificial intelligence teaching assistant adoption in university education: Key drivers through the ability, motivation and opportunity framework. *Education and Information Technologies*, *30*(10), 14123–14164. Advance online publication. DOI: 10.1007/s10639-025-13360-8

Chedrawi, C., Kazoun, N., & Kokkinaki, A. (2024). The role of AI agents in fostering inclusivity for HEIs' students with special needs against backdrops of the accreditation trend. *Quality Assurance in Education*, *32*(4), 582–596. Advance online publication. DOI: 10.1108/QAE-01-2024-0010

Chen, B., Wu, Z., & Zhao, R. (2023). From fiction to fact: The growing role of generative AI in business and finance. *Journal of Chinese Economic and Business Studies*, *21*(4), 471–496. DOI: 10.1080/14765284.2023.2245279

Chen, C. M. (2014). Intelligent web-based learning system with personalized learning path guidance. *Computers & Education*, *56*(1), 209–222. DOI: 10.1016/j.compedu.2010.08.001

Chen, L., Chen, P., & Lin, Z. (2020). Artificial Intelligence in Education: A Review. *IEEE Access : Practical Innovations, Open Solutions*, *8*, 75264–75278. DOI: 10.1109/ACCESS.2020.2988510

Chen, Z. (2023). Ethics and discrimination in artificial intelligence-enabled recruitment practices. *Humanities & Social Sciences Communications*, *10*(1), 567. Advance online publication. DOI: 10.1057/s41599-023-02079-x

Chinta, S. V., Wang, Z., Yin, Z., Hoang, N., Gonzalez, M., Quy, T. L., & Zhang, W. (2024). FairAIED: Navigating fairness, bias, and ethics in educational AI applications. *arXiv preprint arXiv:2407.18745*.

Chiu, T. K. (2021). A holistic approach to the design of artificial intelligence (AI) education for K-12 schools. *TechTrends*, *65*(5), 796–807. https://eric.ed.gov/?id=EJ1309807. DOI: 10.1007/s11528-021-00637-1

Chiu, T. K. F., & Chai, C. S. (2020). Sustainable curriculum planning for artificial intelligence education: A self-determination theory perspective. *Sustainability (Basel)*, *12*(14), 5568. DOI: 10.3390/su12145568

Chiu, T. K. F., Meng, H., Chai, C. S., King, I., Wong, S., & Yam, Y. (2022). Creation and Evaluation of a Pretertiary Artificial Intelligence (AI) Curriculum. *IEEE Transactions on Education*, *65*(1), 30–39. DOI: 10.1109/TE.2021.3085878

Christina, R., & Panagiotidis, P. (2024). Teachers' attitudes towards AI integration in foreign language learning: Supporting differentiated instruction and flipped classroom. *European Journal of Education*, *7*(2), 88–104. DOI: 10.26417/171oob60e

Climent, E. F. (2024, March 5). *Embracing Mindfulness in the age of AI: A Path to Inner Peace*. https://www.linkedin.com/pulse/embracing-mindfulness-age-ai-path-inner-peace-edgardo-zih6e#:~:text=Integrating%20AI%20into%20mindfulness%20practices,but%20unsure%20where%20to%20start

Code.org. (n.d.). *Exploring generative AI*. Code.org. https://code.org/curriculum/generative-ai

Commonwealth of Australia. (2022). *Disability standards for education review: Final report*. https://www.education.gov.au/disability-standards-education-2005/resources

Cooper, J. (2023, September 26). *Stress and Depression*. WebMD. https://www.webmd.com/depression/features/stress-depression

Cooper, G., Tang, K. S., & Fitzgerald, A. (2025). Intersections of Mind and Machine: Navigating the Nexus of Artificial Intelligence, Science Education, and the Preparation of Pre-service Teachers. *Journal of Science Education and Technology*. Advance online publication. DOI: 10.1007/s10956-025-10200-9

Coursera. (n.d.). *Generative AI courses*. Coursera. https://www.coursera.org/campus/generative-ai-courses

Creswell, J. W. (2013). *Qualitative inquiry and research design: Choosing among five approaches* (3rd ed.). SAGE.

Crompton, H. (2017). *Mobile learning and educational theory: Integrating pedagogical strategies with learning technologies*. Routledge.

Cukurova, M., Miao, X., & Brooker, R. A. (2023). Adoption of Artificial Intelligence in Schools: Unveiling Factors Influencing Teachers' Engagement. In Lecture notes in computer science (p. 151). Springer Science+Business Media. https://doi.org/ DOI: 10.1007/978-3-031-36272-9_13

D'Souza, R., Mathew, M., Mishra, V., & Surapaneni, K. M. (2024). Twelve tips for addressing ethical concerns in the implementation of artificial intelligence in medical education. *Medical Education Online*, *29*(1), 2330250. Advance online publication. DOI: 10.1080/10872981.2024.2330250 PMID: 38566608

Dai, R., Thomas, M. K. E., & Rawolle, S. (2024). The roles of AI and educational leaders in AI-assisted administrative decision-making: A proposed framework for symbiotic collaboration. *Australian Educational Researcher*. Advance online publication. DOI: 10.1007/s13384-024-00771-8

Davar, N. F., Dewan, M. A. A., & Zhang, X. (2025). AI chatbots in education: Challenges and opportunities. *Information (Basel)*, *16*(3), 1–25. DOI: 10.3390/info16030235

De Cremer, D., & Kasparov, G. (2022). The ethical AI—paradox: Why better technology needs more and not less human responsibility. *AI and Ethics*, *2*(1), 1–4.

Deveci Topal, A., Dilek Eren, C., & Kolburan Geçer, A. (2021). Chatbot application in a 5th grade science course. *Education and Information Technologies*, *26*(5), 6241–6265. DOI: 10.1007/s10639-021-10627-8

Devineni, S. K. (2024). AI in Data Privacy and Security. In *International Journal of Artificial Intelligence & Machine Learning (IJAIML)* (Vol. 3, Issue 1, pp. 35–49) [Journal-article]. https://iaeme.com/MasterAdmin/Journal_uploads/IJAIML/VOLUME_3_ISSUE_1/IJAIML_03_01_004.pdf

Dianovi, A., Siregar, D., Mawaddah, I., & Suryaningsih, S. (2022). Guidance and Counselling in Education. *World Psychology*, *1*(2), 99–107. DOI: 10.55849/wp.v1i2.95

Digital Education Council. (2025a). *Annual report on digital learning innovations*. Digital Education Council Publications.

Digital Education Council. (2025b). Empowering faculty to experiment, share and learn: Advancing AI literacy in higher education. https://www.digitaleducationcouncil.com/post/empowering-faculty-to-experiment-share-and-learn-advancing-ai-literacy-in-higher-education

Ding, A.-C. E., Shi, L., Yang, H., & Choi, I. (2024). Enhancing teacher AI literacy and integration through different types of cases in teacher professional development. *Computers and Education Open*, *6*, 100178. DOI: 10.1016/j.caeo.2024.100178

Duan, Y., Edwards, J. S., & Dwivedi, Y. K. (2019). Artificial intelligence for decision making in the era of Big Data – evolution, challenges and research agenda. *International Journal of Information Management*, *48*, 63–71. DOI: 10.1016/j.ijinfomgt.2019.01.021

Dyoub, A., Costantini, S., & Lisi, F. A. (2022). Learning domain ethical principles from interactions with users. *Digital Society : Ethics, Socio-Legal and Governance of Digital Technology*, *1*(3), 28.

EDUCAUSE. (2025a). *2025 EDUCAUSE AI landscape study*. https://library.educause.edu/resources/2025/2/2025-educause-ai-landscape-study

EDUCAUSE. (2025b). *Teaching and learning workforce in higher education*. https://www.educause.edu/content/2025/teaching-and-learning-workforce-in-higher-education

Eshaghi, S. (2024, August). *Cooperative Play in Historic Preservation Education: A Theoretical Framework and Game Implementation at the Silk Roads Using Unreal Engine*. Tdl.org. https://ttu-ir.tdl.org/items/a7f435f5-e8f8-4a7b-8bab-4b10912370c8

Espartinez, A. S. (2024). Exploring student and teacher perceptions of ChatGPT use in higher education: A Q-Methodology study. *Computers and Education: Artificial Intelligence*, *7*, 100264. Advance online publication. DOI: 10.1016/j.caeai.2024.100264

Esplugas, M. (2023). The use of artificial intelligence (AI) to enhance academic communication, education and research: A balanced approach. *The Journal of Hand Surgery, European Volume*, *48*(8), 819–822. DOI: 10.1177/17531934231185746 PMID: 37417005

European Commission. (2024). *Artificial Intelligence Act: A European approach to excellence and trust.* https://digital-strategy.ec.europa.eu/en/policies/regulatory-framework-ai

European Parliament. (2020). *The impact of the General Data Protection Regulation (GDPR) on artificial intelligence*. https://www.europarl.europa.eu/RegData/etudes/STUD/2020/641530/EPRS_STU(2020)641530_EN.pdf

Evans, H., & Snead, D. (2024). Understanding the errors made by artificial intelligence algorithms in histopathology in terms of patient impact. *NPJ Digital Medicine*, *7*(1), 89. Advance online publication. DOI: 10.1038/s41746-024-01093-w

Eynden, V. V. den, Corti, L., Woollard, M., Bishop, L., & Horton., L. (2011). *MANAGING AND SHARING DATA BEST PRACTICE FOR RESEARCHERS*. UK Data Archive.

Fadli, R. P., Daharnis, D., & Yusuf, A. M. (2022). How The Implications of Assessment for Guidance and Counseling in Schools? [Jurnal Penelitian Guru Indonesia]. *JPGI*, *7*(1), 148–153. DOI: 10.29210/021875jpgi0005

Fahd, K., Miah, S. J., & Ahmed, K. (2021). *Predicting student performance in a blended learning environment using learning management system interaction data*. Applied Computing and Informatics., DOI: 10.1108/ACI-06-2021-0150

Fahimirad, M., & Kotamjani, S. S. (2018). A Review of the Application of Artificial Intelligence in Teaching and Learning in Educational Contexts. *International Journal of Learning and Development*, *8*(4), 106. DOI: 10.5296/ijld.v8i4.14057

Farhan, A. (2023). The impact of artificial intelligence on human workers. *Journal Of Communication Education*, *17*(2), 93–104. https://jurnal.unipem.ac.id/index.php/joce-ip/article/view/350. DOI: 10.58217/joce-ip.v17i2.350

Farhud, D. D., & Zokaei, S. (2021, October 27). Ethical Issues of Artificial Intelligence in Medicine and Healthcare. *Iranian Journal of Public Health*, *50*(11), i. DOI: 10.18502/ijph.v50i11.7600

Farrell, I. C., Binkley, E. E., Garcia, M. A., & Jackson, T. N. (2022). Advocacy of School Counselors Working With ELL Students. *Professional School Counseling*, *26*(1), 2156759X221134276. Advance online publication. DOI: 10.1177/2156759X221134276

Farzan, M., Ebrahimi, H., Pourali, M., & Sabeti, F. (2024). Artificial Intelligence-Powered Cognitive Behavioral Therapy Chatbots, A Systematic Review. *Iranian Journal of Psychiatry*. Advance online publication. DOI: 10.18502/ijps.v20i1.17395

Feigerlova, E., Hani, H., & Hothersall-Davies, E. (2025). A systematic review of the impact of artificial intelligence on educational outcomes in health professions education. *BMC Medical Education*, *25*(1), 129. DOI: 10.1186/s12909-025-06719-5 PMID: 39871336

Felix, C. V. (2020). The role of the teacher and AI in education. In *International perspectives on the role of technology in humanizing higher education* (pp. 33–48). Emerald Publishing Limited.

Ferrara, E. (2023). Fairness and bias in artificial intelligence: A brief survey of sources, impacts, and mitigation strategies. *Sci*, *6*(1), 1–15. DOI: 10.3390/sci6010003

Fischer, C., Pardos, Z. A., Baker, R. S., Williams, J. J., Smyth, P., Yu, R., Slater, S., Baker, R., & Warschauer, M. (2020). Mining Big Data in Education: Affordances and Challenges. *Review of Research in Education*, *44*(1), 130–160. DOI: 10.3102/0091732X20903304

Fisher, E. J. P., & Fisher, E. (2023). A fresh look at ethical perspectives on artificial intelligence applications and their potential impacts at work and on people. *Business and Economic Review*, *13*(3), 1–22.

Fiske, A., Henningsen, P., & Buyx, A. (2019). Your robot therapist will see you now: Ethical implications of embodied artificial intelligence in psychiatry, psychology, and psychotherapy. *Journal of Medical Internet Research*, *21*(5), e13216. DOI: 10.2196/13216

Fitria, T. N. (2023). The Use of Artificial Intelligence in Education: Can AI replace the teacher's role? *EPIGRAM (e-Journal)*, *20*(2), 165-187. DOI: 10.32722/epi.v20i2.5711

Flores-Viva, J. M., & García-Peñalvo, F. J. (2023). Reflections on the ethics, potential, and challenges of artificial intelligence in the framework of quality education (SDG4). *Comunicar: Media Education Research Journal*, *31*(74), 35–44.

Floridi, L., Cowls, J., Beltrametti, M., Chatila, R., Chazerand, P., Dignum, V., Luetge, C., Madelin, R., Pagallo, U., Rossi, F., Schafer, B., Valcke, P., & Vayena, E. (2018). AI4People—An ethical framework for a good AI society: Opportunities, risks, principles, and recommendations. *Minds and Machines*, *28*(4), 689–707. DOI: 10.1007/s11023-018-9482-5 PMID: 30930541

Foltýnek, T., Bjelobaba, S., Glendinning, I., Khan, Z. R., Santos, R., Pavletić, P., & Kravjar, J. (2023). ENAI Recommendations on the ethical use of Artificial Intelligence in Education. *International Journal for Educational Integrity*, *19*(1), 12. Advance online publication. DOI: 10.1007/s40979-023-00133-4

Francesc, P., Migue, F., & Paula, V. (2019). *Artificial intelligence in education: challenges and opportunities for sustainable development*. Unesco.org. https://unesdoc.unesco.org/ark:/48223/pf0000366994

Fundi, M., Sanusi, I. T., Oyelere, S. S., & Ayere, M. (2024). Advancing AI education: Assessing Kenyan in-service teachers' preparedness for integrating artificial intelligence in competence-based curriculum. *Computers in Human Behavior Reports*, *14*, 100412. Advance online publication. DOI: 10.1016/j.chbr.2024.100412

Gándara, D., Anahideh, H., Ison, M. P., & Picchiarini, L. (2023). Inside the black box: Detecting and mitigating algorithmic bias across racialized groups in college student-success prediction. *arXiv preprint* arXiv:2301.03784. https://arxiv.org/abs/2301.03784

Gardner, M. M., Hickmott, J., & Ludvik, M. J. B. (2023). *Demonstrating student success: A practical guide to outcomes-based assessment of learning and development in student affairs*. Routledge., DOI: 10.4324/9781003444046

Garner, J., & Alley, M. (2013). How the design of presentation slides affects audience comprehension: A case for the assertion-evidence approach. *International Journal of Engineering Education*, *29*(6), 1564–1579.

Garza Schuster, J. E. (2022). A phenomenological investigation of the lived experiences of middle school professional school counselors in addressing student mental health, during the COVID-19 pandemic, after a return to in-person instruction. https://tamucc-ir.tdl.org/server/api/core/bitstreams/8b50554a-9c41-4d73-9554-9b5337de03b9/content

Gašević, D., Siemens, G., & Sadiq, S. (2023). Empowering learners for the age of artificial intelligence. In *Computers and Education: Artificial Intelligence* (Vol. 4). Elsevier B.V. DOI: 10.1016/j.caeai.2023.100130

Ghimire, P., Kim, K., & Acharya, M. (2024). Opportunities and challenges of generative AI in the construction industry: Focusing on adoption of text-based models. *Buildings (Basel, Switzerland)*, *14*(1), 220. DOI: 10.3390/buildings14010220

Gichuki, L. (2025). AI goes to school: The global AI education race, opportunities and perils. *DevelopmentAid*. https://www.developmentaid.org/news-stream/post/194647/ai-transforming-education

Gikandi, J. W., Morrow, D., & Davis, N. E. (2011). Online formative assessment in higher education: A review of the literature. *Computers & Education*, *57*(4), 2333–2351. DOI: 10.1016/j.compedu.2011.06.004

Gimbert, B. G., Miller, D., Herman, E., Breedlove, M., & Molina, C. E. (2023). Social Emotional Learning in Schools: The Importance of Educator Competence. *Journal of Research on Leadership Education*, *18*(1), 3–39. DOI: 10.1177/19427751211014920

Gisonna, N. (2025, February 26). chatbot. Encyclopedia Britannica. https://www.britannica.com/topic/chatbot

Goetz, T., Bieleke, M., Gogol, K., van Tartwijk, J., Mainhard, T., Lipnevich, A. A., & Pekrun, R. (2021). Getting along and feeling good: Reciprocal associations between student-teacher relationship quality and students' emotions. *Learning and Instruction*, *71*, 101349. DOI: 10.1016/j.learninstruc.2020.101349

Gomstyn, A., & Jonker, A. (2024, November 25). Exploring privacy issues in the age of AI. *IBM*. https://www.ibm.com/think/insights/ai-privacy

Goodall, C. (2024, February 11). *Will AI Replace Teachers?* https://www.ai-in-education.co.uk/resources/will-ai-replace-teachers

Google. (n.d.-a). *Gemini*. Google. https://gemini.google.com/app

Google. (n.d.-b). *Google AI essentials*. Grow with Google. https://grow.google/ai-essentials

Google. (n.d.-c) *Notebook LM*. Google. https://notebooklm.google

Gouseti, A., James, F., Fallin, L., & Burden, K. (2024). The ethics of using AI in K-12 education: A systematic literature review. *Technology, Pedagogy and Education*, *1*. Advance online publication. DOI: 10.1080/1475939X.2024.2428601

Grabb, D. (2024). Text-to-Video AI Is Here To Stay: What It Means for Mental Health. *Psychiatric News*, *59*(06), appi.pn.2024.06.6.34. Advance online publication. DOI: 10.1176/appi.pn.2024.06.6.34

Gradescope. (n.d.). *Gradescope*. Gradescope. https://www.gradescope.com

Grammarly. (n.d.). *Grammarly*. Grammarly. https://www.grammarly.com

Grassini, S. (2023). Shaping the future of education: Exploring the potential and consequences of AI and ChatGPT in educational settings. *Education Sciences*, *13*(7), 692. DOI: 10.3390/educsci13070692

Guan, C., Mou, J., & Jiang, Z. (2020). Artificial intelligence innovation in education: A twenty-year data-driven historical analysis. *International Journal of Innovation Studies*, *4*(4), 134–147. DOI: 10.1016/j.ijis.2020.09.001

Guan, L., Zhang, Y., & Gu, M. M. (2025). Pre-service teachers preparedness for AI-integrated education: An investigation from perceptions, capabilities, and teachers' identity changes. *Computers and Education: Artificial Intelligence*, *8*, 100341.

Guerra, A. (2023). *The future benefits of artificial intelligence for students*. Urbe University. https://urbeuniversity.edu/blog/the-future-benefits-of-artificial-intelligence-for-students

Guilherme, A. (2019). AI and education: The importance of teacher and student relations. *AI & Society*, *34*, 47–54.

Gulikers, J. T., Bastiaens, T. J., & Kirschner, P. A. (2008). Authentic assessment, student and teacher perceptions: The practical value of the five-dimensional framework. *Journal of Vocational Education and Training*, *60*(4), 401–412. DOI: 10.1080/13636820802591830

Guo, Q., Feng, R., & Hua, Y. (2021). How effectively can EFL students use automated written corrective feedback (AWCF) in research writing? *Computer Assisted Language Learning*, *35*(9), 2312–2331. DOI: 10.1080/09588221.2021.1879161

Habib, S., Vogel, T., Anli, X., & Thorne, E. (2024). How does generative artificial intelligence impact student creativity? *Journal of Creativity*, *34*(1), 1–7. DOI: 10.1016/j.yjoc.2023.100072

Habsy, B. A., Apriliya, K., Apriliyana, G. S., Zahra, K. F. A., & Mahendra, W. (2024). Concept of Information Service Management Guidance and Counseling. *Jurnal Multidisiplin Indonesia*, *3*(12), 4568–4574. DOI: 10.58344/jmi.v3i12.2075

Hamilton, I. (2024). *Artificial Intelligence In Education: Teachers' Opinions On AI In The Classroom*. https://www.forbes.com/advisor/education/it-and-tech/artificial-intelligence-in-school/

Hamilton, J. (2025). Youper: Your Emotional Health Assistant. https://www.youper.ai

Handini, B. S., Nurhasanah, N., & Panly, F. I. (2022). The effect of artificial intelligent technology used (Duolingo application) to enhance English learning. *ELLITE: Journal of English Language, Literature, and Teaching*, *7*(2), 86–94. DOI: 10.32528/ellite.v7i2.8354

Heaps, T. (2024). *Generative artificial intelligence: Practical uses in education*. The Manitoba Open Education Initiative. https://pressbooks.openedmb.ca/aiineducation/

Hemment, D., Murray-Rust, D., Belle, V., Aylett, R., Vidmar, M., & Broz, F. (2023). Experiential AI: A transdisciplinary framework for legibility and agency in AI. *arXiv preprint arXiv:2306.00635*.

Hennekeuser, D., Vaziri, D. D., Golchinfar, D., Schreiber, D., & Stevens, G. (2024). Enlarged education – Exploring the use of generative AI to support lecturing in higher education. *International Journal of Artificial Intelligence in Education*. Advance online publication. DOI: 10.1007/s40593-024-00424-y

Hepler, R. C., Vecchione, A., Hensley, R., Fensie, A., Sinha, S., Otero, L., Riechers, D., Long, L., Liang, L., Randall, R., & Gladd, J. (2024). Introduction to AI and Ethics in Higher Education. https://edtechbooks.org/introduction_to_ai_and_ethics_in_higher_education

Hickey, D. T., & Harris, T. (2021). Reimagining online grading, assessment, and testing using situated cognition. *Distance Education*, *42*(2), 290–309. DOI: 10.1080/01587919.2021.1911627

Himelfarb, I. (2019, October 01). A primer on standardized testing: History, measurement, classical test theory, item response theory, and equating. *The Journal of Chiropractic Education*, *33*(2), 151–163. DOI: 10.7899/JCE-18-22

Hodges, C., & Ocak, C. (2023, August 30). *Integrating generative AI into higher education: Considerations*. https://er.educause.edu/articles/2023/8/integrating-generative-ai-into-higher-education-considerations

Hodson, N., & Williamson, S. (2024). Can Large Language Models Replace Therapists? Evaluating Performance at Simple Cognitive Behavioral Therapy Tasks. *JMIR AI*, *3*, e52500. DOI: 10.2196/52500

Holmes, W., Bialik, M., & Fadel, C. (2019). *Artificial intelligence in education: Promises and implications for teaching and learning*. The Center for Curriculum Redesign.

Holmes, W., Bialik, M., & Fadel, C. (2019). Artificial Intelligence. In *Education Promises and Implications for Teaching and Learning*. The Center for Curriculum Redesign.

Holmes, W., Porayska-Pomsta, K., Holstein, K., Sutherland, E., Baker, T., Shum, S. B., & Koedinger, K. R. (2022). Ethics of AI in education: Towards a community-wide framework. *International Journal of Artificial Intelligence in Education*, •••, 1–23.

Holstein, K., & Aleven, V. (2022). Designing for human–AI complementarity in K-12 education. *AI Magazine*, *43*(2), 239–248. DOI: 10.1002/aaai.12058

Hornstein, S., Lueken, U., Wundrack, R., & Hilbert, K. (2025). Predicting Satisfaction With Chat-Counseling at a 24/7 Chat Hotline for the Youth: Natural Language Processing Study. *JMIR AI*, *4*(1), e63701. DOI: 10.2196/63701

Huang, M. H., & Rust, R. T. (2018). Artificial intelligence in service. *Journal of Service Research*, *21*(2), 155–172.

Hwang, G. J., Xie, H., Wah, B. W., & Gašević, D. (2020). Vision, challenges, roles and research issues of artificial intelligence in education. *Computers & Education: Artificial Intelligence*, *1*, 100001. DOI: 10.1016/j.caeai.2020.100001

Implementing Artificial Intelligence (AI) in Higher Education. A Narrative Literature Review. (2023). https://www.researchgate.net/publication/376553922_Implementing_Artificial_Intelligence_AI_in_Higher_Education_A_Narrative_Literature_Review

Imran, M., & Almusharraf, N. (2024). Google Gemini as a next generation AI educational tool: A review of emerging educational technology. *Smart Learning Environments*, *11*(1), 22. Advance online publication. DOI: 10.1186/s40561-024-00310-z

Injadat, M., Moubayed, A., Nassif, A. B., & Shami, A. (2021). Machine learning towards intelligent systems: Applications, challenges, and opportunities. *Artificial Intelligence Review*, *54*(5), 3299–3348. DOI: 10.1007/s10462-020-09948-w

International Society for Technology in Education (ISTE). (n.d.). *Artificial intelligence in education*. ISTE. https://iste.org/ai

Iqbal, M. H., Siddiqie, S. A., & Mazid, M. A. (2021). Rethinking theories of lesson plan for effective teaching and learning. *Social Sciences & Humanities Open*, *4*(1), 100172. DOI: 10.1016/j.ssaho.2021.100172

Jadoon, A. I., Khan, F., Syeda Tehmina Naz Bukhari, N. T. S., Gilani, S. Z., Ishfaq, U., & Ullah, M. (2022). Effect of teacher-student relationship on pro-social behavior and academic achievement of secondary school students. *Indian Journal of Economics and Business*, *21*(1), 331–337.

Jafari, E. (2024). Artificial intelligence and learning environment: Human considerations. *Journal of Computer Assisted Learning*, *40*(5), 2135–2149. Advance online publication. DOI: 10.1111/jcal.13011

Jain, A., Kerne, A., Fowler, H., Seo, J., Newman, G., Lupfer, N., & Perrine, A. (2024). *How Could AI Support Design Education? A Study Across Fields Fuels Situating Analytics*.

Jaiswal, C., Jaiswal, L., Kalia, N., & Sharma, O. P. (2025). Artificial Intelligence in Counseling: Evaluating Its Strengths, Limitations, and Ethical Considerations in Indian Schools. *International Journal of Science and Social Science Research*, *2*(4), 328–331. DOI: 10.5281/zenodo.15090441

Jamil, T., Hussain, S., Khan, Z., & Atif, H. (2024). Investigating the Effects of Mindfulness and Meditation on Student Stress Levels and Academic Outcomes with AI. [BBE]. *Bulletin of Business and Economics*, *13*(3), 472–479. https://bbejournal.com/BBE/article/view/1036?articlesBySimilarityPage=53

Jang, S., Kim, J., Kim, S., Hong, J., Kim, S., & Kim, E. (2021). Mobile app-based chatbot to deliver cognitive behavioral therapy and psychoeducation for adults with attention deficit: A development and feasibility/usability study. *International Journal of Medical Informatics*, *150*, 104440. DOI: 10.1016/j.ijmedinf.2021.104440

Janiesch, C., Zschech, P., & Heinrich, K. (2021). Machine learning and deep learning. *Electronic Markets*, *31*(3), 685–695. DOI: 10.1007/s12525-021-00475-2

Jannah, M., Izzati, U. A., Bachri, B. S., & Wismanadi, H. (2023, January). Guidance and Counseling Referral System Initiative. In *Unima International Conference on Social Sciences and Humanities (UNICSSH 2022)* (pp. 383-387). Atlantis Press. https://www.atlantis-press.com/proceedings/unicssh-22/125984046

Jayabhaduri, R., Vijayaraghavan, A., & Ceralaathan, G. (2024, June). AI Powered Chatbot For Mental Health Treatment. In *2024 First International Conference on Technological Innovations and Advance Computing (TIACOMP)* (pp. 168-172). IEEE. **DOI:** DOI: 10.1109/TIACOMP64125.2024.00037

Jemison, J. (2024, October 15). *Mental illness remains taboo in the Philippines, but technology might just help break the stigma — Medicinal Media*. Medicinal Media. https://www.medicinalmedia.com/explore/tech-helps-break-the-stigma-of-mental-illness-in-the-philippines

Jern, K. (2024). *Can AI Replace Teachers?* We Finally Know the Answer.

Jiang, J., Vetter, M. A., & Lucia, B. (2024). *Toward a 'More-Than-Digital' AI Literacy: Reimagining Agency and Authorship in the Postdigital Era with ChatGPT*. Postdigital Science and Education., DOI: 10.1007/s42438-024-00477-1

Jin, Y., Yan, L., Echeverria, V., Gašević, D., & Martinez-Maldonado, R. (2025). Generative AI in higher education: A global perspective of institutional adoption policies and guidelines. *Computers and Education: Artificial Intelligence*, *8*, 100348. DOI: 10.1016/j.caeai.2024.100348

Jisc. (2023). *AI in tertiary education: Challenges and opportunities*. https://www.jisc.ac.uk/reports/artificial-intelligence-in-tertiary-education

Johnson, S. (2013). On the reliability of high-stakes teacher assessment. *Research Papers in Education*, *28*(1), 91–105. DOI: 10.1080/02671522.2012.754229

Johnston, M. (2014). *Secondary Data Analysis: A Method of which the Time Has Come. Qualitative and Quantitative Methods in Libraries*. QQML.

Ka Yuk Chan, C., & Tsi, L. H. (2023). The AI Revolution in Education: Will AI Replace or Assist Teachers in Higher Education? https://arxiv.org/abs/2305.01185

Ka, C., & Colloton, T. (2024). *Generative AI in Higher Education*. Routledge., DOI: 10.4324/9781003459026

Kaharuddin, K., Ahmad, D., Mardiana, M., Latif, I., Arafah, B., & Suryadi, R. (2024). Defining the Role of Artificial Intelligence in Improving English Writing Skills Among Indonesian Students. *Journal of Language Teaching and Research*, *15*(2), 568–678. DOI: 10.17507/jltr.1502.25

Kanungo, A. (2024, March 5). The Green Dilemma: Can AI Fulfil Its Potential Without Harming the Environment? https://earth.org/the-green-dilemma-can-ai-fulfil-its-potential-without-harming-the-environment/

Karaman, M. A., Eşici, H., Tomar, İ. H., & Aliyev, R. (2021). COVID-19: Are school counseling services ready? Students' psychological symptoms, school counselors' views, and solutions. *Frontiers in Psychology*, *12*, 647740. DOI: 10.3389/fpsyg.2021.647740

Karan, B., & Angadi, G. R. (2023). Potential Risks of Artificial Intelligence Integration into School Education: A Systematic Review. *Bulletin of Science, Technology & Society*, *43*(3-4), 67–85. Advance online publication. DOI: 10.1177/02704676231224705

Karataş, F., Eriçok, B., & Tanrikulu, L. (2025). Reshaping curriculum adaptation in the age of artificial intelligence: Mapping teachers' <scp>AI</scp> -driven curriculum adaptation patterns. *British Educational Research Journal*, *51*(1), 154–180. DOI: 10.1002/berj.4068

Karmakar, S., & Das, T. (2024). *Optimization and Computing using Intelligent Data-Driven Approaches for Decision-Making* (1st ed.). CRC Press.

Khan Academy. (n.d.-a). *Khanmigo: AI-powered teaching assistant*. Khan Academy. https://www.khanmigo.ai/

Khan Academy. (n.d.-b). *Khanmigo for educators*. Khan Academy. https://www.khanacademy.org/khan-for-educators/khanmigo-for-educators

Khare, K., Stewart, B., & Khare, A. (2018). Artificial intelligence and the student experience: An institutional perspective. *The International Academic Forum (IAFOR)*.

Khlaif, Z. N., Hamamra, B., & Hussein, E. T. (2025). AI paradox in higher education: Understanding over-reliance, its impact, and sustainable integration. Preprint (Version 1) available at Research Square. DOI: 10.21203/rs.3.rs-6127885/v1

Khosravi, H., Shum, S. B., Chen, G., Conati, C., Tsai, Y.-S., Kay, J., Knight, S., Martinez-Maldonado, R., Sadiq, S., & Gašević, D. (2022). Explainable Artificial Intelligence in education. *Computers and Education: Artificial Intelligence*, *3*(3), 100074. DOI: 10.1016/j.caeai.2022.100074

Kılınç, S. (2024). Comprehensive AI Assessment Framework: Enhancing Educational Evaluation with Ethical AI Integration. Journal of Educational Technology and Online Learning. https://doi.org/DOI: 10.31681/jetol.1492695

Kim, J. (2024). Leading teachers' perspective on teacher-AI collaboration in education. *Education and Information Technologies*, *29*(7), 8693–8724. DOI: 10.1007/s10639-023-12109-5

Kim, J., Klopfer, M., Grohs, J. R., Eldardiry, H., Weichert, J., Cox, L. A.II, & Pike, D. (2025). Examining faculty and student perceptions of generative AI in university courses. *Innovative Higher Education*, *50*(4), 1281–1313. Advance online publication. DOI: 10.1007/s10755-024-09774-w

Kim, J., Lee, H., & Cho, Y. H. (2022). Learning design to support student-AI collaboration: Perspectives of leading teachers for AI in education. *Education and Information Technologies*, *27*(5), 6069–6104. DOI: 10.1007/s10639-021-10831-6

Kim, N. J., & Kim, M. K. (2022). Teacher's Perceptions of Using an Artificial Intelligence-Based Educational Tool for Scientific Writing. *Frontiers in Education*, *7*, 755914. Advance online publication. DOI: 10.3389/feduc.2022.755914

Klimova, B., Pikhart, M., & Kacetl, J. (2023). Ethical issues of the use of AI-driven mobile apps for education. *Frontiers in Public Health*, *10*, 1118116.

Koehler, M., & Mishra, P. (2009). What is technological pedagogical content knowledge (TPACK)? *Contemporary Issues in Technology & Teacher Education*, *9*(1), 60–70. DOI: 10.1177/002205741319300303

Kohli, J. K. (2024). *Impact of Artificial Intelligence on Fashion Education for Future Jobs*. Higher Education for the Future., DOI: 10.1177/23476311241284860

Kolb, D. A. (1984). *Experiential learning: Experience as the source of learning and development.*

Kolluru, V., Mungara, S., & Chintakunta, A. N. (2018). Adaptive learning systems: Harnessing AI for customized educational experiences. [IJCSITY]. *International Journal of Computer Science and Information Technologies*, *6*(1), 13–26. DOI: 10.5121/ijcsity.2018.6302

Kong, S. C., Cheung, W. M. Y., & Tsang, O. (2023). Evaluating an artificial intelligence literacy programme for empowering and developing concepts, literacy and ethical awareness in senior secondary students. *Education and Information Technologies*, *28*(4), 4703–4724. DOI: 10.1007/s10639-022-11408-7

Kong, S. C., Man-Yin Cheung, W., & Zhang, G. (2021). Evaluation of an artificial intelligence literacy course for university students with diverse study backgrounds. *Computers and Education: Artificial Intelligence*, *2*, 100026. Advance online publication. DOI: 10.1016/j.caeai.2021.100026

Kong, S.-C., Cheung, W. M.-Y., & Zhang, G. (2023). Evaluating an Artificial Intelligence Literacy Programme for Developing University Students' Conceptual Understanding, Literacy, Empowerment and Ethical Awareness. *Journal of Educational Technology & Society*, *26*, 16–30.

Kosmala, K., Marszałek, A., & Rudawska, E. (2024). Communication in project team management: Identification of research gaps and direction for future research. *European Research Studies*, *27*(Special Issue A, S2), 732–751. DOI: 10.35808/ersj/3746

Krach, S. K., & Corcoran, S. (2024). Will Computers Replace School Psychologists? An Analysis of Tech-Based Tools for Assessment, Consultation, and Counseling. *Contemporary School Psychology*, *28*(4), 496–508. DOI: 10.1007/s40688-023-00455-7

Krakowski, A., Greenwald, E., Hurt, T., Nonnecke, B., & Cannady, M. (2022, June). Authentic integration of ethics and AI through sociotechnical, problem-based learning. *Proceedings of the AAAI Conference on Artificial Intelligence*, *36*(11), 12774–12782.

Krathwohl, D. R. (2002). A revision of Bloom's taxonomy: An overview. *Theory into Practice*, *41*(4), 212–218. DOI: 10.1207/s15430421tip4104_2

Kruiper, S. M. A., Leenknecht, M. J. M., & Slof, B. (2021). Using scaffolding strategies to improve formative assessment practice in higher education. *Assessment & Evaluation in Higher Education*, *47*(3), 458–476. DOI: 10.1080/02602938.2021.1927981

Kühn, C., Khoo, S., Czerniewicz, L., Lilley, W., Bute, S. J. R., Crean, A., Abegglen, S., Burns, T., Sinfield, S., Jandrić, P., Knox, J., & MacKenzie, A. (2023). Understanding Digital Inequality: A Theoretical Kaleidoscope. *Postdigital Science and Education*, *5*(3), 894–932. DOI: 10.1007/s42438-023-00395-8 PMID: 40479087

Kumar, C. R. (2025). AI-Powered Recruitment: Transforming Talent Acquisition in the Digital Age. *Journal of Informatics Education and Research*, *5*(1). Advance online publication. DOI: 10.52783/jier.v5i1.2166

Labadze, L., Grigolia, M., & Machaidze, L. (2023). Role of AI chatbots in education: A systematic literature review. *International Journal of Educational Technology in Higher Education, 20*(1), 56. Advance online publication. DOI: 10.1186/s41239-023-00426-1

Lacson, J., Kilag, O. K., Sasan, J. M., Groenewald, E., Vidal, E., & Ponte, R. (2024). The Crisis: An In-Depth Analysis of the Shortage of Guidance Counselors and Its Impact on Student Suicide Rates in Philippine Schools. *International Multidisciplinary Journal of Research for Innovation, Sustainability, and Excellence (IMJRISE), 1*(1), 129-135. https://risejournals.org/index.php/imjrise/article/view/15

Ladson-Billings, G. (1995). Toward a theory of culturally relevant pedagogy. *American Educational Research Journal, 32*(3), 465–491. DOI: 10.3102/00028312032003465

Lampou, R. (2023). The Integration of Artificial Intelligence in Education: Opportunities and Challenges. *Review of Artificial Intelligence in Education, 4*(00), e015. Advance online publication. DOI: 10.37497/rev.artif.intell.educ.v4i00.15

Lan, Y. (2024). Through tensions to identity-based motivations: Exploring teacher professional identity in Artificial Intelligence-enhanced teacher training. *Teaching and Teacher Education, 151*, 104736. DOI: 10.1016/j.tate.2024.104736

Latif, E., Mai, G., Nyaaba, M., Wu, X., Liu, N., Lu, G., . . . Zhai, X. (2023). Artificial general intelligence (AGI) for education. *arXiv preprint arXiv:2304.12479*, 1.

Laupichler, M. C., Aster, A., Schirch, J., & Raupach, T. (2022). Artificial intelligence literacy in higher and adult education: A scoping literature review. *Computers and Education: Artificial Intelligence*. DOI: 10.1016/j.caeai.2022.100101

Leach, L. (2016). Enhancing student engagement in one institution. *Journal of Further and Higher Education, 40*(1), 23–47.

Leatherman, A. J. (2024). Exploring How Experienced High School Counselors Make Sense of COVID-19's Impact on their Attitudes and Beliefs about Postsecondary Planning, and their Postsecondary Planning Practices: Two Interpretive Phenomenological Analysis Studies. https://ir.library.oregonstate.edu/concern/graduate_thesis_or_dissertations/tb09jf23h?locale=en

Lee, J. (2025). Smart Solutions for Student Well-being: AI-driven Mental Health Support in a Polytechnic. In *The Rise of Intelligent Machines* (pp. 211-242). Chapman and Hall/CRC. https://www.taylorfrancis.com/chapters/edit/10.1201/9781003469551-9/smart-solutions-student-well-being-jeffrey-lee

Leino, R. K., Kaqinari, T., Makarova, E., & Döring, A. K. (2024). Connectedness with students as a key factor in online teaching self-efficacy. *Computers and Education Open, 6*, 100192. DOI: 10.1016/j.caeo.2024.100192

Li, B., Lowell, V. L., Wang, C., & Li, X. (2024). A systematic review of the first year of publications on ChatGPT and language education: Examining research on ChatGPT's use in language learning and teaching. In *Computers and Education: Artificial Intelligence* (Vol. 7). Elsevier B.V. DOI: 10.1016/j.caeai.2024.100266

Liang, P., Bommasani, R., & Zelikman, E. (2023). AI-detectors biased against non-native English writers. *Stanford HAI.* https://hai.stanford.edu/news/ai-detectors-biased-against-non-native-english-writers

Liang, W., Yüksekgönül, M., Mao, Y., Wu, E. Q., & Zou, J. (2023). GPT detectors are biased against non-native English writers. *Patterns (New York, N.Y.)*, *4*(7), 100779. DOI: 10.1016/j.patter.2023.100779 PMID: 37521038

Lin, C. C., Huang, A. Y. Q., & Lu, O. H. T. (2023). Artificial intelligence in intelligent tutoring systems toward sustainable education: A systematic review. *Smart Learning Environments*, *10*(1), 41. DOI: 10.1186/s40561-023-00260-y

Li, S., & Gu, X. (2023). A risk framework for human-centered artificial intelligence in education: Based on literature review and Delphi–AHP method. *Journal of Educational Technology & Society*, *26*(1), 187–202.

Liu, Y., & Wang, H. Digital Development Global Practice, Research Support Team, & World Bank. (2024). Who on Earth is using generative AI? In World Bank, *Policy Research Working Paper*. https://documents1.worldbank.org/curated/en/099720008192430535/pdf/IDU15f321eb5148701472d1a88813ab677be07b0.pdf

Li, Y., Ding, X., Chen, Y., Li, Y., & Ma, N. (2025, July). Customizable AI for Depression Care: Improving the User Experience of Large Language Model-Driven Chatbots. In *Proceedings of the 2025 ACM Designing Interactive Systems Conference* (pp. 1844-1866). https://doi.org/DOI: 10.1145/3715336.3735795

Lu, J. (n.d.). *Artificial intelligence (AI) LibGuide*. Purdue University Libraries. https://guides.lib.purdue.edu/c.php?g=1371380&p=10135065

Lucietto, A. M., & Peters, D. (2024). Engineering technology and engineering: Incorporating the humanities into the classroom. *Frontiers in Education*, *9*, 1534407. Advance online publication. DOI: 10.3389/feduc.2024.1534407

Luckin, R., Holmes, W., Griffiths, M., & Forcier, L. B. (2016). *Intelligence Unleashed: An argument for AI in Education*. Pearson Education.

Luo, M., Hu, X., & Zhong, C. (2025). The collaboration of AI and teacher in feedback provision and its impact on EFL learner's argumentative writing. *Education and Information Technologies*, *30*(12), 17695–17715. Advance online publication. DOI: 10.1007/s10639-025-13488-7

Ma, Y., & Siau, K. L. (2018). *Artificial intelligence impacts on higher education.* MWAIS 2018 Proceedings, 42. https://aisel.aisnet.org/mwais2018/42

Madigan, D. J., Kim, L. E., Glandorf, H. L., & Kavanagh, O. (2023). Teacher burnout and physical health: A systematic review [Review of Teacher burnout and physical health: A systematic review]. International Journal of Educational Research, 119, 102173. Elsevier BV. https://doi.org/DOI: 10.1016/j.ijer.2023.102173

Maghsudi, S., Lan, A., Xu, J., & van Der Schaar, M. (2021). Personalized education in the artificial intelligence era: What to expect next. *IEEE Signal Processing Magazine*, *38*(3), 37–50. DOI: 10.1109/MSP.2021.3055032

Magic School AI. (n.d.). *Magic School AI: Automated lesson planning and assessments.* Magic School AI. https://www.magicschool.ai

Maher, M. (2024, May 8). U-M launches first university-built generative AI tools. *The Michigan Daily.* https://www.michigandaily.com/news/administration/umich-becomes-first-major-university-to-develop-its-own-generative-ai/

Majjate, H., Bellarhmouch, Y., Jeghal, A., Yahyaouy, A., Tairi, H., & Zidani, K. A. (2023, December 28). AI-Powered Academic Guidance and Counseling System Based on Student Profile and Interests. *Applied System Innovation*, *7*(1), 6. DOI: 10.3390/asi7010006

Ma, K., Zhang, Y., & Hui, B.-H. (2024). How Does AI Affect College? The Impact of AI Usage in College Teaching on Students' Innovative Behavior and Well-Being. *Behavioral Sciences (Basel, Switzerland)*, *14*(12), 1223. DOI: 10.3390/bs14121223 PMID: 39767364

Malik, T., Ambrose, A. J., & Sinha, C. (2022). Evaluating user feedback for an artificial intelligence–enabled, cognitive behavioral therapy–based mental health app (Wysa): Qualitative thematic analysis. *JMIR Human Factors*, *9*(2), e35668. DOI: 10.2196/35668

Mallik, S., & Gangopadhyay, A. (2023). Proactive and reactive engagement of artificial intelligence methods for education: A review. *Frontiers in Artificial Intelligence*, *6*, 1151391. DOI: 10.3389/frai.2023.1151391 PMID: 37215064

Manyika, J., Chui, M., Brown, B., Bughin, J., Dobbs, R., Roxburgh, C., & Hung Byers, A. (2011). *Big Data: The Next Frontier for Innovation, Competition, and Productivity.* McKinsey Global Institute. https://www.mckinsey.com/~/media/McKinsey/Business%20Functions/McKinsey%20Digital/Our%20Insights/Big%20data%20The%20next%20frontier%20for%20innovation/MGI_big_data_exec_summary.pdf

Marr, B. (2022). *Will Artificial Intelligence Replace Teachers?* Rayhan, A., Rayhan, R., & Rayhan, S. (2023). *Revolutionizing Education: The Power of Artificial Intelligence (AI).* DOI: 10.13140/RG.2.2.10716.97924

Marschall, A. M. (2024, June 11). I'm a Therapist Who Tried Headspace to Help Conquer My Stress. *Verywell Mind.* https://www.verywellmind.com/i-tried-headspace-review-7562523

Martone, A., & Sireci, S. G. (2009). Evaluating alignment between curriculum, assessment, and instruction. *Review of Educational Research, 79*(4), 1332–1361. DOI: 10.3102/0034654309341375

Marzano, R. J. (2017). *The new art and science of teaching*. Solution Tree Press.

Marzuki, M., Widiati, U., Rusdin, D., Darwin, D., & Indrawati, I. (2023). The impact of AI writing tools on the content and organization of students' writing: EFL teachers' perspective. *Cogent Education, 10*(2), 2236469. Advance online publication. DOI: 10.1080/2331186X.2023.2236469

McDonald, N., Johri, A., Ali, A., & Collier, A. H. (2025). Generative artificial intelligence in higher education: Evidence from an analysis of institutional policies and guidelines. *Computers in Human Behavior: Artificial Humans, 3*. https://doi.org//arXiv.2402.01659DOI: 10.48550

McDonald, N., Johri, A., Ali, A., & Hingle, A. (2024). Generative artificial intelligence in higher education: Evidence from an analysis of institutional policies and guidelines. *arXiv preprint arXiv:2402.01659*. https://arxiv.org/abs/2402.01659

McKay, C., & Macomber, G. (2021). The Importance of Relationships in Education: Reflections of Current Educators. *Journal of Education, 203*(4), 751–758. DOI: 10.1177/00220574211057044

Meier, S. T. (2025). Initial evaluation of an AI-augmented progress monitoring and outcome assessment. *Counselling & Psychotherapy Research, 25*(1), e12869. DOI: 10.1002/capr.12869

Meli, K., Taouki, J., & Pantazatos, D. (2024). Empowering educators with generative AI: The GenAI education frontier initiative. In *EDULEARN24 Proceedings* (pp. 4289-4299). IATED. https://doi: DOI: 10.21125/edulearn.2024.1077

Merino-Campos, C. (2025a). Privacy by design: Building a data protection culture in higher education institutions. *EDUData Journal, 11*(1), 45–60.

Merino-Campos, C. (2025b). The impact of artificial intelligence on personalized learning in higher education: A systematic review. *Trends in Higher Education, 4*(2), 17. DOI: 10.3390/higheredu4020017

Microsoft. (n.d.). *Copilot.* Microsoft. https://www.microsoft.com/en-us/microsoft-copilot

Mielgo-Conde, I., Seijas-Santos, S., & Grande-de-Prado, M. (2021). Review about online educational guidance during the COVID-19 pandemic. *Education Sciences, 11*(8), 411. DOI: 10.3390/educsci11080411

Milne, L., McCann, J., Bolton, K. A., Savage, J., & Spence, A. C. (2020). Student satisfaction with feedback in a third year Nutrition unit: A strategic approach. *Journal of University Teaching & Learning Practice, 17*(5). Advance online publication. DOI: 10.53761/1.17.5.5

Milossi, M., Alexandropoulou-Egyptiadou, E., & Psannis, K. E. (2021). AI ethics: Algorithmic determinism or self-determination? The GPDR approach. *IEEE Access : Practical Innovations, Open Solutions, 9*, 58455–58466.

Minn, S. (2022). AI-assisted knowledge assessment techniques for adaptive learning environments. *Computers and Education Artificial Intelligence, 3*, 100050. DOI: 10.1016/j.caeai.2022.100050

Mirza, A., & Syed, N. Fatmi, & Pohn, B. (2025). *Integrating artificial intelligence into pre-clinical medical education.* Frontiers in Education. https://www.frontiersin.org/journals/education/articles/10.3389/feduc.2025.1570389/full

Miserandino, M. (2024). Authentic and creative assessment in a world with AI. *Teaching of Psychology*, •••, 1–6. DOI: 10.1177/00986283241260370

Mishra, P., & Koehler, M. J. (2006). Technological pedagogical content knowledge: A framework for teacher knowledge. *Teachers College Record, 108*(6), 1017–1054. DOI: 10.1111/j.1467-9620.2006.00684.x

Moldez, C., Crisanto, M. A., Cerdeña, M. G. R., Maranan, D. S., & Figueroa, R. (2024). Innovation in education: Developing and assessing gamification in the University of the Philippines Open University Massive Open Online Courses. *arXiv preprint* arXiv:2409.03309. https://arxiv.org/abs/2409.03309

Molefi, R. R., Ayanwale, M. A., Kurata, L., & Chere-Masopha, J. (2024). Do in-service teachers accept artificial intelligence-driven technology? The mediating role of school support and resources. *Computers and Education Open, 6*, 100191. DOI: 10.1016/j.caeo.2024.100191

Monteith, S., Glenn, T., Geddes, J. R., Whybrow, P. C., Achtyes, E., & Bauer, M. (2024). Artificial intelligence and increasing misinformation. *The British Journal of Psychiatry, 224*(2), 33–35. DOI: 10.1192/bjp.2023.136

Mortaji, S. T. H., & Sadeghi, M. E. (2024). Assessing the reliability of artificial intelligence systems: challenges, metrics, and future directions. In Iran University of Science and Technology & University of Tehran, *International Journal of Innovation in Management Economics and Social Sciences* (Vol. 4, Issue 2, pp. 1–13). https://ijimes.ir/index.php/ijimes/article/view/133

Moundridou, M., Matzakos, N., & Doukakis, S. (2024). Generative AI tools as educators' assistants: Designing and implementing inquiry-based lesson plans. *Computers and Education Artificial Intelligence*, *7*, 100277. DOI: 10.1016/j.caeai.2024.100277

Moybeka, A. M., Syariatin, N., Tatipang, D. P., Mushthoza, D. A., Dewi, N. P. J. L., & Tineh, S. (2023). Artificial intelligence and English classroom: The implications of AI toward EFL students' motivation. *Edumaspul: Jurnal Pendidikan*, *7*(2), 2444–2454. DOI: 10.33487/edumaspul.v7i2.6669

Muthmainnah, M. (2024). AI-CiciBot as Conversational Partners in EFL Education, focusing on Intelligent Technology Adoption (ITA) to Mollify Speaking Anxiety. *Journal of English Language Teaching and Applied Linguistics, 6*(4), 76-85. ISSN: 2707-756X

Nakao, M., Shirotsuki, K., & Sugaya, N. (2021). Cognitive–behavioral therapy for management of mental health and stress-related disorders: Recent advances in techniques and technologies. *BioPsychoSocial Medicine*, *15*(1), 16. DOI: 10.1186/s13030-021-00219-w

Ng, D. T. K., Leung, J. K. L., Chu, S. K. W., & Qiao, M. S. (2021). Conceptualizing AI literacy: An exploratory review. *Computers and Education: Artificial Intelligence*, *2*, 100041. Advance online publication. DOI: 10.1016/j.caeai.2021.100041

Ng, D. T. K., Leung, J. K. L., Su, J., Ng, C. W., & Chu, S. K. W. (2023). Teachers' AI digital competencies and twenty-first century skills in the post-pandemic world. *Educational Technology Research and Development*, *71*(1), 137–161. DOI: 10.1007/s11423-023-10203-6 PMID: 36844361

Ngeno, G. (2022). Students' Perceptions of the Impact of Guidance and Counselling Programs on Academic Needs Satisfaction in Secondary Schools within the Rift Valley Region, Kenya. *Educational Research Review*, *17*(4), 145–151. https://eric.ed.gov/?id=EJ1344846. DOI: 10.5897/ERR2022.4232

Ngubane, N., Ntombela, B., & Govender, S. (2020). Writing approaches and strategies used by teachers in selected South African English First Additional Language classrooms. *Reading and Writing*, *11*(1). Advance online publication. DOI: 10.4102/rw.v11i1.261

Nguyen, A., Ngo, H. N., Hong, Y., Dang, B., & Nguyen, B. P. T. (2023). Ethical principles for artificial intelligence in education. *Education and Information Technologies, 28*(4), 4221–4241.

Nkedishu, V. C., & Okonta, V. (2024). Unpacking Optimism versus Concern: Tertiary Students' Multidimensional Views on the Rise of Artificial Intelligence (AI). [IRJMS]. *International Research Journal of Multidisciplinary Scope*, *5*(4), 362–37. DOI: 10.47857/irjms.2024.05i04.01261

Nouri, H., & Shahid, A. (2005). The effect of PowerPoint presentations on student learning and attitudes. *Global Perspectives on Accounting Education*, *2*(1), 53–73.

Nwana, H. S. (1990). Intelligent tutoring systems: An overview. *Artificial Intelligence Review*, *4*(4), 251–277. DOI: 10.1007/BF00168958

Nyaaba, M. (2025). *Glocalizing Generative AI in Education for the Global South: The Design Case of 21st Century Teacher Educator AI for Ghana*. arXiv preprint arXiv:2504.07149. https://arxiv.org/abs/2504.07149 DOI: 10.2139/ssrn.5212321

O'Daffer, A., Colt, S. F., Wasil, A. R., & Lau, N. (2022). Efficacy and conflicts of interest in randomized controlled trials evaluating Headspace and Calm apps: Systematic review. *JMIR Mental Health*, *9*(9), e40924. DOI: 10.2196/40924

Ocran, G., Yusuf, S. O., Owusu, P., Boateng, E. A., Krampah, S. O., & Paul-Adeleye, A. H. (2024). AI-driven business analytics for SMES: Unlocking value through predictive and prescriptive analytic. *International Journal of Science and Research Archive*, *13*(1), 3009–3022. DOI: 10.30574/ijsra.2024.13.1.2001

OECD. (2024). The future of education and skills: AI in learning. https://www.oecd.org/education/ai-in-education.pdf

Ofem, U. J., Anake, P. M., Abuo, C. B., Ukatu, J. O., & Etta, E. O. (2025). Artificial intelligence application in counselling practices. A multigroup analysis of acceptance and awareness using gender and professional rank. *Frontiers in Digital Health*, *6*, 1414178. DOI: 10.3389/fdgth.2024.1414178

Ofosu-Ampong, K. (2024). Beyond the hype: Exploring faculty perceptions and acceptability of AI in teaching practices. *Discover Education*, *3*(1), 38. Advance online publication. DOI: 10.1007/s44217-024-00128-4

Oh, S., & Ahn, Y. (2024). Exploring Teachers' Perception of Artificial Intelligence: The Socio-emotional Deficiency as Opportunities and Challenges in Human-AI Complementarity in K-12 Education. In Lecture notes in computer science (p. 439). Springer Science+Business Media. https://doi.org/DOI: 10.1007/978-3-031-64299-9_41

Okeleke, P. A., Ajiga, D., Folorunsho, S. O., & Ezeigweneme, C. (2024). Predictive analytics for market trends using AI: A study in consumer behavior. *International Journal of Engineering Research Updates*, *7*(1), 36. DOI: 10.53430/ijeru.2024.7.1.0032

Okonkwo, C. W., & Ade-Ibijola, A. (2021). Chatbots applications in education: A systematic review. In *Computers and Education: Artificial Intelligence* (Vol. 2). Elsevier B.V. DOI: 10.1016/j.caeai.2021.100033

Olawade, D. B., Wada, O. Z., Odetayo, A., David-Olawade, A. C., Asaolu, F., & Eberhardt, J. (2024). Enhancing mental health with Artificial Intelligence: Current trends and future prospects. *Journal of Medicine, Surgery, and Public Health*, *3*, 100099. DOI: 10.1016/j.glmedi.2024.100099

Ole, F. C. B. (2020). Development and Validation of Teachers' Practices on Formative Assessment Scale (TPFAS): A Measure Using Feedback Loop Model. *International Journal of Education*, *13*(1), 53–62. DOI: 10.17509/ije.v13i1.24715

Onesi-Ozigagun, O., Ololade, Y. J., Eyo-Udo, N. L., & Ogundipe, D. O. (2024). Revolutionizing education through AI: A comprehensive review of enhancing learning experiences. *International Journal of Applied Research in Social Sciences*, *6*(4), 589–607. DOI: 10.51594/ijarss.v6i4.1011

Open, A. I. (n.d.). *ChatGPT.* OpenAI. https://chat.openai.com

Ouédraogo, I. (2024). *Mobile technology and artificial intelligence for improving health literacy among underserved communities* (Doctoral dissertation, Université de Bordeaux; Université Nazi Boni (Bobo-Dioulasso, Burkina Faso)). https://theses.hal.science/tel-04574957/

Ouyang, F., Zheng, L., & Jiao, P. (2022). Artificial intelligence in online higher education: A systematic review of empirical research from 2011 to 2020. *Education and Information Technologies*, *27*(8), 7893–7925. DOI: 10.1007/s10639-022-10925-9

Owan, V. J., Abang, K. B., Idika, D. O., Etta, E. O., & Bassey, B. A. (2023). Exploring the potential of artificial intelligence tools in educational measurement and assessment. *Eurasia Journal of Mathematics, Science and Technology Education*, *19*(8), em2307. Advance online publication. DOI: 10.29333/ejmste/13428

Pack, A., Barrett, A., & Escalante, J. (2024). Large language models and automated essay scoring of English language learner writing: Insights into validity and reliability. *Computers and Education Artificial Intelligence*, *6*, 100234. DOI: 10.1016/j.caeai.2024.100234

Pagliarin, S., La Mendola, S., & Vis, B. (2023). The "qualitative" in qualitative comparative analysis (QCA): Research moves, case-intimacy and face-to-face interviews. *Quality & Quantity*, *57*(1), 489–507. DOI: 10.1007/s11135-022-01358-0

Pahi, K., Hawlader, S., Hicks, E., Zaman, A., & Phan, V. (2024). Enhancing active learning through collaboration between human teachers and generative AI. *Computers and Education Open*, *6*, 100183. DOI: 10.1016/j.caeo.2024.100183

Panadero, E., Broadbent, J., Boud, D., & Lodge, J. M. (2019). Using formative assessment to influence self-and co-regulated learning: The role of evaluative judgement. *European Journal of Psychology of Education, 34*(3), 535–557. DOI: 10.1007/s10212-018-0407-8

Park, E. (2025). I Trust You, but Let Me Talk to AI: The Role of the Chat Agents, Empathy, and Health Issues in Misinformation Guidance. *International Journal of Strategic Communication, 19*(2), 1–30. DOI: 10.1080/1553118X.2025.2462087

Paulauskaite-Taraseviciene, A., Lagzdinyte-Budnike, I., Gaiziuniene, L., Sukacke, V., & Daniuseviciute-Brazaite, L. (2022). Assessing Education for Sustainable Development in Engineering Study Programs: A Case of AI Ecosystem Creation. *Sustainability (Basel), 14*(3), 1702. DOI: 10.3390/su14031702

Pavan, S. (2024). *Devi Manikeswari, Shaikh, Z. H., Mahapatra, D. M., Mohanty, B. S., & Soni, A.* Advances in Educational Technologies and Instructional Design Book Series. Wearables and AI-Smart Technologies., DOI: 10.4018/979-8-3693-7817-5.ch002

Pedro, F., Subosa, M., Rivas, A., & Valverde, P. (2019). Artificial intelligence in education: Challenges and opportunities for sustainable development.

Pedroso, J. E., Siason, A., Ortizo-Roces, C., & Basbas, J. (2022). Implementation of guidance and counseling services during the COVID-19 Pandemic. *ISSRA Journal of Education, Linguistics and Literature, 2*(1), 1-12. https://www.researchgate.net/profile/John-Erwin-Pedroso/publication/358395202_Implementation_of_Guidance_and_Counseling_Services_during_the_COVID-19_Pandemic/links/61ffd980870587329e974b7b/Implementation-of-Guidance-and-Counseling-Services-during-the-COVID-19-Pandemic.pdf

Perkins, M. (2023). Academic integrity considerations of AI large language models in the post-pandemic era: ChatGPT and beyond. *Journal of University Teaching & Learning Practice*, *20*(2), 1–24. DOI: 10.53761/1.20.02.07

Perplexity. (n.d.). *Perplexity.* Perplexity AI. https://www.perplexity.ai/

Personal Data Protection Commission. (2020). *Singapore's approach to AI governance: Model AI governance framework* (2nd ed.). https://www.pdpc.gov.sg/help-and-resources/2020/01/model-ai-governance-framework

Peters, H., Zdravkovic, M., João Costa, M., Celenza, A., Ghias, K., Klamen, D., & Weggemans, M. (2019). Twelve tips for enhancing student engagement. *Medical Teacher, 41*(6), 632–637.

Peterson, L. (2019). School Counselors' Lived Experiences Supporting Students with Mental Health Concerns. https://scholarworks.waldenu.edu/cgi/viewcontent.cgi?article=8696&context=dissertations

Petersson, L., Vincent, K., Svedberg, P., Nygren, J. M., & Larsson, I. (2023). Ethical Perspectives on Implementing AI to Predict Mortality Risk in Emergency Department Patients: A Qualitative Study. *Studies in Health Technology and Informatics, 302*, 676–677. DOI: 10.3233/SHTI230234 PMID: 37203776

Ping, Y. (2024). Experience in psychological counseling supported by artificial intelligence technology. *Technology and Health Care, 32*(6), 3871–3888. DOI: 10.3233/THC-230809

Pohn, B., Mehnen, L., Fitzek, S., & Choi, K. (2025). Integrating AI into medical education: Opportunities and challenges. *Frontiers in Education, 10*, •••. https://www.frontiersin.org/articles/10.3389/feduc.2025.1570389/full. DOI: 10.3389/feduc.2025.1570389

Pokrivcakova, S. (2019). Preparing teachers for the application of AI-powered technologies in foreign language education. *Journal of Language and Cultural Education, 7*(3), 135–153.

Potgieter, I. (2020). Privacy concerns in educational data mining and learning analytics. *International Journal of Information Ethics, 28*. Advance online publication. DOI: 10.29173/irie384

Proudfoot, K. (2021). Panopticism, teacher surveillance and the 'unseen.'. *British Journal of Sociology of Education, 42*(5-6), 812–827. DOI: 10.1080/01425692.2021.1914549

Putri, R. A., Mailana, Z., Fadilah, N., Mardenil, F., & Oktarini, I. (2024). The Effectiveness of Artificial Intelligence Technology in Facing the Challenges of Guidance and Counseling in the Digital Age. *BICC Proceedings, 2*, 213-219. https://doi.org/ DOI: 10.30983/bicc.v1i1.130

Quiroz-Martinez, D., & Rushton, E. A. C. (2024). Exploring strategies to sustain teacher agency in the context of 'hyper-accountability': Reflections from ten experienced chemistry school teachers in Chile. *Teaching and Teacher Education, 152*, 104787. Advance online publication. DOI: 10.1016/j.tate.2024.104787

Rafli, M. F., Syahputra, E., & Yusnadi, Y. (2018). Influence of problem based learning model and early mathematics ability to mathematical communication skills and self-confidence in junior high school. *American Journal of Educational Research*, *6*(11), 1539–1545. DOI: 10.12691/education-6-11-12

Rahman, M. Z. (2024). Leveraging Artificial Intelligence for Enhanced Career Guidance and Development in Bangladesh: Addressing Educational and Employment Gaps. *International Journal of Career Development, 13*. https://www.researchgate.net/profile/Albina-Amin/publication/384243013_International_Journal_of_Career_Development/links/66f05e9a97a75a4b48405bf7/International-Journal-of-Career-Development.pdf#page=13

Rahman, M. A., Das, P., Lam, L., Alif, S. M., Sultana, F., Salehin, M., Banik, B., Joseph, B., Parul, P., Lewis, A., Statham, D., Porter, J., Foster, K., Islam, S. M. S., Cross, W., Jacob, A., Hua, S., Wang, Q., Chair, S. Y., & Polman, R. (2024). Health and wellbeing of staff working at higher education institutions globally during the post-COVID-19 pandemic period: Evidence from a cross-sectional study. *BMC Public Health*, *24*(1), 1848. DOI: 10.1186/s12889-024-19365-1 PMID: 38992680

Rebecchi, K., Todd, L., & Hagège, H. (2024). Teaching responsible creativity: A path to ethical innovation. *Discover Education*, *3*(1), 103. DOI: 10.1007/s44217-024-00164-0

Redecker, C., & Johannessen, Ø. (2013). Changing assessment—Towards a new assessment paradigm using ICT. *European Journal of Education*, *48*(1), 79–96. DOI: 10.1111/ejed.12018

Reich, J., & Ito, M. (2017). *From good intentions to real outcomes: Equity by design in learning technologies*. Digital Media and Learning Research Hub.

Research and Markets. (2024, November 18). *Artificial Intelligence in Education Market Report 2024-2029: Investments in AI-Driven Learning Platforms Fuel Growth with North America Leading*. GlobeNewswire News Room; Research and Markets. https://www.globenewswire.com/news-release/2024/11/18/2982495/28124/en/Artificial-Intelligence-in-Education-Market-Report-2024-2029-Investments-in-AI-Driven-Learning-Platforms-Fuel-Growth-with-North-America-Leading.html

Rezaiee, M., & Kareshki, H. (2024, November). Empowering career pathways: integrating self-regulation strategies with career counseling practices. In *Frontiers in Education* (Vol. 9, p. 1422692). Frontiers Media SA. https://doi.org/DOI: 10.3389/feduc.2024.1422692

Robert, J. (2024). *EDUCAUSE AI landscape study* [Research report]. EDUCAUSE. https://www.educause.edu/ecar/research-publications/2024/2024-educause-ai-landscape-study/introduction-and-key-findings

Robert, J., & McCormack, M. (2024). *EDUCAUSE action plan: AI policies and guidelines*. EDUCAUSE. https://www.educause.edu/research/2024/2024-educause-action-plan-ai-policies-and-guidelines

Robert, J., & Muscanell, N. (2023). Horizon action plan: Generative AI. EDUCAUSE. https://www.educause.edu

Roll, I., & Wylie, R. (2016). Evolution and revolution in artificial intelligence education. *International Journal of Artificial Intelligence in Education*, *26*(2), 582–599.

Roll, I., & Wylie, R. (2016). Evolution and Revolution in Artificial Intelligence in Education. *International Journal of Artificial Intelligence in Education*, *26*(2), 582–599. DOI: 10.1007/s40593-016-0110-3

Romael Haque, M. D., & Rubya, S. (2023, May 22). An Overview of Chatbot-Based Mobile Mental Health Apps: Insights From App Description and User Reviews. *JMIR mHealth and uHealth*, *11*, e44838. DOI: 10.2196/44838

Roshanaei, M., Olivares, H., & Lopez, R. R. (2023). Harnessing AI to Foster Equity in Education: Opportunities, Challenges, and Emerging Strategies. *Journal of Intelligent Learning Systems and Applications*, *15*(4), 123–143. DOI: 10.4236/jilsa.2023.154009

Rossi, A., & Lenzini, G. (2020). Transparency by design in data-informed research: A collection of information design patterns. *Computer Law & Security Review*, *37*, 105402. DOI: 10.1016/j.clsr.2020.105402

Roubini, N. (2023). The AI threat. *Horizons: Journal of International Relations and Sustainable Development*, (24), 26-45. https://www.cirsd.org/en/horizons/horizons-summer-2023--issue-no24/the-ai-threat

Rubin, M., Arnon, H., Huppert, J. D., & Perry, A. (2024, June 11). Considering the Role of Human Empathy in AI-Driven Therapy. *JMIR Mental Health*, *11*, e56529. DOI: 10.2196/56529

Ruiz Viruel, S., Sánchez Rivas, E., & Ruiz Palmero, J. (2025). The role of artificial intelligence in project-based learning: Teacher perceptions and pedagogical implications. *Education Sciences*, *15*(2), 150. DOI: 10.3390/educsci15020150

Saaida, M. B. (2023). AI-driven transformations in higher education: Opportunities and challenges. *International Journal of Educational Research and Studies*, *5*(1), 29–36. DOI: 10.5281/zenodo.8164414

Salinas-Navarro, D. E., Vilalta-Perdomo, E., Michel-Villarreal, R., & Montesinos, L. (2024). Using generative artificial intelligence tools to explain and enhance experiential learning for authentic assessment. *Education Sciences*, *14*(1), 83. DOI: 10.3390/educsci14010083

Salomon, D. (2012). *Data privacy and security*. Springer Science & Business Media.

Sanni, A. B. (2024). *Social Class Factors, Academic Well-Being And Academic Achievement Of Public Secondary School Students In Ekiti State, Nigeria* (Doctoral dissertation, Doctoral Dissertation, University of Ibadan).

Sanusi, I. T., Oyelere, S. S., & Omidiora, J. O. (2022). Exploring teachers' preconceptions of teaching machine learning in high school: A preliminary insight from Africa. *Computers and Education Open*, *3*, 100072. DOI: 10.1016/j.caeo.2021.100072

Sapohov, M. (2024). The characteristics of the educational and digital environment of US universities. *Педевтологія*, *2*(1), 51–58. DOI: 10.31652/3041-1203-2024(1)-51-58

Savitz-Romer, M., Rowan-Kenyon, H. T., Nicola, T. P., Alexander, E., & Carroll, S. (2021). When the kids are not alright: School counseling in the time of COVID-19. *AERA Open*, *7*, 23328584211033600. https://eric.ed.gov/?id=EJ1323994. DOI: 10.1177/23328584211033600

Schiff, D. (2021). Out of the laboratory and into the classroom: The future of artificial intelligence in education. *AI & Society*, *36*(1), 331–348. DOI: 10.1007/s00146-020-01033-8 PMID: 32836908

Schonert-Reichl, K. A. (2017). Social and emotional learning and teachers. *The Future of Children*, *27*(1), 137–155. http://www.jstor.org/stable/44219025. DOI: 10.1353/foc.2017.0007

Schussler, E. E., Bautista, N. U., Link-Pérez, M. A., Solomon, N. G., & Steinly, B. A. (2018). Implementing scientific practices in an introductory biology laboratory class: A mixed-methods evaluation. *Journal of College Science Teaching*, *47*(5), 74–81.

Selwin, S., Saseendran, H., Vemavarapu, K. R., Shaikh, I., Shaikh, Z. H., & Harris, S. B. (2024). AI-Driven Employee Engagement: Transforming Banking Workforce Dynamics Using the BEULA Model. In Awwad, B. (Ed.), *The AI Revolution: Driving Business Innovation and Research. Studies in Systems, Decision and Control* (Vol. 525). Springer., DOI: 10.1007/978-3-031-54383-8_32

Selwyn, N. (2019). *Should robots replace teachers?: AI and the future of education*. John Wiley & Sons.

Selwyn, N. (2019). What's the problem with learning analytics? *Journal of Learning Analytics*, *6*(3), 11–19.

Seo, K., Tang, J., Roll, I., Fels, S., & Yoon, D. (2021). The impact of artificial intelligence on learner–instructor interaction in online learning. *International Journal of Educational Technology in Higher Education*, *18*(1), 54. Advance online publication. DOI: 10.1186/s41239-021-00292-9 PMID: 34778540

Sghir, N., Adadi, A., & Lahmer, M. (2022). Recent advances in Predictive Learning Analytics: A decade systematic review (2012–2022). *Education and Information Technologies, 28*(7), 8299–8333. DOI: 10.1007/s10639-022-11536-0 PMID: 36571084

Shahzad, M. F., Xu, S., Lim, W. M., Yang, X., & Khan, Q. (2024). Artificial intelligence and social media on academic performance and mental well-being: Student perceptions of positive impact in the age of smart learning. *Heliyon, 10*(8), e29523. Advance online publication. DOI: 10.1016/j.heliyon.2024.e29523 PMID: 38665566

Shen, Y., & Shao, W. (2022). Influence of hybrid pedagogical models on learning outcomes in physical education: A systematic literature review. *International Journal of Environmental Research and Public Health, 19*(15), 9673.

Shneiderman, B. (2020a). Bridging the gap between ethics and practice: Guidelines for reliable, safe, and trustworthy human-centered AI systems. *ACM Transactions on Interactive Intelligent Systems, 10*(4), 1–31. DOI: 10.1145/3419764

Shneiderman, B. (2020b). Human-centered AI. *Interactions (New York, N.Y.), 27*(4), 76–81. DOI: 10.1145/3388440

Siau, K., & Wang, W. (2020). Artificial intelligence (AI) ethics: Ethics of AI and ethical AI. [JDM]. *Journal of Database Management, 31*(2), 74–87.

Sienes, M. J. V., & Sarsale, J. C. S. (2024). Revisiting AI in an English Classroom. In Atlantis highlights in social sciences, education and humanities/Atlantis Highlights in Social Sciences, Education and Humanities (p. 37). Atlantis Press. https://doi.org/DOI: 10.2991/978-94-6463-396-2_4

Sierra, C. (2024). A Historical Perspective on Artificial Intelligence in Higher Education. https://doi.org/DOI: 10.13140/RG.2.2.34113.26727

Sinha, C., Meheli, S., & Kadaba, M. (2023). Understanding digital mental health needs and usage with an artificial intelligence–led mental health app (Wysa) during the COVID-19 pandemic: Retrospective analysis. *JMIR Formative Research, 7*(1), e41913. DOI: 10.2196/41913

Slimi, Z., & Carballido, B. V. (2023). Navigating the ethical challenges of artificial intelligence in higher education: An analysis of seven global AI ethics policies. *TEM Journal, 12*(2).

Smith, J. A., Flowers, P., & Larkin, M. (2022). *Interpretative phenomenological analysis: Theory, method and research* (2nd ed.). SAGE. DOI: 10.1037/0000259-000

Smith, J. A., & Osborn, M. (2008). Interpretative phenomenological analysis. In Smith, J. A. (Ed.), *Qualitative psychology: A practical guide to research methods* (2nd ed., pp. 53–80). SAGE.

Sokhanvar, Z., Salehi, K., & Sokhanvar, F. (2021). Advantages of authentic assessment for improving the learning experience and employability skills of higher education students: A systematic literature review. *Studies in Educational Evaluation*, *70*, 1–10. DOI: 10.1016/j.stueduc.2021.101030

Solve Education! (2025). *Dawn of civilization: Bridging educational gaps through gamification*. Solve Education! Publications.

Song, Y., Weisberg, L. R., Zhang, S., Tian, X., Boyer, K. E., & Israel, M. (2024). A framework for inclusive AI learning design for diverse learners. *Computers and Education: Artificial Intelligence*, *100212*, 100212. Advance online publication. DOI: 10.1016/j.caeai.2024.100212

Southworth, J., Migliaccio, K., Glover, J., Glover, J., Reed, D., McCarty, C., Brendemuhl, J., & Thomas, A. (2023). Developing a model for AI across the curriculum: Transforming the higher education landscape via innovation in AI literacy. *Computers & Education: Artificial Intelligence*, *4*, 100127. DOI: 10.1016/j.caeai.2023.100127

Spencer, J. (2024, September 5). *AI Won't Replace Teachers But It Will Transform Nearly Every Aspect of the Job*.

Srinivasan, V. (2022). AI & learning: A preferred future. *Computers and Education: Artificial Intelligence*, *3*, 100062. Advance online publication. DOI: 10.1016/j.caeai.2022.100062

Stahl, B. C. (2021). Artificial intelligence for a better future. In *SpringerBriefs in research and innovation governance*. https://link.springer.com/book/10.1007/978-3-030-69978-9

Stahl, B. C., Antoniou, J., Bhalla, N., Brooks, L., Jansen, P., Lindqvist, B., Kirichenko, A. S., Marchal, S., Rodrigues, R., Santiago, N., Warso, Z., & Wright, D. (2023). A systematic review of artificial intelligence impact assessments [Review of A systematic review of artificial intelligence impact assessments]. *Artificial Intelligence Review*, *56*(11), 12799–12831. DOI: 10.1007/s10462-023-10420-8 PMID: 37362899

Stampfl, R., Geyer, B., Deissl-O'Meara, M., & Ivkić, I. (2024). Revolutionising role-playing games with ChatGPT. *arXiv preprint* arXiv:2407.02048. https://arxiv.org/abs/2407.02048

Strielkowski, W., Grebennikova, V., Lisovskiy, A., Rakhimova, G., & Vasileva, T. (2024). AI-driven adaptive learning for sustainable educational transformation. *Sustainable Development*, •••, 1–27. DOI: 10.1002/sd.3221

Su, J., Ng, D. T. K., & Chu, S. K. W. (2023). Artificial Intelligence (AI) Literacy in Early Childhood Education: The Challenges and Opportunities. In *Computers and Education: Artificial Intelligence* (Vol. 4). Elsevier B.V. DOI: 10.1016/j.caeai.2023.100124

Su, S. W., Hung, C. H., Chen, L. X., & Yuan, S. M. (2024). Development of an AI-based system to enhance school counseling models for Asian elementary students with emotional disorders. *IEEE Access*. https://ui.adsabs.harvard.edu/abs/2024IEEEA.12o9121S/abstract

Sun, J. C., & Pratt, T. L. (2024). Navigating AI Integration in Career and Technical Education: Diffusion Challenges, Opportunities, and Decisions. *Education Sciences*, *14*(12), 1285. DOI: 10.3390/educsci14121285

Suresh, N., Mukabe, N., Hashiyana, V., Limbo, A., & Hauwanga, A. (2021). Career Counseling Chatbot on Facebook Messenger using AI. *DSMLAI : Data Science, Machine Learning and Artificial Intelligence*, 65–73. DOI: 10.1145/3484824.3484875

Swiecki, Z., Khosravi, H., Chen, G., Martínez-Maldonado, R., Lodge, J. M., Milligan, S., Selwyn, N., & Gašević, D. (2022). Assessment in the age of artificial intelligence. *Computers and Education Artificial Intelligence*, *3*, 100075. DOI: 10.1016/j.caeai.2022.100075

Taye, T., & Mengesha, M. (2024). Identifying and analyzing common English writing challenges among regular undergraduate students. *Heliyon*, *10*(17), e36876. Advance online publication. DOI: 10.1016/j.heliyon.2024.e36876 PMID: 39263167

Taylor, D. L., Yeung, M., & Bashet, A. Z. (2021). Personalized and Adaptive Learning. In *SpringerBriefs in statistics* (p. 17). Springer International Publishing., DOI: 10.1007/978-3-030-58948-6_2

Tewari, A., Chhabria, A., Khalsa, A. S., Chaudhary, S., & Kanal, H. (2021, April). A survey of mental health chatbots using NLP. In *Proceedings of the International Conference on Innovative Computing & Communication (ICICC)*. https://papers.ssrn.com/sol3/papers.cfm?abstract_id=3833914

Tian, Y. (2023). Limitations and Advancements of AI Teachers in Classroom Instruction. *Education and Teaching Research*, *3*, 66–72.

Tilala, M. H., Chenchala, P. K., Choppadandi, A., Kaur, J., Naguri, S., Saoji, R., & Devaguptapu, B. (2024, June 15). Ethical Considerations in the Use of Artificial Intelligence and Machine Learning in Health Care: A Comprehensive Review. *Cureus*, *16*(6), e62443. DOI: 10.7759/cureus.62443

Timms, M. J. (2016). Letting artificial intelligence in education out of the box: Educational cobots and smart classrooms. *International Journal of Artificial Intelligence in Education*, *26*(2), 701–712. DOI: 10.1007/s40593-016-0095-y

Toyokawa, Y., Horikoshi, I., Majumdar, R., & Ogata, H. (2023). *Challenges and opportunities of AI in inclusive education: a case study of data-enhanced active reading in Japan*. Smart Learning Environments., DOI: 10.1186/s40561-023-00286-2

Trust, T., Whalen, J., & Mouza, C. (2023). ChatGPT: Challenges, opportunities, and implications for teacher education. *Contemporary Issues in Technology & Teacher Education*, *23*(1), 1–23. https://citejournal.org/volume-23/issue-1-23/editorial/editorial-chatgpt-challenges-opportunities-and-implications-for-teacher-education

Turnitin. (n.d.). *Turnitin*. Turnitin. https://www.turnitin.com/

Tutun, S., Johnson, M. E., Ahmed, A., Albizri, A., Irgil, S., Yesilkaya, I., Ucar, E. N., Sengun, T., & Harfouche, A. (2023). An AI-based decision support system for predicting mental health disorders. *Information Systems Frontiers*, *25*(3), 1261–1276. DOI: 10.1007/s10796-022-10282-5

U.S. Department of Education. (2023). *Artificial intelligence and the future of teaching and learning*. https://www.ed.gov/sites/ed/files/documents/ai-report/ai-report.pdf

UNESCO. (2021a). *AI literacy and the new digital divide: A global call for action*. https://www.unesco.org/en/articles/ai-literacy-and-new-digital-divide-global-call-action

UNESCO. (2021b). *Guidance for AI and education: Recommendations for governments*. https://unesdoc.unesco.org/ark:/48223/pf0000376709

United Nations Educational, Scientific and Cultural Organization (UNESCO). (2021). *Recommendation on the Ethics of Artificial Intelligence*. United Nations Educational, Scientific and Cultural Organization. https://www.unesco.org/en/artificial-intelligence/recommendation-ethics

United Nations Educational, Scientific and Cultural Organization (UNESCO). (2023). *Guidance for generative AI in education and research*. United Nations Educational, Scientific and Cultural Organization., DOI: 10.54675/EWZM9535

University College London. (2023). *Assessment ideas for an AI enabled world*. https://www.ucl.ac.uk/teaching-learning/sites/teaching_learning/files/assessment_menu_040723.pdf

University of Florida. (2023). *AI Across the Curriculum – AI2 Center*. https://ai.ufl.edu

University of Helsinki & MinnaLearn. (n.d.). *Elements of AI*. https://www.elementsofai.com/

University of Maryland College of Education. (2024). *Bridging digital divides in AI-enabled classrooms.*

University of Texas at Austin. (n.d.). *Guidance for using artificial intelligence.* https://tech.utexas.edu/governance/guidance-for-ai

University of Warwick. (2025). *AI and assessment.* https://warwick.ac.uk/fac/cross_fac/academic-development/ai/assessment/

USAHS. (2025). *AI in higher education: How AI is reshaping higher education.* https://www.usa.edu/blog/ai-in-higher-education-how-ai-is-reshaping-higher-education/

van den Berg, G., & du Plessis, E. (2023). ChatGPT and generative AI: Possibilities for its contribution to lesson planning, critical thinking and openness in teacher education. *Education Sciences, 13*(10), 998. DOI: 10.3390/educsci13100998

Varghese, N. N., Jose, B., Bindhumol, T., Cleetus, A., & Nair, S. B. (2025). The power duo: Unleashing cognitive potential through human-AI synergy in STEM and non-STEM education. *Frontiers in Education, 10*, 1534582. Advance online publication. DOI: 10.3389/feduc.2025.1534582

Velander, J., Taiye, M. A., Otero, N., & Milrad, M. (2024). Artificial Intelligence in K-12 Education: Eliciting and reflecting on Swedish teachers' understanding of AI and its implications for teaching & learning. *Education and Information Technologies, 29*(4), 4085–4105. DOI: 10.1007/s10639-023-11990-4

Venkatesh, V., Morris, M. G., Davis, G. B., & Davis, F. D. (2003). User acceptance of information technology: Toward a unified view. *Management Information Systems Quarterly, 27*(3), 425–478. DOI: 10.2307/30036540

Veramuthu, P., & Shah, P. (2020). Effectiveness of Collaborative Writing among Secondary School Students in an ESL Classroom. *Creative Education, 11*(1), 54–67. DOI: 10.4236/ce.2020.111004

Vesna, L., Sawale, P. S., Kaul, P., Pal, S., & Murthy, B. S. N. V. R. (2025). Digital divide in AI-powered education: Challenges and solutions for equitable learning. *Journal of Information Systems Engineering & Management, 10*(21s). https://www.jisem-journal.com/index.php/journal/article/view/3327

Vieriu, A. M., & Petrea, G. (2025). The Impact of Artificial Intelligence (AI) on Students' Academic Development. *Education Sciences, 15*(3), 343. DOI: 10.3390/educsci15030343

Vorobyeva, K. I., Belous, S., Savchenko, N. V., Smirnova, L. M., Nikitina, S. A., & Zhdanov, S. P. (2025). Personalized learning through AI: Pedagogical approaches and critical insights. *Contemporary Educational Technology, 17*(2), ep574. DOI: 10.30935/cedtech/16108

Vygotsky, L. S. (1978). *Mind in society: The development of higher psychological processes.* Harvard University Press., DOI: 10.2307/j.ctvjf9vz4

Wakefield, J. (2020, August 17). A-levels and GCSEs: How did the exam algorithm work? *BBC News.* https://www.bbc.com/news/technology-53810658

Walter, Y. (2024). Embracing the future of artificial intelligence in the classroom: The relevance of AI literacy, prompt engineering, and critical thinking in modern education. *International Journal of Educational Technology in Higher Education, 21*(1), 15. Advance online publication. DOI: 10.1186/s41239-024-00448-3

Wang, D., & Han, H. (2020). Applying learning analytics dashboards based on process-oriented feedback to improve students' learning effectiveness. *Journal of Computer Assisted Learning, 37*(2), 487–499. DOI: 10.1111/jcal.12502

Wang, J., Huang, Y., Chen, C., Liu, Z., Wang, S., & Wang, Q. (2024). Software Testing With Large Language Models: Survey, Landscape, and Vision. *IEEE Transactions on Software Engineering, 50*(4), 911–936. DOI: 10.1109/TSE.2024.3368208

Wang, K., & Lu, W. (2024). AI-induced job impact: Complementary or substitution? Empirical insights and sustainable technology considerations. *Sustainable Technology and Entrepreneurship, 100085.* Advance online publication. DOI: 10.1016/j.stae.2024.100085

Wang, N., & Li, M. (2024). Teachers' perceptions of the risks and benefits of AI in higher education: A case study of ERNIE Bot. *Innovations in Education and Teaching International,* •••, 1–13. DOI: 10.1080/14703297.2024.2432429

Warner, R., & Sloan, R. H. (2021). Making Artificial Intelligence Transparent: Fairness and the Problem of Proxy Variables. *Criminal Justice Ethics, 40*(1), 23–39. DOI: 10.1080/0731129X.2021.1893932

Weber-Wulff, D., Anohina-Naumeca, A., Bjelobaba, S., Foltýnek, T., Guerrero-Dib, J., Popoola, O., Šigut, P., & Waddington, L. (2023). Testing of detection tools for AI-generated text. *International Journal for Educational Integrity, 19*(1), 26. Advance online publication. DOI: 10.1007/s40979-023-00146-z

Westman, S., Kauttonen, J., Klemetti, A., Korhonen, N., Manninen, M., Mononen, A., . . . Paananen, H. (2021). Artificial Intelligence for Career Guidance--Current Requirements and Prospects for the Future. *IAFOR Journal of Education, 9*(4), 43-62. https://eric.ed.gov/?id=EJ1318705

Wiggins, G., & McTighe, J. (2005). *Understanding by design.* Association for Supervision and Curriculum Development.

Willis, M., Duckworth, P., Coulter, A., Meyer, E. T., & Osborne, M. (2020). Qualitative and quantitative approach to assess the potential for automating administrative tasks in general practice. *BMJ Open*, *10*(6), e032412.

Wilson, E. (2023, September 12). I tried the Smiling Mind app to see if it could help me stop worrying constantly. *Verywell Mind*. https://www.verywellmind.com/i-tried-smiling-mind-app-review-7643815

Winkler, C., Hammoda, B., Noyes, E., & Van Gelderen, M. (2023a). Entrepreneurship education at the dawn of generative artificial intelligence. *Entrepreneurship Education and Pedagogy*, *6*(4), 579–589. DOI: 10.1177/25151274231198799

Winkler, J., Koehler, M. J., & Theodore, R. (2023b). Reimagining professional development for AI-driven classrooms. *Educational Technology Research and Development*, *71*(2), 355–373. DOI: 10.1007/s11423-023-10102-9

Winkler, R., Koehler, M. J., & Theodore, R. M. (2023c). Empowering educators to be AI-ready: Opportunities and cost considerations. *Journal of Educational Technology Policy and Practice*, *21*(2), 115–134. DOI: 10.1007/s12345-023-00678-x

Wong, L. P. (2024). Artificial Intelligence and Job Automation: Challenges for Secondary Students' Career Development and Life Planning. *Merits*, *4*(4), 370–399. DOI: 10.3390/merits4040027

Wong, M. F., Guo, S., Hang, C. N., Ho, S. W., & Tan, C. W. (2023). Natural language generation and understanding of big code for AI-assisted programming: A review. *Entropy (Basel, Switzerland)*, *25*(6), 888. DOI: 10.3390/e25060888

World Bank. (2024). *Artificial intelligence in education: Challenges and opportunities*. https://documents1.worldbank.org/curated/en/099734306182493324/pdf/IDU152823b13109c514ebd19c241a289470b6902.pdf

Wu, C., Zhang, H., & Carroll, J. M. (2024). AI Governance in Higher Education: Case Studies of Guidance at Big Ten Universities. *Future Internet*, *16*(10), 354. DOI: 10.3390/fi16100354

Xiang, D., Qin, G., & Zheng, X. (2022). The influence of student-teacher relationship on school-age Children's empathy: The mediating role of emotional intelligence. *Psychology Research and Behavior Management*, *15*, 2735–2744. DOI: 10.2147/PRBM.S380689

Xu, Z. (2024). AI in education: Enhancing learning experiences and student outcomes. *Applied and Computational Engineering*, *51*(1), 104–111. DOI: 10.54254/2755-2721/51/20241187

Yadav, N. (2025, May 27). *IBM is cutting around 8000 jobs likely because of AI, major losses in HR department*. India Today. https://www.indiatoday.in/technology/news/story/ibm-is-cutting-around-8000-jobs-likely-because-of-ai-major-losses-in-hr-department-2544873-2025-05-27

Yan, L., Martinez-Maldonado, R., Jin, Y., Echeverria, V., Milesi, M., Fan, J., Zhao, L., Alfredo, R., Li, X., & Gašević, D. (2024b). *The effects of generative AI agents and scaffolding on enhancing students' comprehension of visual learning analytics*. arXiv preprint arXiv:2409.11645. https://arxiv.org/abs/2409.11645

Yang, H., & Kyun, S. (2022). The current research trend of artificial intelligence in language learning: A systematic empirical literature review from an activity theory perspective. *Australasian Journal of Educational Technology*, *38*(5), 180–210. DOI: 10.14742/ajet.7492

Yan, L., Sha, L., Zhao, L., Li, Y., Martinez-Maldonado, R., Chen, G., Li, X., Jin, Y., & Gašević, D. (2024a). Practical and ethical challenges of large language models in education: A systematic scoping review. *British Journal of Educational Technology*, *55*(1), 90–112. DOI: 10.1111/bjet.13370

Yarrington, J. S., Lasser, J., Garcia, D., Vargas, J. H., Couto, D. D., Marafon, T., Craske, M. G., & Niles, A. N. (2021). Impact of the COVID-19 Pandemic on Mental Health among 157,213 Americans. *Journal of Affective Disorders*, *286*, 64–70. DOI: 10.1016/j.jad.2021.02.056

Yeh, P. L., Kuo, W. C., Tseng, B. L., & Sung, Y. H. (2025). Does the AI-driven Chatbot Work? Effectiveness of the Woebot app in reducing anxiety and depression in group counseling courses and student acceptance of technological aids. *Current Psychology (New Brunswick, N.J.)*, *44*(9), 1–13. DOI: 10.1007/s12144-025-07359-0

Ye, J. (2021). Advancing mental health and psychological support for health care workers using digital technologies and platforms. *JMIR Formative Research*, *5*(6), e22075. DOI: 10.2196/22075

Yola, R., Azizah, W., Azizah, N., & Sabarrudin. (2024). Implementation of Use Deep Artificial Intelligence (AI) Guidance and Counseling Student Learning Process . *BICC Proceedings*, *2*, 138–142. https://doi.org/DOI: 10.30983/bicc.v1i1.118

Yu, L., & Yu, Z. (2023). Qualitative and quantitative analyses of artificial intelligence ethics in education using VOSviewer and CitNetExplorer. *Frontiers in Psychology*, *14*, 1061778.

Zaman, B. U. (2023). Transforming education through ai, benefits, risks, and ethical considerations. *Authorea Preprints*.

Zawacki-Richter, O., Marín, V. I., Bond, M., & Gouverneur, F. (2019). Systematic review of research on artificial intelligence applications in higher education – Where are the educators? *International Journal of Educational Technology in Higher Education, 16*(1), 1–27.

Zawacki-Richter, O., Marín, V. I., Bond, M., & Gouverneur, F. (2019). Systematic review of research on artificial intelligence applications in higher education – where are the educators? *International Journal of Educational Technology in Higher Education, 16*(1), 39. Advance online publication. DOI: 10.1186/s41239-019-0171-0

Zee, M., Rudasill, K. M., & Bosman, R. J. (2021). A cross-lagged study of students' motivation, academic achievement, and relationships with teachers from kindergarten to 6th grade. *Journal of Educational Psychology, 113*(6), 1208–1226. DOI: 10.1037/edu0000574

Zeide, E. (2019, August 26). Artificial intelligence in higher education: Applications, promise and perils, and ethical questions. *EDUCAUSE Review, 54*(3), 31–39. https://ssrn.com/abstract=4320049

Zeren, G., Erus, S. M., Amanvermez, Y., Genç, A. B., & Duy, B. (2022). Client's experiences of online counseling: Satisfaction and therapeutic alliance. *Cukurova University Faculty of Education Journal, 51*(1), 634–658. DOI: 10.14812/cuefd.843542

Zhaı, X., Yin, Y., Pellegrino, J. W., Haudek, K. C., & Shi, L. (2020). Applying machine learning in science assessment: a systematic review [Review of Applying machine learning in science assessment: a systematic review]. Studies in Science Education, 56(1), 111. Taylor & Francis. https://doi.org/DOI: 10.1080/03057267.2020.1735757

Zhai, X., Chu, X., Chai, C. S., Jong, M. S. Y., Istenic, A., Spector, M., & Li, Y. (2021). A Review of Artificial Intelligence (AI) in Education from 2010 to 2020. *Complexity, 2021*(1), 8812542.

Zhang, K., & Aslan, A. B. (2021). AI technologies for education: Recent research & future directions. *Computers and Education Artificial Intelligence, 2*, 100025. DOI: 10.1016/j.caeai.2021.100025

Zheng, C., Yuan, K., Guo, B., Hadi Mogavi, R., Peng, Z., Ma, S., & Ma, X. (2024, May). Charting the future of AI in project-based learning: a Co-design exploration with students. In *Proceedings of the 2024 CHI Conference on Human Factors in Computing Systems* (pp. 1-19). DOI: 10.1145/3613904.3642807

Zhou, P., Wang, L., Liu, Z., Hao, Y., Hui, P., Tarkoma, S., & Kangasharju, J. (2024). A survey on generative AI and LLM for video generation, understanding, and streaming. *arXiv (Cornell University)*. https://doi.org//arxiv.2404.16038DOI: 10.36227/techrxiv.171172801.19993069/v1

About the Contributors

Shahnawaz Khan is currently serving as the Head of Applied Research at Bahrain Polytechnic in Bahrain. He holds a Ph.D. in Computer Engineering from Indian Institute of Technology (BHU), India. He has held academic, leadership, and administrative positions in esteemed universities and software industry across multiple countries. His academic experience extends to directing various committees, including those focused on research, faculty development, and accreditation. He has also been actively involved in education quality and accreditation (such as ABET, BQA, NCAAA, and NACC) for multiple esteemed universities across multiple countries. Dr. Khan is a recognized expert in Artificial Intelligence, Blockchain, and Islamic FinTech. He brings nearly two decades of experience in research, teaching, and industry in computer science, and app development. He has co-founded a vocational training institute, and two IT companies and has served as a chief technical officer. With a strong track record in Artificial Intelligence, his research has resulted in over 70 peer-reviewed publications with over 2000 citations, four patents, and seven edited books. He has also served as an editor for several special issues of SCI and Scopus indexed journals. Dr. Khan has supervised numerous postgraduate and graduate researchers and is a frequent reviewer for top-tier journals and conferences. Dr. Khan is passionate about applying AI to solve real-world problems. He leads a team of researchers focused on developing innovative solutions (by applying artificial intelligence) for real-world problems in areas such as Islamic fintech, healthcare and global warming. He is committed to fostering the next generation of researchers.

Philippe Pringuet is an assistant professor in computer science at Bahrain Polytechnic, teaching on multiple courses of the Programming major. Philippe has 15 years experience in education in European and Middle Eastern contexts and is an Apple Certified trainer and a Senior Fellow of the Advanced Higher Education, UK. Philippe led the development of the Bachelor of ICT Programme at Bahrain Polytechnic and in his roles as Head of School of ICT and then as

Dean of the Faculty of Engineering, provided the leadership to guide the ICT and Engineering programmes towards international accreditation with the British Computer Society and the Institution of Engineering and Technology. Personable and energetic academic with 10+ years management experience establishing a new Polytechnic in a multicultural environment. An active participant in National Education Reform, creating and delivering programmes in a Problem Based Learning approach following student-centred principles and, contributor to the establishment of the Labour Market Observatory. Areas of interest include Education Leadership, Problembased Learning, Quality & Accreditation, Assessment & Moderation, Change Managemen

***

Sally Abualgasim Associate Professor on Computer Science. Experienced Computer Science Ph.D. with 20+ years in academia, research and solve problem by programming, excelling in AI, System and Object-Oriented Programming. Adept in lecturing, research supervision, and academic leadership.

Zeinab Ahmed holds a Ph.D. in Computer Engineering and Networks from the University of Gezira, Sudan. Since June 2020, she has served as an Assistant Professor in the Department of Computer Engineering at the same university. Currently, she is a Postdoctoral Fellow at the Department of Electrical and Computer Engineering, International Islamic University Malaysia (IIUM), Malaysia. With extensive academic leadership experience, Dr. Zeinab has previously held the position of Head of the Department of Computer Engineering at the Faculty of Engineering Technology, University of Gezira, Sudan. She has actively contributed to various projects in computer engineering and networking and has authored more than thirty research papers and book chapters in peer-reviewed journals and conferences. Her primary research interests lie in wireless communication networks. As an accomplished academic, she brings expertise in research, e-learning, programming, and lecturing, with a strong track record in higher education.

Andi Asrifan is an accomplished educator and academic leader with a Doctorate in Education, specializing in English Language Education from Universitas Negeri Makassar. With a strong academic foundation, he holds a Master's degree in the same field and a Bachelor's degree in Secondary Education. His dissertation focused on developing bilingual educational materials, reflecting his commitment to enhancing language education. Dr. Asrifan has extensive experience in various educational roles, including serving as the Head of the International Affairs Office at Politeknik Negeri Nunukan and as the Head of the Institute for Student Development and

Alumni at Universitas Muhammadiyah Sidenreng Rappang. He is also an active member of several professional organizations, including the Linguistics Society of Indonesia and TEFLIN. In addition to his administrative roles, Dr. Asrifan is a passionate advocate for educational innovation and has participated in numerous international conferences and webinars, sharing his insights on language teaching and curriculum development. His dedication to professional development is evident through his participation in various training programs.

Vaishnavi Balaji Holding a Doctor of Philosophy in Machine Learning and GIS and a Master of Science in Software Technology both from Vellore Institute of Technology, Vellore. and a Master of Science in Machine Learning & AI - Executive PG, a dual credential program from Liverpool John Moores University and IIIT Bangalore. Other Skill Set: Proficient in Python and familiar with frameworks like Django and Streamlit. Expertise extends to deep learning with Keras, Scikit-learn, TensorFlow, and Torch, as well as computer vision and natural language processing. Experience in generative AI includes AI chatbot creation, data analysis, and fine-tuning LLMs. Additionally, skilled in RDBMS, cloud services like AWS, and MLops tools such as Airflow and CI/CD pipelines.

Michael Finetti is an Associate Professor of Education at Saint Peter's University in Jersey City, NJ, where he serves as the Director of Special Education Programs and oversees the Endorsement Program for Teacher of Students with Disabilities Certification. Dr. Michael Finetti teaches both face-to-face and online undergraduate and graduate courses in the Caulfield School of Education. Dr. Michael Finetti has conducted numerous presentations at the Faculty Resource Network National Symposium, Association of Mathematics Teachers of New Jersey, New Jersey Association for Colleges of Teacher Education (NJACTE), New Jersey Education Association (NJEA) annual convention, and NJ Edge. In addition to these presentations, he conducted many special education and technology webinars. His own research discusses the effectiveness of collaborative instruction and assistive technology for students with disabilities in inclusive settings. Dr. Michael Finetti received his B.S. degree from Rutgers University and his M.A. in Education and Ed. D. in Educational Leadership degrees from Seton Hall University.

Jay C. Garrels is an accomplished academic and researcher currently serving as the Chair of the Department of Health & Physical Education and Exercise Science at Saint Peter's University. He holds a Ph.D. in Health Science with a Specialization in Movement Science from Seton Hall University, as well as a Master's in Exercise Science from East Stroudsburg University. Dr. Garrels has dedicated his career to teaching and advising students, with a focus on the holistic development of each individual, guided by the principle of cura personalis. His expertise spans a range of areas, including exercise physiology, biomechanics, and public health. In addition to his academic roles, he has actively contributed to the growth of the Exercise Science program at Saint Peter's and has participated in numerous community health initiatives. Dr. Garrels has published in peer-reviewed journals, presented at national conferences, and engaged in various research projects, particularly in areas related to sports performance and health promotion. His new research interest focuses on investigating the impact artificial intelligence is having on teaching methods for instructors and the learning process for students.

Sanjit Ghosh has over 22 years of extensive industrial and academic experience. He previously served as Deputy General Manager with Edtech vertical of HCLTech, He was also with Infosys ltd for 16 years, worked as Senior Principal Consultant -Learning and led the competency certification program of Infosys. He has expertise in technical training deliver, development and implementation of employee competency development program, certification content management and delivery. Sanjit is also experienced in need analysis, stakeholder management, talent management, LMS implementation and administration.

Marie Grace A. Gomez is Professor 11 at the Counselor Education Area, College of Education, University of the Philippines-Diliman. She teaches counseling and research courses at the undergraduate and graduate levels. She has a bachelor's degree in Political Science, a Master of Arts in Education (Guidance) degree, a Doctor of Philosophy degree in Guidance, and another doctorate in Special Education. She has served as a classroom teacher, guidance counselor, and administrator in the basic and tertiary education settings. Her community extension projects involve counseling and assessment of children, persons with disability, children in conflict with the law, drug surrenderees, development of sexual health literacy programs for teens with disabilities, sexually abused children, medical personnel, women with mental health issues in institutional settings, and persons affected by COVID-19. She has been the lead researcher for the Philippines in a UNESCO research led by Leonard Cheshire UK on Comprehensive Sexuality Education for persons with disabilities. She has received the 2022 Most Outstanding Professional Teacher Award in the field of Academe and Research from the Philippine Federation for Professional Associations.

Juvrianto Chrissunday Jakob is a dedicated English lecturer at the Civil Engineering Department of Ambon State Polytechnic, Indonesia. With a strong academic background and a passion for education, his areas of expertise encompass Teaching English as a Foreign Language (TEFL), integrating Technology in

Language Learning, Discourse Analysis, and English for Specific Purposes (ESP). These fields reflect his commitment to equipping students with language skills tailored to their professional and academic needs. He holds a master's degree in English Education from Universitas Negeri Makassar, Indonesia, where he honed his skills in pedagogy and research. His scholarly pursuits focus on exploring innovative teaching methodologies and the application of modern tools in language instruction, ensuring his teaching methods align with the evolving demands of education in the digital era. Beyond his role as a lecturer, He is an active contributor to academic communities. He serves as a tutor and language instructor, helping learners enhance their English proficiency. His dedication to academic excellence is further evident in his role as a reviewer for several local and international journals, where he evaluates and supports the dissemination of research in his field. His professional journey is driven by his belief in lifelong learning and his desire to foster effective communication skills in students and professionals alike. His contributions to the intersection of language, technology, and education underscore his impact as an educator and scholar.

Rusdiana Junaid, Grad.Dipl. in TESOL., M.Hum., M.A., is a distinguished academic leader and scholar in the field of English language education, applied linguistics, and cultural studies. Currently serving as the Rector of the Institute of Health and Business Kurnia Jaya Persada Palopo, she brings decades of academic, administrative, and international experience to her role. She holds multiple postgraduate degrees in English Language Studies and Applied Linguistics from Hasanuddin University and Curtin University, Australia, where she also completed specialized training in TESOL. Her professional development includes participation in international programs such as the SUSI Program at New York University, the JICA-sponsored Lesson Study Training in Japan, and the Ph.D. Sandwich Program with Griffith University, Australia. Prof. Rusdiana has held various leadership positions, including Dean of the Faculty of Education and Dean of Computer Engineering at Universitas Cokroaminoto Palopo. She is actively involved in professional organizations such as TEFLIN, WALS, ALSI, ALTI, and MLI. In addition to her teaching and research roles, she contributes as an assessor in national academic quality assurance programs, including PPG, BKD, JAFUNG, and LAMDIK

Nicole Luongo is a Professor of Education at Saint Peter's University in Jersey City, NJ. Currently, she is teaching graduate, doctoral, and undergraduate education courses in the Caulfield School of Education. Dr. Luongo has authored several anthologies, including Foundations of Teaching and Learning: A Comprehensive Guide to Assessment In The K-12 Classroom and The New K-12 Classroom:

Teaching Reading and Language Arts In A Digital World. Also, she has authored an Open Education Resource entitled Online Teaching & Learning: Course Design Basics. Dr. Luongo received a B.S. in elementary education from Bucknell University and an M.A. in education from Seton Hall University. Most recently, she graduated from Nova Southeastern University with an Ed.D. in instructional technology and distance education.

Devi Manikeswari A competent and dedicated educator with extensive teaching/training experience in tertiary, higher and senior secondary education levels. Areas of research expertise include Business Management, HR, OB, Higher education and Psychometric testing.

Satya Pavan Kumar. Ratnakaram is an accomplished academician currently employed as an Assistant Professor in the Faculty of Business and Logistics, Bahrain Polytechnic since September 2022. Prior to this, he has worked as a Program Manager and IQA member in the Commercial Studies Division, Bahrain Training Institute, Kingdom of Bahrain for more than 16 years. With over two decades of teaching/training/industry experience across three countries, published more than 25 articles in national and international journals in the field of Accounting, banking, insurance, CSR and ESG.

Rismawati Sudirman is a distinguished academic and consultant with a robust focus on sustainability reporting. She currently holds the position of lecturer and Head of the Quality Assurance Institute at Universitas Muhammadiyah Palopo, where she has been pivotal in ensuring the quality of university processes and outputs since February 2020. Additionally, she serves as an Assurer for Sustainability Reporting at the National Center for Sustainability Reporting in Jakarta, specializing in the evaluation of sustainability reports for mining companies across Indonesia. Her academic qualifications are extensive, comprising a Bachelor's degree in Economics and Accounting, a Master's degree in Accounting Science, and a Doctorate in Accounting from Universitas Brawijaya, Malang. Rismawati is also a certified specialist in sustainability reporting, risk management, and tax planning, holding several prestigious certifications including Certified Sustainability Reporting Specialist (CSRS) and Certified Risk Management Practitioner (CRMP). In her professional capacity, she has provided consultancy services in financial management and tax compliance for companies such as PT. Reski Barito Timur and PT. Helay Raya. Furthermore, she has authored multiple publications on taxation and management, contributing significantly to the academic community. Her interests in reading, writing, and travel reflect her commitment to lifelong learning and professional growth in her field.

Harris Saseendran is a seasoned academic with over 17 years of experience spanning higher education, corporate training, and HR management. He is currently an Asst. Professor at the Faculty of Business and Logistics, Bahrain Polytechnic, Kingdom of Bahrain, where he serves as a course coordinator and moderator for HR and business management degree programs, and contributes to academic program development. Previously, Dr. Saseendran was a Program Manager at Bahrain Training Institute, Ministry of Education, Kingdom of Bahrain, overseeing CIPD-certified and NQF-aligned HR and business diploma programs. His corporate experience includes roles as HR recruiter and operations manager specializing in IT and ITES recruitment for major MNCs in India. Dr. Saseendran has published extensively in research journals and popular outlets like Economic Times and Bahrain Confidential. He has also presented at international conferences on AI, organizational behavior, HR, and education.

Sonia Selwin is an accomplished educator, community leader, and advocate for women's empowerment with over 23 years of experience in education and organizational development. Her dual passions for teaching and project development have driven her to make significant contributions to academia, community building, and social impact initiatives. Dr. Selwin has taught business management courses to diverse groups, including CIPD and Edexcel programs in the Kingdom of Bahrain, where she also played a vital role in developing qualifications for the National Qualifications Framework. At the Bahrain Training Institute, Bahrain, she introduced impactful initiatives such as the Annual Research Symposium and facilitated faculty workshops to enhance research skills. Currently pursuing post-doctoral research at Andrews University, USA, Dr. Selwin serves as the Director of Women Ministries at HopeSide Ministries in Maryland, USA, and is the President & Founder of PEACE (People Empowerment Alliance for Creativity & Education), a globally operating nonprofit established to empower marginalized communities, including women, minorities, and individuals with intellectual and developmental disabilities. Her initiatives focus on creating transformative impacts through education, entrepreneurship, and spiritual guidance.

Zakir Shaikh is an Assistant Professor, Department of Accounting and Finance, School of Business Administration, Kingdom University, Bahrain. Prior to this, he worked more than 28 years in commercial and academic industry. He has published numerous articles in referred journals and presented many papers in various conferences, both local and abroad in the different area of Accounting, management and Islamic Banking and Finance. He has also participated in a variety of seminars, forums, workshops and international conferences. He obtained his Ph.D. (Islamic Banking and Finance) from India in 2018. His doctoral thesis explored the entrepreneurial phenomenon from an Islamic perspective and argued for profit and loss sharing (PLS) contracts as viable alternatives to conventional interest-based financing instruments. He holds Master degree in Commerce, Business Administration & Finance and Control. He is a member of AAA, Chartered Institute of Islamic Finance Professionals (CIIF), Malaysia; Indian Accounting Association; Orissa Commerce Association, India and associated with Accounting & Auditing Organization for Islamic Financial Institution (AAOIFI), Bahrain

K. Siva Kumar Gowda is an Assistant Professor, Department of Computer Science and Engineering - IOT, Sreenidhi Institute of Science and Technology, Hyderabad, Telangana, India.

Anand Soni is a seasoned educator and researcher at Bahrain Polytechnic's School of Business & Logistics, with nearly 20 years of teaching experience. He holds a Ph.D. in Management and master's degrees in Business Management and Commerce (ABST). He authored the book Business Analytics and Data Science for Decision Making and has contributed to a patent, journal articles, and book chapters. Dr. Soni has co-guided Ph.D. students, supervised master's theses, and helped develop NQF qualifications. He actively organizes academic events and frequently serves as a keynote speaker, reflecting his commitment to research, education, and professional engagement.

I. Sowmyasri is a Student at the Department of Computer Science and Engineering - IOT, Sreenidhi Institute of Science and Technology, Hyderabad, Telangana, India.

Venkat T is Professor and Head, Department of Computer Science and Engineering - IOT, Sreenidhi Institute of Science and Technology, Hyderabad, india

Joe Terantino, Ph.D. is associate professor of Second Language Education at Oklahoma State University. His research focuses on online language learning and the meaningful integration of technology in language teaching and learning. His work has been published in CALICO and Language Learning & Technology.

Koteswara Rao Vemavarapu has been working as Assistant Professor at the School of Business in Bahrain Polytechnic since 2022 and he worked as Faculty in the Commercial Studies Division, Bahrain Training Institute (BTI), Ministry of Education, Kingdom of Bahrain from 2006 to 2022. He has over 24 years of teaching experience and five years of industry experience. He was involved in delivering courses of Edexcel, BNQF, Association of Accounting Technicians (AAT, UK), and the Chartered Institute of Personnel and Development (CIPD, UK). His experience as a Program Manager (HR and Accounting), Internal Verifier, Chairman of a Mapping Panel and Conformation Panel Member, Divisional Timetable Coordinator, and Social Committee member is remarkable. His specialization is setting up accounting systems and controls for an organization. His research interests include Performance Management and the impact of technological advancement on HR. He has published research papers in reputed journals, presented papers at conferences, conducted workshops, and served as a resource person for national and international conferences.

Joshua Williams is a faculty member at Saint Peter's University, where he teaches courses in Exercise Science, Nutrition, and Health and Physical Education. He also leads AI-focused Master Classes for educators and is actively involved in AI research within higher education. He has a decade of secondary education teaching experience and a background in curriculum design, AI integration in pedagogy, and innovative assessment strategies. His current research explores how faculty members utilize AI to enhance productivity, instructional efficiency, and student engagement. Outside of AI research, he is interested in human health and wellness on an individual and community level.

Om Prakash Yadav is an Associate Professor at the School of Computer Science and Engineering, Lovely Professional University, Punjab, India. With 19 years of academic experience, he has previously served at ISL Engineering College, Sri Sarada Institute of Science and Technology, and Grahmbell P.G. College in Hyderabad, Telangana. He has authored 29 international and 7 national research papers, with expertise in Networking, IoT, and AI/ML

Sidra Zaheer is a second-year Ph.D. student in the Language, Literary, and Culture program at Oklahoma State University, serving as a graduate teaching and research assistant. Her research focuses on integrating AI into curricula to enhance the learning experiences of multilingual students. She aims to develop and foster a facilitative framework that leverages AI to enrich and personalize learning in diverse, multilingual settings.

Yimeng Zhu is a second-year Language, Literacy, and Culture student at Oklahoma State University. As a teaching and research assistant at the OSU Reading and Math Center, he explores using AI tools to support English learners. His research focuses on enhancing learning for students from diverse cultural backgrounds, especially international students.

Index

www.ingramcontent.com/pod-product-compliance
Lightning Source LLC
LaVergne TN
LVHW080900300926
849162LV00003B/499

* 9 7 9 8 3 3 7 3 0 3 9 6 3 *